The 2000s in America

The 2000s in America

Volume 1
Abortion—*Freakonomics*

Editor
Craig Belanger
University of Advancing Technology

SALEM PRESS
A Division of EBSCO Publishing
Ipswich, Massachusetts

GREY HOUSE PUBLISHING

The 2000s in America, 2013, published by Grey House Publishing, Inc., Amenia, NY, under exclusive license from EBSCO Publishing, Inc.

∞ The paper used in these volumes conforms to the American National Standard for Permanence of Paper for Printed Library Materials, Z39.48 1992 (R1997).

Library of Congress Cataloging-in-Publication Data

The 2000s in America / editor, Craig Belanger, University of Advanced Technology.
    volumes cm
  Includes bibliographical references and index.
   ISBN 978-1-4298-3883-2 (set) -- ISBN 978-1-4298-3884-9 (volume 1) -- ISBN 978-1-4298-3885-6 (volume 2) -- ISBN 978-1-4298-3899-3 (volume 3) 1. United States--Civilization--1970---Encyclopedias. 2. United States--Civilization--21st century--Encyclopedias. 3. United States--History--1969---Encyclopedias. 4. Two thousands (Decade)--Encyclopedias. I. Belanger, Craig. II. Title: Two thousands in America.
  E169.12.A178 2013
  973.93--dc23
                                                                                              2012045422

■ Contents

■ Publisher's Note

The 2000s in America is a two-volume encyclopedic reference work that comprehensively covers the impact of the first decade of the twenty-first century, including the most significant people, institutions, events, and developments spanning both the United States and Canada. This set is the ninth in Salem Press's acclaimed Decades in America series, which encompasses every decade from the 1920s through the 2000s. Librarians and teachers have praised this series for its ability to help students understand the most important aspects of each decade's history—precisely the goal of the series.

The essays in The 2000s in America have been written to meet the needs of high school students and college undergraduates, but the set's clear and innovative approach to the decade and its authoritative articles should also make it useful to more advanced students and scholars. Its more than four hundred alphabetically arranged essays cover the full breadth of North American history and culture throughout the decade, and its supporting features include fifteen appendixes and helpful finding aids such as detailed indexes and a list of articles by subject category.

Scope and Coverage

Each decade is closely identified with at least one, if not several, landmark event or major turning point. While one of the key events of the 2000s, a decade often referred to as the "Aughties," was certainly the terrorist attacks of September, 2011, a defining catastrophe to be sure, the decade was also punctuated by the devastation of Hurricane Katrina, costly wars in both Afghanistan and Iraq, and a late recession rivaling the economic devastation of the Great Depression. Compounded with an ever evolving and socially pervasive technological world and the meteoric rise of all things digital, from smartphones and tablets to the startups that help to create and sustain them, the American landscape has undergone a radical transformation, literally and metaphorically.

While these volumes devote a great deal of their space to the aforementioned topics, the work itself does not do so at the expense of neglecting other noteworthy subjects. Indeed, one of the fascinating aspects about Salem Press's Decades sets is what they reveal about the many unique contributions and developments to history of each decade. In The 2000s in America, for example, readers will find articles on such varied subjects as animal cloning and the organic food industry; the beginnings of medical tourism and tangible green technology; the popularization of reality television and the advent of blogging; the rise of multimedia empires such as the Twilight series and Harry Potter that boast multigenerational appeal; digital inventions innovations such as the BlackBerry and the iPod; and polarizing events such as the Indian Ocean earthquake and tsunami and the Virginia Tech Massacre.

The breadth of the set's more than 400 articles can be seen in the variety of some of the categories under which they fall:

- African Americans
- Art & Architecture
- Business
- Canada Court Cases & the Law
- Crime & Punishment
- Disasters
- Economics
- Education Environmental Issues
- Film
- Health & Medicine
- International Relations
- Journalism
- Latinos
- Legislation
- Literature
- Military & War
- Music
- Native Americans
- People
- Politics & Government
- Popular Culture
- Religion & Spirituality
- Science & Technology
- Sexuality
- Social Issues
- Sports
- Television
- Terrorism
- Transportation
- Women's Issues

The appendix section at the end of volume 2 contains the complete list of category headings, followed by the articles to which they apply.

As with Salem Press's other Decade sets, The 2000s in America combines long overview essays on broad subjects with shorter articles discussing people, books, films, fads, inventions and scientific discoveries, and other events and important topics representative of the decade. Every article focuses on its subject within the context of the 2000s, devoting only such attention to what happened before and after that decade as is needed to place the subjects within their fuller historical contexts.

Organization and Format

Ranging in length from one to six pages, each article in The 2000s in America begins with a concise title followed by a brief definition or description of the person, organization, work, concept, or event. Headwords are selected to help users find articles under the titles they expect, and additional help in locating topics can be found the extensive Personage and Subject Indexes in volume 2.

After their titles, articles provide a variety ready-reference top matter tailored to the individual topics. For example, articles on individual persons provide brief identifications and their subjects' birth and death dates and places. Articles on events give brief descriptions of the events and their dates and places. Other types of articles provide similar information. Under the subheading "Significance," all articles provide summary statements about the importance of their subjects within the context of the 2000s.

The main body of each concludes with an "Impact" section that reviews the subject's broader importance during the 2000s. Every article also offers bibliographical notes, which include annotations in articles of one thousand or more words, and every article is signed by its contributor. The affiliations of the contributors can be found in the list following this note.

Special Features

Volume 2 contains fifteen appendixes that provide additional information about selected aspects of the decade: major films and film awards; best-selling US books; top-selling video games; winners of major sports events; major Broadway plays and awards; the most-watched US television shows; major literary and music awards; a glossary of decade-defining words and slang; a detailed time line; an annotated general bibliography; a chronological list of major scandals; and the top names given at birth.

The encyclopedia also contains a number of useful tools to help readers find entries of interest. A complete list of all essays in The 2000s in America appears at the beginning of each volume. A list of entries sorted by category appears at the end of each volume. Volume 2 also has a comprehensive personage and subject index.

Online Access

Salem Press provides access to its award-winning content both in traditional, printed form and online. Any school or library that purchases The 2000s in America is entitled to complementary access to a fully supported online version of the set. Online features include a simple intuitive interface, user-profile areas for students and patrons, sophisticated search functionality, and complete contents, including appendixes. Access is available through a code printed on the inside cover of the first volume, and that access is both unlimited and immediate.

Acknowledgments

The editors of Salem Press would like to thank the numerous scholars who contributed essays and appendixes to The 2000s in America. Their names and affiliations are listed in the front matter to volume 1. The editors especially wish to thank Professor Craig Belanger, University of Advancing Technology, for serving as the project's editor and for bringing to the project his special expertise on technology and society.

■ Introduction

It is human nature to try to make sense of the disparate events, moods, tones, and colors of the past, to seek within the chaos of time and prior human activity some outstanding threads we can pull on to tie it all up in a neat enough package so that we can understand the world around us. There is even a word for this contextualizing tendency: zeitgeist, or the spirit of the times. Observing the zeitgeist presents the challenge of considering the present, ascribing to it varied meanings, and perhaps even using our history as a lesson for those who may someday need to know what we know now about the times in which we have lived.

The hunt for the zeitgeist continues apace at the end of each annual cycle. As evidence, witness the best-ofs and significant event listings that appear like mass-media perennials the week between Christmas and New Year's Day, and then watch as the tone toward the decade's close becomes more solemn, presumably because more things happened and thus more meaning can be found. This tendency provides consolation, of course, since retrospection offers opportunities to contextualize—to make sense of—the times which have recently passed us by.

But it can be trouble nonetheless—trouble because we've only got our time-bound selves to believe; trouble because we cannot know whether today is the doomsday of tomorrow or the "moment it all changed" or just somehow not that interesting in the grand scheme (and thus folly); trouble because we only have the past as a guide for meaning; and trouble because in attempting to identify the zeitgeist of an era you must indulge in the notion that we can, in fact, make sense of it all.

Indulge this premise, then—forgetting about the zeitgeist for a moment, there is still some meaning to be had from the moments we call the 2000s. Let's see if there is some other way of accounting for the people, things, events, and actions. If it's true we can, from the vantage point of the second decade of this century, look back upon the first decade and understand it, this volume offers an opportunity to start down that path.

* * *

In retrospect, the vast social, technological, and political changes of the first decade of the twenty-first century, accelerated by the events of September 11, 2001, were impossible to predict: a United States congressman suspected of having an illicit affair with a missing intern; the scientific community locked in a battle of wills with President George W. Bush's restrictions on embryonic stem cell lines; and a waning energy crisis in California. Such were the rousing stories of the day in the late spring and summer of 2001, none of which indicated a world on the brink of an irrevocable global transformation.

Yet readers venturing past the headlines and the predicaments of the day got a glimpse of the nation's—and the world's—destiny. For example, hiding deep in the international news section of the *New York Times* the morning of September 11 was a seemingly minor story ("Taliban Foe Hurt and Aide Wounded by Bomb") about an explosion in northern Afghanistan two days previous which had injured Ahmad Shah Massoud, a leader of local resistance against the Taliban. Massoud died of his wounds, as reported a few days later after the towers fell, and his former comrades-in-arms became vital to our efforts in Iraq.

The Taliban themselves were known to readers of the *Times* and other Western periodicals that summer as the extremists who had ordered the destruction of a vast collection of antiquities, including two grand statues of the Buddha, all in the name of Islam. Only the most acute national security watchers would have made any but the most cursory connection between the heroic figure of Massoud, the acts of religious extremists against representations of the Buddha, and a series of bombings against American targets abroad, and even one in New York City itself, in the previous decade. After September 11, only the least aware could have failed to predict how government reactions the world over would stoke the classic tension between national security and privacy. The days of imagining and believing that what was happening in the Middle East was of regional concern ended that morning in September.

As the world was soon to learn, these events constituted granular parts of the story as we understand it today, so far. Yet they do not tell the entire story of the first decade of the twenty-first century. In any other decade, it would have been difficult to argue that a global "War on Terror," which began with an attack on American soil, constituted two lengthy wars across four continents, and saw an end to the regime of two of the developed world's most notorious leaders, is *not* the central point of view from which we should define the times in which we live.

From a vantage point just past the end of the first decade of the century, a case can be made that the "War on Terror," though monumental, was only part of what makes the 2000s unique from previous decades, but that we can't begin to describe this decade without acknowledging the vast social shifts brought about by three other influences on our daily lives during the 2000s: the Internet, social media, and the ongoing economic crises of the latter half of the decade.

True, the Internet was a game changer as far back as the 1980s, so it was certainly nothing new at the turn of the century. However, large growth in consumer spending on personal computers and rising penetration rates, coupled with advancements in delivery speeds, methods, and the sheer number of Internet-capable devices, led directly to a burgeoning second decade in which it is nearly impossible to find someone who does not consume a portion of the Internet for at least a few minutes daily on a device more powerful, computationally speaking, than those which once put mankind on the moon (and at far less the cost).

This was also the decade of social media, a sociotechnological force so strong it reshaped the notion of interpersonal relationships and accelerated the most revolutionary series of political and social changes the Middle East has ever seen—Arab Spring. Not even in existence at the dawn of the 2000s, social media platforms such as Facebook, YouTube, and Twitter quickly became vital mediums in the social life of people around the world, not only because they helped us realize dreams born in science fiction of interacting with media and communicating around the world, but they also allowed us to do so *instantaneously* and *dynamically*, with moving pictures, playlists, and even commentary from anyone with an Internet connection.

Aside from the persistent wars, the 2000s was also a time bookended by recession, a decade in which the world's economy took a tumble from atop a seeming house of cards, causing drastic declines in employment and the net worth of millions of homeowners in the United States and, as the devastation curled outward, worldwide. Sometime in the future, we may be able to look back at the financial crises and count our blessings for the hard lessons learned, but chances are that anyone reading this book at the time of publication has a family member or friend who either lost a home or a job, or they themselves have found it very difficult to buy a home, find a job, and pay for college during this decade. As competition for the main protagonist of the decade goes, alongside a global military and intelligence effort and exponential sociotechnological change, economic crisis seems a more-than-worthy candidate for where to begin describing how we got where we are today.

If none of the above convinces you of the uniqueness of the 2000s, consider that this was also the decade in which the fundamental dream of the civil rights era was realized with the election of the first African American president of the United States. Not to mention that his primary competition on the way to office included two women—one of his own party and the other a running mate for the opposition. After centuries of rule by one segment of the socioeconomic sphere, it seemed US voters were more than willing to participate when neither gender nor race determined one's ability to lead the nation.

Of course it is not just the large political and economic events by which we understand our times. To this decade, we can also credit some interesting social changes that promise to shape the world moving forward. With respect to our seemingly endless capacity to indulge entertainment needs, we need to examine the radical alterations to our media landscape. Video gaming, an esoteric entertainment pursuit as recently as the 1980s, can now claim not just entire families, but generations of families as aficionados across several powerful platforms that double as internet portals and often telephones. Despite the drastic decline of video stores during the decade (not to mention the apparent "demise" of other forms of physical media, such as books and periodicals), there seems no apparent end to the amount and type of entertainment media available for viewing, reading, or listening to once we get bored with the gaming console—that is, if we are not already viewing, reading, and/or listening simultaneously. In the event one is pulled away from home to attend to other matters, no worries—you can always pull out a smartphone or tablet computer and resume your activities.

While social media and gaming environments provide ample opportunities for anonymity online (via avatars or just plain lying about who you are), this decade is also marked by a new appreciation for the act of sharing, whether it is in the form of a picture of dinner, a play-by-play description of, well, practically anything you wish to describe, or comments on the inevitable changes to moods, relationships, and the waistline that afflict all of humanity. It is advised, of course, that users of said technologies and the Internet be wary of the copyright issues involved in playing, modifying, downloading, uploading, remixing, mashing up, sharing, or just plain innocently interacting with ubiquitously accessible media. Pay heed as well to the security of these devices, since failure to do so could result in susceptibility to the millions of hackers worldwide who threaten to steal your identity or simply ensnare your computer into a botnet with which they can attack more computers and put individual users, or perhaps entire corporations, in jeopardy in an act of cybercrime. To top all of this off, one of the most profound technology movements of the decade was one that had some people claiming Human Being 1.0—me and you, that is—might progress so far beyond our current intelligence and capabilities that we could look back someday and not even recognize what came before Human Being 2.0.

* * *

Let's not suggest these volumes are an attempt to capture the zeitgeist. If anything, by the sheer diversity of topics on hand, they may support a case against doing so. What they offer instead is an invaluable accounting for particular events, people, artifacts, trends, and other particulars of the decade.

Given the numerous financial and military crises of the era, documented in detail throughout this volume, it might be an appropriate conclusion to say these were times of great confusion and anxiety, a decade of turmoil and insecurity. As evidence for this particular (some might say pessimistic) spin on the decade, one could point to the events of September 11, the flow of devastating financial meltdowns, and the high levels of unemployment, which at decade's end still loomed.

A different spin—one not somehow magically divorced from the realities of war and financial peril—disposes us to an optimistic view that we are capable of overcoming the worst of times. We might, in this regard, look back and frame the decade as a time of promising sociotechnological changes and the realization of, in the presidency of Barack Obama and the emergence of ubiquitous computing, decades of social and scientific progress. In this latter view, despite the fact that some things like war and suffering will always be part of our world, there is nothing we cannot see our way through.

Even as the second decade progresses, we are still in some ways living through the first decade, and we are likely to be doing so for a while to come. The 2000s will very much be a part of the daily lives of hundreds of millions of people who will come after us and, glancing back in time, see what happened and know at least one kind of truth about these times.

Craig Belanger, Associate Professor
University of Advancing Technology

■ Contributor List

Anna Accettola, MA
Wilton, California

Elizabeth Adams
Naples, Florida

Richard Adler, PhD
University of Michigan–Dearborn

Carolyn Anderson, PhD
University of Massachusetts
  Amherst

Jamie Aronson Tyus
Phoenix, Arizona

Michael P. Auerbach, MA
Marblehead, Massachusetts

Eric Badertscher, MA
Annapolis, Maryland

Beverly Ballaro
Lynnfield, Massachusetts

Craig Belanger
University of Advancing Technology

Adam J. Berger, PhD
New York, New York

Kathleen Berlew
Duryea, Pennsylvania

Veronica Bray
Newbury, Massachusetts

Tanya Brown
Independent Scholar

Michael H. Burchett
Limestone College

Cait Caffrey
Scranton, Pennsylvania

Ann Cameron
Essex, Massachusetts

Josephine Campbell
Wilkes-Barre, Pennsylvania

Lori Cavanaugh
Independent Scholar

Tamela N. Chambers
University of Illinois at Urbana-
  Champaign

Lynn-nore Chittom
Nashville, Tennessee

Lindsay M. Christopher
University of Denver

Patrick G. Cooper
Orlando, Florida

Chris Cullen
New York, New York

Tracey M. DiLascio, Esq.
Framingham, Massachusetts

Jonathan E. Dinneen
Bridgewater, Massachusetts

Desiree Dreeuws, MA
Los Angeles, California

Sally Driscoll
State College, Pennsylvania

Wendy Evans
Independent Scholar

Jack Ewing
Boise, Idaho

Miroslav Farina
Scranton, Pennsylvania

Molly Hagan
New York, New York

Randall Hannum, PhD
New York City College of
  Technology, CUNY

Angela Harmon
Pittston, Pennsylvania

Karen Hunter
Independent Scholar

Micah L. Issitt
Philadelphia, Pennsylvania

Edward Johnson, PhD
University of New Orleans

Mark S. Joy, PhD
Jamestown College

Linda M. Kelley
University of Illinois,
  Urbana-Champaign

Hope L. Killcoyne
South Salem, New York

Brenda Kim
Marblehead, Massachusetts

Grove Koger
Boise State University

Gina Kuchta
Richmond, Virginia

Jack Lasky
Jenkins Township, Pennsylvania

M. Lee, MA
Boston, Massachusetts

Christopher Mari
Jackson Heights, New York

Andrew Maul
Phoenix, Arizona

Laurence W. Mazzeno, PhD
Alvernia University

Terri McFadden
Boston, Massachusetts

Richard Means
Portland, Maine

Matthew Mihalka
University of Minnesota, Twin
 Cities

Kassundra Miller
Montclair Public Library

Steve Miller
Somerville, Massachusetts

Jennifer Monroe
Independent Scholar

Ellen Moser
Brooklyn, New York

Leslie Neilan
Virginia Polytechnic Institute and
 State University

Donna Norman
Independent Scholar

Monica Osborne, PhD
University of California,
 Los Angeles

Ian Paul
Tel Aviv, Israel

Matt Pearce
Independent Scholar

John Pearson
Boston, Massachusetts

Lucia Pizzo
Cambridge, Massachusetts

Colin Post
Arequipa, Peru

John Pritchard
Burlington, Vermont

Joshua Pritchard
Somerville, Massachusetts

Pilar Quezzaire
Boston, Massachusetts

Richard M. Renneboog, MSc
Strathroy, Ontario

Bill Rickards
Amesbury, Massachusetts

James Ryan
Hackensack, New Jersey

Kerry Skemp, MA
San Francisco, California

Brad C. Southard
Appalachian State University

Rebecca Sparling
Kingston, Pennsylvania

Leland Spencer
Ipswich, Massachusetts

Keira Stevenson
New York, New York

James Tackach
Roger Williams University

Lee Tunstall, PhD
University of Calgary

Nicole Van Hoey PharmD
Arlington, Virginia

Andrew E. Walter, JD
Hartford, Connecticut

Maddie Weissman, MA
La Canada, California

George Whitson, PhD
University of Texas at Tyler

Anne Whittaker
Wenham, Massachusetts

Amy Witherbee PhD
University of Arkansas

■ Complete List of Contents

Volume 1

Volume 2

Volume 3

The 2000s
in America

A

■ Abortion

Definition: The process of intentionally terminating a pregnancy

Since the Supreme Court's Roe v. Wade *decision in 1973, which gave women the right to have an abortion, the debate over this issue has divided the United States. Abortion has remained a polarizing issue into the twenty-first century, which has witnessed protests at abortion clinics, restricted access to abortions, and death threats against abortion providers. Legislative and judicial action has also been taken to limit reproductive rights.*

For Americans, views on abortion extend from strict considerations of women's health and bodies into the political, economic, social, and moral spheres. While all American women are allowed the right to a safe, legal abortion, the ability to access such procedures varies from state to state. In addition to restrictive state policies, women seeking abortions often face a social stigma. And as pro-choice and pro-life groups accuse each other of politicizing the issue, the question of women's health is often left out of the conversation.

Upholding Women's Rights

The early 2000s saw an expansion of women's options when considering an abortion. In 2000, the Food and Drug Administration approved RU-486, a pill used to terminate early pregnancies. Also that year, in *Stenberg v. Carhart*, the US Supreme Court overturned a Nebraska law that prohibited partial-birth abortions. The court's decision rejected the law, which was based on morality and contained no exception for women whose lives were threatened by their unviable fetus, for the sake of women's health.

In 2004, the Supreme Court upheld the legality of abortion under *Roe v. Wade* by maintaining the decision made by the Fifth Circuit Court of Appeals in *McCorvey v. Hill*. In this case, Norma McCorvey (the pseudonymous plaintiff "Jane Roe" in the original

case, who later became pro-life) attempted to have *Roe* overturned, but the court denied her request. The court's decision confirmed the vitality of the *Roe* decision for all women.

Rights of the Fetus

After the retirement of Supreme Court Justice Sandra Day O'Connor and the appointment of Samuel Alito to replace her, the Supreme Court's stance on abortion began to shift. In 2007, the court heard *Gonzales v. Carhart*, which addressed the constitutionality of the Partial-Birth Abortion Ban Act of 2003. This act, signed by President George W. Bush, became the first piece of federal legislation to ban abortion after *Roe v. Wade*. While lower courts had ruled that the law was unconstitutional based on its vague language, burden on women, and omission of any medical exception, the Supreme Court narrowly decided to uphold it. In her dissenting opinion, Ruth Bader Ginsburg affirmed her alarm at this move to empower a fetus above a woman and her own health.

Seeking to expand the rights of the fetus, in 2008, the Colorado-based group Personhood USA began a nationwide campaign to build support for an amendment to the US Constitution extending fetal rights to the moment of conception and thereby banning abortion. By invoking the concept of personhood, the group spoke directly to the *Roe* decision, which allows abortion based on the lack of personhood in a nonviable fetus.

Impact

As the decade progressed, the endurance of *Roe v. Wade* came increasingly into question. From state to state, a woman's right to an abortion was restricted. States considered measures to mandate counseling, bolster the legal status of the fetus, restrict options for minors, and refuse medical services to women.

Abortion opponents also continued to target providers. In 2009, George Tiller, a pro-life physician known as one of the few providers of late-term abortions, was shot and killed in Wichita, Kansas. While his murder was condemned by President Barack Obama, the US Conference of Catholic Bishops, the Family Research Council, and the American Jewish Congress, the event demonstrated the extreme views represented in the abortion debate.

The end of the decade saw an increase in anti-abortion legislation. As the debate over the Affordable Care Act, designed to extend health care to all Americans, raged in 2009, members of Congress questioned the role of insurance providers in covering abortion and contraceptives. While the decade opened by addressing abortion with a focus on preserving a woman's health, this focus seemed to shift to the basic morality of abortion.

In subsequent years, groups have advocated for fetal rights through personhood amendments at the state level. Groups have also sought to strengthen fetal rights through legislation such as fetal heartbeat bills, which recognize the rights of a fetus from the moment of its first detectable heartbeat. These restrictive practices, among other developments, have led some to declare that there is a "war on women" in America, and that women's rights, specifically the right to abortion, are far from certain.

Further Reading

Bonavoglia, Angela, ed. *The Choices We Made: Twenty-Five Women and Men Speak Out About Abortion.* New York: Random, 1991. Print. A collection of personal narratives about abortion from women and men speaking from a wide range of social, economic, and moral viewpoints.

Boston Women's Health Book Collective. *Our Bodies, Ourselves.* New York: Simon, 2011. General reference for women's health, outlining abortion procedures and the history of abortion while providing an extensive compilation of additional resources from the perspective of women's rights.

Cohen, Adam. "The Next Abortion Battleground: Fetal Heartbeats." *Time.* 17 Oct. 2011. Web. 7 Aug. 2012. Presents a balanced view of restrictions on abortion and the states considering heartbeat bills and personhood amendments.

Joffe, Carole. *Dispatches from the Abortion Wars: The Costs of Fanaticism to Doctors, Patients, and the Rest of Us.* Boston: Beacon, 2009. Provides an on-the-ground look at the experience of abortion providers and the women who seek abortions.

Schroedel, Jean R. *Is the Fetus a Person? A Comparison of Policies Across the Fifty States.* Ithaca: Cornell UP, 2000. Schroedel examines views on the vulnerability of the fetus by state, laying the foundation for the debate over fetal personhood in the 2000s.

Lucia Pizzo

■ Abramoff, Jack

Identification: American lobbyist
Born: February 28, 1958; Atlantic City, New Jersey

Abramoff was the central figure in what became one of the biggest congressional corruption scandals in decades. The federal investigation into his work as a lobbyist led not only to his own guilty plea, but to the conviction of numerous politicians.

As a lobbyist, Jack Abramoff was skilled at cultivating connections. He offered jobs to those who were politically connected, and promoted his own associates for government positions. Ambitious and bold, Abramoff funneled millions of dollars from American Indian casinos to the coffers of political groups in Washington, DC, lavishing trips and favors on influential politicians.

Following the election of George W. Bush as president in 2000, Abramoff was named to the Interior Department transition team, where his influence as a lobbyist and political operative grew. At the peak of his lobbying career, Abramoff represented the business interests of ten different American Indian tribes. He also did lobbying work for the governments of Sudan and Malaysia, and for several telecommunications companies.

In 2004, the *Washington Post* published a report on Abramoff's lobbying work for an American Indian casino group. According to the report, Abramoff and former House Majority Leader Tom Delay earned more than $45 million from gaming interests. Subsequently, Abramoff became the focus of an investigation by the Senate Indian Affairs Committee. He also came under scrutiny by authorities for his involvement in the sale of the cruise ship company SunCruz Casinos. Following the announcement of the investigation into Abramoff, many politicians hastily returned campaign contributions from groups affiliated with his lobbying network.

In January 2006, Abramoff pleaded guilty to fraud in the SunCruz Casinos case, admitting that he had

Jack Abramoff. (Tom Williams/Roll Call/Getty Images)

Schmidt, Susan, and James V. Grimaldi. "The Fast Rise and Steep Fall of Jack Abramoff." *Washington Times.* Washington Times LLC, 29 Dec. 2005. Web. 9 July 2012.

Stone, Peter H. Heist: *Superlobbyist Jack Abramoff, His Republican Allies, and the Buying of Washington.* New York: Farrar, 2006. Print.

Josephine Campbell

■ Abu Ghraib torture scandal

Definition: The torture and physical and psychological abuse of Iraqi prisoners at Abu Ghraib prison in Iraq in 2003

Reports of prisoner abuse at Abu Graib began to circulate in 2003 after the US invasion of Iraq. To investigate these claims, the United States Army launched a criminal investigation in January 2004. The investigation reports contained graphic images confirming the abuse of Iraqi prisoners by US Army personnel. Such pictures launched an international and political scandal that tarnished the public image and military integrity of the United States.

filed false documents as a buyer of the company. He also pleaded guilty to three felony counts of fraud and corruption related to his dealings with American Indian gaming interests.

Impact

On March 29, 2006, Abramoff was sentenced to five years and ten months in prison. As a result of his conviction and plea deal, several lawmakers, congressional aides, government officials, and other associates of Abramoff's were also subject to federal investigations. Republican Congressmen Tom DeLay and Robert Ney were both forced to step down due to their connections with Abramoff's lobbying network. Ney later pleaded guilty to corruption charges. In the end, the Abramoff scandal resulted in over twenty separate convictions.

Further Reading

Abramoff, Jack. *Capitol Punishment: The Hard Truth about Washington Corruption from America's Most Notorious Lobbyist.* Washington, DC: WND, 2011. Print.

Leibovich, Mark. "Abramoff, From Prison to a Pizzeria Job." *New York Times.* New York Times Co., 23 June 2010. Web. 9 July 2012.

At Abu Ghraib Prison

Following the terrorist attacks of September 11, 2001, President Bush launched the War on Terrorism, which embroiled the United States in separate wars in Afghanistan and Iraq. During the dictatorship of Saddam Hussein in Iraq, Abu Ghraib, located just west of Baghdad, had emerged as an internationally infamous prison demarked by bloodshed, torture, and filthy living conditions caused by overcrowding. The United States entered the war in Iraq predicated on the premise of eliminating such autocratic brutality and ushering in a democratic free society for the oppressed Iraqi people. However, the impulsive nature of US war plans led to several missteps that the Bush administration would have to address and served as a major hindrance to the establishment of peace in the Middle East.

After the collapse of Saddam Hussein's regime in 2003, Janis Karpinski, an Army reserve general and intelligence and operations officer, was placed in charge of all military prisons in Iraq, a service novel to her despite her experience in the Gulf War and in Special Services. Soon thereafter, Karpinski was formally suspended pending an investigation of the

An unidentified Iraqi detainee suffering abuse at Abu Ghraib prison in Baghdad, in late 2003. (AP Photo/File)

Army's prison system, which would uncover a widespread, systematic abuse of power. A fifty-three page report written by Major General Antonio M. Taguba and leaked by the *New Yorker* elucidated a plethora of instances of blatant and criminal abuses against the Iraqi prisoners at Abu Ghraib. Soldiers belonging to the 372nd Military Police Company perpetrated such acts as beating and sodomizing prisoners as well as threatening rape of male inmates. Graphic evidence, including eyewitness accounts and photographs, backed up the alleged wrongdoings. The Department of Defense subsequently dishonorably discharged and prosecuted seventeen of the soldiers and officers who had participated in the abuse. Participants from various government agencies also resigned.

US Exceptionalism in the Twentieth and Twenty-First Centuries

The notion of US exceptionalism, in which the United States would elevate itself above international protocol with regard to humane treatment of the incarcerated abroad, arose out of this and subsequent torture scandals. During the 1980s, when the United

States was still engaged in the Cold War, one differentiating factor between the enemy Russian communist state and the "good," civilized United States was that the United States did not torture foreign detainees. The Abu Ghraib torture scandal and the graphic photographs released thus shocked the American public and launched a national debate over the meaning and function of torture in US foreign policy.

The rhetoric of the 1980s regarding torture faded away during the 2000s, when American conservatives and exceptionalists alleged that the United States had a right to torture—the practice was already a normalized facet of US foreign policy. The Pentagon conceded in 1996 that the School of the Americas used training manuals on torture based on the methods utilized during the Vietnam War. In addition, various cases during the twentieth century demonstrated US-sponsored torture and abuse, such as the civil war in El Salvador (1979–92). Public opinion polls of the 2000s revealed that over half of the US population believed torture should be used in certain situations.

The Abu Ghraib torture scandal was therefore in line with the policies embraced by the US government since the Cold War, while it also resulted from the culmination of various policies approved by President Bush that allowed for US aggression during the War on Terrorism. The United States deployed a systematic chain of abuse of foreign detainees at various sites: Afghanistan, Iraq, Guantanamo Bay, and other US-sponsored foreign autocracies.

Cultural Implications, Political Crisis, and Public Opinion

The political scandal that emerged in light of the Abu Ghraib prison scandal pertained largely to the anti-Arab sentiment articulated by US sociocultural attitudes after the September 11 attacks. Abu Ghraib became emblematic of a salient American attitude of superiority that rendered Arabs as violent terrorists whose cultural practices were inferior to those of the United States. The dehumanization of the prisoners was particularly humiliating and denigrating because homosexuality in the Arab world violates Islamic law.

Critics of US foreign policy viewed such behavior as illustrative of the United States' disregard toward non-Westerners. The scandal worsened with the Bush administration's response to the crisis as they tried to lessen the damage to America's reputation both at home and abroad. Bush's official apology deflected responsibility for the acts, asserting that such treatment was not indicative of the US Army's protocol abroad and was reprehensible. He did so to buttress the credibility of the United States in foreign affairs; the nation's position within the international community was already tenuous because of the War on Terrorism. Bush's apology created a chasm between US forces in Iraq and the Iraqi people, which heightened the brutality of attacks on US forces during the Iraq War. There were mixed reactions to Bush's apology from the American public, as it both repaired his public image at home and further destroyed his credibility.

Impact

International outrage at the treatment of Iraqi prisoners held at Abu Ghraib led to institutional changes within the US military prison system in Iraq. The scandal was also indicative of broader problems with the US campaign in Iraq and exacerbated negative public opinion about the nature of the war itself. White House officials acknowledged the consequences of the scandal as other countries perceived the United States as dedicated to denigrating Islam and the Arab world. The Abu Ghraib torture scandal soiled the already tenuous relationship between the Middle East and the United States and forced the United States to revive its public image within the international community with regard to the War on Terrorism.

Further Reading

Benvenisti, Meron, et al. *Abu Ghraib: The Politics of Torture.* Berkeley: North Atlantic, 2004. Print. Essays explore a variety of perspectives on the Abu Graib scandal, from the soldiers and prisoners involved, to the US government and the occupied culture of Iraq.

Greenberg, Karen J., and Joshua L. Dratel, eds. *The Torture Papers: The Road to Abu Ghraib.* New York Cambridge UP, 2005. Print. Documents the reports written by US government officials to establish the legality of, prepare for, and document interrogation and torture in Abu Ghraib, Afghanistan, and Guantanamo Bay.

Hersh, Seymour M. *Chain of Command: The Road from 9/11 to Abu Ghraib.* New York : Harper, 2004. Print. Hersh wrote a number of pieces for the *New Yorker* regarding prisoner abuse at Abu Ghraib. His book explores the scandal from a wider scope, examining how the United States ended up in Iraq.

Mokhtari, Shadi. *After Abu Ghraib: Exploring Human Rights in America and the Middle East.* New York: Cambridge UP, 2009. Print. Uses speeches, news reports, and interviews with human rights NGO officials to examine three human rights struggles in the United States and the Middle East that occurred after the Abu Ghraib prison scandal.

Tétreault, Mary Ann. "The Sexual Politics of Abu Ghraib: Hegemony, Spectacle, and the Global War on Terror." *NWSA Journal* 18.3 (2006): 33–50. *Academic Search Complete.* Web. 26 Dec. 2012. Analyzes the photographic evidence of the Abu Ghraib prison scandal in terms of orientalism, the concept of Western superiority.

Maddie Weissman, MA

■ Academy Awards

Definition: Annual awards ceremony hosted by the Academy of Motion Picture Arts and Sciences to honor achievements in the film industry.

The Academy Awards ceremony has been a yearly tradition since it was first held in 1929. It has become a televised event watched by several million viewers in more than one hundred countries. During the 2000s, several milestones in the history of the awards occurred.

The 2000–2009 Academy Awards

The seventy-second Academy Awards in 2000 honored achievements for films released in 1999, with comedian Billy Crystal returning to host the show for a seventh time. The drama *American Beauty* won the most awards with a total of five, including best picture, and best director for Sam Mendes. Actor Kevin Spacey received the award for best actor for his starring role in the film. *The Matrix*, *The Cider House Rules*, and *Topsy-Turvy* also won multiple awards.

The following year, comedian Steve Martin hosted the ceremony for the first time. The film *Gladiator* received the most nominations with twelve, winning five awards, including best picture. Actor Russell Crowe took home the best actor award for his role in the film. Also in 2001, the film *Crouching Tiger, Hidden Dragon* became the first martial-arts film to be nominated for best picture.

The 81st Annual Academy Awards. (Courtesy Greg Hernandez)

Comedian Whoopi Goldberg, who had hosted three times before, returned to host the seventy-fourth Academy Awards in 2002. The films *A Beautiful Mind* and *The Lord of the Rings: The Fellowship of the Ring* each won four awards, including best picture for the former. Actress Halle Berry became the first African American woman to win the best actress award, doing so for her role in *Monster's Ball.*

In 2003, Martin returned to host the seventy-fifth Academy Awards. The musical *Chicago* won best picture and five other awards. There were two milestones at the ceremony: Actor Adrien Brody, who was twenty-nine at the time, became the youngest person to win the best actor award, doing so for his role in *The Pianist.* Also, the song "Lose Yourself" by rapper Eminem became the first hip-hop song to win best song.

Crystal returned for the eighth time to host the seventy-sixth Academy Awards in 2004. The big winner was *The Lord of the Rings: The Return of the King,*

the third film in the Lord of the Rings trilogy. The film won all eleven awards for which it was nominated, including best picture. It became the first film with more than ten nominations to win all of them. Actor Sean Penn won his first Academy Award, best actor for his role in *Mystic River.* South African Charlize Theron became the first African person to win best actress, for her role in *Monster.*

Million Dollar Baby was the big winner at the seventy-seventh Academy Awards in 2005. It won best picture, best actress for Hilary Swank, and best director for Clint Eastwood. Thus, Eastwood, at seventy-four years old, became the oldest director to win the award. Director Martin Scorsese's biopic *The Aviator*, about Howard Hughes, won the most awards with five.

The seventy-eighth Academy Awards, hosted for the first time by comedian Jon Stewart, were notable because several independently financed, low-budget films were nominated, including *Crash* and *Brokeback Mountain*. Although *Brokeback Mountain* was the favorite to win best picture, that honor went to *Crash*. However, *Brokeback Mountain* director Ang Lee became the first Asian person to win the best director award.

At the seventy-ninth Academy Awards in 2007, hosted by comedian Ellen DeGeneres, Martin Scorsese won his first best director award, after previously being nominated five times, for his film *The Departed*, which also won best picture. The film was the first remake of a foreign film (the 2002 Hong Kong crime thriller *Infernal Affairs*) to win best picture.

Stewart returned to host the eightieth Academy Awards in 2008. The film *No Country for Old Men* won the most awards with four, including best picture, and tied *There Will Be Blood* with the most nominations with eight. For the first time since 1964, non-American actors and actresses won all of the major acting awards. For her role in *Elizabeth: The Golden Age*, actress Cate Blanchett became the only actress to be nominated twice for the same role, that of Britain's Queen Elizabeth I, whom she had also portrayed in 1998's *Elizabeth*.

For the eighty-first Academy Awards ceremony in 2009, the Academy of Motion Picture Arts and Sciences brought in a new production team to revamp the ceremony in hopes of bringing in more viewers. An actor—Hugh Jackman—rather than a comedian, hosted the ceremony. The film *Slumdog Millionaire* won the most awards with eight, including best picture, and best director for Danny Boyle. Sean Penn won his second best actor award, for his role as openly homosexual politician Harvey Milk in the film *Milk*.

Scientific and Technical Awards

The Academy Awards for technical achievement are generally not televised. They are commonly held on the evening prior to the televised Academy Awards at a dinner and ceremony. The Scientific and Technical Awards honor those who contribute to the technological innovations of the motion-picture industry.

Throughout the 2000s, several people were honored at these special awards ceremonies. In 2001, Advanced Digital Systems Group won a scientific and engineering award for their design and development of the Sony DADR 5000 digital audio dubber. Gerald Cotts won a technical achievement award in 2005 for his engineering of the Satellite-X HMI Softlight. The

same year, Nelson Tyler won a technical achievement award for his development of the Tyler Gyro Platform boat-mount stabilizing instrument for use in films.

Impact

Throughout the 2000s, the Academy of Motion Picture Arts and Sciences continued to honor achievements in the motion-picture industry with the Academy Awards. Several milestones were reached in the decade: For the first time an African American person won a best actress award and an Asian person won a best director award. The Academy also gave highest honors to several genre films for the first time, with *The Lord of the Rings: The Return of the King* being the first fantasy film to win best picture.

Further Reading

Adalian, Josef. "Oscar TV Ratings: Better, but Not Good." *TV Week.* 24 Feb. 2009. Web. 1 Aug. 2012. Presents several statistics and discusses the increase in ratings of the 2009 Academy Awards, after the producers revamped the show to pull in more television viewers.

Kinn, Gail, and Jim Piazza. *The Academy Awards: The Complete Unofficial History—Revised and Up-to-Date.* New York: Black Dog, 2011. Covers every Academy Awards through 2010. Each entry features an examination of the year in film and a look at that year's ceremony; also profiles the winners in major categories.

Levy, Emanuel. *All About Oscar: The History and Politics of the Academy Awards.* New York: Continuum, 2003. Presents inside stories from the Academy Awards, facts, and interesting trivia. Also examines what it means to win an Academy Award and how popularity is a factor in who wins.

Osborne, Robert. *Eighty Years of the Oscar: The Official History of the Academy Awards.* New York: Abbeville, 2008. Written by a film critic for the *Hollywood Reporter*; contains complete lists of every nominee and winner since the first Academy Awards in 1929.

Pond, Steve. *The Big Show: High Times and Dirty Dealings Backstage at the Academy Awards.* New York: Faber, 2005. Provides a behind-the-scenes look at the Academy Awards, from 1994 to 2004, and examines how the awards show changed during that time.

Patrick G. Cooper

■ Adelphia scandal

Definition: A corporate scandal involving corruption within the cable company Adelphia Communications Corporation, which led to the arrest of owner John Rigas

The Adelphia Communications Corporation was one of the largest cable companies in the United States before filing for Chapter 11 bankruptcy and being bought off by other companies. John Rigas had founded Adelphia in 1952 and, along with his son Timothy Rigas, was sentenced to jail for several counts of fraud. The Adelphia scandal was one of several corporate scandals that occurred in the United States in 2002.

Adelphia was the fifth largest cable provider in the United States in the early 2000s. Founded by brothers John and Gus Rigas in 1952, the company saw large growth in the 1980s and 1990s. By the early 2000s the company was offering its clients high-speed Internet access, digital cable, and phone services. On March 27, 2002, Adelphia employees reported $2.3 billion in undisclosed debt. It was revealed that the Rigas family had used their private trust, Highland Holdings, to borrow money from Adelphia, creating this debt. Shortly after the disclosure, stock in Adelphia dropped nearly 65 percent and the Securities and Exchange Commission launched an investigation into the company.

Investigators, led by US Attorney James Comey, found that the Rigas family had used much of the loans to buy more stock in Adelphia. The Rigas family created false receipts showing payments made from their personal funds, not from money borrowed from Adelphia. The investigation also uncovered that Adelphia funds were used to purchase several exorbitant luxuries, including a private golf course, the use of company jets, and a personal chef for the family.

Adelphia stakeholders also filed a suit against the Rigas family for $1 billion. The suit claimed that the entire Rigas family was in violation of the Racketeer Influenced and Corrupt Organizations Act of 1970. They argued that the Rigas family, including John's wife, Doris, and his daughter Eileen, had frequently taken part in insider trading in order to make themselves wealthier.

John and his son Timothy Rigas were found guilty of several counts of fraud and conspiracy. On June 20, 2005, John was sentenced to fifteen years in federal prison and Timothy was sentenced to twenty years. Adelphia was forced to file bankruptcy, with its competitors Time Warner and Comcast buying out nearly all of Adelphia's assets. The funds taken by the Rigas family amounted to more than $3 billion.

Impact
The Adelphia scandal and the subsequent incarcerations of John and Timothy Rigas are examples of the federal government's efforts to investigate corporate corruption in the 2000s. The actions of the Rigas family cost stakeholders billions of dollars. The scandal was heavily covered in the media, bringing the issues of corporate ethics and insider trading to the public. The scandal helped to garner support for the Sarbanes-Oxley Act of 2002, which is a federal law that strengthened standards for US public company boards, management, and public accounting firms.

Further Reading
Frank, Robert, and Jerry Markon. "Adelphia Officials Are Arrested, Charged With 'Massive' Fraud." *Wall Street Journal.* Dow Jones & Co., 25 July 2002. Web. 27 Oct. 2012.

Grant, Peter, and Christine Nuzum. "Adelphia Founder and One Son Are Found Guilty." *Wall Street Journal.* Dow Jones & Co., 9 July 2004. Web. 27 October 2012.

Patrick G. Cooper

■ Airline industry

Definition: The combination of rising costs and decreasing numbers of passengers led to significant changes to the airline industry during the 2000s

The US airline industry experienced several major setbacks during the 2000s, including terrorist attacks, increased operating costs, and labor disputes. Some airlines sought bankruptcy protection, while others negotiated mergers in the hopes of returning their companies to viability. By the end of the decade, most US airlines had significantly cut their labor force and decreased their passenger capacity in attempts to regain financial stability.

The 2000s were a difficult decade for the airline industry. US airlines carried approximately 665 million passengers domestically and internationally in

A traveler is screened as he passes through a security checkpoint. (©iStockphoto.com/Tim Boyle)

2000. By 2009, that number had reached only 703 million—a decrease of 60 million passengers from its peak in 2007—and growth was much slower than anticipated. The terrorist attacks of September 11, 2001, along with several other attempted terrorist acts, led to tighter federal regulation of airport security procedures and increased security costs. Skyrocketing fuel costs further harmed the airlines' financial stability, leading to layoffs and labor disputes that threatened to drive several major airlines into bankruptcy before the end of the decade.

Terrorism and Security
On September 11, 2001, nineteen terrorists hijacked four airplanes and flew them into the World Trade Center in New York City and the Pentagon in Washington, DC, killing thousands of people. In response to these attacks, Congress passed the Aviation and Transportation Security Act on November 19, 2001, which established the federal Transportation Security Administration (TSA) within the Department of Transportation. The TSA assumed responsibility for passenger airline security from the Federal Aviation

Administration (FAA). When the Homeland Security Act was passed by Congress in November 2002, the TSA was moved into the newly formed Department of Homeland Security. The TSA became responsible for screening all passengers and carry-on baggage before boarding the plane, screening checked baggage and cargo for hazardous materials, cross-checking passenger lists with a terrorist watch "no-fly" list, and conducting background checks on millions of employees in the transportation industry.

In December 2001, another terrorist named Richard Reid attempted to detonate explosives hidden in his sneakers while on an American Airlines flight from Paris, France, to Miami, Florida. Passengers and crew members stopped him, but the attempt led to a new TSA-imposed security requirement that all passengers remove their shoes for X-ray inspection prior to boarding the plane. The TSA enacted further restrictions on carrying liquids through security checkpoints in August 2006, following the interception of a terrorist plot to detonate explosive devices on ten planes bound for the United States from the United Kingdom.

While some credit these additional precautions with preventing further terrorist attacks, others criticize the measures for causing significant delays at airport check-in and security, mistaken-identity issues regarding the no-fly list, and civil rights violations caused by racial profiling.

Decreased Ridership and Increased Operating Costs

These high-profile attacks caused a noticeable decrease in ridership during the months that followed; it took nearly three years to return to normal levels following September 11, 2001. Many airlines struggled to maintain profitability while selling fewer tickets, especially since the new security requirements were costly to implement. Several major airlines, including US Airways (2002–3 and 2004–5), United Airlines (2002–6), Northwest Airlines (2005–7) and Delta Airlines (2005–7), filed for bankruptcy protection while they restructured their companies in attempt to regain profitability. This period also saw several mergers between major US airlines, including US Airways and America West Airlines in 2005, and Northwest Airlines and Delta Airlines in 2008.

Many consumers expressed frustration with airline travel during this time: Increased security measures combined with staffing cuts often led to long lines at ticket counters and security checkpoints. Travelers were also frustrated with the perceived lack of customer service. Nonetheless, US airlines continued to carry more than 600 million passengers annually throughout the decade.

Unfortunately, as the industry struggled to recover, skyrocketing fuel costs further damaged profitability. In 2005, Hurricane Katrina dramatically reduced the oil refinement capacity of the United States, while the ongoing wars in the Middle East and political tension with Venezuela reduced oil supplies worldwide. By 2008, financial market speculators were actively trading options for oil, which further drove up the price: A barrel of crude oil that sold for $20 to $40 per barrel at the beginning of the decade spiked to a high of over $147 in July 2008, before crashing back down to $40 only a few months later.

This enormous increase in fuel cost drove many smaller regional airlines out of business and led to continued financial struggles for larger carriers. Southwest Airlines emerged as a surprising winner in this debacle: The airline had locked in its fuel purchase price, and Southwest's risky bet that fuel costs would continue to rise paid off. Because Southwest's fuel costs were less than half that of other airlines, it was one of the few airlines to post a profit in 2008 while still offering bargain fares. This competitive advantage helped the airline gain significant market share.

Labor Disputes

Unsurprisingly, labor disputes arose amid the financial turmoil. Many airlines reduced their workforce, and demanded pay cuts and benefit reductions from their remaining employees. Delta Airlines faced off with its pilots in 2005, when it demanded concessions in pay and benefit in an unsuccessful attempt to avoid bankruptcy. A strike was narrowly avoided with the help of the bankruptcy court. In August 2005, the mechanics for Northwest Airlines went on strike due to difficulties with contract negotiations.

Impact

The combination of terrorist threats, increased operating costs, and labor difficulties left many airlines struggling financially throughout the 2000s. Tickets prices increased, but consumer perception of the quality of airline customer service declined as people became frustrated with long wait times due to increased security measures, additional baggage restrictions, and decreased staffing levels. While the industry did experience growth in total annual ridership over the course of the decade, that growth was significantly smaller than expected, and financial problems led to several bankruptcies and mergers in order to keep the companies afloat.

Further Reading

Bethune, Gordon. *From Worst to First: Behind the Scenes of Continental's Remarkable Comeback*. New York: Wiley, 1998. Print. Examines how Continental Airlines adjusted its business model in the 1990s and reviews the state of the airline industry at the beginning of the 2000s.

Pae, Peter. "Hedge on Fuel Prices Pays Off." *Los Angeles Times*. Los Angeles Times, 20 May 2008. Web. 29 Nov. 2012. Describes the fuel hedging efforts undertaken by Southwest Airlines during the mid-2000s.

Shaw, Stephen. *Airline Marketing and Management.* Burlington: Ashgate, 2011. Print. Offers an overview of the airline industry from a marketing perspective.

Transportation Security Administration. "About TSA." *Transportation Security Administration.* Department of Homeland Security, n.d. Web. 29 Nov. 2012. Provides an overview of the history and responsibilities of the TSA.

Wensveen, John G. *Air Transportation: A Management Perspective.* Burlington: Ashgate, 2011. Print. Explores the airline industry from the perspective of corporate managers.

Tracey M. DiLascio, Esq.

■ Alaska Airlines Flight 261

The Event: Fatal airplane crash off the California coast resulting from a mechanical failure due to inadequate maintenance procedures
Date: January 31, 2000
Place: Pacific Ocean, near Anacapa Island

On January 31, 2000, the horizontal stabilizer of Alaska Airlines Flight 261 jammed, causing the aircraft to plunge into a nosedive. The airplane, a McDonnell Douglas MD-83, hit the waters of the Pacific Ocean with sufficient force to destroy the aircraft, killing everyone on board. The malfunction was caused by a worn-out critical component that was not replaced during maintenance. This component did not have a fail-safe backup in case of an emergency.

Alaska Airlines Flight 261 departed from Licenciado Gustavo Díaz Ordaz International Airport in Puerto Vallarta, Mexico. It was scheduled to reach its final destination at Seattle-Tacoma International Airport in Washington state, with a planned stop at San Francisco International Airport in California. Captain Ted Thompson and First Officer William Tansky were flying the aircraft, which carried three cabin crew members and eighty-three passengers.

Approximately two hours after takeoff, Flight 261 contacted dispatch to inform them of a jammed horizontal stabilizer. The crew requested a landing at Los Angeles International Airport in California. Half an hour later, the pilots lost partial control of the aircraft, and it descended rapidly almost ten thousand feet. They managed to fly for another ten minutes

before completely losing control and crashing into the ocean. All eighty-three passengers and five crew members were killed.

The National Transportation Safety Board's investigation revealed that the accident was not caused by human error or adverse weather. A combination of factors contributed to the failure of a critical component in the horizontal stabilizer, called a jackscrew assembly, which is essential in the vertical control of an airplane. The component did not have a fail-safe backup in the event of a malfunction. The scheduled maintenance and lubrication of the jackscrew assembly, although approved by the Federal Aviation Administration, were found to be insufficient. John Liotine, a mechanic for Alaska Airlines, had recommended the replacement of the plane's jackscrew two years prior to the crash. His decision was overruled by other mechanics, who performed further testing and deemed that the part was within the acceptable limits of wear.

Impact
Both the aircraft manufacturer, Boeing, and the carrier, Alaska Airlines, accepted responsibility for the accident. They agreed to compensate the relatives of the victims. Both pilots were posthumously awarded gold medals for heroism from the Air Line Pilots Association. Several safety measures and maintenance procedures were improved as a result of the National Transportation Safety Board's findings and recommendations. The Federal Aviation Administration was required to conduct better oversight of future maintenance operations.

Further Reading
Dodd, Chris. "Alaska Flight 261 Pilots Awarded ALPA Gold Medal." *Air Line Pilot.* Air Line Pilots Association International, Mar. 2001. Web. 7 Aug. 2012.

Malnic, Eric, and Li Fellers. "Firms Accept Liability in Flight 261 Crash." *Baltimore Sun.* Baltimore Sun Media Group, 4 June 2003. Web. 7 Aug. 2012.

National Transportation Safety Board. *Loss of Control and Impact with Pacific Ocean Alaska Airlines Flight 261 McDonnell Douglas MD-83, N963AS About 2.7 Miles North of Anacapa Island, California January 31, 2000.* Washington: National Transportation Safety Board, 30 Dec. 2002. PDF file.

PBS. "Alaska Air Crash." *PBS.* MacNeil/Lehrer Productions, 1 Feb. 2000. Web. 7 Aug. 2012.

Miroslav Farina

■ Alito, Samuel

Identification: Associate justice of the US Supreme
Court, beginning in 2006
Born: April 1, 1950; Trenton, New Jersey

*Samuel Alito was confirmed as the 110th justice of the Su-
preme Court of the United States in January 2006. Alito is
poised to decide on a number of longstanding social and
civil-rights issues expected to come before the court. His confirmation as Justice Sandra Day O'Connor's successor has
made the Supreme Court's composition significantly more
conservative.*

US Court of Appeals Judge Samuel Alito Jr. was
nominated by President George W. Bush to the US
Supreme Court on October 31, 2005. That July, Supreme Court Justice Sandra Day O'Connor had sent
her letter of resignation to President Bush. Any nomination to the Supreme Court of the United States is
fraught with political ramifications. A Supreme
Court appointment is for life, and the justices have
an impact on US law and social policy long after the
president who submits the nomination has left office. Justice O'Connor's retirement, however, was of
particular concern. Throughout her years of service, O'Connor famously represented the court's
swing vote. Her moderate opinions kept a degree of
balance on the court between liberal and conservative political positions.

Most legal experts agree that Alito's career and
public statements place him firmly in the conservative tradition. Nevertheless, Alito was not President
Bush's first nominee. On July 20, Bush had nominated US Court of Appeals Judge John Roberts to fill
O'Connor's seat on the Court. On September 3, 2006,
however, Supreme Court Chief Justice William
Rehnquist died suddenly after nearly nineteen years
on the court. Bush quickly moved to withdraw Roberts's nomination for associate justice and instead
nominated him to fill Chief Justice Rehnquist's seat.

President Bush next nominated White House
Counsel Harriet Miers to the associate justice seat
being vacated by O'Connor. On October 27, Miers
withdrew her acceptance of the nomination after
objections from both political parties and the American Bar Association about her qualifications for the
Supreme Court.

On October 31, President Bush announced his
nomination of Alito to fill the position of associate

Samuel Alito. (Collection of the Supreme Court of the United
States/Photograph by Steve Petteway)

justice. Unlike Miers, Alito had the necessary legal
experience to serve on the Supreme Court. The debate about Alito's fitness for the bench revolved
around a few social and political issues, such as
abortion rights, affirmative action, and civil rights
during times of war.

On the Issues

Many American liberals were alarmed by Alito's
staunchly conservative views, particularly his belief
that constitutional law does not protect an individual's right to an abortion. In response to these concerns, several Democratic senators, led by Senator
John Kerry of Massachusetts, tried unsuccessfully to
garner support for a filibuster to block the nomination of Alito. In spite of the debates over Alito's suitability, the Senate Committee confirmed Alito as the
110th justice of the Supreme Court on January 31,
2006, by a vote of 58 to 42.

With Alito's nomination secured, the Supreme
Court became decidedly more conservative than
when Justice O'Connor had served. In all of the
5-to-4 Supreme Court rulings from 2006 until the
end of the decade, Alito never once sided with the

liberal half of the court. In 2007, Alito joined the majority opinion in a 5-to-4 ruling on *Gonzales v. Carhart*, which upheld the federal Partial-Birth Abortion Ban Act as constitutional. Just seven years earlier, Justice O'Connor had voted to strike down a similar statewide ban in *Stenberg v. Carhart*. In addition, Alito joined the majority opinion on several other landmark cases decided by a 5-to-4 ruling, including *District of Columbia v. Heller* (2008), *Montejo v. Louisiana* (2009), and *Ricci v. DeStefano* (2009).

Impact

Samuel Alito's nomination and subsequent confirmation to the Supreme Court will have an impact on US law and politics for years to come. Nominated during a time of bitterly partisan political dialogue, Alito is poised to rule on a number of modern history's defining issues. As a conservative voice on the court, Alito has, on occasion, broken rank. Alito was the lone dissenting vote in *Snyder v. Phelps*, a closely watched case involving the infamous Westboro Baptist Church, in which he argued that protesting at funerals is not protected speech under the First Amendment.

Further Reading

Bazelon, Emily. "Mysterious Justice." *New York Times* 20 Mar. 2011, Sunday Magazine: MM13. Print.

Brust, Richard. "No More Kabuki Confirmations." *ABA Journal* 95.10 (2009): 39–43. Print.

Gibson, James L., and Gregory A. Caldeira. "Confirmation Politics and the Legitimacy of the U.S. Supreme Court: Institutional Loyalty, Positivity Bias, and the Alito Nomination." *American Journal of Political Science* 53.1 (2009): 139–55. Print.

Amy Witherbee

■ Al-Qaeda

Definition: A jihadist Islamic network founded by Osama bin Laden in the late 1980s and led by him until his death on May 2, 2011

The effort to eliminate al-Qaeda in Iraq, Afghanistan, and elsewhere has severely affected the domestic and foreign affairs of the United States, and has added more than $1 trillion to the US national debt. The War against Terrorism strained relations between the United States, Canada, and many other western nations, though they remained united in their alliance against the terrorist organization.

The name *al-Qaeda* is taken from the Arabic word meaning "the base." During the Soviet occupation of Afghanistan in the 1980s, it referred to the camp that had been established for the training of the mujahideen, Islamic volunteers who joined the fight against the invading Soviet forces. The terrorist movement that uses the name was formed at that time by Osama bin Laden, who was the group's leader and figurehead, advised by a council of Islamic fundamentalist clerics and other supporters. Al-Qaeda functions as a network of isolated cells that receive funding and direction from the organization. Funding has come from numerous sources around the world, including bin Laden's personal wealth, and is directed to different cells by various means. Each cell is anonymous; within each cell no member knows all of the other members of the cell, nor do members know who is in other cells. Thus each cell is essentially an autonomous body that uses the name of al-Qaeda.

Al-Qaeda Goals and Purposes

The principal goal of al-Qaeda, as stated by various members of the organization, is to end the involvement and influence of the United States and other Western countries in the Middle East and to establish a global Islamic state. Al-Qaeda operatives have stated they plan to accomplish these goals primarily through effecting the collapse of the United States and global economies. To achieve these goals, al-Qaeda's presumed strategy was to carry out an attack in the United States that would prompt the US military to invade a Middle Eastern country. Al-Qaeda operatives would then incite local resistance and expand the conflict into neighbouring countries as a long war of attrition, while simultaneously carrying out attacks within allied nations so as to fragment international support for the United States. The purported belief then is that the ongoing economic strain of these accumulated factors would result in the collapse of the US and world economies, after which a fundamentalist Islamic state could be established throughout the world. While the strategy may seem to involve a rather large leap of faith in its last stage, it is worth noting that similar strategies were used during the Soviet occupation of Afghanistan and effectively destroyed the economy of the former Soviet Union, resulting in its eventual collapse.

A poster of Osama bin-Laden at a rally in Islamabad, Pakistan, November 16, 2001. (Visual News/Getty Images)

Activities during the 2000s

Al-Qaeda carried out numerous actions during the 1990s, but the organization became the most notorious terrorist network in history with the attacks on the United States on September 11, 2001. Some three thousand people were killed in these attacks, which targeted the World Trade Center in New York and the Pentagon in Washington, DC. Subsequently, the United States and allied nations instituted the War on Terrorism that has consumed trillions of dollars of the world economy throughout the 2000s. The 2003 invasion of Iraq, ostensibly on the grounds that the country had become a stronghold of al-Qaeda, was preceded by invasion of Afghanistan to root out al-Qaeda supporters there. Throughout the 2000s, US forces worked diligently in Afghanistan, along with forces from Canada, Great Britain, Germany, Spain, the Netherlands, and several other nations, to dismantle the oppressive rule of the Taliban, an alleged supporter of al-Qaeda, and to restore a stable democratic government. The effort was equal in

importance to the ongoing search for Osama bin Laden and the destruction of al-Qaeda.

While the War on Terrorism was ongoing in Iraq and Afghanistan, al-Qaeda carried out attacks in countries allied with the United States and on US holdings. On October 12, 2000, al-Qaeda operatives successfully exploded a bomb alongside the USS *Cole* as the ship refueled off-shore, killing seventeen American service members and severely damaging the ship itself. This attack was followed by the September 11 attacks. Several bombings were also carried out in 2003 in Istanbul, Turkey, by a group with close ties to al-Qaeda; these attacks killed sixty-seven people and injured about seven hundred others. On March 11, 2004, al-Qaeda bombings in railway stations in Madrid, Spain, killed nearly two hundred people and injured more than one thousand others. The Spanish people reacted in outrage, with many Spanish citizens blaming the event on the Spanish government's support for the United States and their military presence in Iraq. On July 7, 2005, a similar attack was carried out in London, United Kingdom, that killed more than fifty people and injured approximately seven hundred.

As the Taliban lost its stranglehold on major portions of Afghanistan, its fighters withdrew to the mountainous wilds in the borderlands with Pakistan, where the organization could regroup and mount an insurgency into Afghanistan. Osama bin Laden evaded capture in Afghanistan, and removed himself and much of the leadership of al-Qaeda to Pakistan. For some time, bin Laden and members of his family lived in seclusion in the city of Abbottabad, in a walled villa only a short distance from the Pakistan military academy. He was eventually traced to that location, where he was ultimately killed by US Navy Seals on May 2, 2011. His death, and the deaths of several other top-level al-Qaeda agents who would have been his successors, severely disrupted al-Qaeda activities, though the al-Qaeda terror network continues to be a powerful presence in world affairs.

Al-Qaeda in Canada and the United States

The actions taken by allied nations against al-Qaeda in the 2000s strained their relations with the United States. Actions taken by the United States against al-Qaeda during that same time also had major and costly effects, such as the establishment of the US Department of Homeland Security and enactment of much stricter controls along the border between Canada and the United States. Tension between the two nations also arose over several issues involving border security and the disposition of individuals associated with al-Qaeda in Canada. These ranged in severity from the relatively minor inconvenience of requiring Canadian citizens to have a current passport in order to enter the United States, to the serious issues raised by the prolonged detention of Canadian citizens Maher Arar and Omar Khadr by the US government on terrorism charges. The refusal of the United States government to return Khadr to Canada for trial was a source of contention between the two nations, which was finally resolved in 2012 with the return of Khadr to Canada, where he would carry out the remainder of his sentence in a maximum-security Canadian prison.

One important aspect of the difference in constitutional jurisdiction that remained contentious for both Canada and the United States throughout the 2000s was the perceived ease with which terrorist agencies such as al-Qaeda seemed able to use Canada's immigration system and border crossings to enter the United States. In many areas, the border runs through wide-open spaces where it is possible to walk across from one nation into the other undetected, and this is in fact a method that has been used by terrorist agents on occasion to enter the United States from Canada. The dissension helped to promote the passing of new federal antiterrorism laws in Canada that would circumvent the difficulties in bringing terrorism suspects to trial in Canada, with regard to the protection of rights guaranteed by the Canadian Charter of Rights and Freedoms.

Impact

The impact of al-Qaeda on the United States and Canada throughout the 2000s was immense. While the citizenry of the two nations remained united in their stance against terrorism in general and al-Qaeda in particular, the economy of the United States suffered a serious blow through the costs associated with the War on Terrorism. Actions against al-Qaeda have added, both directly and indirectly, more than $1 trillion to the national deficit in the United States. The effort also cost the lives of several thousands of American, Canadian, and other allied soldiers, and untold numbers of civilian casualties. At the end of 2009, al-Qaeda continued to be a major presence in Afghanistan and Pakistan, and the ter-

rorist organization had spread its influence into numerous locations around the world, particularly Algeria, Yemen, and Somalia.

Further Reading

Atwan, Abdel Bari. *The Secret History of al-Qaeda.* Berkeley: U of California P, 2006. Print. In this book, Atwan describes the political agenda and plans that have driven al-Qaeda throughout the decade and since its formation, examining its origins.

Bergen, Peter. *The Longest War: The Enduring Conflict Between America and al-Qaeda.* New York: Free, 2011. Print. As the first Western journalist to personally interview Osama bin Laden as the leader of al-Qaeda, Bergen provides a unique perspective on the subject of this book.

Lawrence, Bruce, ed. *Messages to the World: The Statements of Osama bin Laden.* London: Verso, 2005. Print. In this book the reader can obtain a firsthand look into the mind of the leader of the most feared and reviled terrorism network in history.

Riedel, Bruce. *The Search for al-Qaeda: Its Leadership, Ideology and Future.* Washington: Brookings Institution, 2008. Print. Riedel's book describes the difficulty of comprehending the workings of al-Qaeda and locating its leadership after the failure to capture Osama bin Laden in Afghanistan.

Williams, Paul L. *Al Qaeda: Brotherhood of Terror.* New York: Pearson, 2002. Print. Williams's book provides an insightful overview of the terrorist network known as al-Qaeda, discussing its origins, methods of operation, and the people who were its leaders.

Richard M. Renneboog, MSc

■ American Airlines Flight 587

The Event: Fatal crash resulting from pilot error and mechanical failure
Date: November 12, 2001
Place: Queens, New York

On November 12, 2001, American Airlines Flight 587 was scheduled to fly from New York City to Santo Domingo, Dominican Republic, before it crashed shortly after takeoff in the Belle Harbor neighborhood of Queens, New York, killing everyone on board and five others on the ground. The cause of the crash was later ruled to be mechanical failure resulting from pilot error.

American Airlines Flight 587 was an early-morning flight scheduled to depart John F. Kennedy International Airport in New York and arrive at Las Americas International Airport in Santo Domingo, Dominican Republic, on November 12, 2001. The flight was commanded by Captain Edward States and First Officer Sten Molin, who was acting as pilot. In addition, there were seven other crew members and 251 passengers on board.

Upon takeoff, the Airbus A300 plane encountered turbulence believed to be the wake of a Japan Airlines plane that had taken off just before Flight 587. First Officer Molin struggled to keep the plane level through the turbulence, but he ultimately lost control, and Flight 587 crashed into a residential section of Belle Harbor.

According to the National Transportation Safety Board's official report on the incident, the crash was attributable to Molin's response to the turbulence. The report states that Molin attempted to compensate for the turbulence by using his rudder controls so aggressively that his actions caused the vertical stabilizer, or tail fin, to separate from the plane. This sent the aircraft out of control and caused both engines to separate prior to impact.

Impact

Because the crash of Flight 587 occurred only two months after the terrorist attacks of September 11, 2001, and in the midst of a series of anthrax poisonings in the United States, there was initial speculation that the incident might have been an act of terrorism. Investigators quickly dismissed this possibility, however, as the evidence showed no indication of terrorist activity.

Because the pilot's rudder control technique was responsible for the accident, American Airlines began a special rudder control training program and, in 2009, the airline retired its A300 fleet.

Further Reading

Airbus. "American Airlines Retires Its A300 fleet." *Airbus*. EADS Group, 10 Sept. 2009. Web. 6 Aug. 2012.

Airlines Flight 587 Airbus Industrie A300-605R, N14053, Belle Harbor, New York, November 12, 2001. Washington: National Transportation Safety Board, 26 Oct. 2004. PDF file.

Kleinfield, N. R. "The Crash of Flight 587: The Overview; 260 on Jet Die in Queens Crash; 6 to 9

Missing as 12 Homes Burn; US Doubts Link to Terrorism." *New York Times*. New York Times, 13 Nov. 2001. Web. 6 Aug. 2012.

Levin, Alan. "NTSB Blames Pilot Error for Flight 587 Crash." *USA Today*. Gannett, 26 Oct. 2004. Web. 6 Aug. 2012.

Miller, Leslie. "Pilot Error Blamed by NTSB for American Airlines Crash That Killed 265 in November 2001." *San Diego Source/The Daily Transcript*. San Diego Source/The Daily Transcript, 26 Oct. 2004. Web. 6 Aug. 2012.

National Transportation Safety Board. *In-Flight Separation of Vertical Stabilizer American*

Jack Lasky

■ *American Idol*

Identification: Television reality series in which singers compete, are critiqued by a three-person panel of celebrity judges, and are eliminated by viewers
Executive Producer: Simon Fuller (b. 1960)
Date: Premiered on June 11, 2002

Beginning in 2002, the unmatched success of the reality show American Idol greatly affected the FOX network. The show targeted the youth demographic and quickly became part of FOX's regular-season lineup. The show's blend of emotional and entertaining elements contributed to its success and increased the ratings of other FOX programs.

Executive producer Simon Fuller created *American Idol* based on shows that were successful in other countries. Though summer television viewership had traditionally been low in the United States, when *American Idol* debuted in June 2002, it was received enthusiastically by teens and children, and it became an immediate success. Over the years, FOX heavily promoted upcoming seasons, which debuted each January. A few years after the show debuted, advertisements sold by FOX during *American Idol* were the most expensive for a television series.

Initial episodes of each *American Idol* season included highlights of open auditions, which were held at venues across the United States. Some performers gained fame merely for their terrible auditions. Each week selected contestants performed and received criticism and advice from the judges. Viewers were encouraged to vote by both phone and text message, and results were announced on a second

Ryan Seacrest and Kelly Clarkson during the Season 2 finale of American Idol, *2003.* (S. Granitz/WireImage/Getty Images)

weekly episode. Winners received solo recording contracts and were managed by Fuller's company, 19 Entertainment. The series was coproduced by FremantleMedia North America.

For the first few seasons, the age range for contestants was quite young—sixteen to twenty-four. In later years, the format was expanded and adjusted. The hosts and judges changed slightly over time. The first season was hosted by Brian Dunkleman and Ryan Seacrest. By the second season, Seacrest was the solo host. Initial judges were Simon Cowell, Paula Abdul, and Randy Jackson. It was widely acknowledged that Cowell's caustic comments and callous treatment of contestants accounted for much of the show's success. Abdul, who was a judge until 2009, treated competitors more gently, as did Jackson. The combination of nurturing and nastiness was a key component of *American Idol.*

Fuller also developed similar shows for other countries and signed licensing agreements for products ranging from backpacks to Barbie dolls. Other FOX series enjoyed increased ratings as a result of both their proximity to *American Idol* on the schedule and heavy promotion during the show. The network was not alone in profiting—product placement and

mentions of major sponsors were extremely lucrative for the producers, and FOX affiliates were allocated three minutes an hour to sell local ads. The show experienced small ratings declines beginning in 2007.

Idol Winners

Contestants signed contracts in advance, giving 19 Entertainment the right to manage them for three years, and Fuller guided several winners successfully. Runners-up who wanted to pursue singing careers were also contractually obligated to be managed by Fuller if he was interested in signing them. The contestants who performed on *American Idol* tour to large crowds. Kelly Clarkson, Carrie Underwood, Clay Aiken, Fantasia Barrino, Kellie Pickler, and Chris Daughtry were among the contestants who achieved some post-*American Idol* fame. Season-one winner Clarkson's "A Moment Like This" made chart history with its swift rise to the number-one position on Billboard Hot 100.

Successes and Setbacks

Winning the competition was no guarantee of success, and such top finishers as Taylor Hicks and Ruben Studdard lost their record contracts as a result of poor sales. Several contests who did not win were triumphant in their careers, however. Though season 3 contestant Jennifer Hudson did not win *American Idol,* she earned a supporting role in the film *Dreamgirls* (2006), for which she received a 2007 Academy Award, a Golden Globe, and other awards. She also earned a Grammy Award for best rhythm-and-blues album in 2009. Though Daughtry came in fourth place in the fifth season of *Idol,* he sold 3.6 million copies of his first album.

Impact

The success of *American Idol* and of many of the singers featured on the show changed the music industry. Numerous young people aspired to be pop singers. Though a few, such as Hudson, went on to perform soul music or achieved success on the country or rock charts, most contestants brought a pop style to the show. Music teachers saw increasing numbers of students who wanted to be famous pop singers as a result of to the show's popularity among teenagers.

The *American Idol* phenomenon extended to charity. Several special fund-raising episodes drew donations for such organizations as Feeding America,

Malaria No More, and Save the Children. Guests including President Barack Obama, U2's Bono, and NFL quarterbacks Eli and Peyton Manning appeared on fund-raising episodes. By the end of the decade, the Idol Gives Back program had raised more than $140 million for charitable organizations.

Further Reading

Austen, Jake. *TV a-Go-Go: Rock on TV from American Bandstand to American Idol.* Chicago: Chicago Review, 2005. Print. Examines the relationship between popular music and television through the decades.

Canfield, Jack, Mark Victor Hansen, and Debra Poneman. *Chicken Soup for the American Idol Soul.* Deerfield Beach: Health, 2007. Print. Inspirational accounts of the personal experiences of previous *American Idol* participants.

Caro, Mark. "The 'Idol' Effect." *Chicago Tribune.* Chicago Tribune, 16 Jan. 2007. Web. 2 Aug. 2012. Analyzes cultural changes since the series debuted.

Greene, Andy. "Chris Daughtry: 'American Idol' Is 'in a State of Decline.'" *Rolling Stone.* Rolling Stone, 14 Jan. 2008. Web. 3 Aug. 2012. Interview with the rock singer Daughtry, who criticizes the series.

Halperin, Shirley. *American Idol: Celebrating Ten Years—The Official Backstage Pass.* New York: Abrams, 2011. Print. Collection of photos of, facts about, and updates on the performers.

Lieberman, David. "'American Idol' Zooms from Hit Show to Massive Business." *USA Today.* USA Today, 29 Mar. 2005. Web. 3 Aug. 2012. Information about the financial success of the series and its producers.

Josephine Campbell

■ American Recovery and Reinvestment Act of 2009

The Law: Federal legislation that was designed primarily to create jobs and stimulate economic growth in an effort to end the serious and protracted recession then existing in the United States

Date: Enacted February 17, 2009.

Also Known As: ARRA; Economic Stimulus Act; Economic Stimulus Bill; Recovery Act

The American Recovery and Reinvestment Act of 2009 was Congress's response to the economic downturn, or financial crisis, that began approximately in 2007, and continued several years thereafter. The Act—essentially a government spending bill—was primarily designed to create new jobs, to save existing jobs, and to provide financial resources to federal, state, and local government programs that had been adversely impacted by the protracted economic downturn.

Beginning approximately in late 2007, the United States began to experience a financial crisis second in severity only to the Great Depression. Generally, this period saw the so-called housing bubble burst, leading to a decline in housing prices and a rise in home foreclosures. Simultaneously, unemployment rates increased. Banks and other financial institutions suffered significant losses, with some filing for bankruptcy, and consumers began to experience losses on their investments, including retirement funds. Additionally, capital investment declined, and, for most individuals, income levels decreased. The overall result was a widespread and protracted economic downturn that negatively affected millions of Americans, as well as businesses across the country. The economic downturn was not limited to the United States. To be sure, many countries, including several of the United States' trading partners, experienced similar economic problems during this period in time.

Passage and Scope of the Recovery Act

After being elected president, but before taking office in 2009, Barack Obama had considered, and had convened studies concerning, the possible effect of a comprehensive economic stimulus bill. In January 2009, shortly after Obama's inauguration, the House of Representatives and the Senate each proposed versions of what would eventually become the American Recovery and Reinvestment Act (ARRA). After the bills were compared, a conference report of the bills passed the House of Representatives, and shortly thereafter, the bill was passed by the Senate in a 60–38 vote. On February 17, 2009, approximately one month into his presidency, President Obama signed ARRA into law. Importantly, nearly all Congressional Democrats supported the act, and nearly all Congressional Republicans opposed it. Accordingly, the act itself was both contentious and divisive from the beginning.

As passed, ARRA is primarily a spending bill that was designed to jumpstart the US economy after the protracted recession. The act had several enumerated purposes, namely, to save and create jobs and stimulate economic recovery; to help Americans who had been adversely affected by economic conditions; to invest in technology, science, and health-related endeavors; to fund transportation and environmental protection initiatives that were believed to have long-term economic benefits; and to prevent shortfalls in state and local governmental budgets with the goal of avoiding the elimination of important government services and state or local tax increases. At the time of passage, the total cost of ARRA was estimated at $787 billion. According to a February 2012 report from the Congressional Budget Office, the total financial impact of the act between 2009 and 2019 will be approximately $831 billion—$44 billion more than the initial estimates.

Spending and Investment Provisions of the Recovery Act

ARRA included hundreds of provisions specifically designed to implement the stated purposes. Specifically, the act included tax incentives for individuals and families, such as a payroll tax credit, the expansion of the child tax credit, a homebuyer tax credit, and an energy tax credit. The act appropriated approximately $87 billion to fund Medicaid, and $25 billion to aid in subsidizing health care premiums for the Consolidated Omnibus Budget Reconciliation Act (COBRA), a health benefit program for the unemployed. Other key provisions concerned funding for education. Nearly $54 billion was allocated to prevent layoffs and other budget cuts in schools; approximately $16 billion was earmarked to increase the value of Pell Grants, which are funds available to certain college students.

Another major arm of ARRA included funding for the unemployed, the poor, and the retired. At the time the act was passed, unemployment and underemployment figures were at extremely high rates. Specifically, $40 billion was allocated to extend unemployment benefits and to increase the value of such benefits. Additionally, nearly $20 billion was directed to the Food Stamp program whereby low-income Americans could more easily purchase certain food items. Further, $14 billion was allocated to one-time, $250 payments to those receiving Social Security, as well as veterans who were receiving disability payments. Lesser amounts were allocated to fund food banks and to provide job training for groups such as the elderly and the disabled.

A further stated goal of ARRA was to put Americans back to work. To that end, $27.5 billion was used to fund construction projects related to highways and bridges, and another $8 billion was set aside to fund railway projects. Many of these projects were considered "shovel-ready," in the sense that the projects had been deemed ready to be completed, but had lacked funding or approval until specifically authorized by the act.

Other provisions included funding for Army Corps of Engineer environmental projects; approximately $7 billion allocated to improve governmental facilities; $1 billion to fund explosive detection systems at United States airports; $6 billion to clean up hazardous waste sites; $27 billion dedicated to renewable energy and other energy related efficiency projects, which included $6 billion in guarantees for renewable energy sources; $4 billion to the Department of Housing and Urban Development to repair public housing; $3 billion to the National Scientific Foundation for research; and $4 billion to state and local law enforcement.

Impact

As previously noted, ARRA was highly controversial at the time of its passage, with almost all House and Senate Democrats supporting it, and nearly all House and Senate Republicans in opposition. Not surprisingly, there still exists great divide among economic scholars, politicians, and members of the general public as to whether ARRA was successful or, rather, whether it simply was an example of wasteful government spending that provided no meaningful benefit for most Americans.

In July 2011, President Obama stated: "I'm absolutely convinced, and the vast majority of economists are convinced, that the steps we took in the Recovery Act saved millions of people their jobs or created a whole bunch of jobs." Dylan Matthews of the *Washington Post* analyzed nine economic studies of ARRA in 2011, and noted that, in six of the nine studies, the economists had concluded that the act did have a significant and positive impact on employment and growth. The economists who conducted the remaining three studies concluded that the overall impact of the act was negligible or impossible to detect.

In May 2012, the Congressional Budget Office, a federal agency whose chief task is to provide objective and nonpartisan economic data and analysis to

Congress, released statistics related to the practical impact of ARRA with respect to the first quarter of 2012 only. These statistics are interesting because they begin to analyze the long-term effects of the act, rather than the immediate effect that it had in 2009. Among the findings for the first quarter of 2012 were the following: ARRA raised the United States' real gross domestic product between 0.1 percent and 1 percent; it lowered unemployment by between 0.1 percent and 0.8 percent; it resulted in between 200,000 and 1.5 million people being employed; and it increased by between 300,000 and 1.9 million the number of full-time jobs. The findings also noted, however, that the effects of ARRA peaked in early 2010, and had since diminished.

The long-term success or failure of ARRA likely will not be known for some time, however. For example, it is impossible to accurately gauge the billions invested in programs such as clean energy and energy efficiency until the overall feasibility of clean energy itself—a program in a relative stage of infancy—is more accurately calculable. Additionally, as some economists have noted, it is difficult to separate with complete accuracy, for example, the number of jobs created in 2009 that were a result of ARRA, and the number of jobs created in 2009 that were a product of the economic supply and demand that existed at that specific time. Some created jobs, in fact, may have been a combination of both ARRA and the prevailing economic conditions at that time. As with any controversial political decision, the successes and the failures of ARRA will be debated for years to come.

Further Reading

Gandel, Stephen. "Obama's Stimulus Plan: Failing by its Own Measure." *Time.* Time Inc., 14 July 2009. Web. 3 Nov. 2012. Using economic figures released after the first several months of ARRA's passage, Gandel argues that the act is off to a slow start and, may in fact be failing.

Grabell, Michael. *Money Well Spent?: The Truth Behind the Trillion-Dollar Stimulus, the Biggest Economic Recovery Plan in History.* New York: Perseus, 2012. Print. A relatively objective analysis of the manner in which funds for ARRA were distributed, its impact on the economy, and its effect on US citizens.

Grunwald, Michael. *The New New Deal: The Hidden Story of Change in the Obama Era.* New York: Simon, 2012. Print. The author, a correspondent for *Time* magazine, provides a meticulously detailed and well-researched account of ARRA's passage, and argues that it has been responsible for preventing the United States from entering a protracted depression.

Leonhardt, David. "Judging Stimulus by Job Data Reveals Success." *New York Times.* New York Times Co, 16 Feb. 2010. Web. 3 Nov. 2012. Argues that, although ARRA had certain flaws, it essentially accomplished exactly what its intended purpose was, namely, to create jobs at a time when the US economy was struggling greatly.

Tellis, Paul G, Ed. *American Recovery and Reinvestment Act: History, Overview, Impact.* Happauge: Nova, 2010. Print. A comprehensive look at the provisions and history of ARRA, as well as an examination into its overall impact after its first half-year in effect.

Andrew E. Walter, JD

■ Anderson, Wes

Identification: American film director
Born: May 1, 1969; Houston, Texas

Having written or co-written and directed all of his films, Anderson is one of modern cinema's true auteurs. His distinctive artistic vision and understated brand of humor have solidified his place in the canon of American moviemaking.

With films such as the cult classic *Bottle Rocket* (1996) and the critically acclaimed *Rushmore* (1998) under his belt, Wes Anderson's star was already on the rise by the time he released *The Royal Tenenbaums* in 2001. Chronicling the story of an eccentrically dysfunctional Manhattan family, the film was a hit with audiences and critics alike. The screenplay, which Anderson cowrote with cast member Owen Wilson, was nominated for an Academy Award and a British Academy of Film and Television Arts Award. The success of the movie elevated Anderson to a new level of fame.

Anderson followed up *The Royal Tenenbaums* with *The Life Aquatic with Steve Zissou* (2004). The film is loosely based on the life of deep-sea explorer Jacques Cousteau, a person whom Anderson has always admired. Although the film was not as commercially successful as its predecessor, it was nominated for a few minor awards.

Wes Anderson. (©iStockphoto.com/Kevin Winter)

In 2007, Anderson released *The Darjeeling Limited,* which tells the story of three brothers traveling throughout India. The film was well received by critics, who praised its narrative and aesthetic appeal. That same year, Anderson directed an advertising campaign for AT&T and directed and starred in an ad for American Express. He also worked with actor Brad Pitt on a commercial for a French bank in 2008.

For his next film project, Anderson made use of a different filmmaking process: stop-motion animation. *The Fantastic Mr. Fox* (2009), based on the character created by author Roald Dahl, was both a critical and commercial success. The movie earned Anderson his second Academy Award nomination, this time, for Best Animated Feature.

Impact
Throughout his career, Anderson has demonstrated a unique ability to connect with audiences through his portrayal of flawed yet relatable characters. Anderson's use of unique set designs and innovative camera work give his films an inimitable sense of

endearing refinement that sets him apart from other filmmakers and has earned him prestige among audiences, critics, and industry professionals.

Further Reading
Adweek. "10 Great TV Spots Directed by Wes Anderson." *Adweek.* Adweek, 3 July 2012. Web. 6 July 2012.
Crosley-Marra, Benjamin. "NYFF Interview: Wes Anderson." *Ion Cinema.* IonCinema.com, 4 Oct. 2007. Web. 6 July 2012.
Harcourt, Nic. "Tête-à-tête: Wes Anderson." *Los Angeles Times Magazine.* Los Angeles Times Communications LLC, February 2010. Web. 6 July 2012.
Mackenzie, Suzie. "Into the Deep." *Guardian* [UK]. Guardian News and Media Ltd., 11 Feb. 2005. Web. 6 July 2012.
NPR. "Wes Anderson: Creating a Singular Kingdom." *NPR.* NPR, 29 May 2012. Web. 6 July 2012. Reuters. "AT&T Plans Edgy Wireless Campaign." Reuters. Thomson Reuters. 11 Sept. 2007. Web. 6 July 2012.

Cait Caffrey

■ Anthrax attacks

The Event: A series of letters containing anthrax spores sent to the offices of two United States senators and a number of American news media outlets
Date: September 18, 2001–October 9, 2001
Place: Boca Raton, Florida; New York, New York; Washington, DC

The anthrax attacks of 2001 represented the first extensive use of a bioterror weapon in the United States, demonstrating the vulnerability of the country to such an attack. The FBI investigation of the attacks was among the most extensive in the history of the organization.

Between September 18 and October 9, 2001, letters containing spores of the deadly anthrax bacterium were mailed to the Washington, DC, offices of Senators Tom Daschle of South Dakota and Patrick Leahy of Vermont. Letters containing anthrax were also mailed to the offices of ABC, CBS, and NBC News, and to media offices in New York and Florida. While neither senator was harmed, the letters infected twenty-two people with anthrax spores; five died. Following their initial investigation, the FBI established the letters were mailed from a postal drop box in Trenton, New Jersey. Several persons became infected with anthrax through inhalation upon opening the letters, though none was among the intended targets; several were postal workers. The method of exposure by two of the victims was never established.

In the wake of the September 11, 2001, terrorist attacks in New York, Washington, and Pennsylvania, the focus of the investigation into the anthrax attacks was initially centered on the Islamic terrorist group al-Qaida. The group, led by Osama Bin Laden, had claimed responsibility for the September 11 attacks, and several of the infected letters included anti-Israeli and anti-American comments. In the months following the anthrax infections, the FBI was criticized for being unable to link either Iraq or al-Qaida to the attacks. In 2002, the FBI's investigation began to focus on a specific person of interest, Steven Hatfill, a virologist who was at one time employed by the National Institutes of Health. Hatfill was thought to have both the expertise to produce the anthrax spores and access to the material and equipment necessary to manufacture them. However, no evidence pointing to his involvement in the anthrax attacks was ever found.

In 2008, the media reported that the focus of the FBI's investigation had shifted to Bruce Ivins, a researcher at the US Army Medical Research Institute of Infectious Diseases (USAMRIID) at Fort Detrick, Maryland. The FBI was preparing to file charges against Ivins when, in July 2008, he committed suicide. At the time of his death, Ivins was aware he was the prime suspect in the anthrax attacks. This fact, and his history of psychological problems, is believed to be the basis for his suicide. The evidence against Ivins was circumstantial—no confession or "smoking gun" was ever discovered—but many investigators, journalists, and scientific experts believe the FBI had built a strong case establishing Ivins's guilt.

Impact

Funding for the study of biological terrorism was significantly increased following the anthrax attacks of 2001, including the Project Bioshield Act in 2004, which funded vaccine development. The FBI received significant criticism for its focus on Hatfill, whose connection with the anthrax attacks was largely circum-

stantial. Though Hatfill was eventually exonerated, his designation as a "person of interest" resulted in a significant level of notoriety and disruption of his life. His subsequent lawsuits against the federal government and the news media were settled for significant sums of money.

Further Reading

Guillemin, Jeanne. *American Anthrax: Fear, Crime and the Investigation of the Nation's Deadliest Bioterror Attack.* New York: Holt, 2011.

Willman, David. *The Mirage Man: Bruce Ivins, the Anthrax Attacks, and America's Rush to War.* New York: Random, 2011.

Richard Adler, PhD

■ Apatow, Judd

Identification: American film producer, director, and writer
Born: December 6, 1967; Syosset, New York

Judd Apatow was the creative force behind a number of critically acclaimed television series and box-office hits. His popular and financially successful films are often male-bonding comedies, or "bromances," that expose the vulgar as well as the sentimental sides of men.

Screenwriter Judd Apatow's big breakthrough came in 1999, when he and Paul Feig produced the television series *Freaks and Geeks*. Although a critical hit, the show was cancelled after one season. The show continues to have a large cult following, and it was named one of the best one hundred television series of all time by Time magazine in 2007.

Realizing that television was not the perfect place for his brand of humor, Apatow contacted comedian Steve Carell, whom Apatow had worked with while producing the film *Anchorman: The Ron Burgundy Story* (2004). At the time, Apatow asked Carell if he had any ideas for a film. Carell responded with a plot based on his stand-up character, a middle-aged guy who has never had sex. The two went on to cowrite *The 40-Year-Old Virgin* (2005) based on this material, which Apatow also directed. The film was a big hit, earning both critical and popular acclaim; it earned more than four times its production cost at the box office. This success allowed Apatow to begin production on a backlog of projects. Between 2004 and 2009

Judd Apatow. (©iStockphoto.com/EdStock)

he produced, wrote, or directed more than ten hit films, including *Knocked Up* (2007), *Superbad* (2007), *Walk Hard: The Dewey Cox Story* (2007), *Forgetting Sarah Marshall* (2008), *Step Brothers* (2008), *Pineapple Express* (2008), and *Funny People* (2009).

Working with people he met on *Freaks and Geeks*, such as Seth Rogen, Jason Segel, and James Franco, Apatow created a circle of friends and coworkers whom he encouraged to write and to direct. His films are often collaborations, beginning with improvisation, moving on to a working script, and continuing with improvisations through the completion of the film. His wife, Leslie Mann, and their two children are often featured in his films, as are his good friends, Seth Rogen and Adam Sandler, among others. In a typical Apatow film, the main character achieves happiness through family and friendship. When Apatow's male characters are introduced, they have the maturity of an adolescent and refuse to grow up. The plot of the film takes them through experiences that force them into a happy and fulfilling adulthood.

Impact

Apatow became a powerhouse in Hollywood because of his personal achievements and the enormous success of his creative circle. He actively mentors new talent, encouraging young comedians to break out of stand-up and begin writing, directing, and producing their own films. His roster of protégés had a near-monopoly on early 2000s comedy culture, cementing Apatow's status as one of the most influential people working in Hollywood.

Further Reading

Hymowitz, Kay S. "The Child-Man." *Dallas Morning News.* Manhattan Inst. for Policy Research, 1 Feb. 2008. Web. 20 Aug. 2012.

Rodrick, Stephen. "Judd Apatow's Family Values." *New York Times.* New York Times Co., 27 May 2007. Web. 19 Aug. 2012.

Stein, Joel. "Taking Judd Apatow Seriously." *Time.* Time Inc., 20 July 2009. Web. 19 Aug. 2012.

Leslie Neilan

■ Apple Inc.

Definition: American consumer electronics company that manufactures and sells computer hardware, software, and electronic gadgets

In 2007, Apple Computer changed its name to Apple Inc., reflecting a shift from creating primarily personal computing devices to providing a full line of consumer electronics, such as the iPod and iPhone, as well as content marketplaces to support these devices. Throughout the 2000s, the company enjoyed financial success due to its successful marketing and unwavering focus on developing beautifully designed, easy-to-use consumer products.

From its inception, Apple occupied a unique place among technology companies by typically both manufacturing the hardware and programming the software for its devices. This contrasted with companies such as Microsoft, which developed the Windows operating system and licensed it for use on personal computers (PCs) manufactured by other companies. Although Apple experienced difficulties in the 1990s due to some failed partnerships and product launches, the return of cofounder Steve Jobs in 1997 was widely credited with getting the company back on track for dramatic success in the 2000s. Beginning

Apple store in New York City. (Courtesy Jorge Lascar)

with the redesigned iMac desktop computer in 1998, Apple went on to develop a series of popular consumer products that helped transform the nature of personal computing and media consumption.

Macintosh

Mac OS X, the tenth version of the Macintosh operating system, was released on March 24, 2001. It combined a stable Unix-based platform with a visually appealing user interface called "Aqua." For software developers, OS X introduced the Carbon application programming interface (API) and the Xcode integrated development environment (IDE) for writing code.

OS X was a key step in making Macs a central focus of consumer computing culture. Cat-themed names for OS X releases were popular with enthusiasts and eventually became marketing devices. OS X versions progressed from Cheetah (version 10.0) and Puma (10.1) in 2001 to Jaguar (10.2) in 2002, Panther (10.3) in 2003, Tiger (10.4) in 2005, Leopard (10.5) in 2007, and Snow Leopard (10.6) in 2009. In 2011

and 2012, Lion (10.7) and Mountain Lion (10.8) were released. Each update brought new features, including chat programs, customizable widgets (such as a calculator or dictionary), a file and application search, or a simple backup system.

In 2006, Apple replaced PowerPC microprocessors with Intel microprocessors in all of its computers. This shift was accompanied by name changes: the PowerMac desktop, iBook, and PowerBook laptops became the Mac Pro, MacBook, and MacBook Pro, respectively, while the iMac desktop kept its name. Black MacBooks marked the first time Mac laptops were made available in black, an option that continued until 2008.

The iMac desktop computer evolved from its signature egg shape to a more modern monitor-based appearance, including a transition from colored plastic to white plastic and then aluminum. The iMac was designed by Jonathan Ive, whose aesthetic played a leading role in distinguishing the company.

Thanks in part to Ive, Mac computers were generally perceived as aesthetically appealing as well as easy to use, and were popular choices for purposes such as graphic design. Critics alleged limited processing power for resource-intensive activities, particularly games; bemoaned Apple's tight control over all components of the hardware and software; and found the computers overpriced—even though some direct comparisons found Apple computers to be faster and less expensive than PCs.

Throughout the 2000s, Apple offered a set of email, web publishing, and remote storage services first named iTools (2000 to 2002), then .Mac (pronounced "dot Mac"; 2002 to 2008), and finally MobileMe (2008 to 2012). These services were in a sense a precursor to consumer-friendly cloud computing services (and would eventually be succeeded by Apple's own iCloud offering in 2012).

iPod

The iPod, a portable media player, was released on October 23, 2001. The first iteration of the device held just 5 gigabytes (GB) of music, or 1,000 songs (later versions would hold up to 64 GB, or 15,000 songs). Competitors included the Windows-compatible Creative ZEN and Diamond Rio media players, the Sony Walkman, and (later) the Microsoft Zune, but a unique design, aggressive marketing, and unmatched content availability helped the iPod achieve more than 70-percent market share by 2009.

The iPod evolved rapidly, with many new iterations: the iPod photo, which could display images; the iPod Mini (later iPod Nano) and iPod Shuffle, smaller versions of the iPod available in multiple colors; and the iPod Touch, a wireless-enabled touchscreen device. Beginning with fifth-generation (late 2005) iPods and third-generation (2007) iPod Nanos, the devices supported video content.

The iTunes Store, launched in 2003, created a marketplace for consumers to legally purchase music online and transfer it to an iPod or other media player. Files were initially available in advanced audio coding (AAC) format and used digital rights management (DRM) restrictions to prevent distribution of copyrighted content, although DRM-free content would become available in 2007 and DRM would be eliminated from music files by 2009. Single songs were typically sold for $0.99 and full albums for $9.99. A version of iTunes for Windows was also released in 2003 to help Windows users enjoy iTunes Store offerings.

BMG, EMI, Sony Music Entertainment, Universal, and Warner supplied the initial content; independent and other major labels later joined. Due to international laws and consumer preferences, each country has its own iTunes Store, typically with a different selection of content. The first international iTunes Stores (for the United Kingdom, France, and Germany) launched in June 2004, and twenty-two countries had stores by the end of 2009. In addition to purchased content, the iTunes Store also offered free subscriptions to user-submitted audio or video podcast recordings.

The American iTunes Store went on to sell audiobooks (through a partnership with Audible.com), video content in 2005, and games in 2006. Apple TV, a device for streaming media content from the iTunes Store and other sources such as Netflix and YouTube to a traditional television, was released in March 2007. In the same year, iTunes U made educational content from major institutions available through the iTunes Store.

The iTunes Store was a hit with consumers, selling more than one million songs in its first five days, seventy million songs in its first year, and eight billion songs by July 2009. The store also boosted iPod sales: after selling fewer than 400,000 devices in 2001, more than 20 million iPods were sold worldwide in 2005, and more than 50 million per year from 2007 to 2010.

iPhone

The iPhone, a revolutionary touchscreen smartphone, was announced in January 2007 and released in June 2007. The day after the initial announcement, Apple stock hit a then-record high of $97.80 per share, a preview of later peaks that would reach over $300. Before the introduction of the iPhone, smartphone penetration seemed largely relegated to the corporate market, with more than 80 percent of the market using Blackberry, Windows, and Palm devices in 2006. After the introduction of the iPhone, general smartphone adoption grew more quickly, reaching 17 percent in 2009 (from 8 percent in 2007). Blackberry devices still outnumbered iPhones two to one, but the iPhone's growth trajectory suggested the ratio had the potential to change: nearly 25 million iPhones were sold in 2009, more than doubling 2008 sales.

A sleek style and aluminum casing made the iPhone visually distinctive. Initially available in 4 GB or 8 GB, later versions would run to 16 GB and even 32 GB. Later iterations included the iPhone 3G, released in July 2008, and the iPhone 3GS, released in June 2009. Both were available in white or black plastic and added assisted GPS (global positioning system) navigation and an upgraded 3-megapixel camera with tap-to-focus, among other features.

The iPhone used the iOS platform, a version of the core Mac OS X operating system. The iPhone interface featured icons that open up different applications such as messaging, calendar, email, camera, photos, video, maps, music, and weather. The iPhone did not support Adobe Flash videos, a conscious decision made by Apple to promote the development of mobile-friendly HTML5 video solutions. Apple was one of the first smartphone vendors to popularize the "pinch-to-zoom" gesture, and the device supported many other gestures, such as shaking the phone to undo an act.

The iPhone was marketed as a user-friendly way to access the internet and all types of media, and the iOS platform made it possible to do so in unprecedented ways. Just as anyone could record and submit a podcast for free distribution through the iTunes Store, anyone could develop and submit an iPhone application for inclusion in the App Store. Apple's success with the iPhone was, in part, because the device was more a computer than a phone, and changed consumer expectations regarding how they interacted with the web.

Retail Stores and Events
The first retail Apple Stores opened on May 19, 2001, creating another channel for Apple to attract customers. The retail stores, which would number 273 in the United States by the end of 2009, were typically located in malls or areas with heavy foot traffic. Apple products prominently displayed at the front of the stores allowed consumers to conduct hands-on trials. Apple exercised careful control over the layout and appearance of each store.

To further the image of Apple as a consumer-friendly company, Apple Stores featured Genius Bars—tables staffed with dedicated technical support. Consumers could drop in unscheduled to receive free support and repairs for Apple products under warranty. Apple Stores also hosted classes to help consumers learn to use their new Apple products. This customer-focused, brand-driven approach was distinctive in a world where computer support

had often been provided by independent vendors, not necessarily the computer manufacturers themselves. In 2006, Apple Stores phased out traditional point-of-sale cash registers in favor of small mobile payment devices carried by staff members, increasing the high tech feel of being in an Apple Store.

The stores were widely credited for building a base of popular support for Apple products, and were also financially successful, grossing upwards of $4,000 per square foot according to some estimates. When new stores opened or new Apple products were released, many consumers waited in long lines to be the first to enter or get the product. The popularity of product launches echoed the popularity of events such as Apple's Worldwide Developers Conference (WWDC) and Macworld Expo, where major product announcements and releases often took place until 2009. CEO Steve Jobs was particularly known for his understated but emotional presentation style at such events, as well as for his tendency to wear denim pants and black turtlenecks.

The Apple Store concept was emulated by other companies, including Sony and Microsoft, which opened stores with similar visual details such as glass storefronts, long tables displaying products, and enthusiastic employees in colorful t-shirts.

Criticism and Lawsuits
Significant criticism was leveled at Apple throughout the 2000s, including complaints about tight controls over application programming (specifically restrictions on the use of Adobe Flash) and unexplained app rejections; reports of labor abuses by Apple suppliers, particularly in China; and allegations of monopolizing content distribution. Apple was also criticized for environmentally unfriendly practices. A tightly controlled and somewhat secretive company, Apple rarely responded directly to criticism, but did launch an investigation of working conditions at suppliers and began publishing annual labor reports in 2008.

Apple was also involved in several lawsuits, primarily regarding technology patents. The company also pressured or sued several websites (including Think Secret) regarding the release of private product information or unauthorized product instructions.

Some have posited the existence of a "Cult of Mac," consisting of devoted Apple users who are unreceptive to criticism of the company, avidly follow company news, and typically buy the latest products.

The concept reveals how deeply popular and sometimes divisive Apple products can be.

Impact

Apple's emphasis on design and the customer experience made it a standout consumer electronics company in the 2000s. Its cutting-edge devices and online marketplaces for music, apps, and other content transformed the way that consumers interacted with media and the internet.

Further Reading

Isaacson, Walter. *Steve Jobs*. New York: Simon, 2011. Print. A prominent biography of the Apple cofounder and chief executive officer.

Lashinsky, Adam. *Inside Apple: How America's Most Admired—and Secretive—Company Really Works*. New York: Business Plus, 2012. Print. An in-depth examination of the notoriously secretive company, based on unprecedented access to insiders.

Linzmayer, Owen. *Apple Confidential 2.0: The Definitive History of the World's Most Colorful Company*. San Francisco: No Starch, 2004. Print. A comprehensive background on Apple's early years, which set the stage for later success.

Segall, Ken. *Insanely Simple: The Obsession That Drives Apple's Success*. New York: Portfolio Hardcover, 2012. Print. Insights from the cocreator of the iMac and iPod, contrasting Apple with other tech companies.

Kerry Skemp, MA

■ Arcade Fire

Definition: Popular Canadian indie rock band

Arcade Fire officially formed in 2001, taking its name from a rumored fire. Under the leadership and enthusiasm of Win Butler, Arcade Fire offered a contrast to the mainstream music scene. In particular, the band set itself apart through the use of broad instrumentation, from mandolins to accordions, and through infectious energy.

While Win Butler first began performing in Boston, Massachusetts, with Josh Deu under the name Arcade Fire, the band did not begin to truly coalesce until the duo relocated to Montreal, Quebec, in 2001. From its early days, Arcade Fire experienced multiple iterations, evolving as members left and joined the band. Deu did not stay with Arcade Fire; another founding member, however, Régine Chassagne, became the band's drummer and in 2003, Butler's wife. The band eventually came to include Will Butler, Richard Parry, Tim Kingsbury, Jeremy Gara, and Sarah Neufeld.

In 2004, Arcade Fire released its debut album, *Funeral*, with independent label Merge Records. The album was highly anticipated in smaller circles, and a raving review in the indie music website *Pitchfork* galvanized the album's positive reception. Fueled by the Internet, *Funeral* became Merge's fastest-selling album up to that point. The Internet also fostered a wider global audience for the band. The success of Arcade Fire's first album, as energetic as it was personal—named in reference to the many band members who lost relatives during its recording—confirmed that independent music could legitimately compete with the mainstream.

Arcade Fire's second album, *Neon Bible*, was officially released in March of 2007. The band utilized the Internet to leak songs early and provided a limited release on iTunes to promote the album. *Neon Bible* was recorded in an old church that the band had converted into an apartment and recording studio outside of Montreal. Widely popular, *Neon Bible* was shortlisted for the Polaris Music Prize the year of its release. In 2008, it won the Meteor Music Award for Best International Album and the Juno Award for Alternative Album of the Year. Throughout the band's quick rise to success, Arcade Fire retained the intensity that might characterize a lesser-known indie band fighting for survival and relevance.

Impact

Whether driving around on tour or assuming all costs to renovate the band's recording studio, Arcade Fire modeled self-sufficiency as a means of retaining artistic control. Independence let the band retain its own vision without deference to a record label's desires. Continuing to act in accordance with band members' values, Arcade Fire preformed free concerts for Democratic contender Barack Obama during the 2008 presidential campaign. The band was further popularized through appearances on *Saturday Night Live* and the *Late Show with David Letterman*, and the use of the song "Wake Up" in the trailer for the movie *Where the Wild Things Are* (2009).

Although the band's success has largely depended on the Internet, Arcade Fire's ethic challenged digital music distribution. The band emphasized each album's physicality, considering liner notes and album art essential to any complete album. While individual songs are available for purchase online, Arcade Fire produced albums as full compositions reliant on all aspects rather than as a loose collection of songs.

Further Reading

Cook, John, Mac McCaughan, and Laura Ballance. *Our Noise: The Story of Merge Records.* Chapel Hill: Algonquin, 2009. Print.

Kot, Greg. *Ripped: How the Wired Generation Revolutionized Music.* New York: Scribner, 2009. Print.

Lucia Pizzo

■ Armstrong, Lance

Identification: Professional cyclist
Born: September 18, 1971; Plano, Texas

As a professional cyclist, Lance Armstrong was one of the most iconic athletes of the decade. He dominated in international competitions and, despite an ongoing fight with cancer, went on to win seven consecutive Tour de France titles. He later became embroiled in a doping scandal that cost him endorsements and forced him to step down as chair of his charity, Livestrong. Armstrong was subsequently stripped of his Tour de France titles.

In the early 1990s, Lance Armstrong emerged as the US national amateur cycling champion, winning the Thrift Drug Classic and the First Union Grand Prix. By the late 1990s, he was ranked among the top ten international cyclists. He won the Tour du Pont in 1995 and again in1996 for an unprecedented second time, while also establishing records for the fastest average time-trial speed and the largest margin of victory.

In October 1996 Armstrong was diagnosed with advanced testicular cancer. When doctors discovered that the tumors had spread to his lungs, lymph nodes, and brain, they gave him a 40 percent chance of survival. He began an aggressive regimen of chemotherapy, and after a series of successful surgical procedures, was declared cancer-free in the early weeks of 1997. Unable to remain idle in the months

Lance Armstrong. (©iStockphoto.com/Sylvain Gaboury)

following his diagnosis, he created the Lance Armstrong Foundation, also known as the Livestrong Foundation, an international organization dedicated to the promotion of cancer research, awareness, and early detection.

Armstrong returned to racing in 1998, competing in a number of international events. In May of that year, he married Kristin Richard, whom he had met the previous year at a charity function for his foundation. With a new contract with the United States Postal Service Pro Cycling team, Armstrong was ready to resume his place among the world's best cyclists. He returned to the Tour de France in the summer of 1999, garnering media attention for his plans to compete in the prestigious race so soon after his ordeal with cancer. After dominating the majority of the race, Armstrong became the first American to win the event since Greg LeMond in 1990, finishing with a margin of more than seven minutes over his closest competitor. Firmly denying the French media's accusations that he had used illegal performance-enhancing drugs to win the race, Lance returned the following year to a second Tour de France victory, once again joining LeMond as the only American to repeat as champion. In 2000, Armstrong competed at the Summer Olympics in Sydney, Australia, earning a bronze medal for road cycling in the men's individual time trial.

Armstrong continued to make cycling history by winning the Tour de France seven consecutive times, from 1999 to 2005. In 2002, he was named "Sportsman of the Year" by *Sports Illustrated* magazine, and from 2002 through 2005, the Associated Press named Armstrong "Male Athlete of the Year." However, Armstrong's professional accomplishments took a toll on his personal life. Lance and Kristin Armstrong filed for divorce in September 2003. Following his 2005 Tour De France victory, Armstrong retired from cycling, saying he wanted to focus his efforts on the work of his charitable foundation. In 2007, he joined a large contingent of other well-known sports figures in the founding of Athletes for Hope, a nonprofit organization that coordinates and supports the philanthropic efforts of professional athletes.

In September 2008, Armstrong announced that he would return to cycling and stated that he hoped to earn another Tour de France victory in 2009. While competing in a race in Spain in March 2009, however, Armstrong fell and broke his collarbone, an injury that would eventually require surgery. Nonetheless, Armstrong would go on to compete in the 2009 Tour de France, finishing in third place. In 2010, Armstrong again competed in the Tour de France, this time on racing team sponsored by electronics retailer RadioShack. However, his effort was thwarted by another injury after a crash, and he completed his final Tour in twenty-third place.

For years, Armstrong was dogged by accusations that he had used performance-enhancing drugs throughout his career. In June 2012, the US Anti-Doping Agency (USADA) formally charged Armstrong and several other members of his team with doping. At first, Armstrong denied the charges and filed a lawsuit to block the USADA's proposed punishment. When a federal judge dismissed the suit, Armstrong announced he would no longer contest the charges against him. In late August, the USADA stripped Armstrong of all competitive results from August 1998 to August 2012. Union Cycliste Internationale, the international governing body of professional cycling, quickly ratified the USADA's sanctions against Armstrong, ultimately stripping Armstrong of all his Tour de France titles and banning him from professional cycling for life. Armstrong was also later stripped of his 2000 Olympic bronze medal.

After vehemently denying all allegations for years, Armstrong admitted to using performance-enhancing drugs in an Oprah Winfrey interview in early 2013.

Impact

While the fate of Armstrong's legacy remains uncertain, his nearly unrivaled dominance during the height of his career will be hard to forget. He raised professional cycling's profile in the United States to unprecedented levels, and his trademark Livestrong bracelets have become a ubiquitous symbol of solidarity with the fight against cancer.

Further Reading

Bissinger, Buzz. "WINNING. (Cover Story)." *Newsweek* 160.10 (2012): 26–33. *Academic Search Complete.* Web. 23 Oct. 2012.

Edwards, Elizabeth. "Lance Armstrong. (Cover Story)." *Time* 171.19 (2008): 66–67. *Academic Search Complete.* Web. 23 Oct. 2012.

Osborne, Sue. "It's Not About The Bike: A Critique Of Themes Identified In Lance Armstrong's Narrative." *Urologic Nursing* 29.6 (2009): 415–43. Print.

James Ryan

■ *Arrested Development*

Identification: Mockumentary-style television sitcom about a dysfunctional family
Executive Producer: Mitchell Hurwitz (b. 1963)
Date: November 2, 2003–February 10, 2006

Arrested Development *garnered great critical praise, but the show did not draw a large enough audience to keep it from cancellation following its third season. The show focuses on the dysfunctional Bluth family, who loses its real-estate riches and is forced to live in a model home.*

Arrested Development was conceived by producer Ron Howard and writer Mitchell Hurwitz. Inspired by the accounting fraud scandal of the Enron

Corporation energy company, the two created a sitcom centered on the fictional "riches to rags" Bluth family. The show was shot using handheld cameras in the style of a reality television show and presented multiple, elaborate comedic plotlines. It garnered nearly universal critical acclaim, and during its first season in 2003, it was nominated for seven Emmy Awards, winning five. Despite praise from critics and a large cult following, *Arrested Development* was canceled after its third season, which aired in 2006. The series was revived, however, and a fourth season started streaming on Netflix in early 2013. A film based on the series is also forthcoming.

Jason Bateman plays Michael Bluth, a recent widower and the most levelheaded member of the Bluth family. While the rest of the family insists on living excessively in spite of their financial troubles, Michael is not materialistic and struggles to keep the family together. Many of the show's conflicts revolve around which family member will take over the Bluth Company's home construction business while father George Bluth Sr. (Jeffrey Tambor) is in prison for defrauding investors. His wife Lucille (Jessica Walter) is the chief executive officer of the company, and Michael is the manager. Vying for Michael's position is his older brother George Oscar Bluth, or "Gob" (Will Arnett), who is a failed magician. Other family members include the youngest brother Byron "Buster" Bluth (Tony Hale), sister Lindsay Bluth Fünke (Portia de Rossi), and Michael's son, George-Michael Bluth (Michael Cera).

Impact

The show has been praised for its layered approach to comedy, featuring elaborate scenarios and several interweaving plots that often carry over into subsequent episodes. The show is frequently self-referential and is told in linear fashion, although it often utilizes a variety of storytelling tools such as flashbacks and narration. While *Arrested Development* is not the first sitcom to use the mockumentary style, its unique use of the format helped popularize the mockumentary on American television and paved the way for subsequent sitcoms to utilize the style. Hurwitz and Howard borrowed comic sensibilities from many influential shows while also subverting the traditional sitcom genre. The show's self-awareness, use of wordplay, and absurdity have influenced the direction of the television situation comedy.

Further Reading

Schilling, Mary Kaye. "Jason Bateman, Act Two." *New York* 23 Aug. 2010: 145–47. Print.
Wren, Celia. "Crimes and Banana Stands." *Commonweal* 26 Mar. 2004: 19–20. Print.

Patrick G. Cooper

■ Art movements

Definition: Trends and major developments in the art world in North America in the 2000s

Trends in North American art in the 2000s continued the course set forth by the new media, digital, and Internet art trends of the 1990s. Artists of the 2000s also continued to adopt the distinctly twenty-first-century notion of disavowing loyalty to any single medium, immersing themselves across various methods and subject matter. The period was also marked by a new popularity of guerilla-style street art by notable artists such as Barry McGee and the development art-as-brand imagery in works by designers such as Shepard Fairey.

Notable Figures and Works

The early 2000s marked the completion of one of the previous decade's most ambitious works of American contemporary art, the epic *Cremaster Cycle* by Matthew Barney (b. 1967). The artist's elaborately constructed aesthetic universe utilizes themes of mythology and biography to construct a narrative based on the biological process of embryonic sexual development. While many in the art world lauded the project's ambition, grandiose scale, and imagination, skeptics panned the films and their accompanying work as disengaging, laborious, and egotistic.

Sculptor Sarah Sze (b. 1969), one of the decade's most prominent female sculptors, was awarded a MacArthur grant in 2003 for her similarly ambitious works and grandiose scale. Sze's work in the early 2000s was best known for its dominance of gallery space, typified by towering formations formed through a reappropriation of everyday objects such aluminum ladders, massive scaffolding, and halogen lights.

While Barney and Sze were embraced for their work in the sphere of gallery-centered, theatrical exhibition, many prominent North American artists of the 2000s were schooled in and discovered from movements beyond such traditional realms.

The Gates, an installation by Christo and Jeanne-Claude, February 2008. (Courtesy of Martin van den Berg)

Painter and graffiti artist Barry McGee (b. 1966) is the decade's most prominent and noteworthy example of the transition from street artist to artistic celebrity. Like his socially conscious graffiti-art predecessors Jean-Michel Basquiat (1960–1988) and Keith Haring (1958–1990), McGee successfully transformed his natural talent as an illustrator into commercial and critical success with little formal training. McGee's imagery concentrates on the frustrations of modern American urban living, including urban blight, rampant commercialism, homelessness, addiction, and crumbling infrastructure.

Similar themes were addressed throughout the decade by the British street artist Banksy (b. 1974), whose subversive, antiestablishment graffiti art in public spaces made him the decade's best-known artist. In 2008, Banksy created a variety of works on damaged and abandoned buildings in New Orleans decrying the American government's response to Hurricane Katrina.

New York City would once again assume its international status as the centerpiece of the North American art world midway through the decade, when the city's venerated Central Park became home to an ambitious installation, *The Gates*, by the husband and wife sculpture team of Christo (b. 1935) and Jeanne-Claude (1935–2009) during the month of February 2005.

The Gates was an installation of over 7,500 doorway structures, each sixteen feet high, constructed over twenty-three miles of pathways throughout the park. From each "gate" hung a saffron colored nylon sheet. The piece, like much of Christo and Jeanne-Claude's celebrated installations in previous years, was part current happening, part environmental sculpture, and part engineering marvel. The work is considered by many the largest, most discussed, and most visited work of public art in the 2000s. The piece transformed the normally bland February Central Park landscape into a magnificent field of color, while offering Christo and Jean-Claude's social commentaries on the notion of public space, travel, and destination.

Social commentary and subversion are paramount to the work of the street artist turned graphic artist Shepard Fairey (b. 1970), one of the 2000s best-known figures in the North American art world. Fairey gained notoriety in the 1990s for his *Obey* sticker campaigns featuring imagery of the venerated wrestler Andre the Giant.

Fairey then gained international notoriety with his series of *Hope* posters created for the 2008 presidential campaign of Barack Obama. The red, white, and blue posters feature a stoic portrait of the candidate above motivational words such as "hope" and "change." Though not originally commissioned by the Obama campaign, the posters nonetheless became one of the most iconic images of the campaign. Fairey would later face accusations of copyright infringement for the origin of the image, which was later found to be an Associated Press photograph.

While Fairey's work was reproduced and imitated by millions of people across the United States, one of the decade's most significant gallery draws was that of the American sculptor and commercial artist Jeff Koons (b. 1955). Koons achieved fame through his reappropriation of objects from American kitsch, from sculptures of balloon animals and giant puppies, to steel rabbits, to giant aluminum flowers and porcelain figures of pop music icons.

Koons's work throughout the 2000s was lauded by admirers as a celebration of American culture that drew new audiences to contemporary galleries. This was thanks in large part to his works' celebrative nature, phantasmal, childlike subject matter, and overall positivity. But to a vocal contingent of skeptics, Koons's sculptures were dismissed throughout the decade as mere trinkets of self-merchandising that evoke no deep meaning beyond eccentricity and camp. Nonetheless, Koons remained one of the largest exhibit draws throughout the 2000s; his work continued to sell at huge prices throughout the decade. His sculpture *Hanging Heart* sold at auction in 2007 for over $23 million dollars, the largest price paid for the work of a living artist at that time.

Major Sales and Museum Attendance

The realm of private art collection remained extremely lucrative and exclusive throughout decade. As in previous centuries, masterworks were the objects of desire to the wealthy, fetching never-before-seen prices at both private sale and auction. In fact, the 2000s saw the highest price ever paid for a painting repeatedly shattered.

That title had long been held by Van Gogh's *Portrait of Dr. Gachet*, which fetched $82.5 million at auction in 1990. That amount was trumped in May of 2004, when Pablo Picasso's *Garçon à la Pipe* fetched $104.2 million at a private auction in New York. In June of 2006, Gustav Klimt's *Portrait of Adele Bloch-Bauer* set the record anew with an auction sale of $135 million. A short five months later, the record fell again with the November sale of Jackson Pollock's *No. 5, 1948*, which sold to an anonymous buyer for $140 million.

Museum visitation continued to rise throughout the 2000s. In addition to newly constructed contemporary art museums in Boston and New York, the National Gallery of Art in Washington, DC, and the Metropolitan Museum of Art in New York City remained two of the most frequently visited museums in the United States.

Impact

All of the major artists of the 2000s speak to an evolution in the art world toward widespread social commentary and the tendency of artists, regardless of medium, to attempt to convey universal messages. This concept is a stark difference from previous decades, during which contemporary art remained a somewhat insular realm of intellectuals, private collectors, and art historians.

Bolstered in part by trends in social networking, branding, and newly formed digital communities, art in the 2000s seems to have reestablished painting, sculpture, and design as major instruments of social communication and change—broadening both the audience and potential of artists throughout the continent.

Further Reading

Baedeker, Rob. "America's 25 Most Visited Museums." *USA Today*. USA Today, 4 Oct. 2007. Web. 10 Aug. 2012. An overview of America's most popular museums in 2007.

Cottor, Holland. "Depending on the Culture of Strangers." *New York Times*. New York Times, 31 Dec. 2009. Web. 10 Aug. 2012. A discussion of art trends of the 2000s.

Dietch, Jeffery, Roger Gatsman, et al. *Art in the Streets*. New York: Rizzoli, 2011. eBook. Covers an exhibition survey of the history of the international graffiti and street art movements.

"Explore Artists." *Art 21: Art of the 21st Century*. Public Broadcasting Service, 2012. Web. 10 Aug. 2012. Biographies of prominent artists of the 2000s.

Kimmelman, Michael. "In a Saffron Ribbon, a Billowy Gift to the City." *New York Times*. New York Times, 13 Feb. 2005. Web. 10 Aug. 2012. Discusses *The Gates* by Christo and Jeanne-Claude.

"Shepard Fairey." *New York Times*. New York Times, 11 Aug. 2011. Web 10 Aug. 2012. An overview of Fairey's major works; includes both praise and criticism of Fairey.

Thomkins, Calvin. "Koons at Fifty." *New Yorker*. Condé Nast, 7 Feb. 2005. Web. 10 Aug. 2012. Discusses Koons's artistic achievements.

"Visual Artist Sarah Sze Among MacArthur 'Genius Award' Recipients." *Columbia News*. Columbia University, 8 Oct. 2003. Web. 10 Aug. 2012. Brief biography of Sze, announcing the MacArthur Fellowship awarded to her in 2003.

John Pritchard

■ Ashcroft, John

Identification: Former attorney general of the United States

Born: May 9, 1942; Chicago, Illinois

John Ashcroft was a prominent Missouri politician before ascending to national politics. He served as the state's governor, as well as state senator before President George W.

Bush selected him to head the US Department of Justice in 2001. His deeply conservative beliefs caused considerable controversy during his tenure as attorney general.

John Ashcroft came to prominence during his two terms as governor of Missouri (1985–1993), where he focused on fiscal restraint and managed to balance the budget throughout his tenure. In 1994, Ashcroft was elected to the US Senate, where his support for strong anti-abortion measures, including a constitutional amendment, sparked controversy. Ashcroft faced a tough reelection campaign in 2000 against Mel Carnahan, Missouri's Democratic governor. Carnahan was killed in a plane crash in October, less than a month before the election. Acting Governor Roger Wilson appointed Carnahan's widow, Jean, to fill the vacancy after Carnahan posthumously won the election. Ashcroft chose not to contest his defeat.

John Ashcroft. (©iStockphoto.com/Mario Tama)

Not long after Ashcroft's failed reelection bid, newly inaugurated US President George W. Bush nominated him as attorney general. The nomination brought another storm of criticism, relating to Ashcroft's record on abortion and civil rights, as well as his strong conservatism and religious beliefs. Eventually, despite the criticism, the Senate confirmed Ashcroft by a vote of 58 to 42.

Concerns about civil rights came to a head following the September 11, 2001, terrorist attacks against the United States. Under Ashcroft's leadership, the US Justice Department sought expanded powers to track and arrest suspected terrorists. This led to the creation of the USA PATRIOT Act, also known as the Patriot Act, which Congress passed not long after the attacks. Ashcroft also faced criticism during the military campaign against the Taliban regime of Afghanistan. Ashcroft was criticized over how the United States treated captured enemy combatants. Despite these criticisms, Ashcroft maintained that the US government had a right to expand its law enforcement activities to protect against further attacks.

In 2002, Operation TIPS was proposed by Ashcroft in an attempt to encourage employees to inform law-enforcement agencies of suspicious activity that they may encounter while at work. The proposal was widely criticized and eventually abandoned. In 2003, Ashcroft promoted Operation Pipe Dreams and Operation Headhunter, in which investigations were conducted on businesses that were suspected of selling drug paraphernalia. He also pushed for mandatory minimum-sentencing laws for drug-related crimes and offenses. Ashcroft resigned as attorney general in 2004. He was succeeded by Alberto Gonzales. After his departure, he founded the consulting firm Ashcroft Group LLC.

Impact

As attorney general, Ashcroft played a pivotal role in a post–September 11 counterterrorism and law-enforcement efforts in the United States. He was a driving force behind the push to expand federal powers, which culminated in the passing of the Patriot Act. Ashcroft's controversial stances on social issues were emblematic of the Bush administration's more conservative leanings, and his record on matters of civil liberty was heavily scrutinized.

Further Reading

Cole, David. "Hold Ashcroft Accountable." *Nation* 289.10 (2009): 6–8. Print.

Isikoff, Michael, and Mark Hosenball. "Ashcroft On Triumphs—And Threats." *Newsweek* 145.4 (2005): 6. Print.

Mosimann, James E. "Al-Kidd V. Ashcroft: Clearly Established Confusion." *Iowa Law Review* 96.1 (2010): 331–55. Print.

Eric Badertscher

■ Autism

Definition: A developmental disorder that affects behavior, communication, and social interaction beginning in infancy or early childhood. As the severity can range from very mild to severe, it is now encompassed by the umbrella term, autism spectrum disorders (ASDs), which includes the related Asperger's syndrome and other similar disorders

The number of autism spectrum disorder cases rose alarmingly in recent decades, creating what many referred to as an epidemic. As parents and health professionals searched for causes and effective treatment plans, increased funding allowed for public and private research to expand in many different directions, while a national dialogue formed around the safety of early-childhood vaccinations and resulted in new policies, as well as public health fears.

Autism has always been one of the most puzzling disorders. Although it has long existed, it was not defined as a developmental disorder until 1943, and not included as a unique entry in the American Psychiatric Association's *Diagnostic and Statistical Manual of Mental Disorders* (*DSM-III*) until 1980. The *DSM-IV-TR* (2000) specifies the criteria for autistic disorder as encompassing six or more characteristics drawn from a longer list of social impairments, communication/language impairments, and restricted, repetitive behaviors or abnormal interests, with an onset beginning before age three, characterized also by abnormal functioning in social interaction, language, or imaginative play. Some of the more common symptoms of autism include flapping the hands and the inability to maintain eye contact or understand feelings. The disorder is often marked by the addition of gastrointestinal disorders, sleep problems, sensitivities to light or other external stimuli, and a weak immunological system that can cause ear infections, skin problems, and other issues. Although it develops before the age of three, it is often diagnosed later. In some cases, toddlers appear to be developing normally, but then begin to exhibit unusual behavior, stop communicating, or regress socially or intellectually. For reasons that are yet unknown, most autistic children are male.

Related to autism is the more recently identified Asperger's syndrome, a milder form that is defined more by social or behavioral impairments rather than intellectual abilities. In fact, many children and adults with Asperger's have above average abilities or interests, while a tiny percent are savants. By the end of the decade, as revisions to the fifth edition of the *DSM* were under discussion, it appeared that autism and Asperger's disorders would be encompassed by the umbrella term of autism spectrum disorders (ASDs) to reflect the wide variety of symptoms and levels of severity, along with the milder pervasive developmental disorder not otherwise specified (PDD-NOS) and childhood disintegrative disorder (CDD).

During the 1990s, the number of ASD cases began to increase drastically. In 1991, one in every 2,500 children was diagnosed with autism. In 2000, the number had soared to one in every 150. As parents, educators, and mental health professionals were raising the alarm, the US Congress passed the Children's Health Act, which mandated the establishment of a new autism research network. The National Institute of Mental Health (NIMH) and four other government organizations then founded the Studies to Advance Autism Research and Treatment (STAART) program, one of the premier programs in the world. Funding in the private sector paid for other dedicated research studies. Much of the research undertaken was driven by advancements in neuroscience and genetics while other research studied behavioral therapy or environmental links. Despite the concerted effort to solve the puzzle of autism, the number of cases continued to rise. By 2004, one in 125 children was diagnosed with an ASD. Most experts explained that the increase was largely, but not completely, the result of more children being screened, reclassification of disorders, and better diagnoses. Still, parents and some health professionals had their doubts and looked elsewhere for answers.

The Link between Autism and Vaccinations

During the 1990s, some parents noticed their infants or toddlers exhibiting signs of autism soon after receiving early-childhood inoculations, such as MMR (measles/mumps/rubella) and DPT (diphtheria/tetanus/pertussis). Their fears were supported by a 1988 British study conducted by Dr. Andrew Wakefield that showed a causal link between the MMR vaccine and autism. (The research was later found to be fraudulent and Wakefield lost his license to practice medicine.) The primary culprit was alleged to be thimerosal, a preservative

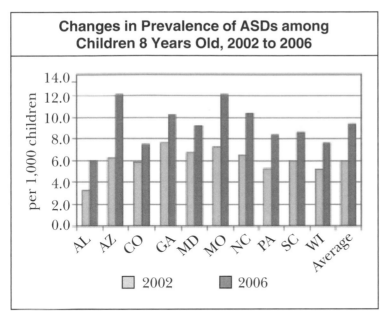

Changes in Prevalence of ASDs among Children 8 Years Old, 2002 to 2006

☐ 2002   ☐ 2006

Source: Centers for Disease Control and Prevention.

used in vaccinations since the 1930s with a composition of 49.6 percent ethyl mercury. Thimerosal was widely known to be toxic by the pharmaceutical industry and by governments throughout the world, many of whom had banned the use of it in vaccines, although the United States apparently believed it was safe in the small doses used for infrequent vaccinations. The problem was that children were receiving more and more vaccines, with the addition of flu shots, hepatitis B (HepB), *Haemophilus influenzae* (Hib), and others, making the link between thimerosal and autism more plausible. After an investigation, the US government ordered manufacturers to remove thimerosal from some vaccinations as a precautionary measure, although they could continue to use up lots that were stockpiled.

By this time, an antivaccination movement was well under way and thousands of lawsuits were being filed, mostly targeting Eli Lilly and Co. The controversy was fueled in 2002, when US House of Representatives Majority Leader Dick Armey admitted to inserting a last-minute provision into the Homeland Security Act that removed liability for any injuries resulting from vaccinations, similar to a bill sponsored earlier by Senator Bill Frist. President George W. Bush signed the Act. Armey justified the inclusion as being necessary for national security in the case of "germ weapons" and feared settlements could

deplete the supply of vaccinations needed by the military. Parents who had filed lawsuits were in an uproar, and convinced Congress to repeal the rider the following year, although attempts to pass a similar bill continued.

In 2005, as the controversy moved from law journals and medical newsletters to television programs, talks shows, and popular magazines, journalist David Kirby published *Evidence of Harm: Mercury in Vaccines and the Autism Epidemic: A Medical Controversy* that blamed the pharmaceutical industry, the FDA, and the American Academy of Pediatrics (AAP) of negligence and incompetence, while an article written by Robert F. Kennedy Jr. for *Rolling Stone* and *Salon.com* spoke about an alleged government cover-up over thimerosal, also stoking the growing fear and anger among the general public. Numerous research studies were undertaken that failed to establish a link, although some pointed to the possibility of vaccines operating as a trigger. Nevertheless, states began to take matters into their own hands, and by the end of the year 34 states had either banned mercury in vaccines for infants or had pending legislation.

As the decade came to an end, several lawsuits that had made it to trial also failed to prove the link between vaccines and autism. Lawyers then started to prepare for a Supreme Court case that would determine whether or not parents could even sue over child vaccines.

Beyond Vaccinations

Despite the removal of thimerosal from early-childhood vaccinations, the rate of autism continued to climb. Researchers were as stymied as parents. They considered a multitude of prenatal factors, including viruses, bacterial infections, maternal hormones, and the use of antibiotics, as well as breastmilk and bottled formula. Several studies showed some connection to German measles (rubella) during pregnancy, while others showed a link to terbutaline, a drug taken during pregnancy to prevent premature labor. Researchers also looked into other suspected environmental factors, including food allergies, exposure to cleaning products, mercury in fish, insecticides, phthalates, antibacterial soaps, aspartame, flame retardants, television viewing, Wi-Fi, and cell phones. While additional studies disproved the link with mercury, as well as lead, arsenic, and other metals, it remained a leading cause in the public eye.

As there is no drug that will cure autism, only medicine that can alleviate some of the symptoms, frustrated parents began to seek out alternative treatment programs, including chelation, a process used to rid the body of mercury and other toxic chemicals. Chelation poses a danger to the kidney, heart, and other parts of the body, and was known to have caused at least one death among autistic children. Parents also tried neurofeedback, hyperbaric oxygen chambers, acupuncture, craniosacral therapy, reiki, nutritional supplements, special diets, steroids, and the hormone secretin.

Some parents claimed to have found success with one or more alternative treatment plans, while others continued to search for something effective. In the meantime, the greatest success was being reached with behavioral therapy, and experts advised that the earlier it was started, the better. Programs such as applied behavior analysis (ABA), sensory integration therapy, or the Early Start Denver Model (ESDM) were giving parents hope that their children would one day be normal, but the programs required a vast investment in time and money, leaving tens of thousands of families frustrated.

Impact

By the end of the decade, the numbers were sobering: one in every eighty-eight children was diagnosed with an autism spectrum disorder. While a cure for autism remained elusive, the increase in public awareness resulted in a new approach to viewing the disorder without the social stigma previously attached. In fact, attitudes towards Asperger's syndrome have been elevated in those cases where the affected individuals accomplished major musical, artistic, or intellectual achievements.

During the decade, many autism and Asperger's organizations were founded, including Autism Speaks, which has raised millions of dollars for advocacy and research. In 2006, the US Congress passed the Combating Autism Act, which dedicated $1 billion for research, screening, treatment, education, and early intervention. Increased funding has supported numerous research projects, including clinical trials for new drugs, behavioral therapy initiatives, and the

Study to Explore Early Development (SEED) program, funded by the Centers for Disease Control and Prevention and being carried out by the Centers for Autism and Developmental Disabilities Research and Epidemiology (CADDRE) Network, the largest initiative yet to identify risk factors in developmental disabilities. While a cure has yet to be found, the research has proven that early intervention is key to helping autistic children live full lives, and thus routine screening for children under the age of two has become the standard.

Perhaps the greatest impact on all of society resulted from the antivaccination movement. As the decade came to a close, outbreaks of whooping cough (pertussis), measles, mumps, polio, and other diseases that had been eradicated in the United States and elsewhere were reappearing, hinting at a major public health hazard yet to come.

Further Reading

Attwood, Tony. *The Complete Guide to Asperger's Syndrome.* London: Kingsley, 2008. Print. Good introductory book with a glossary and a list of resources for further reading.

Bock, Kenneth and Cameron Stauth. *Healing the New Childhood Epidemics: Autism, ADHD, Asthma, and Allergies.* New York: Ballantine, 2008. Print. Builds the case here for the linkage between these four conditions and sets a healing program to reverse the toxicity in the brain and metabolic dysfunction that he believes is responsible.

Kennedy, Robert F. "Deadly Immunity." *Rolling Stone* 29 June 2005: 57. Print. Details an alleged cover-up by the CDC, FDA, and the pharmaceutical industry to downplay any potential link between thimerosal and autism.

Kirby, David. *Evidence of Harm: Mercury in Vaccines and the Autism Epidemic: A Medical Controversy.* New York: St. Martin's, 2005. Print. This controversial bestselling book by a journalist presents the case for the vaccination-autism link.

Neimark, Jill. "Autism: It's Not Just in the Head." *Discover Magazine* Apr. 2007: 32. Print. Explores research into the causes, diagnosis, and therapy of autism undertaken by the middle of the decade, with an emphasis on genetic and biomedical research.

Offit, Paul A. *Autism's False Prophets: Bad Science, Risky Medicine, and the Search for a Cure.* New York: Columbia UP, 2008. Print. Debunks any link between vaccinations and autism and provides an historical account of ineffective and sometimes dangerous treatment undertaken by parents.

Parsell, Diana. "Assault on Autism." *Science News* 166.20 (2004): 311. Print. Details the many possible environmental links to autism being explored early in the decade.

Sally Driscoll

■ Automotive industry crisis

Definition: A major downturn in the US automotive industry from 2008 to 2010, resulting from a global financial crisis, high fuel costs, and poor vehicle sales, and ultimately forcing Chrysler and General Motors to file for bankruptcy despite receiving government support

The automotive crisis demonstrated the central role of the industry in the US economy, but also revealed that US automakers had been slow to respond to changes in economic conditions and consumer demand. After receiving approximately $80 billion in emergency government loans, US automakers would recover from the crisis in part by streamlining their brands, offering purchase incentives, and developing smaller, more fuel-efficient vehicles.

Decline in Sales and Lending

Automotive sales by US automakers held relatively steady throughout the early part of the 2000s, growing between 2 and 4 percent per year. However, the distribution of sales was shifting steadily from the Big Three US companies (Chrysler, Ford, and General Motors) to foreign automakers, particularly Asian companies such as Honda and Toyota, which were offering better product lines of fuel-efficient vehicles than their US competitors. Beginning in 2001, rising gas prices began to negatively affect consumer demand for larger vehicles, which represented the bulk of US automakers' product lines. Heightened competition from affordable and reliable foreign brands put pressure on US automakers, but a relatively healthy economy enabled total vehicle sales to continue increasing. In 2006, the Japanese automaker Toyota surpassed Chrysler and Ford in US sales, heightening the competition between US and foreign automakers. Two years later, Toyota surpassed General Motors (GM) as the

world's largest automaker, a distinction GM had held since 1931.

Before the United States entered into a recession in 2007, the Big Three were already in a difficult situation. All three companies lost money in 2006: Chrysler, $1.5 billion; GM, $2 billion; and Ford, $12.7 billion. (In part because of this major loss in 2006, Ford may have been better prepared to weather the crisis of 2008: It had applied for and received a $23.5 billion line of credit in 2006, even offering up its famed blue oval logo as collateral.)

In 2008, a spike in fuel prices and an economic recession combined to devastate the US automotive industry. The economic collapse, sparked by interrelated housing and financial factors, made financial institutions reluctant to extend credit, complicating the ability of many consumers to receive auto loans. Additionally, many automobile purchases had typically been financed by home equity lines of credit—lines of credit offered based on home values—a practice that became less viable as home values decreased.

These factors combined to reduce US auto sales from 17 million in 2006 to 10.6 million in 2009, a decrease of nearly 40 percent. The rapid decline in sales hit Chrysler and GM particularly hard, in part because of their labor structure and product mix and because they did not have adequate cash reserves to respond effectively to the crisis.

Other Factors

In addition to declining auto sales, several other economic factors influenced the progression of the automotive crisis, including higher unemployment, reduced access to credit, reduced consumer spending, and higher fuel costs. All of these factors negatively affected consumer ability and willingness to purchase and maintain automobiles.

Chrysler and GM were especially affected by rising fuel costs and the resulting decline in truck and sport utility vehicle (SUV) sales. Since the late 1990s, these companies had made more than half of their profits from trucks and SUVs, particularly because these larger vehicles typically offered more profit per vehicle than smaller cars. As a result, the companies had continued to invest in the design and production of these large, fuel-inefficient vehicles throughout the 2000s.

With the dual economic and energy crises of the late 2000s, and gas prices exceeding four dollars per

The U.S. House of Representatives's Financial Services Committee hearing on the bailout of the Big Three automakers, November 19, 2008. (Courtesy CODEPINK Women for Peace)

gallon across the United States in July 2008, Chrysler and GM were caught without a sufficient line of fuel-efficient passenger vehicle models to attract buyers, as well as a surplus of fuel-inefficient vehicles for which there was little demand. As a result, dealerships were forced to sell many vehicles at a loss. Truck sales dropped 17 percent from 2007 to 2009, while large SUV sales declined 29 percent. In contrast, Toyota capitalized on its Prius hybrid, which featured both electric and gasoline-powered engines and sold one million vehicles by May 2008.

The struggles of GM and Chrysler may also have been related to their multiple vehicle brands: more than eight for GM and four for Chrysler. Developing and marketing separate brands was not only expensive, but also may have caused internal sales cannibalization as consumers switched from one GM or Chrysler brand to another.

In response to the crisis, GM sold its Saab brand and phased out Saturn, Hummer, and Pontiac, leaving the company to work with its Chevrolet, Cadillac, Buick, and GMC brands. Chrysler did not shut down brands entirely, but heavily retooled most of its vehicle lines and eliminated some models. Ford also made multiple brands but sold its luxury brands—Aston Martin in March 2007,

Jaguar Land Rover in June 2008, and Volvo in August 2010—to concentrate on Lincoln and Mercury.

Labor costs were also perceived as a problem for the automakers. In contrast to foreign countries, where automobiles could be produced with much cheaper labor, companies building cars in the United States typically pay higher wages for similar work, in part because of the negotiating power of unions such as the United Auto Workers (UAW). Automakers were also paying wages to some autoworkers whose plants were closed or who were otherwise out of work, as well as the health insurance premiums and pensions of many retired workers.

Government Involvement

The large and sudden drop in auto sales put Chrysler and GM in a difficult situation regarding how to continue operations in a resource-intensive industry. Due to the credit freeze, Chrysler and GM were unable to borrow the cash they needed to maintain operations through the crisis. The situation was so dire that in the fall of 2008, the two competitors even considered merging. Instead, in a congressional hearing before the House Financial Services Committee on November 19, 2008, the companies requested $25 billion in government-subsidized loans out of the $700 billion approved by Congress in October for the Troubled Asset Relief Program (TARP). GMAC Financial Services, the financing arm of General Motors, also applied for assistance. Congressional leaders doubted the companies' ability to use funds effectively and requested detailed recovery plans.

There was widespread popular opposition to any form of "bailout" for the auto industry. Many voiced the idea that the bailout was unnecessarily propping up a dead or dying industry. Government support was perceived as working to discourage innovation and competition, as well as to "reward" the automakers' poor financial and product planning. Public opinion of the automakers was already negative when media reports revealed that the Big Three auto executives had all traveled to the congressional loan meetings in private luxury jets. When the automakers returned to DC to submit their recovery plans, the company CEOs all arrived in American-made hybrid vehicles.

The automakers submitted their plans by December 2, 2008, along with a $15 billion short-term loan proposal on December 9, 2008. This proposal was rejected by the Senate on December 11, but President George W. Bush approved a $17.4 billion loan ($9.4 billion for GM and $4 billion for Chrysler, with $4 billion in conditional funds) on December 19. On the same day, Fitch Ratings downgraded Chrysler and GM to a "C" default rating, emphasizing the dire financial situation of the companies. GMAC received $5 billion in aid on December 29, 2008.

Despite negative public opinion of the bailout, jobs were the major motivator for the government to support the automotive industry. Government analysis uncovered three million jobs linked to the Big Three in some way. The anticipated loss of these jobs, combined with an anticipated increase in the number of vehicles imported (which alone was expected to take $25 billion out of the US economy) and a 7.3 percent unemployment rate in December 2008 played a large part in the government's decision to fund Chrysler and GM.

Initial Outcomes

The money loaned to the companies was only a short-term solution, however, and in exchange for the bailout, GM and Chrysler were required to submit long-term restructuring plans by March 2009. Just weeks after President Barack Obama took office, on February 15, 2009, he announced the creation of the Presidential Task Force on the Auto Industry, which would assume responsibility for reviewing the viability plans submitted by Chrysler and GM. That same month, GM and Chrysler requested an additional $14 billion, saying that their loaned funds would run out by the end of March. In March, the US Treasury and the presidential task force determined that the automakers' proposed plans were insufficient to achieve long-term viability and required the companies to restructure more thoroughly, with conditions such as limitations on CEO pay and UAW benefits, in order to continue to receive government assistance.

In January 2009, Italian automaker Fiat had proposed a deal in which it would take a 35 percent stake in Chrysler to help the company develop fuel-efficient vehicles and share resources with the European company, which was interested in moving back into the US market. When the task force rejected Chrys-

ler's restructuring plan in March, it determined that Chrysler was no longer viable as a stand-alone company, giving the automaker thirty days to solidify its partnership with Fiat or risk being denied additional government funding.

In April, Chrysler and Fiat completed their partnership. However, despite Fiat's involvement and major concessions made by the company and the UAW, a small number of Chrysler's creditors refused to accept the terms of the restructuring plans. On April 30, 2009, Chrysler filed for Chapter 11 bankruptcy—the first major automaker to do so since Studebaker in 1933. In response, the government announced a plan that allowed UAW, Fiat, and the US and Canadian governments to take stakes in the company, and committed $8 billion in additional government support. In May, a bankruptcy court approved the sale of Chrysler's assets to "new Chrysler," formally known as Chrysler Group LLC, thus overturning the objections of a small group of Chrysler's creditors. On June 10, 2009, forty-two days after filing for bankruptcy protection, Chrysler emerged from bankruptcy.

As part of its restructuring, Chrysler announced plans to close 25 percent of its US dealerships in May 2009. GM followed with similar news, closing a total of 1,100 GM dealerships representing 18 percent of its total outlets but just 7 percent of sales. General Motors Corporation filed for bankruptcy on June 1, 2009, reporting more than $91 billion in assets and $172 billion in debt—the fourth largest bankruptcy in US history.

General Motors Corporation became Motors Liquidation Company, the organization that would handle bankruptcy restructuring. Core GM assets were repurchased by General Motors Company (the "new GM"). The US Treasury offered an additional $30 billion in government funds to facilitate the company's restructuring; the governments of Canada and Ontario contributed an additional $9.5 billion in assistance. GM emerged from bankruptcy proceedings after forty days, on July 10. Having contributed nearly $50 billion to the company, the US government now owned a 61 percent stake in GM, with a UAW health benefits fund, the Canadian governments, and bondholders taking up the remaining stakes.

Cash for Clunkers

To help encourage the purchase and use of fuel-efficient vehicles, the US government initiated the Car

Allowance Rebate System (CARS), nicknamed "Cash for Clunkers," in the summer of 2009. The program allowed consumers to trade in vehicles no more than twenty-five years old with an average fuel economy rating of less than 18 miles per gallon (mpg) for new vehicles with an economy of at least 22 mpg. Consumers then received a purchase credit of anywhere from $3,500 to $4,500 to use toward new, more fuel-efficient vehicles.

The program required the scrapping of the old vehicles through engine disablement to prevent resale. The program officially launched on July 1, 2009, and claims were first processed on July 24. The initial $1 billion in funds allocated was used by July 30, 2009, prompting Congress to approve an additional $2 billion in funds. The program ended August 24, 2009.

CARS was viewed as successful in motivating many visits to car dealerships and stimulating the US economy. About twenty-three thousand dealerships participated and thousands of cars were sold as many consumers downsized from SUVs or trucks to passenger vehicles. The Department of Transportation reported that the average trade-in vehicle's fuel efficiency was 15.8 mpg, while the new vehicles purchased as part of the program averaged 24.9 mpg. Additionally, trucks represented 84 percent of the trade-in vehicles, while 59 percent of the newly purchased vehicles were passenger cars, confirming the consumer trend toward smaller vehicles.

Although sales increased for the Big Three during the promotion, the top ten cars (and all trucks, vans, or jeep vehicles) traded in were all Big Three vehicles. Worse yet, eight of the top ten new cars that replaced them were Asian brands (Honda, Hyundai, Nissan, and Toyota), with only the Ford Focus and Ford Escape cracking into the top ten new vehicles. These top ten lists starkly showed the emphasis on large vehicles that had been so pervasive—and problematic—for the Big Three. The final tally for the program saw 690,114 cars traded in for $2.88 billion in rebates.

Impact

After emerging from bankruptcy, both Chrysler and GM quickly moved to retool their product lines. All three major US automakers placed a new emphasis on fuel-efficient vehicles after the crisis. Chrysler launched several significantly redesigned vehicles in 2009, including the highly successful redesign of the Jeep Grand Cherokee, which offers a significantly better fuel economy than previous models. Chrysler also introduced a number of compact cars, such as the Fiat 500, to the US market. GM continued developing the Chevrolet Volt hybrid vehicle, which went on sale in 2010.

Although the auto industry did not fully recover by the end of 2009, Chrysler and GM both returned to profitability within two years of filing for bankruptcy protection. In addition, both fully repaid their government loans several years ahead of schedule. However, the majority of the US government's investment in GM was in stock holdings; for the government to break even on that bailout, GM's share price would have to exceed $51 a share. Also, the several billion dollars the US government invested into the "old" GM and Chrysler is unlikely to ever be repaid. The bailout represented unprecedented government intervention into the private market, and the crisis showed that even large companies must respond to, not dictate, changes in economic markets and consumer demand.

Further Reading

Hoffman, Bryce G. *American Icon: Alan Modally and the Fight to Save Ford Motor Company.* New York: Crown Business, 2012. Print. An overview of the crisis based on close interaction with Ford CEO Alan Mulally, who brought the company through that problematic period.

Lutz, Bob. *Car Guys vs. Bean Counters: The Battle for the Soul of American Business.* New York: Portfolio Hardcover, 2011. Print. Describes the automotive crisis in the context of larger trends in corporate America. Written by a former General Motors CEO.

Roth, Gregory, and Seth Feaster. "Milestones in the Carmakers' Crisis." *New York Times.* New York Times, 16 Feb. 2009. Web. 15 Oct. 2012. An interactive month-by-month timeline of the automotive industry crisis, including short overviews, related photographs, and links to in-depth news articles.

US Dept. of the Treasury. "Auto Industry." *Treasury. gov.* US Dept. of the Treasury, 22 Aug. 2012. Web. 15 Oct. 2012. An overview of US government assistance to the automotive industry. Also features a graph showing the spike in vehicles sold during Cash for Clunkers program.

Vlasic, Bill. *Once Upon a Car: The Fall and Resurrection of America's Big Three Automakers—GM, Ford, and Chrysler.* New York: Morrow, 2011. Print. Provides a comprehensive take on the automotive crisis.

Kerry Skemp, MA

■ Auto-Tune

Definition: Antares Audio Technology'sAuto-Tune is audio production software used to correct vocal or solo instrumental pitch one semitone at a time. Other brands of similar software are also referred to as "auto-tune."

Auto-Tune rose in popularity in the 2000s. At first, it was used to compensate for a flawed performance; by the end of the decade, however, it had developed into a stylized technique utilized by many popular artists.

Auto-Tune was designed and developed by Andy Hildebrand in 1997 for his company, Jupiter Systems, which was later renamed Antares Audio Technology. In 1998, Cher's song "Believe" became the first published song in which the technology was used to correct vocal pitch.

For the first half of the 2000s, Auto-Tune was mostly used subtly by music producers and sound engineers, with the exception of some electronic musicians. Blatant use of Auto-Tune software became popular in 2005, with the release of singer T-Pain's debut album *Rappa Ternt Sanga*. Nearly every song on the record featured Auto-Tune, including lead single "I'm N Luv (Wit a Stripper)," which highlights the software's tendency to snap notes to an exact pitch, especially in ascending or descending melodies.

Soon artists from many different musical genres were exploring Auto-Tune as a medium. For some artists, such as rapper Snoop Dogg, the software allowed them to express themselves through singing for the first time. Auto-Tune also enabled artists to extend their range of expression. Indie folk artist Bon Iver's track "Woods" is composed solely of Auto-Tuned vocals layered on top of one another. In 2008, Rapper Kanye West released *808s and Heartbreak*, a concept album based around an 808 drum machine and Auto-Tuned vocals. For West, Auto-Tune was not just a new way to sing; but a gateway to an entirely new kind of music. Other musicians, such as the indie band Death Cab for Cutie and the rapper Jay-Z, were critical of the software, however.

Auto-Tune usage expanded beyond music. In 2009, members of the band the Gregory Brothers created the viral video series *Auto-Tune the News*. The band took debate footage and news interviews, applied Auto-Tune to the people speaking, and set it to music. Popular clips include footage of the 2008 presidential debates and news anchor Katie Couric.

Impact

Auto-Tune is widely used in popular music, whether it is used subtly or featured prominently. Smartphone apps that simulate the Auto-Tune sound, such as I Am T-Pain and Songify, remain popular, allowing any aspiring artist or music fan to experiment with the effect.

Debate continues about whether Auto-Tune is detrimental or beneficial to music and musicians. Detractors say that the software should be used discretely or not at all. Some feel that using it is akin to cheating and that it cheapens the performance of musicians who can sing or play in tune on their own. Advocates state that the technology has broadened musical expression and made music production more efficient and less costly.

Further Reading

Jurgensen, John. "The Battle Over Bionic Vocals." *Wallstreet Journal* [Washington] 9 Sep. 2009, n. pag. Web. 19 July 2012.

Katz, Mark. *Capturing Sound: How Technology Has Changed Music.* Berkeley: U of California P, 2010. Print.

Milner, Greg. *Perfecting Sound Forever: An Aural History of Recorded Music.* New York: Faber, 2010Print.

Leland Spencer

■ *Avatar*

Identification: Science fiction film about a paraplegic Marine sent to the planet Pandora, where he becomes engaged in a war between natives and humans

Director: James Cameron (b. 1954)

Date: Released on December 18, 2009

Avatar was one of the most anticipated movies of 2009 and quickly became one of the biggest hits of the year. Its use of advanced motion-capture technology and stereoscopic 3-D was regarded as a groundbreaking innovation in the motion-picture industry.

Avatar was written and directed by James Cameron, best known for the epic *Titanic* (1997). Cameron was to begin production on *Avatar* immediately following *Titanic*'s release, but he waited several years because he did not think the available technology was advanced enough to support his artistic vision. He resumed work on *Avatar* in 2005, and production was completed four years later.

The movie, set in the near future, tells the story of Jake Sully (played by Sam Worthington), a disabled war veteran. Jake journeys to the world of Pandora on a mission for a dubious corporation that is mining the planet for its valuable minerals. Jake is tasked with infiltrating the Na'vi, the planet's native inhabitants. In order to explore the planet and communicate with the natives, Jake must transfer his consciousness into the genetically-grown body of a Na'vi, known as an avatar. Jake's interactions with the Na'vi introduce him to Neytiri (Zoe Saldana), a Na'vi princess, with whom he falls in love. When the humans threaten the Na'vi people's existence, Jake becomes torn between his human self and his avatar.

Avatar was one of the most expensive productions in history, with an estimated budget of more than $300 million. However, it was an instant commercial hit, grossing more than $200 million worldwide during its opening weekend.

Impact

Overall, critics hailed *Avatar* as a breakthrough in the art of filmmaking. After its release, Cameron announced his plans to make two more films focusing on Jake and Neytiri. The director said the two sequels would take less time to make than the original because he had already mastered the

Sam Worthington at a screening of Avatar. (Frazer Harrison/ Getty Images Entertainment/Getty Images)

technology involved. In addition to being a commercial and critical success, *Avatar* was nominated for many awards, including four Golden Globes.

Further Reading

Child, Ben. "You Review: Avatar." *Guardian* [UK]. Guardian News and Media, 18 Dec. 2009. Web. 15 Aug. 2012.

Ditzian, Eric. "James Cameron Talks 'Avatar' Sequel Plans." *MTV*. Viacom Intl., 21 Dec. 2009. Web. 15 Aug. 2012.

Duncan, Jody and Lisa Fitzpatrick. *The Making of Avatar*. New York: Abrams, 2010. Print.

Cait Caffrey

B

◼ Banned books

Definition: Published books deemed inappropriate and subsequently withheld

Whether instituted by the government, school board officials, or concerned parents, book banning has influenced the lives of all readers. Even those not directly affected by bans are subject to the surrounding culture of censorship that bans necessarily create. While some argue that books should be banned to protect children, others worry about the broader impact of censorship on any free society.

In a democracy, ideas of freedom and censorship continually redefine each other. In the case of book banning, censorship takes the form of physically limiting access. In 1939, the American Library Association (ALA) sought to address this issue through its Library Bill of Rights. It defined the book's purpose as a tool "for the interest, information, and enlightenment of all people" and determined that books should not be banned "because of the origin, background, or views of those contributing to their creation." Furthermore, it affirmed that "materials should not be proscribed or removed because of partisan or doctrinal disapproval." In 1982, the ALA instituted Banned Books Week, a national event that raises awareness about the harms of censorship. As libraries declared their commitment to spreading knowledge through unrestricted reading, government and citizen groups expressed growing concern over the suitability of some texts for young minds.

Banning Trends in the 2000s

Typically, banned books fall into four categories of offense: political, religious, sexual, or social. The 2000s were no exception to this pattern. Tim O'Brien's *The Things They Carried* (1990) depicts the Vietnam War through the experiences of soldiers. While it was criticized on political grounds shortly after publication, grievances continued into the 2000s. In 2001, 2003, and 2006, schools challenged the book for its strong language.

Widely popular and the target of a number of bans, the Harry Potter series has met opposition since publication of the first volume in 1998. Most often criticized on religious grounds, the series has found opponents in Focus on the Family, Family Friendly Libraries, Freedom Village USA, and other conservative Christian groups. Across the country, church groups shredded and burned copies of the texts publicly to signal opposition. From 1999 to 2002, books from the series were the most challenged in the United States, with challenges continuing throughout the decade.

Another controversial series, Cecily von Ziegesar's *Gossip Girl* (2002–2011) has irked parents since 2004 because of its sexual content. Chronicling the lives of Manhattan's teen socialites, the book's mature content has been derided as inappropriate for youth.

Particularly relevant to the 2000s, Khaled Hosseini's *The Kite Runner* (2003) depicts the relationship between two boys in Afghanistan separated by social class and religion. Although a New York Times Best Seller, the book was widely challenged in 2008. Critics of the book claimed that its scenes of sexual violence were inappropriate, while defenders argued that such scenes accurately depicted social aspects of a particular culture.

While those seeking to ban books often hold firm convictions, a broad look at trends reveals that the desire to ban depends as much on the social climate of a particular time and place as on a book's content. Many classic texts were once, or still are, banned.

Protecting the Idea of Childhood

While books may occasionally be banned from all readers, young and old alike—particularly when governments feel threatened by texts—most book bans are partial, intended to protect children specifically. Books may thus be banned from a school curriculum or a school library. Books deemed inappropriate may require parental permission for children to read

Most Frequently Banned Books of the Decade

Title	Author	Publish Date
Harry Potter (series)	J.K Rowling	1999–2007
Arming America	Michael Bellasiles	2000
Life is Funny	E.R Frank	2000
The Facts Speak for Themselves	Brock Cole	2000
I Saw Esau	Iona Opte, Peter Opie, and Maurice Sendak	2000
What My Mother Doesn't Know	Sonya Sones	2001
Whale Talk	Chris Crutcher	2001
Rainbow Boys	Alex Sanchez	2001
Daughters of Eve	Lois Duncan	2001
You Hear Me?	Betsy Franco and Nina Nickles May	2001
Crazy: A Novel	Benjamin Lebert	2001
Cut	Patricia McCormick	2001
King and King	Linda de Haan and Stern Nijland	2002
Gossip Girl (series)	Cecily von Ziegesar	2002–2009
The Adventures of Super Diaper Baby	Dav Pilkey, George Beard, and Harold Hutchins	2002
The Lovely Bones	Alice Sebold	2002
The Earth, My Butt, and other Big, Round Things	Carolyn Mackler	2003
The Kite Runner	Khaled Hosseini	2003
When Dad Killed Mom	Julius Lester	2003
Fat Kid Rules the World	K.L Going	2003
Olive's Ocean	Kevin Henkes	2003
Staying Fat for Sarah Byrnes	Chris Crutcher	2003
America	E.R Frank	2003
Ttyl; ttfn; l8r g8r (series)	Lauren Myracle	2004–2007
And Tango Makes Three	Justin Richardson and Peter Parnell	2005
Always Running	Luis Rodriguez	2005
What's Happening to My Body	Linda Madaras, Area Madaras, and Simon Sullivan	2007
Anastasia (series)	Lois Lowry	2008

them, or bookstores may relocate them to the adult section.

In rare instances, books are banned in the interest of children's physical health. Congress's Consumer Product Safety Improvement Act (CPSIA) of 2008 effectively bans certain illustrated books printed before 1985, because of the lead content in some of the ink used for the illustrations.

Impact

Whether one supports or opposes censorship, the act of banning books acknowledges the power of reading.

A banner backdrop for the Banned Books Week Read-Out cosponsored by the American Library Association and the McCormick Freedom Museum, Chicago, 2008. (Courtesy of Jim Rettig)

The ALA considers this power one best held by readers. To the ALA, censorship includes not only an outright ban on a book but also any denial of access through the decision not to purchase a certain book or the intentional withholding of information from a library patron. Each of these actions leads to the same result: barring readers from knowledge.

Other groups have viewed book banning as a direct affront to First Amendment freedoms, considered necessary to maintaining a free society. If books, and their ideas, are banned, then power is given to those able to restrict reading. From this perspective, the issue of book banning becomes less about protecting children from books deemed inappropriate and more about ensuring the freedom to read (and to write) for all Americans.

Further Reading

American Library Association, Office for Intellectual Freedom. *Intellectual Freedom Manual.* Chicago: ALA, 2002. Print. Examines the Library Bill of Rights (and includes the full text), addressing accessibility, the freedom to read, and censorship.

Heins, Marjorie. *Not in Front of the Children.* New York: Hill, 2001. Print. Relates the history of censorship across art forms, particularly focusing on the assumption of innocence and helplessness in childhood.

Karolides, Nicholas J., Margaret Bald, and Dawn B. Sova. *120 Banned Books.* New York: Checkmark, 2005. Print. Categorizes and examines books banned based on political, religious, sexual, and social grounds. Each entry includes a book's summary, censorship history, and related sources.

Lewis, Anthony. *Freedom for the Thought That We Hate.* New York: Basic, 2007. Print. Outlines challenges to First Amendment freedoms, referencing court cases to explain the development of censorship and the affirmation of freedom.

Morrison, Toni, ed. *Burn This Book.* New York: HarperStudio, 2009. Print. Collection of essays by prominent authors on writing and meaning of censorship.

Olson, Walter. "The New Book Banning." *City Journal* 12 Feb. 2009. Web. 8 Aug. 2012. Elaborates on the threat of CPSIA to old books.

Lucia Pizzo

■ Beck, Glenn

Identification: American radio and television personality

Born: February 10, 1964; Everett, Washington

Glenn Beck is a conservative television and radio personality who gained prominence in 2000 as a popular yet highly controversial political commentator. A best-selling author, he released six books in the 2000s, beginning in 2003. Despite frequently drawing criticism for his incendiary rhetoric, he was a highly influential figure in the growing conservative movement during the 2000s.

Glenn Beck got his start in radio broadcasting at the age of thirteen, when he entered a contest with a local radio station and won an hour of airtime. Beck later leveraged that early experience, earning a job at Seattle's FM station KUBE 93 while he was still in high school. Throughout the 1980s and 1990s, Beck worked as a DJ at various radio stations in Phoenix, Houston, and Baltimore. He eventually found work hosting morning shows at KC101 in New Haven, Connecticut. During Beck's tenure at KC101, Clear Channel Communications, which at the time was a small but growing media venture, purchased the station. Clear Channel's growing number of affiliated stations would give Beck the opportunity to transition away from his role as a DJ into political talk radio.

Beck began to express an interest in moving into talk radio, as he felt he had outgrown the "morning

Glenn Beck. (Courtesy Luke X. Martin)

zoo" format of Top 40 music stations. He was given a small gig at Clear Channel's New Haven AM station in return for avoiding political conversations during the morning zoo show. This concession helped him hone his talk skills and gain some experience in a different format. Beck left New Haven for Tampa, Florida, where he landed his first talk radio spot, *The Glenn Beck Program,* in 2000. The show gained an enormous following during the Bush-Gore presidential election controversy and attracted new viewers following the terrorist attacks of September 11, 2001. *The Glenn Beck Program* went national in 2002 and relocated to WPHT in Philadelphia, Pennsylvania. In 2006, Beck broke into television as a nighttime commentator with CNN Headline News. The Fox News Channel offered him a job in January 2009, where his show quickly attracted more than two million viewers.

Beck's Fox News program garnered a wide audience, as he struck a chord with conservatives who shared his concerns about the actions of the Obama administration. In 2009, Beck led the 9-12 Project, a movement seeking to recapture what Beck calls the "American values" that united the country on September 12, 2001, the day after the terrorist attacks on the World Trade Center and the Pentagon. In the summer of 2009, Beck came under fire for claiming that President Obama was a racist, prompting a number of advertisers to pull their ads from Beck's program. Beck also drew attention to poor practices at the Association of Community Organizations for

Reform Now (ACORN), a community activism organization that subsequently lost congressional funding.

Beck is also an author of several books, including *The Real America: Messages from the Heart and Heartland* (2003), *An Inconvenient Book: Real Solutions to the World's Biggest Problems* (2007), and *Arguing with Idiots: How to Stop Small Minds and Big Government* (2009). In addition, he created *Fusion Magazine* and formed his own media organization, Mercury Radio Arts, which handles his media pursuits. In April 2011, Beck announced that he was ending his daily television show on Fox News. While Beck's critics stated the show was cancelled by the network because of lack of supporting advertisers, Beck himself stated that was going to continue to work with Fox on other projects.

Impact

Glenn Beck was one of the most visible and influential pundits in the conservative movement against the Obama administration. His wildly successful television program earned him a spot among the Fox News right-wing commentators, joining the likes of Sean Hannity and Bill O'Reilly. Several of his books have topped New York Times Best Sellers lists, and his Restoring Honor rally drew an estimated eighty-seven thousand people to Washington, DC, in August 2010.

Further Reading

Gottfried, Paul. "Glenn Beck's Revisionism." *American Conservative* 9.9 (2010): 36–38. Print.

Parker, James. "Glenn Beck in Exile." *Atlantic Monthly* June 2012: 40–41. Print.

Poniewozik, James. "Glenn Beck." *Time* 18 Apr. 2011: 21. Print.

Ann Cameron

■ Beltway snipers

The Event: A series of shootings in the greater Washington, DC, area perpetrated in October 2002 by John Allen Muhammad and Lee Boyd Malvo

Date: October 2–24, 2002

Place: Maryland, Virginia, Washington, DC

For twenty-three days in October 2002, Washington, DC, Maryland, and Virginia were gripped by fear as a series of

random shootings took the lives of ten people. A widely publicized FBI investigation ensued. The news media devoted hours of airtime and pages of print to the shootings, as a nation still reeling from the terrorist attacks of September 2001 looked on.

The crime spree perpetrated by forty-one-year-old John Allen Muhammad, a convert to the Nation of Islam with a troubled past, and seventeen-year-old Lee Boyd Malvo, Muhammad's protégé, began in August 2002, when the pair conducted a series of shootings and robberies in Louisiana and Alabama in which one person was murdered and three injured.

The first of the October shootings—most of which happened around the section of Interstate 495 known as the Capital Beltway, giving the spree its common name—occurred on October 2, 2002, when a fifty-five-year-old man was shot dead in a parking lot in Wheaton, Maryland. On October 3, five more people were shot and killed while conducting everyday tasks, including pumping gasoline, reading a book at a bus stop, and operating a lawn mower. The random nature of the shootings sowed panic and fear throughout the Washington area and inspired nationwide media coverage. The Montgomery County Police Department in Maryland helmed the investigation, backed up by hundreds of FBI agents around the country. From October 4 to October 19, six more people were shot, three fatally.

Investigators received their first break in the case when someone called a tip line claiming to be the sniper and claiming responsibility for the two shootings in Alabama. Police followed up on this tip, examining fingerprint and ballistic evidence from the Alabama crime scene. Public unrest reached a fever pitch after communications from the snipers began to be discovered at the scenes of the shootings, including a letter that threatened children.

On October 17, police announced that they had matched a fingerprint from one of the Alabama crime scenes to Malvo. One of Malvo's previous arrest records connected him with Muhammad, whose name investigators recognized from a tip. Investigators discovered that Muhammad had a 1990 Chevrolet Caprice registered in his name. A description of the car was released to the media. On October 22, a tenth victim was shot and killed in Aspen Hill, Maryland. Two days later, the Caprice

was spotted at a rest stop in Maryland, and Malvo and Muhammad were arrested. Further investigation revealed that the pair had operated a sniper rifle through a hole in the trunk of the automobile, allowing them to shoot at people and flee without notice.

Officials in Virginia and Maryland agreed to try Muhammad in Maryland, where he was found guilty of murder in May 2006. He was executed by lethal injection in November 2009. Malvo, who pled guilty and agreed to testify against Muhammad, was sentenced to life in prison without parole.

Impact

The Beltway snipers' killing spree gripped the United States for three weeks in October of 2002, terrorizing residents of the greater Washington area. Before Muhammad and Malvo's capture, security was heightened around government buildings such as the White House and the Capitol building. In all, ten people were killed and three people suffered severe injuries. The investigation into the shootings is remembered as collaborative effort between the region's local law enforcement officers, federal agents, the public, and the news media.

Further Reading

Cannon, Angie. *23 Days of Terror: The Compelling True Story of the Hunt and Capture of the Beltway Snipers.* New York: Pocket, 2003.

Horwitz, Sari, and Michael Ruane. *Sniper: Inside the Hunt for the Killers Who Terrorized the Nation.* New York: Ballantine, 2004. Print.

Moose, Charles, and Charles Fleming. *Three Weeks in October.* New York: Penguin, 2003.

Patrick G. Cooper

■ Benoit, Chris

Identification: Canadian professional wrestler
Born: May 21, 1967; Montreal, Quebec, Canada
Died: June 25, 2007; Atlanta, Georgia

As a professional wrestler, Benoit made a lasting impression in the ring. His double murder–suicide, however, serves as an example of the dangers of brain damage caused by exposure to head trauma in contact sport and also prompted investigations into drug use by members of wrestling organizations.

Chris Benoit became a star of professional wrestling in part due to his wholesome image as a family man. His first wife was wrestling stage manager, Nancy Sullivan. When Benoit won the World Wrestling Entertainment (WWE) heavyweight championship in 2004, his wife and son shared the moment with him on the mat. The appearance stood in sharp contrast to events that occurred a year earlier, when Nancy filed for divorce and requested a restraining order against Benoit, citing her husband's violent and threatening behavior. Nevertheless, the wrestler and his spouse had patched things up and all seemed well. Benoit's success in the WWE continued, and he was slated to appear on a WWE special telecast in June of 2007.

Benoit, nicknamed the Canadian Crippler, had two sons from a previous relationship. He and Nancy also had a son, Daniel. As an infant, Daniel was undersized and was reportedly treated with growth hormones. On the weekend before his planned telecast appearance, Benoit, then forty, changed his plans. He sent several unusual text messages, one of which indicated his family was sick. Friends and family became concerned when they had not heard from him for a long period of time. The police visited the family's home in Atlanta, where they discovered that Nancy and Daniel had been murdered, and Benoit had committed suicide.

Investigators discovered prescription anabolic steroids in Benoit's home. However, toxicology reports conducted as part of the murder investigation indicated that it was unlikely that Benoit's behavior was caused by the substances found in his system. Doctors with the Center for the Study of Retired Athletes conducted a later study of Benoit's brain. The team posthumously diagnosed him with chronic traumatic encephalopathy (CTE), a type of dementia. Experts at the center concluded this condition had likely impaired Benoit's behavior and judgment.

Impact

Following the Benoit double murder–suicide, US congressional committees began investigating drug policies of wrestling organizations. The testosterone level in Benoit's body was found to be about ten times the normal level. As a result, wrestling organizations made efforts to address the health concerns of their athletes. Investigations into steroid purchases also resulted in the suspensions of eleven WWE wrestlers in late 2007.

Further Reading

Randazzo, Matthew V. *Ring of Hell: The Story of Chris Benoit and the Fall of the Pro Wrestling Industry.* Beverly Hills: Phoenix, 2008. Print.
"Steroids Discovered in Probe of Slayings, Suicide." *ESPN.* ESPN Internet Ventures, 27 June 2007. Web. 9 July 2012.
Swartz, Jon. "Doping Still an Issue in Wrestling." *USA Today.* USA Today, 19 Nov. 2007. Web. 9 July 2012.

Josephine Campbell

■ Bernanke, Ben

Identification: Chair of the Federal Reserve
Born: December 13, 1953; Augusta, Georgia

Economist Ben Bernanke became chair of the Board of Governors of the Federal Reserve System in 2006 and was reappointed in 2010. Because Bernanke's tenure as chair coincided with the global economic downturn that began in 2008, his efforts were largely focused on economic recovery.

In 2002 Ben Bernanke, chair of the economics department at Princeton University, was appointed a member of the Board of Governors of the Federal Reserve System by President George W. Bush. The Federal Reserve is the central bank of the United States; its Board of Governors comprises seven members, each of whom is appointed to serve a fourteen-year term. The board is responsible for supervising the twelve regional Federal Reserve banks and establishing consumer credit and banking regulations. In 2005, Bernanke resigned from the Board of Governors to become chair of the Council of Economic Advisors, a group of economists who advise the president. Many speculated that, if Bernanke did well in this position, he would likely succeed Federal Reserve Chair Alan Greenspan, who was slated to retire the following year.

In 2006, President Bush appointed Bernanke chair of the Federal Reserve Board of Governors, a four-year term. At the same time, Bernanke was appointed to a fourteen-year term as a member of the board. He stated that one of his main objectives was to increase transparency within the Federal Reserve; however, the difficulty surrounding this goal was soon apparent. At the 2006 White House Correspondents' Association Dinner, he discussed interest rate

Ben Bernanke. (©iStockphoto.com/Jonathan Ernst)

policy with a CNBC anchor who then broadcast the information, causing a sharp drop in the stock market. Bernanke called the incident a "lapse in judgment," and stated that, in the future, his would communicate to the public using only the established, formal channels.

Bernanke's first term as chair of the Board of Governors was marked by the global economic recession that began in 2008. Some have criticized Bernanke's response to the recession, stating that he did not adequately anticipate the effects of the housing market downturn and subprime mortgage loan delinquencies on the national and global economy. Bernanke also faced criticism for letting Lehman Brothers declare bankruptcy in September 2008 instead of bailing out the large investment bank (as institutions such as AIG and Bear Stearns would later be bailed out or funded by the US government). Bernanke defended the decision, however, stating that Lehman Brothers did not have sufficient collateral to support a bailout. Bernanke also defended the government's

role in stabilizing AIG and Bear Stearns, stating that their failures would have greatly impeded economic recovery and stability. However, Bernanke has clearly stated that he feels AIG was taking advantage of gaps in regulation and that, while a bailout was necessary, he was frustrated and angered by AIG's fiscal irresponsibility.

In early 2010, President Barack Obama appointed Bernanke to a second term as chair of the Federal Reserve. Shortly after his reappointment, Bernanke voiced concern over economic recovery in the United States, citing high foreclosure rates and unemployment. He resolved to lower interest rates, increase the Federal Reserve's transparency and accountability in matters of monetary policy, and prevent inflation.

Impact

Bernanke was a central figure in the federal scramble to mitigate the effects of the economic downturn of 2008. Bernanke's decisions helped to shape the financial climate of the United States and the world in the following years. Bernanke oversaw unprecedented government bailouts of private businesses and the management of the housing crisis fallout, setting the stage for a rocky recovery and significantly affecting the political tone in America.

Further Reading

Grunwald, Michael. "Ben Bernanke. (Cover Story)." *Time* 174.25 (2009): 44–62. Print.
Hummel, Jeffrey Rogers. "Ben Bernanke versus Milton Friedman the Federal Reserve's Emergence as the US Economy's Central Planner." *Independent Review* 15.4 (2011): 485–18. Print.
Isikoff, Michael. "Ben Bernanke's Identity Crisis." *Newsweek* 154.10 (2009): 9. Print.

Elizabeth Adams

■ Bernie Madoff Ponzi scheme

Definition: The largest Ponzi scheme in history, in which financier Bernie Madoff defrauded his investors of billions of dollars over twenty years

On December 11, 2008, Bernie Madoff was arrested and charged with eleven felony counts, including securities fraud, wire fraud, money laundering, and perjury. These stemmed from his massive Ponzi scheme, which over the

course of twenty years involved approximately $64 billion in capital, and resulted in more than $18 billion in direct losses for its victims. Shockingly, the largest Ponzi scheme in history was perpetrated by a trusted Wall Street insider, and went undiscovered for years despite several tips to the Securities and Exchange Commission from concerned citizens.

When the scandal surrounding his trading company broke at the end of 2008, Bernard "Bernie" Madoff was one of the most venerated people in American finance. He began his securities trading career at the age of twenty-two, in 1960, when he used his modest savings of $5,000 to start a company called Bernard L. Madoff Investment Securities LLC. By the early 1980s, his company had grown into an industry leader. In1989, his company was responsible for approximately 5 percent of all trading activity on the New York Stock Exchange.

Madoff was considered a brilliant entrepreneur and a visionary. He was made chair of the NASDAQ exchange in 1990. This honor was a sign of the respect he was given in the financial sector. In this role, he forged a close relationship with the Securities and Exchange Commission (SEC) that continued throughout his later career.

Madoff's Hedge Fund's Apparent Success

In the 2000s, Madoff was at the height of his career. The investment management division of Madoff Investment Securities was considered to be one of the best investment houses in the world. It apparently presented investors with consistent returns of 10 to 15 percent.

In general terms, Madoff's securities firm was said to be engaging in a complex trading approach, in which the company claimed it was purchasing stocks from the largest and most stable American companies, and making careful position adjustments through purchasing secondary options. Theoretically, Madoff's company was innovative, but a safe place for clients to invest. This perception was bolstered by its ability to show amazingly consistent, if not spectacularly high, returns to clients.

Madoff's investment firm represented a limited number of clients, and was an exclusive firm. At first, investors mainly came from those with personal connections to Madoff and his family through country clubs and other social institutions. Later, as demand for access to the fund grew, it began to take on investors from secondary networks, often called feeder funds.

Warning Signs and the End of the Madoff Scam

Although Madoff's company enjoyed a strong reputation overall, there were some individuals who were skeptical of the Madoff firm's legitimacy. Among these was a financial investigator named Harry Markopolos. While working for an investment firm called Rampart Investment Management in 2000, he became aware of the Madoff fund's unusual ability to make money even when the overall markets were down.

Markopolos publicly expressed concerns about the Madoff company. He also submitted multiple complaints to the SEC over several years, but they dismissed his allegations. On November 7, 2005, Markopolos sent a report to the SEC outlining his concerns that Madoff was running a Ponzi scheme, basing his allegations on fourteen years of revenue reports from the Madoff company. SEC officials once again announced that the claims were wrong, and that Madoff was not engaged in illegal activities.

The Madoff scam ultimately ended not because of SEC investigations, but because of the global recession that began in 2008. Beginning in September 2008, as securities markets suffered steep declines, investors scrambled to retrieve their money from the Madoff fund in order to cover losses elsewhere. Between September and December 2008, investors pulled approximately $7 billion from the company.

As a Ponzi scheme, the firm was set up to pay departing investors with money coming in from new ones. As long as it continued to grow, the ruse could continue. With the sharp market downturn in 2008, however, and the massive investor exodus from the securities markets that followed, growth stopped. Despite several desperate attempts to secure money from associates, the Madoff fund was finally in a position where it could not continue its scam.

Bernie Madoff admitted his wrongdoing to his family members on December 9, 2008. They alerted the FBI, and Madoff was arrested two days later. On March 12, 2009, Madoff pleaded guilty to the charges, admitting that he had not been doing legitimate securities trading since the 1990s. On June 29, 2009, Madoff was sentenced to 150 years in prison.

Bernie Madoff. (Jin Lee/Bloomberg/Getty Images)

Impact

The Madoff scandal had a powerful impact on the American financial sector. The fact that such a large-scale scam could take place despite repeated calls for SEC investigations has caused many to question the integrity of that regulatory agency. Following the scandal, two victims of the scam committed suicide, after they realized the extent of their financial losses. Madoff's son, Mark, also committed suicide after a lawsuit was filed against him and his brother Andrew, accusing them of being aware of and profiting from their father's illegal activity. The scandal also significantly damaged investor confidence worldwide, and resulted in the loss of billions of dollars for charitable foundations, businesses, and individuals.

Further Reading

Kirtzman, Andrew. *Betrayal: The Life and Lies of Bernie Madoff.* New York: Harper, 2009. Print. This is a thorough account of Bernie Madoff's career.

Markopolos, Harry. *No One Would Listen: A True Financial Thriller.* Hoboken: Wiley, 2010. Print.

Would-be whistleblower Markopolos presents an account of his quest to stop Madoff.

Nasaw, Daniel. "Timeline: Key Dates in the Bernard Madoff Case." *Guardian* 16 Feb. 2011. Web. 25 Oct. 2012. The Guardian provides a chronology of key events in the Ponzi scheme scandal.

Times Topics. "Bernard L. Madoff." *New York Times.* New York Times Co., 28 June 2012. Web. 25 Oct. 2012. This is an easy to follow, interactive timeline of the major events of the Madoff case from the New York Times.

Adam J. Berger, PhD

■ Biden, Joe

Identification: US vice president
Born: November 20, 1942; Scranton, Pennsylvania

Joseph R. Biden Jr. was elected as the forty-seventh vice president of the United States on November 4, 2008. His election as vice president was the culmination of a lifelong career in politics and public service in the United States Senate.

Joe Biden. (Library of Congress, LC-DIG-ppbd- 00359/Photograph by Andrew Cutraro)

Joe Biden was born on November 20, 1942, in Scranton, Pennsylvania. The Biden family relocated to Delaware in 1953. Biden majored in history and political science at the University of Delaware, graduating in 1965, and went on to earn his law degree from Syracuse Law School in 1968. After graduation, he returned home to Wilmington, Delaware, where he practiced law until 1970, when he won election to the New Castle County Council. In 1972, rather than pursue reelection to the county council, Biden decided to run for the US Senate. This was considered a brash move, given his youth and limited political experience. Biden won the 1972 election and became one of the youngest senators in US history.

Biden was elected to his fifth term in the Senate in 1996. When Senator Jim Jeffords of Vermont left the Republican Party to become an independent, giving Democrats control of the Senate in June 2001, Biden became chair of the Foreign Relations Committee. He soon became involved in the national debate over the viability of the Strategic Defense Initiative, a "Star Wars"–like defense shield for the United States, which had been proposed in the 1980s by President Ronald Reagan and advanced by President George W. Bush in the early 2000s. Biden made clear his view, arguing that the "missile defense delusion" would damage international nonproliferation efforts.

Biden was reelected to a sixth term in November 2002 by a margin of 17 percentage points. However, he would lose the chairmanship of the Foreign Relations Committee to Senator Richard Lugar as the Republicans took back majority control of the Senate in January 2003. He again became the ranking minority member of the committee. In mid-2003, Biden was mulling over his prospects for another run for the presidency in 2004, but decided that he did not have enough time to prepare financially.

Beginning in 2004, Biden became involved in efforts to improve the National Domestic Violence Hotline. Biden also introduced a bill in 2007 called the National Domestic Violence Volunteer Act in order to establish a network of volunteer lawyers willing to represent domestic violence victims in court, but the bill was not enacted. In 2007, Biden assumed the chairmanship of the International Narcotics Control Caucus and resumed the chairmanship of the Senate Foreign Relations Committee.

Biden declared his candidacy in the 2008 presidential election on January 31, 2007. Biden made news during the Democratic Party primaries debate for his sense of humor and his use of one-liners to criticize both his colleagues and his Republican challengers. Nonetheless, Biden received only a small percentage of votes in the 2008 Democratic Party caucus in Iowa, placing fifth. He announced his withdrawal from the presidential primaries on January 3, 2008. In June, Senator Barack Obama secured the Democratic presidential nomination.

Biden began focusing his efforts on running for a seventh Senate term against Republican challenger Christine O'Donnell. However, on August 23, Democratic nominee Obama announced that he had selected Biden as his running mate. Obama's campaign stressed Biden's experience in foreign policy and national security when citing his credentials to be vice president. Others cited Biden's popularity among blue-collar American workers as a reason Obama had selected Biden as his running mate. Biden was heavily involved in campaigning leading up the election, particularly in swing states such as Pennsylvania and Ohio.

The 2008 US presidential election was held on November 4. Senators Obama and Biden defeated Republican Party nominees Senator John McCain of Arizona and Governor Sarah Palin of Alaska. Biden was also reelected to his Senate seat. The governor of Delaware named Biden's former chief of staff, Edward Kaufman, to fill Biden's vacant Senate seat. Biden cast his last Senate vote on January 15, 2009, and began serving as vice president following his inauguration on January 20, 2009. Biden is the first vice president from Delaware and the first Catholic to hold the office.

As vice president, Biden held regular interviews with various media outlets to help inform the public of the White House strategy to improve the national economy following the 2008 financial crisis. Biden also travelled overseas extensively on diplomatic visits; he was worked extensively with Central and South American political leaders to address the issues of drug trafficking and violence. He had a key role in ending the war in Iraq, travelling to that country more than a half dozen times. Biden was also heavily involved in implementing the American Recovery and Reinvestment Act of 2009 to alleviate the impact of the 2008 financial crisis. In early 2010, Biden also worked hard to promote President Obama's healthcare reform act.

Impact

Biden is recognized for his role in shaping US foreign policy, crime and drug control measures, and environmental protection and education policy. In his thirty-six years as a senator, Biden built a reputation for earnest, off-the-cuff politicizing—a tone which he has maintained throughout his vice presidency. Following Obama and Biden's reelection in November 2012, Biden indicated that he would continue to be active in US politics after he completed his second term as vice president.

Further Reading

Gelb, Leslie H. "Joe Biden, Out Loud." *Newsweek* 158.26 (2011): 42–45. Print.

Heilemann, John. "Joe Biden Isn't Finished." *New York* 45.28 (2012): 28–116. Print.

Scherer, Michael. "Mo Joe." *Time* 179.23 (2012): 26–30. Print.

John Pearson

■ Biofuel

Definition: A type of renewable fuel made from plants and animal products and wastes; the most common types include ethanol and biodiesel

Many countries began using and developing alternate sources of liquid fuel, known as biofuel, in the late 2000s due to nations' dependence on petroleum and the spike in price of the fuel. While biofuel may have been better for the environment and cost less than fossil fuels, it was not without drawbacks. Producing biofuel used exorbitant amounts of energy as well as large volumes of crops. This consumption of resources may have outweighed the benefits of using biofuel.

Early in the twenty-first century, biofuel quickly became one of the leading alternative fuels in the world. As of 2009, the United States consumed about 100 billion gallons of oil each year, and this number continued to grow. This coupled with the rising cost of petroleum in the late 2000s led researchers to develop biofuel as a more sustainable energy source. The main difference between biofuels and fossil fuels is that biofuels are made from plants grown just prior to production, while fossil fuels are made of decomposed plants and animals that were compressed underground for millions of years. Biofuel can be produced very quickly.

Although several types of biofuels were developed, ethanol and biodiesel were the most common. Ethanol is an alcohol made by fermenting a crop, such as corn or sugar cane, and then distilling it. The United States and Brazil were the top producers of ethanol in the world as of 2009. The United States used mainly corn, while Brazil used sugar cane to produce ethanol. Ethanol can be used as a substitute for gasoline or blended with gasoline. In the United States, gasoline was blended with 10 percent ethanol (E10), which increased the octane of the gasoline and reduced pollution-causing emissions. To further the use of biofuels, in 2007, the United States passed the Energy Security and Independence Act, which mandated that the country would produce and use thirty-six billion gallons of biofuels each year by 2022.

Biodiesel is typically a mixture of an alcohol, such as methanol, and an oil, such as animal fat, recycled cooking grease, soybean oil, or vegetable oil. It can be used as an additive to diesel or by itself. Its use has been shown to reduce vehicle emissions. During the

2000s, scientists began researching the production of second-generation biofuels, which used plant waste products. They claimed that using plant cellulose or microscopic algae to produce biofuel would eliminate the need to use food crops. In the meantime, however, ethanol and biodiesel continued to be produced using food crops.

Pros

Using biofuels offered many advantages. The cost of petroleum was rising, which made the cost of biofuel much less in comparison. Fossil fuels took billions of years to form under the ground, while biofuels were renewable. Biofuels were produced from crops that could be continually grown and took much less time to produce.

Because crops can be grown in most parts of the United States, the production of biofuels boosted local and national economies. This reduced the nation's dependence on foreign fuel. Using biofuel was also better for the environment. When biofuels were burned, less carbon was released into the environment. The production of biofuels also recycled products such as used cooking oils and crop wastes. In addition, biodiesel made with soybeans did not hurt the food supply because only the oil of the soybean was used, leaving the rest of it for consumption.

Cons

Despite the advantages of biofuels, many disadvantages existed as well. Because large amounts of crops such as corn were grown to produce ethanol, fewer crops were grown for food. This could be potentially devastating to countries where food is scarce and possibly lead to severe food shortages. Biofuel manufacturing plants also used large volumes of water. Three gallons of water were needed to produce one gallon of ethanol. The National Academy of Sciences estimated that producing one hundred million gallons of ethanol required the same amount of water used in a year by a town of about five thousand people. This could be disastrous to the millions of people worldwide who lack clean drinking water and could further exacerbate the worldwide water crisis.

Although the use of biofuels has been shown to decrease carbon emissions, ethanol produced from corn crops often polluted the environment. Corn farming required larger amounts of fertilizer and pesticides than any other type of biofuels farming. Runoff from fertilizer and pesticides harmed waterways, leading to "dead zones" in the Gulf of Mexico and along the Atlantic Coast. The entire process of making biofuels consumed exorbitant amounts of energy, too. Much debate existed about whether biofuels generated enough energy to make up for resources used to produce them—especially since the energy output of biofuels was much lower than traditional fuels.

Impact

Biofuels have been a reliable alternative form of energy used throughout many countries. While the development of biofuels did not eliminate the need for fossil fuels during the 2000s, it lessened the United States' dependence on fossil fuels. Biofuels also reduced the amount of carbon released into the environment. With more development and research into second-generation biofuels, it may be possible to readily substitute biofuels for fossil fuels in the future and even end dependence on fossil fuels altogether.

Further Reading

"Biodiesel Myths Busted." *Biodiesel.org*. National Biodiesel Board, n.d. Web. 3 Dec. 2012. PDF file. A report debunking the myths about biodiesel.

"Biofuels." *New York Times*. New York Times, 17 June 2011. Web. 3 Dec. 2012. An overview on biofuels.

"Biofuels and Renewable Energy: What Is a Biofuel Anyway?" *Living Green and Saving Energy*. Living Green and Saving Energy, 17 Nov. 2010. Web. 3 Dec. 2012. A blog post explaining how biofuels work.

"Biofuels: The Original Car Fuel." *National Geographic*. National Geographic Soc., 2012. Web. 3 Dec. 2012. Details the history of biofuels.

"FAQ's." *BioFuel Energy Corp*. BioFuel Energy Corp, 2008. Web. 3 Dec. 2012. Explains the basics of biofuel production and uses.

"Learning about Renewable Energy: Biofuels Basics." *National Renewable Energy Laboratory*. Alliance for Sustainable Energy, LLC, 18 May 2012. Web. 3 Dec. 2012. Explains the difference between biofuels and other renewable energy sources. Also includes a video, "Converting Biomass to Liquid Fuels."

Skye, Jared. "Advantages and Disadvantages of Biofuels." *LoveToKnow Green Living*. LoveToKnow Corp. Web. 3 Dec. 2012. Weighs the pros and cons of biofuel production and usage.

Angela Harmon

■ BlackBerry

Definition: A popular wireless-device brand based out of Ontario, Canada, and known for its smartphones

After creating their first wireless device in 1999, BlackBerry's parent company Research in Motion developed the first-generation smartphones for which the brand is known. While these phones offered typical features of mobile phones, they also enabled users to send emails and instant messages, and served as personal digital assistants, cameras, and media players. Smartphones expanded cell phone capabilities, creating a robust market for the product while changing expectations about the pace of communication in the twenty-first century.

BlackBerry devices have significantly altered wireless communication. Initially named for the arrangement of its keypad, as the keys of a BlackBerry are arranged in bulbous clusters, resembling the fruit. By providing a full keyboard, users were more easily able to type out messages than on a standard cell phone. The ease of communication was then tempered by "BlackBerry thumb," a term referring to thumb pain caused by excessive use of the device.

In addition to facilitating typed communication, BlackBerry devices are particularly known for their encryption features. These allow messages to be sent and received under high security. This secrecy has endeared the phones to government officials and drug dealers alike. The phone, while already a prominent player among wireless devices of the early 2000s, gained further popularity through Barack Obama's use of his BlackBerry during his 2008 campaign and subsequent presidency. The phone has also been adopted for use among federal agents and police officers.

The addictive nature of BlackBerry use earned it the name "CrackBerry" among users of the device. This term encapsulates the phone's effect during the early 2000s, which was to create and expand the market for such versatile wireless devices. Globally appealing, BlackBerry created nearly 100 million devices between 2000 and 2010. Although BlackBerry initially held the bulk of the market for smartphones, its success invited competition. Google's Android and Apple's iPhone, both released in 2007, largely cut into BlackBerry's market share with their new and highly capable smartphones.

A BlackBerry Bold 9650 cell phone. (Courtesy Evan-Amos)

Impact

The early 2000s saw the ascent and decline of the BlackBerry. Still, while BlackBerry smartphones no longer enjoyed market dominance, and as smartphone usage increased, the brand continued to attract new users. Perhaps less noticeably, but more pervasively, BlackBerry devices have rewired the expectations of communication. Cell phones created the expectation of constant social accessibility, and smartphones expanded this expectation, offering access to email and the Internet. The capability to be always connected cultivated a dependence on wireless products while simultaneously granting users access to information with a constancy not seen prior to the twenty-first century.

As technological development accelerates, the long-term effects of BlackBerry and smartphone use remain to be seen. New and evolving devices may render BlackBerry devices obsolete, or perhaps greater societal dependence on smartphones will facilitate the brand's revival. Either way, the rise of smartphones has had an undeniable effect on the pace of communication in the 2000s.

Further Reading

Joyce, Amy. "For Some, Thumb Pain is BlackBerry's Stain." *Washington Post* 23 Apr. 2005. Web. 1 Nov. 2012.

Noguchi, Yuki. "Government Enters Fray Over Black-Berry Patents." *Washington Post* 12 Nov. 2005. Web. 2 Nov. 2012.

Sweeny, Alastair. *BlackBerry Planet: The Story of Research in Motion and the Little Device that Took the World by Storm.* Mississauga: Wiley, 2009. Print.

Lucia Pizzo

■ Blagojevich, Rod

Identification: Governor of Illinois, 2003–9
Born: December 10, 1956; Chicago, Illinois

Rod Blagojevich was the fortieth governor of Illinois and the first Democrat to hold the office in twenty-five years. His career abruptly ended with his impeachment in 2009 on charges of criminal corruption and bribery.

The Illinois Republican Party's twenty-five year hold on the governor's office suggested that Ron Blagojevich, who had represented Chicago's Fifth District in the US House of Representatives since 1997, would have little chance of success when he proposed running for governor in 2002. But with the endorsement of popular Chicago Mayor Richard M. Daly and a number of significant trade unions, Blagojevich was able to raise a record $25 million dollars in campaign contributions, and beat out his opponent, Illinois Attorney General Jim Ryan.

The beginning of Blagojevich's first term as governor presented a whole new set of challenges. Blagojevich inherited a large budget deficit and a wide gap between Chicago's urban economy and the rural communities that make up most of Illinois. To address the state's economic problems, Blagojevich's administration developed a number of proposals, including a state venture capital plan to give financial assistance to new businesses located in rural areas, a sales tax on services, licensing more casinos, and seeking more federal funding.

He won reelection in 2006 after defeating Edwin Eisendrath in the Democratic Party primary and defeating Judy Baar Topinka and Rich Whitney in the general election.

Rod Blagojevich. (©iStockphoto.com/David Banks)

On December 9, 2008, Blagojevich and his chief of staff John Harris were arrested for soliciting bribes and conspiracy to commit fraud. The charges were related to the Governor's responsibility to appoint a replacement for the US Senate seat being vacated by former Illinois Senator and US President-elect Barack Obama. According to the charges, wiretaps of phone conversations taken from Blagojevich's office revealed an effort to offer the vacant seat to someone who could arrange a lucrative job for the governor or his wife. Blagojevich allegedly stated that he would appoint himself to the seat if an arrangement suitable to him could not be reached. The charges also included allegations that Blagojevich threatened the editorial board of the *Chicago Tribune* and a Chicago children's charity. Following his arrest, calls for Blagojevich's resignation came from Democrats and Republicans nationwide. Although Blagojevich made bail, impeachment proceedings against him began in January 2009.

On January 29, 2009, Blagojevich was convicted at his impeachment trial by a unanimous vote of 59–0 in the Illinois state senate. He was immediately succeeded as governor by Lieutenant. Governor Patrick Quinn. In September 2009, Blagojevich published a book entitled *The Governor: The Truth Behind the Political Scandal That Continues to Rock the Nation.* He also appeared on the reality television series *The Celebrity Apprentice.*

Blagojevich's trial began on June 10, 2010. On August 17, 2010, he was convicted of lying to FBI investigators. However, the jury was deadlocked on the remaining twenty-three corruption charges.

On June 27, 2010, a jury found Blagojevich guilt on seventeen criminal counts, including wire fraud, bribery and corruption. The verdict ended two and a half years of legal wrangling surrounding the former governor.

Impact

Blagojevich was a notoriously unpopular governor even prior to the breaking of the Obama Senate seat scandal. The corruption story made for an odd backdrop to the early days of Obama's presidency, drawing unfavorable attention to the Chicago political landscape. The spotlight trained on Blagojevich afforded him a bizarre run as a pop culture reference point. He appeared as a contestant on *The Celebrity Apprentice* and performed with Chicago's Second City improv group in a show titled *Rod Blagojevich Superstar.* He was repeatedly mocked on *Saturday Night Live* and was even offered a job with professional wrestling company TNA Wrestling.

Further Reading

Coen, Jeff, Rick Pearson, and David Kidwell. "Blagojevich arrested; Fitzgerald calls it a 'politcal corruption crime spree'." *Chicago Tribune.* Tribune Newspaper, 10 Dec. 2008. Web. 26 Oct. 2012.

Davey, Monica and Jack Healy. "Illinois Governor Charged in Scheme to Sell Obama's Seat." *New York Times.* New York Times, 9 Dec. 2008. Web. 26 Oct. 2012.

Queenan, Joe. "The Real Blagojevich Scandal." *Washington Post* 14 Dec. 2008: B01. Print.

Amy Witherbee

■ Blogging

Definition: The regular posting of opinions, observations, video, links, images, or other content on a web-based log, or blog

The act of blogging has come a long way since its beginnings in the late 1990s. What was once used mainly as an online diary for people to express their thoughts and feelings evolved into a multipurpose communication tool used for recreation and business. With the expansion of computer technology throughout the 2000s, web accessibility increased and blogging became the primary Internet publishing channel for the masses.

The term "blog" sprouted from the word "weblog," which was first used in the late 1990s to describe the logging of web links a person had visited while perusing the Internet. Before the blogging environment existed, many people logged stories of their personal lives in online diaries. From these online diaries the art of blogging was born. Blogging was initially limited to those with at least some technological skill. Websites such as Blogger, LiveJournal, and Tumblr soon enabled anyone with an Internet connection to create and maintain a blog. In October 2004, blog tracker David Sifry estimated that approximately twelve thousand new blogs were being created each day. Many types of blogs have developed since the early 2000s. Corporations began using blogs for marketing and public relations. Politicians used blogs to spread their political views. All blogging activities were conducted in what came to be known as the "blogosphere."

With the advent of self-starter blogging tools, the number of bloggers rapidly swelled. Blogs were soon regarded as an important medium in self-publishing. The personal nature and tone of blog entries was considered a primary factor in their increased popularity. The function of blogs quickly extended beyond purely personal use. Many used the space to call attention to various news reports and other world events. As an alternative to traditional news outlets, some blogs became sources of cultural commentary. Blogging soon became recognized for its ability to disseminate information on a much wider basis. Bloggers garnered credibility early in the decade when users began employing blogs to challenge the status quo. American bloggers paid particular attention to political affairs. The collaborative approach such blogs utilized gave readers a broader dialogue than regular news media allowed and blogs became influential agents for newsgathering.

Blogging the News

In December 2002, the blog *Talking Point Memos* (*TPM*), founded by Josh Marshall, posted running criticisms of then Senate majority leader Trent Lott, who had stated that America would have been better off had Senator Strom Thurmond's segregationist 1948 presidential campaign succeeded. The blog was the first to contribute substantial coverage to the incident, with major media organizations picking up the story only after the news was made public by *TPM*. As a result of *TPM*'s coverage, Lott was forced to step down from his leadership position.

Blogs continued to impact the political world in ways that regular news reporting could not. Because bloggers had the capability to discuss the stories via the blog's commenting section, users could debate and analyze news. Such interactive analyses led to what is known as the Rathergate scandal. Blogs including *Power Line* questioned the authenticity of military documents presented by news anchor Dan Rather on *60 Minutes* in 2004. Based on these documents, Rather had reported that President George W. Bush may have received special treatment while in the military. When the documents turned out to be forgeries, Rather's reputation as a journalist was forever damaged.

Blogger Matt Drudge's *Drudge Report* significantly contributed to the coverage of a Washington scandal in the late 1990s. His reporting on the Bill Clinton–Monica Lewinsky affair on the *Drudge Report* received national attention, largely for the information he divulged. Mainstream media commentators cited his blog as their source for information, and as a result, the *Drudge Report* became one of the first nationally known blogs. When Drudge was named to *Time* magazine's list of the 100 Most Influential People in the World in 2006, the magazine noted Drudge's significance as an inspiration—many people were motivated to begin blogging about the news due to his success.

Blogging Enters the Mainstream

In time, major news organizations' websites soon housed blog sections where writers and readers could interact over breaking news. Media outlets such as the *Huffington Post*, the *New York Times*, MSNBC, and CNN all started blogs dedicated to various topics.

Blogging also played an important role in global news coverage. Live updates and behind-the-scenes coverage were more accessible than ever as people used blogs to spread their stories. Crises such as Hurricane Katrina in 2005 and the 2004 tsunami in South Asia received wider exposure in the United States as survivors posted updates and photos to their blogs.

As blogging became increasingly common among Internet users, businesses began using it for commercial means. Corporations, recognizing the potential to expand their customer bases, began promoting their products on popular blogs. Businesses created company-sponsored blogs for public relations, building trust with consumers, and obtaining feedback about products.

Politicians began using blogs to their benefit in the first few years of the decade. In 2002, US representative Ray Cox of Minnesota was one of the first major politicians to start a blog. He touted blogging for its ability to broaden political dialogue and connect voters to their government. Some politicians used blogs as forums to counter what they considered biased reporting by the mainstream media.

Microblogging became a popular form of blogging with the launch of Twitter in July 2006. Microblogging involves much shorter postings of a few hundred characters that provide brief updates to blog readers. Users could also post links to other web content, including pictures and videos. During the 2007 wildfire outbreak in San Diego, California, people used Twitter to post updates about the fires and inform their families about their situations.

Impact

Blogging has had a tremendous effect on public discourse and the way news is circulated. Many bloggers have gained large followings, and some have even published books or crossed over into other media. Advances in computer technology have allowed bloggers to go beyond the written word and create video blogs. Numerous celebrities, corporations, and public figures gained large followings—often millions of fans—through Twitter. While seeking the presidency in 2008, Democratic candidate Barack Obama's campaign kept in touch with his young voters through tweets.

Though some observers are concerned that the growing popularity of social networking websites will undermine the use of blogs, others consider blogging its own form of social networking and have confidence in its resilience. Bigger concerns involve the issues of copyright infringement, and there is discussion as to how much trust should be placed in bloggers as credible news outlets. Several bloggers have been accused of defamation, and some have been criminally charged; others have been the targets of threatening cyberbullying campaigns. In 2007, a bloggers' code of conduct was proposed in response to such concerns.

Further Reading

Memmott, Mark. "Scoops and Skepticism: How the Story Unfolded." *USA Today.* USA Today, 21 Sept. 2004. Web. 10 Dec. 2012. Presents live updates of the days surrounding the Rathergate scandal.

Naone, Erica. "Microblogging Timeline." *MIT Technology Review.* MIT Technology Review, 19 Aug. 2008. Web. 5 Dec. 2012. Follows the various stages of microblogging and its evolution.

"The Rise and Rise of Corporate Blogs." *CNN.* Cable News Network, 20 Dec. 2005. Web. 5 Dec. 2012. Discusses the reasons why corporations create blogs and how they affect corporations' relations with employees and customers.

Sappenfield, Mark. "More Politicians Write Blogs to Bypass Mainstream Media." *Christian Science Monitor.* Christian Science Monitor, 24 Mar. 2005. Web. 5 Dec. 2012. Discusses politicians' use of blogs as a way to counter mainstream media.

Wortham, Jenna. "After 10 Years of Blogs, the Future's Brighter than Ever." *Wired.* Condé Naste, 17 Dec. 2007. Web. 5 Dec. 2012. Provides a brief history of blogging and discussion of how blogs have been instrumental in the development of alternative news outlets.

Cait Caffrey

■ Blu-ray Discs

Definition: Optical discs that can store a large amount of data and present high-definition video

Seeking to develop a successor to the popular but technologically limited DVD format, several major electronics companies began exploring the possibility of using blue lasers to store and read information on disc storage systems in the 2000s. Blu-ray Discs competed with the HD DVD format early in the decade but eventually gained the support of major film studios and consumer electronics manufacturers, becoming the prevalent format for high-definition home video.

Prior to the introduction of Blu-ray Discs, optical disc technology such as DVDs used red lasers to read and store data. Blue lasers, as used in Blu-ray technology, have shorter wavelengths and focus on a smaller area of a disc, reading a greater amount of data more precisely. This allows such discs to play back recorded video in high definition.

Electronics manufacturers Sony and Pioneer first introduced the DVR-Blue, a high-capacity DVD that used blue laser technology, at a trade show in October of 2000. Two years later, Sony and Pioneer joined with seven other leading electronics companies to form the Blu-ray Disc Founders, devoted to developing the Blu-ray Disc format; the group changed its name to the Blu-ray Disc Association (BDA) in 2004. To help boost consumer interest, Sony announced that the PlayStation 3 video game console would be able to play Blu-ray Discs. Electronics manufacturer Toshiba introduced a rival format, HD DVD; however, with the support of film studios such as Walt Disney Pictures and Warner Brothers Pictures as well as retailers such as Walmart and Best Buy, Blu-ray Disc was successful in becoming the predominant format for high-definition home video viewing.

Blu-ray Disc players became available for purchase in June 2006, and films in the format were released beginning in the same month. Sales of Blu-ray Discs increased dramatically as the format gained popularity with consumers. Panasonic introduced the first portable Blu-ray Disc player in 2009. That same year, the BDA introduced 3-D film technology on Blu-ray Discs, which allowed the discs to be played back in 3-D on compatible televisions.

Impact

The introduction of Blu-ray Discs has increased the visual and auditory quality of films, television programs, and other recorded materials available to consumers. Supported by the leading producers of consumer electronics and the major film studios as well as several independent studios, the medium has gained popularity as Blu-ray players have become more prevalent and affordable. In response to this increase in popularity, many studios have begun to restore older titles digitally and release them on Blu-ray Disc for audiences to experience in high definition.

Further Reading

Nazarian, Bruce. *Fast Path to Blu-ray.* Las Vegas: Digital Guy, 2009. Print.

Taylor, Jim, Charles Crawford, and Michael Zink. *Blu-ray Disc Demystified*. New York: McGraw, 2008. Print.

Patrick G. Cooper

■ Bonds, Barry

Identification: American baseball player
Born: July 24, 1964; Riverside, California

Barry Bonds was one of the most successful, dynamic, and controversial baseball players of the late twentieth and early twenty-first century. Late in his career, however, rumors of steroid use prompted questions about the legitimacy of his numerous career records.

In 2001, at the age of thirty-seven, when most baseball players' careers are in decline, San Francisco Giants outfielder Barry Bonds made an assault on Mark McGwire's record of seventy single-season home runs. He homered twenty-eight times in the Giants' first fifty games. By the midseason All-Star game, Bonds had thirty-nine home runs, a record for that point in the season. By the end of August, he had fifty-seven; by the end of September, he had sixty-nine home runs, one off McGwire's mark with a week left to play. Home run number seventy came on October 4. The next day, in a game against the rival Los Angeles Dodgers, Bonds belted numbers seventy-one and seventy-two. He finished the 2001 season with seventy-three home runs and another Most Valuable Player Award.

In 2002, the Giants reached the World Series for the first time since Bonds joined the team. Bonds batted .294 with three home runs in the five-game National League Divisional Series against the Atlanta Braves, then batted .273 with one homer during the National League Championship Series against the St. Louis Cardinals. In the World Series against the Anaheim Angels, Bonds performed even better, batting .471 with four home runs, but the Giants lost the series to the Angels in seven games.

Because of his increased home run output after age thirty-five, Bonds's name often surfaced during discussions of steroid use in baseball. In 2003, Bonds's personal trainer, Greg Anderson, was indicted in a federal court for illegally distributing steroids to his clients as part of the Bay Area Laboratory Co-operative (BALCO) case. During grand jury proceedings in the case, Bonds reportedly

Barry Bonds. (Courtesy Kevin Rushforth)

testified that he did not knowingly receive steroids from Anderson. Outside of court, Bonds maintained that his increased home run output late in his career resulted from a strict exercise regimen and legal nutritional supplements.

Bonds continued to play amid the controversy. He hit his seven-hundredth career home run in 2004. By 2006, he had 734 career home runs, only 21 short of Hank Aaron's record. That record fell in 2007, Bonds's last season. He completed his baseball career with 762 home runs and a record 2,558 bases on balls. Just after that 2007 season, Bonds was indicted for perjury and obstruction of justice in his grand jury testimony in the BALCO case. He did not return to baseball. In the major American professional sports leagues, only the hockey sensation Wayne Gretzky has won his league's most valuable player award more times than Bonds.

Impact

Bonds was one of the most talented and controversial athletes of his time. He set home run records, was named to the National League All-Star team fourteen times, and won his league's Most Valuable Player Award seven times. However, rumors of his steroid use and his 2011 conviction on the obstruction of justice charge for his testimony in the BALCO case made many followers of the game question the validity of Bonds's records and achievements. Bonds becomes eligible for the Baseball Hall of Fame in

2013; on statistics alone, he is a sure selection, but the steroid controversy might give pause to the sportswriters who vote on the honor.

Further Reading

Bloom, John. *Barry Bonds.* Santa Barbara: Greenwood, 2004. Print.

Pearlman, Jeff. *Love Me, Hate Me: Barry Bonds and the Making of an Antihero.* New York: HarperCollins, 2006. Print.

Williams, Lance, and Mark Fainaru-Wada. *Game of Shadows: Barry Bonds, BALCO, and the Steroid Scandal That Rocked Professional Sports.* New York: Gotham, 2006. Print.

James Tackach

■ Border security

Definition: A nation's ability to control who and what crosses into its lands

Though illegal immigration has long been a priority of the US Border Patrol, drug smuggling was an ongoing concern as well. In 2001, border security drew intense public interest. Additional funds and legislation were directed at securing the nation's borders against potential terrorist attacks. Manpower, technology, and razor wire were employed to stop illegal crossings.

Border security encompasses land, sea, and air enforcement. The United States has many land and sea borders, all of which fall under the jurisdiction of US Customs and Border Protection (CBP). The US Border Patrol, US Coast Guard, and other agencies and departments work under CBP on the front lines of border security.

When the Border Patrol was first established in 1924, its agents primarily patrolled isolated areas on horseback. By the twenty-first century, agents worked on foot, bicycles, horseback, motor vehicles, watercraft, and aircraft to prevent people and contraband—including weapons and drugs—from illegally entering the country and to apprehend lawbreakers who succeed in crossing the borders. A variety of technological devices—including motion detection equipment, night vision cameras, and unmanned drone aircraft—alerted agents to possible intrusion.

The role of the border patrol became significantly more important after the September 11, 2001,

terrorist attacks. Suddenly, the public became aware of the large number of people in the United States illegally and the possibility that they were planning terrorist strikes. Even the Canadian border, which had been patrolled but was largely disregarded by the public, was a concern. More resources were directed at securing ports of entry, including border crossings, marine ports, and airports.

Establishment of the US Department of Homeland Security

Following the 2001 terrorist attacks, twenty-two agencies or departments were combined under a new umbrella agency. The Department of Homeland Security (DHS), established in 2002, was allotted a number of responsibilities, among them administering immigration laws, disaster response, national security, and securing cyberspace. Agencies including CBP, Immigration and Customs Enforcement (ICE), Transportation Security Agency (TSA), Coast Guard, and Federal Emergency Management Agency (FEMA) operated under DHS to secure the nation and its citizens.

Though the US Border Patrol generally takes the lead in patrolling the borders, the US Coast Guard is also an active participant in border security. The Homeland Security Act of 2002 established ports, waterways, and coastal security as the Coast Guard's primary mission. The Coast Guard protects the US Marine Transportation System (MTS) and those within it through aircraft and watercraft patrols. The agency works to prevent the MTS from being used by terrorists targeting the country, infrastructure, people, resources, and vessels. The Coast Guard engages in both counterterrorism (offensive) and antiterrorism (defensive) activities. The Border Patrol and Coast Guard frequently work together in operations, particularly in securing the southwestern border of the United States. In addition, Coast Guard agents safeguard the commercial and recreational fisheries along the US coast in the Gulf of Mexico, thereby protecting the country's economic interests in the region.

CBP agents maintain crossings. They inspect cargo traversing the borders and ensure individuals have the proper authorization to enter the United States. They frequently search vehicles for individuals being smuggled into the country. Human trafficking has been a significant issue, particularly along the southern US border shared by Mexico. In such cases,

A small fence, shown in 2007, separates densely populated Tijuana, Mexico (right), from the United States in the Border Patrol's San Diego Sector. (National Guard/Photograph by Sergeant First Class Gordon Hyde)

the work of the Border Patrol often includes rescuing individuals abandoned by human traffickers.

The Border Fence

In 2006, US lawmakers passed the Secure Fence Act. The legislation required the DHS to establish 700 miles of double fencing along the 1,951-mile border separating the United States from Mexico and to monitor the border with technology. The ambitious $1.2 billion undertaking progressed quickly at first, but by the 2008 deadline, much was incomplete. Plans that year were to secure about 300 miles of the border against vehicular crossings, while 370 miles of barriers would prevent pedestrian traffic.

In Yuma, Arizona, and other populous areas, twenty-foot-high steel walls were erected with nearby secondary razor-wire barriers. Illegal immigrant apprehensions in Yuma dropped from 5,571 in March 2007 to 751 in March 2008. The border at San Luis, Arizona, was reinforced with three walls. Between them, a vast flat area was under continuous surveillance using lights, cameras, and other technology.

Migrants who traversed one barrier were essentially stalled in an area where border agents could easily capture them. Elsewhere, little more than metal mesh—or even picket fencing—blocked the way between Mexico and the United States. Though officials touted the decrease in illegal crossings in well-fortified areas, elsewhere authorities reported increased border traffic.

Much of the initial fence construction was completed on federal land. Local landowners often objected to the intrusion of the barriers and asked why local communities were not allowed to give input on the building projects. Many ranchers in Texas, who owned land on both sides of the US–Mexico border, refused to give the government access to their property. Some property owners—including some universities in Texas—were sued by the government when they objected to construction that would divide their properties.

Environmental activists argued that the substantial barriers designed to keep humans from passing also obstructed wildlife and interfered with migrating and endangered species. Many were angered that DHS was not bound by environmental laws, and several organizations, including the Sierra Club, filed lawsuits. In 2007, members of the Tohono O'odham nation argued against a barrier being built on an ancient burial site on their lands, calling it desecration. The Cocopah and Kickapoo nations also protested against the division of their lands by the border fence.

Officials in Texas formed the Texas Border Coalition, which filed a federal lawsuit in May 2008. They charged the head of DHS with not consulting with local authorities and owners of private property in establishing the fences in Texas and asked the courts to cease work on the barriers.

All of these objections set the project back, yet official figures indicated fewer people were crossing into the United States illegally. At about this time, however, the American economy entered a recession, and many experts noted that fewer Mexicans would attempt the trip when so few jobs were available in the United States.

The fence project yielded the best results when the barriers were supplemented by increased patrols and electronic surveillance. Heavier penalties for those apprehended—including detention for as long as two months—also were regarded as a deterrent. When faced with a difficult border crossing, however, many individuals simply moved to a less secure area to cross. Paradoxically, San Diego, California, where fences had defined the border since 1993, reported a 20 percent increase in apprehending illegal border crossers in 2007.

Though the federal government faced much opposition to the fence project, other Americans voiced objections to the slow progress being made on the border barriers. In Tucson, Arizona, the Techno Patriots began electronic surveillance of the border in 2007. Members of the group placed thermal imaging cameras in the border area and monitored them from their homes. Other groups, such as the Cochise County Militia of Naco, Arizona, vowed to patrol the border and apprehend illegal immigrants who bypassed the barriers.

Impact

In 2009, the US Border Patrol employed more than 20,000 agents—up from about 9,651 agents in 2001. DHS reported significantly fewer individuals were apprehended by the Border Patrol. DHS, which had committed large amounts of resources to the Southwest borders, attributed the decrease to its success in deterring illegal border crossings with barriers and penalties. At the same time, rates of seizure of contraband rose sharply. In 2009, CBP agents confiscated nearly 11,000 pounds of cocaine and more than 2.6 million pounds of marijuana.

The border fence, initially funded with $1.2 billion, cost considerably more as the project developed. The DHS had spent about $2.1 billion by mid-2008, with only a portion of the barriers complete. In January 2009, the US Government Accountability Office estimated that the border fence's per-mile costs to date had varied between $200,000 and $15.1 million, depending on the type of fence, materials, land purchase price, labor costs, topography, and other factors.

Further Reading

Archibold, Randal C., and Julia Preston. "Homeland Security Stands By Its Fence." *New York Times*. New York Times, 21 May 2008. Web. 5 Dec. 2012. Reports on the debate between supporters and detractors of the fence along the US–Mexico border.

"Border Patrol Overview." *CBP*. US Department of Homeland Security, 5 Jan. 2011. Web. 5 Dec. 2012. Describes the Border Patrol's mission, staffing, operations, apprehensions, and drug seizures.

Hataley, Todd, Christian Leuprecht, and Kim Richard Nossal, eds. "Evolving Transnational Threats and Border Security." *Centre for International and Defence Policy*. Kingston, Ontario: Queen's U, 2012. PDF file. A report about Canadian national security with particular focus on the US–Canada border.

Porier, Shar. "Cochise County Militia Ready to Patrol." *Douglas Dispatch*. Douglas Dispatch, 3 Feb. 2009. Web. 5 Dec. 2012. A militia group briefs volunteers on what they can and cannot do to apprehend individuals illegally crossing from Mexico into Arizona.

"Where Should I Look for 'Suspicious Activity'?" *America's Waterway Watch*. US Coast Guard, 19 June 2012. Web. 5 Dec. 2012. Information about detecting and reporting suspicious activity that could indicate possible terrorist activities along US waterways.

Josephine Campbell

■ *Boy Scouts of America v. Dale*

The Case: US Supreme Court ruling on the constitutionality of excluding openly gay individuals from serving as Boy Scout leaders

Date: Decided on June 28, 2000

By classifying Boy Scouts as a private group rather than a public entity, the Supreme Court ruled that excluding Scout leaders on the basis of sexual orientation is protected under the First Amendment. The ruling declared that these restrictive policies do not violate antidiscrimination laws.

James Dale had been a Boy Scout member from a young age. In 1989, he became an assistant scoutmaster in New Jersey. But in 1990, in response to public acknowledgement of his homosexuality in a newspaper, Dale was dismissed from his position in Boy Scouts of America (BSA). Citing discrimination, Dale and his lawyers from Lambda Legal, a group committed to protecting gay rights, filed a lawsuit against BSA in 1992.

Boy Scouts of America holds its scouts and leaders to the Scout Oath, a commitment to "keep myself . . . morally straight." This phrase, "morally straight," is expounded upon in the 1959 and 1979 versions of the *Boy Scout Handbook*, which specifically tie morality among members to heterosexuality. As moral role models, BSA argues, leaders must commit to the morality implicit in the Scout Oath.

Initially, the New Jersey Superior Court ruled in favor of BSA. Following this, the state appeals court and state supreme court cited the New Jersey

---

The Boy Scouts Respond

In a press release on June 28, 2000, the Boy Scouts of America responded to the Supreme Court's decision to uphold the organization's policy of excluding openly gay leaders.

We are very pleased with the U.S. Supreme Court's decision in the *Boy Scouts of America v. Dale* case. This decision affirms our standing as a private association with the right to set its own standards.

This decision allows us to continue our mission of providing character-building experiences for young people, which has been our purpose since our founding.

For more than 20 years, the Boy Scouts of America has defended its membership standards. We went to the highest court in the land, the U.S. Supreme Court, in order to do so. As a private organization, the Boy Scouts of America must have the right to establish its own standards of membership if it is to continue to instill the values of the Scout Oath and Law in boys. Thanks to our legal victories, our standards of membership have been sustained.

We believe an avowed homosexual is not a role model for the values espoused in the Scout Oath and Law.

Boy Scouting makes no effort to discover the sexual orientation of any person. Scouting's message is compromised when prospective leaders present themselves as role models inconsistent with Boy Scouting's understanding of the Scout Oath and Law.

Scouting's record of inclusion is impressive by any standard. However, we do ask all of our members to do their best to live the Scout Oath and Law. Today, boys from every ethnic, religious, and economic background in suburbs, farms, and cities know and respect each other as they participate in our program.

We thank the parents, volunteers, and friends of Scouting who have supported us in this case and others. We respect other people's right to hold differing opinions and ask that they respect ours.

In a support brief filed by three of Scouting's largest chartered organizations, they addressed why Scouting has been so effective for 90 years: "Scouting's program for character development is effective precisely because it teaches through both precept and concrete examples of its adult leaders. . . . Scoutmasters exist not only to espouse the ideals of Scouting, but more importantly to live and embody them; they are the role models of the Scouting movement."

Law Against Discrimination (LAD), favoring Dale. Appealing this ruling, BSA took the case to the US Supreme Court, where a divided court upheld BSA's First Amendment freedom of association on a vote of five to four. Justice William Rehnquist wrote the majority opinion, affirming BSA as a private entity entitled to hold its leaders to its own standards.

During the proceedings, the American Psychological Association (APA) filed a brief in support of gay Scout leaders. The brief promotes antidiscrimination policies as an effective way to reduce hate crimes and the resulting psychological harm. The brief also cites research that demonstrates how leadership ability is not affected by sexual orientation and refutes claims that homosexuality causes dangerous behavior. The real danger, the APA contended, is the threat of discrimination to the public wellbeing.

Impact

While the Supreme Court's decision in *Boy Scouts of America v. Dale* maintained the constitutionality of discrimination in the BSA and, implicitly, any private group, the case garnered attention for the issue of discrimination based on sexual orientation. Gay rights advocates saw this case as a milestone when two New Jersey courts recognized and condemned such discrimination. Additionally, arguments surrounding the Supreme Court case filtered into the public mind and discourse. The case also revealed specific policies and biases inherent in Boy Scouts of America, which led some donors to cut ties with the organization.

Further Reading

"Boy Scouts of America v. Dale." *Lambda Legal.* Lambda Legal, 2012. Web. 10 Aug. 2012.

McHugh, James L., and Nathalie F. P. Gilfoyle. "Brief of *Amicus Curiae* American Psychological Association in Support of Respondent." *American Psychological Association.* American Psychological Association, 29 Mar. 2000. Web. 10 Aug. 2012.

Mechling, Jay. *On My Honor: Boy Scouts and the Making of American Youth.* Chicago: U of Chicago P, 2001. Print.

Lucia Pizzo

■ Brady, Tom

Identification: American football player
Born: August 3, 1977; San Mateo, California

Tom Brady was one of the best football players of the early 2000s. He is widely regarded to be one of the best quarterbacks to ever play the game, leading the New England Patriots to four Super Bowls, of which they won three.

After graduating from the University of Michigan, quarterback Tom Brady was picked in the sixth round of the 2000 NFL draft by the New England Patriots. The Patriots had star quarterback Drew Bledsoe and two other quarterbacks on the roster, but Coach Bill Belichick liked Tom's poise and loved his intelligence.

Matched against the St. Louis Rams in Super Bowl XXXVI in 2002, the Patriots had a quarterback dilemma. Many fans wanted Bledsoe to play, but the team wanted Brady, who had led them throughout the season. Belichick chose Brady, who helped the Patriots to the first Super Bowl victory in franchise history. For his efforts, Brady earned most valuable player (MVP) honors for the game. Brady had officially established himself as the

Tom Brady. (Courtesy Keith Allison)

Patriots' starting quarterback; Bledsoe was traded to the Buffalo Bills months later.

In 2002, the Patriots finished 9–7 and missed the playoffs. Brady required postseason shoulder surgery. In the first game of 2003, the team was shut out 31–0 against Bledsoe's Bills. The Patriots rallied and won all fifteen of the remaining regular season games, fighting injuries and the weight of the winning streak. Brady drove his team through the playoffs to defeat the Carolina Panthers in Super Bowl XXXVIII, again earning the game's MVP award. He had become a superstar and his team, a dynasty. He developed a knack for comeback wins, and comparisons to his childhood hero, Montana, abounded.

Brady and the Patriots maintained momentum into 2004, as the team cruised through the regular season to a victory over the Philadelphia Eagles in Super Bowl XXXIX. In 2005 and 2006, he led the Patriots to the playoffs, but the team did not appear in the Super Bowl.

In 2007, Brady was given his strongest complement of offensive players and responded, setting the regular-season touchdown-passing record with 50 and winning the NFL MVP award. His Patriots became the first team in history to finish the regular season 16–0. However, the team was upset by the New York Giants in Super Bowl XXLI. After this remarkable year, however, his 2008 season ended abruptly in the very first game when he sustained a season-ending knee injury.

Brady, recovered from his injury, returned to the Patriot's active lineup in 2009. In October, he led the Patriots to a spectacular 59–0 win over the Tennessee Titans, throwing his personal best of six touchdowns during the game. Although Brady suffered his first NFL home playoff loss to the Baltimore Ravens, he was named the 2009 NFL Comeback Player of the Year.

Brady became an international celebrity during the 2000s. The star quarterback was named among *People* magazine's 2002 list of the world's fifty most beautiful people, hosted *Saturday Night Live* in 2005, and appeared as a guest star on several television shows. Brady dated actor Bridget Moynahan in the mid-2000s and has a son, John Thomas Edward Moynahan, with her. In February 2009, Brady wed supermodel Gisele Bündchen. The couple have a son, Benjamin Rein Brady, and are expecting another child in December 2012.

In addition to his stellar football career, Brady was involved with a number of charitable interests during the decade and has stated an interest in one day becoming a US senator.

Impact

Tom Brady was arguably the most popular and best player in the NFL in the first decade of the 2000s. In his first four Super Bowl appearances, he and the Patriots won three times. His 2007 season was the best for a quarterback in NFL history to that time. Brady's football success was congruent with Joe Montana's, his football idol.

Further Reading

Donaldson, Jim. *Then Belichick Said to Brady: The Best New England Patriots Stories Ever Told*. Chicago: Triumph, 2009. Print.

Glennon, Sean. *Tom Brady vs. the NFL: The Case for Football's Greatest Quarterback*. Chicago: Triumph, 2012. Print.

Pierce, Charles P. *Moving the Chains: Tom Brady and the Pursuit of Everything*. New York: Farrar, 2007. Print.

Jonathan E. Dinneen

■ Brin, Sergey and Larry Page

Identification: American computer engineers and entrepreneurs

Sergey Brin
Born: August 21, 1973; Moscow, Soviet Union (now Russia)

Larry Page
Born: March 26, 1973; East Lansing, Michigan

Brin and Page created the search engine Google in the late 1990s. As the site gained popularity in the 2000s, the two entrepreneurs expanded their company to encompass projects such as mapping and digitization of books. Brin and Page also became known for their philanthropic work in areas such as renewable energy and public health during the decade.

Business partners Sergey Brin and Larry Page met while attending Stanford University as graduate students. Together they developed the search engine Google, incorporating their company in 1998. Brin

Sergey Brin (left), and Larry Page of Google, May 2008. (Courtesy Joi Ito)

and Page quickly expanded Google from its basic search engine origins, adding features such as an image search and launching versions of Google in a variety of languages.

Growth of Google

Throughout the 2000s, Brin and Page focused on expanding Google further, developing new functions for the search engine itself and also moving into new areas. In 2001, they recruited Eric Schmidt to manage the business, naming him chief executive officer (CEO). The following year, the company partnered with AOL and added such applications as Google News.

Over the course of the decade, Brin and Page dedicated themselves to creating a work environment and company culture that encouraged inno-

vation and experimentation. Employees, known as Googlers, enjoyed a lively work environment at the company headquarters, which featured game rooms, cafés, and an outdoor volleyball court. They were encouraged to spend a percentage of their work time pursuing what interested them, regardless of profitability, and a number of the resulting small projects became major developments for the company.

Many of Google's innovative ideas generated discussion and even controversy. For example, Google began scanning books in 2004, preserving digital copies of works both out of copyright and more recently published. Though Brin and Page defended the project, noting that digitization was the best way to preserve books, critics were concerned about the rights of copyright holders and possible effects on sales. Further controversy arose, even among Brin,

Page, and Schmidt, as Google negotiated the tricky decision of whether to launch a service in China. The executives knew that Google would be subjected to censorship by the Chinese government; however, they ultimately determined that providing good service in China was preferable to providing substandard service from without, and entered the Chinese market in 2005.

Philanthropy and Personal Lives

In 2004, Brin and Page announced that they would dedicate 1 percent of Google's stock and 1 percent of the company's profits to philanthropic efforts. Disease, global warming, and poverty were among the issues to be addressed by the new philanthropic division of the business, Google.org, which would remain a for-profit charity business venture. Developing renewable energy was on the agenda, as was commercializing plug-in hybrid cars. In 2006 they hired a public health expert, physician Larry Brilliant, as executive director of the venture. Google.org focused on efforts such as tracking disease outbreaks and developing aid locators for areas hit by natural disasters. The initiative also developed tools such as Google Flu Trends, which predicted flu outbreaks using data from searches about symptoms.

In addition to their philanthropic efforts through Google.org, Brin and Page were also active philanthropists in their personal lives. Brin, who cofounded the Brin Wojcicki Foundation with his wife, Anne Wojcicki, became a supporter of such charitable organizations as the Michael J. Fox Foundation, which funds research related to Parkinson's disease, and the Hebrew Immigrant Aid Society, which had helped Brin's family emigrate from the Soviet Union when he was a child. In 2005, Page was elected to the board of trustees of the X PRIZE Foundation, a non-profit organization that funds prizes for developments in fields such as education and space exploration.

In 2007 Brin married Wojcicki, cofounder of genetic analysis company 23andMe. The couple went on to have two children. After participating in genetic testing carried out by 23andMe, Brin learned that he possessed a gene that gave him a significant chance of developing Parkinson's disease later in life. His mother had previously been diagnosed with the disease. In light of this development, Brin directed a significant portion of his philanthropic efforts toward related medical research. Page married Lucy

Southworth in December of 2007, and the couple later had a child.

Impact

With the creation of a search engine that allowed users to find the most relevant results simply and quickly, Brin and Page revealed the potential of the Internet and allowed users greater access to information. Though the search engine remained the core focus of the Google business into the second decade of the twenty-first century, the leadership team continued to encourage innovation and develop applications that increased communication and access to information. They also continued to take a lead role in the management of the company, with Page replacing Schmidt as CEO in 2011.

Further Reading

Albanesius, Chloe. "Brin Defends Google Books, Talks Unicorns." *PC*. Ziff Davis, 9 Oct. 2009. Web. 11 July 2012.

Hafner, Katie. "Philanthropy Google's Way: Not the Usual." *New York Times*. New York Times, 14 Sept. 2006. Web. 12 July 2012.

Hammonds, Keith H. "How Google Grows . . . and Grows . . . and Grows." *Fast Company*. Mansueto Ventures, 31 Mar. 2003. Web. 12 July 2012.

Malseed, Mark. "The Story of Sergey Brin." *Moment*. Center for Creative Change, Feb. 2007. Web. 11 July 2012.

Serwer, Andy. "Larry Page on How to Change the World." *CNN Money*. Cable News Network, 1 May 2008. Web. 12 July 2012.

Stross, Randall. *Planet Google: One Company's Audacious Plan to Organize Everything We Know*. New York: Simon, 2009. Print.

Josephine Campbell

■ *Brokeback Mountain*

Identification: Film about a secret twenty-year love affair between two cowboys in the American West
Director: Ang Lee (b. 1954)
Date: Released on September 2, 2005

Brokeback Mountain *was a 2005 feature film based on the 1997 short story of the same name by the American author Annie Proulx. The film depicts the meeting and subsequent secret romantic relationship that develops across de-*

cades between Ennis Del Mar (Heath Ledger) and Jack Twist (Jake Gyllenhaal), two livestock laborers working on the Wyoming plains in 1963.

In *Brokeback Mountain*, the young Wyoming cowboys Ennis Del Mar and Jack Twist are hired to herd sheep in the open range near Brokeback Mountain throughout the summer. During this time, they form a close connection which culminates in a sexual relationship. The film was one of the first produced by a major Hollywood studio (Universal) to depict bisexuality outside the confines of a plot based around the struggle for gay civil rights. It was also one of the first widely released films to depict gay sex scenes.

Brokeback Mountain primarily centers on the struggle of both men to carry on with their lives in the wake of their summer romance; both men eventually marry women and start families, continuing their connection through annual fishing trips. Each of their marriages deteriorates. While Twist insists the two could live together in seclusion, Del Mar balks at the suggestion for fear of retaliation from outsiders if their secret is discovered. Del Mar also maintains a close relationship with his two children despite a falling out with his wife, who uncovers the nature of his relationship with Twist.

When a postcard from Del Mar to Twist is returned to him stamped "Deceased," Del Mar envisions Twist being murdered as the victim of a hate crime. Twist's wife explains to Del Mar that his death was the result of an accident while repairing an automobile. The audience is left to decide which was his true fate.

Impact
Upon its release, a small but vocal group of conservative film critics and pundits encouraged boycotts of *Brokeback Mountain* due to its unapologetic portrayals of homosexuality. Many critical of the film were also shocked by its filmic undressing of the myth of the American cowboy. Nonetheless, the majority of audiences and film scholars lauded the film, both for its cinematic beauty and its tender love story. The film was nominated for eight Academy Awards, including best picture; it won best director, best adapted screenplay, and best original score. Despite the controversy surrounding its release, *Brokeback Mountain* became one of the most acclaimed and highest grossing films of the 2000s. It also became a landmark in the acceptance of gay romantic

themes by both Hollywood filmmakers and audiences alike.

Further Reading
Ehrenstein, David. "'Brokeback's' Tasteful Appeal." *Los Angeles Times.* Los Angeles Times, 1 Feb. 2006. Web. 9 Aug. 2012.

Needham, Gary. *Brokeback Mountain.* Edinburgh: Edinburgh UP, 2010. Print.

Patterson, Eric. *On Brokeback Mountain: Meditations about Masculinity, Fear, and Love in the Story and the Film.* Plymouth: Lexington, 2008. eBook.

John Pritchard

■ Bush administration scandals

Definition: A number of high-profile scandals linked to the two-term presidency of George W. Bush during the 2000s

The scandals of the Bush administration included the incorrect intelligence gathered to support a war in to Iraq, the seemingly unjustified firing of US attorneys, and the administration's close relationship with contractors that were charged with a wide range of improprieties and mismanagement in Iraq after President Saddam Hussein's removal. These scandals directly affected Bush's popularity and helped foster a Democratic Party revival.

The presidency of George W. Bush (2001–9) was distinguished by a number of key events, most notably the terrorist attacks of September 11, 2001, an economic recession, and active military operations in both Iraq and Afghanistan. Amid these events, the Bush administration was embroiled in a number of scandals. Some of these scandals involved the Iraq and Afghanistan wars, while others were related to events in the United States.

Weapons of Mass Destruction
President Bush and his administration believed that the regime of Iraqi president Saddam Hussein was connected to al-Qaeda, the terrorist group behind the September 11 attacks, or was at least enabling the group to operate in the remote regions of Iraq. Moreover, the administration believed that long-standing sanctions against Iraq—which were applied by the United Nations to halt Iraq's efforts to build and use nuclear, biological, and chemical

I. Lewis "Scooter" Libby with his lawyer, Theodore Wells Jr. (left), February 3, 2006. (AP Photo/Manuel Balce Ceneta)

weapons—were poorly enforced and that Hussein continued to pursue a weapons program.

In February 2003, Bush sent Secretary of State Colin Powell to the United Nations to argue for US military action against Iraq. Powell brought with him satellite photos and other evidence that suggested that Iraq was indeed developing weapons of mass destruction. A key piece of evidence the administration presented was a letter, written on official letterhead by the president of Niger, that argued that Iraq was already gathering weapons-grade uranium. This letter, along with other pieces of intelligence intercepted and gathered by American operatives, provided Bush with the justification for forcibly disarming and removing Hussein from power.

However, the Italian Letter, so named because it was intercepted and delivered to the US embassy in Rome, was soon revealed to be fake. In fact, once American troops were in Iraq, their search for weapons of mass destruction proved fruitless; although Hussein hoped to develop and/or obtain such weapons, there was no sign that he was close to his goal. The intelligence failure undermined the credibility of both the Bush administration and the intelligence community.

Compounding the Iraq situation was the Plame scandal. In 2003, former US ambassador Joseph C. Wilson IV wrote a scathing editorial in the *New York*

Times, alleging that the Bush administration manipulated intelligence and information to help justify the invasion of Iraq. Shortly after the piece was published, news leaked that Wilson's wife, Valerie Plame, was a CIA covert operative. The leak was traced to the office of Vice President Dick Cheney. Cheney's chief of staff, Lewis "Scooter" Libby, was believed to have leaked the information as retaliation for Wilson's comments. He was soon found guilty of perjury and obstruction of justice and sent to prison for his actions.

Firings of US Attorneys

On the domestic front, one of the more significant scandals affecting President Bush's administration was a series of highly visible firings in the Department of Justice (DOJ). In 2006, eight US attorneys were dismissed from their jobs with little public explanation. However, news leaked to the media that the employees were fired not for any misdeeds or incompetence but because they held political ideologies that were counter to those in the Bush administration.

The DOJ, like any other executive branch agency, had employees who acquired their jobs because they were supporters of the president. However, the position of US attorney (along with other sensitive positions) has long been considered nonpartisan and independent of politics in general, thus fostering an evenhanded approach to the law. If the allegations were true, the case of the US attorneys suggested not only that this tradition was being disregarded but also that the Bush administration had created an environment in which the DOJ was being used to support the president's agenda rather than to uphold the law.

As more information about the attorneys came to light, the scandal took on an ominous tone. New Mexico–based US attorney David Iglesias, for example, had been contacted by the Republican senator Pete Domenici and congressional representative Heather Wilson to expedite a corruption investigation into Wilson's campaign opponent (with whom Wilson was in a close race) so that, ideally, charges would be filed before the November election. According to reports, Iglesias did not act in as rapid a fashion as Domenici and Wilson had requested, and White House Chief of Staff Karl Rove interceded. Shortly afterward, Iglesias was removed from his post, while Domenici quickly offered a list of potential successors to the DOJ for Iglesias's position.

The scandal continued to grow, as more evidence of political gamesmanship came to bear. Attorney General Alberto Gonzales was a close political ally and friend of President Bush and, according to observers, allowed that relationship to break down the traditional walls between the White House staff and the DOJ, thereby fostering an environment in which such politically motivated firings could take place. Even the responsibilities of the DOJ seemed to be prioritized according political motivations. One piece of evidence supporting this charge was the fact that, over a six-year period from 2001 to 2006, not a single case of voter discrimination was brought before US attorneys on behalf of a minority. However, voter-fraud cases (about which civil rights groups frequently complained because they often target minority voting districts, from which Democratic votes are more likely) were made a priority. Gonzales resigned in 2007 amid the scandal, while investigations into the firings and the culture at his department continued to reveal evidence of political contamination.

US Contractors in Iraq

Before becoming vice president, Cheney sat in a position of significance at Texas-based Halliburton Corporation. Halliburton is a multinational corporation with subsidiaries operating in a number of areas, including oil-field development and military support. It is in these two fields that Cheney's former company was given lucrative contracts after the US-led invasion of Iraq. Halliburton provided logistical and supply support to troops in that war-torn country. The company was also charged with helping to reestablish Iraq's oil fields, which were heavily damaged during the conflict.

Because Halliburton was so closely aligned with Cheney and quickly won these contracts, the Bush administration was charged with favoritism. However, more serious complaints about Halliburton's activities in Iraq and elsewhere were issued by not only Bush's political adversaries but also his own military and supporters. One complaint said that Halliburton charged the Department of Defense millions

of dollars to deliver meals that were never delivered to American troops in the Middle East theater. There were also charges that Halliburton manipulated the price of Iraqi oil delivered to neighboring Kuwait. Furthermore, in 2004, American and European officials began investigating a Halliburton payment of nearly $200 million to the government of Nigeria; this payment may have enabled Halliburton and its consortium partners to obtain special tax breaks for a natural gas project. By the mid-2000s, Halliburton was under a microscope for its dealings; many senior-level employees were called before special investigating committees, and many others were charged formally with criminal activities.

Meanwhile, another major contractor selected by the Bush administration for work in Iraq worsened the US presence there. Private security contractor Blackwater was assigned to protect certain members of the provisional government in that country, including American ambassadors and personnel. In 2007, Blackwater security guards opened fire on Iraqi civilians, killing seventeen innocent people in a crowded area of Baghdad. The guards claimed that they were firing in self-defense, but investigations into the shootings revealed that there was no threat and that the guards were not even protecting their clients at the time. After the shooting, more allegations surfaced about Blackwater personnel; there were complaints of corruption, brutality, and attempts to cover up evidence of this brutality. However, because Blackwater was a contractor to the State Department, little was done to prosecute the company's employees or hold Blackwater accountable.

Blackwater's contract raised major questions about the use of contractors in Iraq. It also undermined the American presence in Iraq, seemingly validating the claims of Hussein loyalists and other Iraqis that US troops were attempting to take over Iraq using heavy-handed means. In the United States, Blackwater's connections to several key Bush administration officials (some of whom later worked for the contractor) and other political figures suggested that Blackwater was taking advantage of its political alliances while engaging in shadowy activity.

Impact

President Bush's administration, like those of other presidents, frequently became the target of purported scandal. To be sure, many scandals are the product of political forces working to unseat the incumbent. However, many of the myriad charges against the Bush administration were highly publicized and did not appear to be politically motivated. Among them were the mistakes of the intelligence community with regard to Iraq, the awarding of military contracts to corporations later revealed to be involved in a number of questionable (if not illegal) activities, and the alleged political manipulation of one of Washington's traditionally nonpolitical agencies.

Many of the parties involved, including senior administration staff, were forced to resign and/or were successfully prosecuted for their roles. Public opinion of President Bush, which surged briefly after the September 11 attacks, trended downward as a result of these and other scandals.

Further Reading

Chatterjee, Pratap. *Halliburton's Army: How a Well-Connected Texas Oil Company Revolutionized the Way America Makes War.* New York: Nation, 2010. Print. Outlines both the connection between Halliburton and the Bush administration and the list of complaints made against the company's work in Iraq.

Eisner, Peter, and Knut Royce. *The Italian Letter: How the Bush Administration Used a Fake Letter to Build a Case for War in Iraq.* Emmaus, PA: Rodale, 2007. Print. Describes the use of one of the central pieces of "evidence," a forged letter from the Nigerian embassy in Rome, as grounds for the US invasion of Iraq.

Gibbs, Nancy, and Mike Allen. "A Time to Regroup." *Time* 31 Oct. 2005: 24–31. Print. Discusses how the Bush administration reacted to and moved on from its failures and scandals during the mid-2000s.

Iglesias, David, and Davin Seay. *In Justice: Inside the Scandal That Rocked the Bush Administration.* New York: Wiley, 2008. Print. Written by one of the attorneys fired in the US attorney scandal. Provides his perspectives as an observer and a victim of the firings.

Krugman, Paul. "How Bush Gets Away with It." *Rolling Stone* 2 Oct. 2003: 53–55. Print. Describes how, in the author's opinion, the Bush administration was able to parlay its public support after September 11 and a period of relative economic stability to move beyond its scandals.

Tumulty, Karen, and Massimo Calabresi. "Inside the Scandal at Justice." *Time* 10 May 2007: 44–49. Print. Focuses on both the eight US attorneys fired in 2007 for reasons not publicly disclosed and the Bush administration's role in the scandal.

Michael P. Auerbach

■ Bush v. Gore

The Case: US Supreme Court ruling on constitutionality of Florida recount after the 2000 presidential election
Date: Decided on December 12, 2000

While the 2000 presidential election between George W. Bush and Al Gore was a tight race across the country, it was closest in Florida. After a battle between the US Supreme Court and Florida's judiciary and legislature, the court declared Bush the winner. This decision called into question the relative power of states and the federal government and revealed flaws in America's election process.

In addition to Republican George W. Bush and Democrat Al Gore, the 2000 election featured a number of fringe candidates, including Ralph Nader of the Green Party and the Reform Party's Patrick Buchanan. Only 55.6 percent of eligible Americans voted. At the end of Election Day on November 7, Gore won the popular vote, but the Electoral College, which elects the president by a vote of electors from each state, was another question. While both sides tallied their votes, it became clear that Florida's twenty-five electoral votes would decide the election. Like most states, Florida awards all electoral votes to one candidate, according to the popular vote. While news stations named Gore and then Bush as winner, a difference of fewer than 1,800 votes ultimately referred the issue to Florida's state constitution, which mandates a recount when the difference between candidates is less than 0.5 percent of votes cast.

Progression through the Courts

After a machine recount of votes and the inclusion of overseas ballots, the outcome in Florida was even less definitive. Citing a failure in ballot punch-card machines in Broward, Miami Dade, and Palm Beach counties, as well as mistakes in Volusia County, Gore's legal team, led by Warren Christopher, requested a manual recount. Heading up Bush's legal team,

James Baker argued against the need for this recount. Critics accused Democrats of attempting to gain votes by only considering liberal counties, while Democrats defended the call to recount due to faulty voting machines. On November 21, the Florida Supreme Court approved the manual recount, setting a deadline of November 26.

Breaking with the Republican tradition of deference to states' rights, the Bush team requested that the US Supreme Court review the recount issue, and the high court agreed. Republicans claimed that since there was no consistency in the manual recount process (recount protocol was determined by county), the recount violated the "equal protection" of voters under the 14th Amendment. They also contended that the state legislature, not the judiciary, was granted power to determine electors under the US Constitution's Article II. While arguments continued, on November 26, Florida secretary of state Katherine Harris, who had chaired Bush's Florida campaign, certified Bush as winner of Florida by 537 votes. At that time, manual recounts were still ongoing in Miami Dade and Palm Beach counties.

Arguments continued at the US Supreme Court, and the justices asked the Florida Supreme Court for an explanation of its actions in allowing a recount. On December 8, the Florida court responded by mandating a continued manual recount, focusing on voter intent. A day later, the US Supreme Court's conservative justices overruled the Florida court's decision and demanded that the recount stop. On December 12, the Supreme Court justices, by a vote of 5–4, confirmed that the manual recount did violate the equal protection of voters. On December 13, Gore conceded the election to Bush.

Voter Intent

Discerning voter intent might be viewed as the purpose of elections. Yet confusion in Florida revealed that intent is not always straightforward, and that not every vote counts. Questions of intent surfaced as machine recounts commenced. Some counties using punch-card ballots—such as Palm Beach, Broward, and Miami-Dade—showed high numbers of unusable ballots. Voters had either overvoted, by punching holes for multiple candidates, or undervoted, by not fully punching a hole for any candidate. Statewide, Florida recorded over 61,000 undervotes and 113,000 overvotes. In order to consider these votes,

---

Gore Concedes the Election

In one of the most controversial elections in U.S. history, Democratic candidate Al Gore lost to Republican candidate George W. Bush following the Supreme Court's decision to halt the recount of Florida ballots. The following excerpt is from Gore's concession speech, delivered on December 13, 2000:

Now the U.S. Supreme Court has spoken. Let there be no doubt, while I strongly disagree with the court's decision, I accept it. I accept the finality of this outcome which will be ratified next Monday in the Electoral College. And tonight, for the sake of our unity as a people and the strength of our democracy, I offer my concession.

I also accept my responsibility, which I will discharge unconditionally, to honor the new President-elect and do everything possible to help him bring Americans together in fulfillment of the great vision that our Declaration of Independence defines and that our Constitution affirms and defends....

This has been an extraordinary election. But in one of God's unforeseen paths, this belatedly broken impasse can point us all to a new common ground, for its very closeness can serve to remind us that we are one people with a shared history and a shared destiny.

---

the Florida courts ruled in favor of a manual recount, including votes where the intent was evident.

Manual recounts could also discern voter intent in Optical Character Recognition (OCR) ballots, which were used in Volusia County. These ballots function like standardized test bubble sheets. If a voter uses the wrong type of pencil or pen, or if the voter marks an "x" instead of filling in a bubble, the vote is invalidated by machine recounts. Manual recounts could decipher these mistakes and include the vote.

The Florida recount became famously associated with the state of its chads. Chads, the pieces of a punch-card ballot meant to pop off as voters make their selections, can remain attached to ballots, invalidating the vote. Whether machines are old, overused, or merely stuck, a ballot's chad can be called

David Boies presents oral arguments in the Florida presidential ballot recount case to Justice Leander J. Shaw Jr. (left) and Chief Justice Charles T. Wells, December 7, 2000. (AP Photo/Charles Archambault, Pool)

"hanging," "dimpled," or "pregnant" to refer to its relative detachment. Evaluating the chads in Florida was key to determining voter intent.

Intent was also confused by new ballot formats. Typically, Florida ballots grouped all candidates for a position on one page. But as new rules allowed additional candidates, counties were faced with the problem of accommodation. To retain the single-page format, they would be forced to shrink the font size. To retain the font size, important for elderly Floridians, candidates would spill out onto two pages. This two-page format, termed the "butterfly ballot," led to widespread confusion. Many voters voted on both pages—causing invalidation by overvoting—or voted for Buchanan when they intended to vote for Gore, due to confusion regarding name placement. Even Buchanan acknowledged the faulty votes in counties where he did surprisingly well among populations known for voting Democrat and in places where he had not campaigned.

Partisan Politics

Bush v. Gore revealed the divisive potential of elections. Every level of argument regarding recounts was motivated by political bias. In her rush to certify Bush, Katherine Harris acted as both a public servant and as a vital part of Bush's Florida campaign. In demanding a manual recount, Gore was both a man fighting for the recognition of every vote as well as a candidate seeking uncounted votes that might win him the presidency. Even in the Supreme Court, the justices showed themselves to be interpreters of law as well as activists. Dissenting Justice John Paul Stevens viewed the court's decision to halt the recount as a mark of partisanship and a degradation of law, stating, "Although we may never know with complete certainty the identity of the winner of this year's presidential election, the identity of the loser is perfectly clear. It is the nation's confidence in the judge as an impartial guardian of the rule of law."

By ending the recount, the Supreme Court effectively chose the 43rd president. In the eyes of Gore supporters, George W. Bush, who had campaigned as a unifier, ascended to the presidency on the back of partisanship.

Impact

Largely unmentioned by scholars, critics, or the Supreme Court, *Bush v. Gore* has inspired little action. While another recount of votes was attempted in 2001, many ballots had disappeared. The results were deemed inconclusive, although a recount based on voter intent indicated a win for Gore. To address election reform, Congress passed and Bush signed the Help America Vote Act in 2002, requiring states to upgrade their voting systems, but the law's effectiveness is unclear.

While the *Bush v. Gore* case exposed legal discrepancies in Florida's recount process regarding when and how votes would be recounted, it also implied the need for a national protocol. To this end, some states have passed voter ID laws, requiring identification to vote, though some claim these depress minority voter turnout. The case questioned the modern utility of the Electoral College and winner-take-all system for electoral votes that most states use. Activists pushed for change in these areas, though unsuccessfully. Beyond America's electoral system, the way the case was argued and decided revealed deep biases inherent in the administration of elections, partisanship that privileged candidates over fixing a flawed system, and vast procedural disparities between states and counties. Deciding elections in court, instead of by the people, was seen by many as undercutting the essence of democracy.

Further Reading

Boies, David. *Courting Justice.* New York: Hyperion, 2004. Print. Memoir chronicling the author's law career, devoting considerable attention to his role as one of Gore's advocates in *Bush v. Gore.*

Keyssar, Alexander. *The Right to Vote: The Contested History of Democracy in the United States.* Rev. ed. New York: Basic, 2009. Print. Revised edition of a history of suffrage in the United States that includes perspectives on the contested 2000 election.

Patterson, James T. *Restless Giant: The United States from Watergate to* Bush v. Gore. New York: Oxford UP, 2005. Print. A history of the United States since Richard Nixon's presidency, culminating in the confusion of the 2000 election.

Poundstone, William, *Gaming the Vote: Why Elections Aren't Fair (and What We Can Do about It).* New York: Farrar, 2008. Print. Examines the factors that influence elections, particularly political calculations to manipulate voters with fringe candidates, and proposes a method to simplify America's voting system.

Zelden, Charles L. Bush v. Gore: *Exposing the Hidden Crisis in American Democracy.* Lawrence: UP of Kansas, 2008. Print. Thoroughly investigates the recount process in Florida during the 2000 election.

Lucia Pizzo

■ Bush, George W.

Identification: American president, 2001–09
Born: July 6, 1946; New Haven, Connecticut

George Walker Bush, businessman and former Texas governor, became the forty-third president of the United States in 2000, following the closest and most contentious presidential election in United States history. While in office, President Bush enjoyed extremely high approval ratings among Americans, but by the end of his second term, his ratings were the lowest recorded for any previous US president.

During his second term as governor of Texas, George W. Bush enjoyed wide support among minority voters, which helped to attract the attention of the national Republican Party in its search for a presidential candidate. In June 1999, Governor Bush announced that he would campaign for the 2000 Republican Party presidential nomination.

2000 Presidential Campaign

During the campaign, Bush described himself as a "compassionate conservative" and stressed his intentions to limit the size of the federal government, reduce taxes, and improve education. His critics commented on his relative inexperience, his controversial past, and his habit of speaking in general terms about complex issues. In addition, many Democratic critics were against Bush's strong anti-abortion stance and his opposition to hate-crime legislation. Liberals also criticized his support for the death penalty, emphasizing the fact that Texas had conducted record numbers of executions during Bush's term as governor.

Despite Arizona Senator John McCain's victory in the politically important New Hampshire primary, Bush went on to win the Republican presidential nomination in August 2000. He chose former US Secretary of Defense Dick Cheney as his running mate, hoping that the veteran politician would lend an air of experience to the campaign. Bush and Cheney faced Democrats Vice President Al Gore and Connecticut senator Joseph Lieberman in the general election.

The 2000 presidential election proved to be one of the closest elections in American history. Although election night brought calls from various media outlets declaring victory for each party, it was eventually determined in the days following the election that the majority of electoral college votes needed to win the presidency would be decided by the winner of the state of Florida. A month-long legal and political dispute over voting irregularities and recounts in Florida ensued. The battle over which candidate would lay claim to Florida's twenty-five electoral votes, and thus the presidency, eventually reached the Supreme Court. The court ruled in a 5–4 decision to officially end all recounts of the Florida presidential ballots. The decision made official previous vote counts that determined the Bush/Cheney ticket as the winner in Florida and served to officially and legally determine them as the winners of the presidential election. Critics of Bush and supporters of the Gore/Lieberman ticket were bitter about the Supreme Court ruling and noted the fact that Bush/

President George W. Bush confers with his National Security Council at Camp David, November 8, 2006. (Left to right) Vice President Dick Cheney; the president; Colin Powell, Secretary of State; Donald Rumsfeld, Secretary of Defense; and Paul Wolfowitz, Deputy Secretary of Defense. (National Archives/P7389-27A)

Cheney had lost the popular vote. In addition, many critics of the election outcome were critical of the role that Green Party candidate Ralph Nader played in the election, stating that Nader votes in Florida resulted in a decrease in votes for Gore. Gore publicly conceded the election in a speech to the nation that occurred on December 13, 2000.

Bush's First Term

Although Bush emphasized cooperation between Democrats and Republicans and vowed to heal the divisions caused by the controversial election, many of his critics still doubted the validity of his presidency when he was inaugurated on January 20, 2001. The occasion marked the first time since the administrations of John Adams (1797–1801) and John Quincy Adams (1825–29) that both a father and son had been elected president.

During his first several months in office, Bush worked with a Democratic majority in Congress to get his tax-cut proposal passed. He was criticized for his proposal to expand oil exploration in protected nature reserves in Alaska as well as for his decision to withdraw from the 1972 antiballistic missile (ABM) arms control treaty. However, the biggest test of Bush's administration came following the terrorist attacks of September 11, 2001. During the attacks, terrorists hijacked four commercial jet airliners from US airports, crashing one plane into each of the two World Trade Center towers in New York City and a third into the Pentagon building in Washington, DC, the headquarters of the US Department of Defense. A fourth plane, later determined to be headed for the White House, crash landed in Shanksville, Pennsylvania. No one traveling aboard the four planes survived. The two World Trade Center towers

Excerpt from George W. Bush's Inaugural Address, delivered on January 20, 2005

"On this day, prescribed by law and marked by ceremony, we celebrate the durable wisdom of our Constitution and recall the deep commitments that unite our country. I am grateful for the honor of this hour, mindful of the consequential times in which we live, and determined to fulfill the oath that I have sworn and you have witnessed.

At this second gathering, our duties are defined not by the words I use but by the history we have seen together. For a half a century, America defended our own freedom by standing watch on distant borders. After the shipwreck of communism came years of relative quiet, years of repose, years of sabbatical, and then there came a day of fire.

We have seen our vulnerability, and we have seen its deepest source. For as long as whole regions of the world simmer in resentment and tyranny, prone to ideologies that feed hatred and excuse murder, violence will gather and multiply in destructive power and cross the most defended borders and raise a mortal threat. There is only one force of history that can break the reign of hatred and resentment and expose the pretensions of tyrants and reward the hopes of the decent and tolerant, and that is the force of human freedom.

We are led, by events and common sense, to one conclusion: The survival of liberty in our land increasingly depends on the success of liberty in other lands. The best hope for peace in our world is the expansion of freedom in all the world."

collapsed within an hour and a half of the initial impact. In addition, the Pentagon building sustained significant damage, and the country was gripped with a sense of nationwide panic. As a result of the September 11 attacks, 2,998 people, both Americans and foreign nationals, were killed and over six thousand were injured.

President Bush declared the attacks on the United States to be an act of war, and in response, his administration launched the global war on terror," which aimed to destroy terrorist enclaves worldwide and declared as a hostile entity any nation that knowingly harbored terrorist groups. Investigations and intelligence reviews following the attacks determined that they were conducted by the Islamic fundamentalist terrorist organization known as al-Qaeda, led by Saudi Arabian exile Osama bin Laden. Intelligence reports confirmed that the group had trained in areas of Afghanistan, under the auspice of that country's Islamic fundamentalist government, known as the Taliban.

In October 2001, Bush ordered the US military to launch air strikes in Afghanistan. The military campaign toppled the Taliban regime, removing them as the country's central governing power. Although various al-Qaeda camps were targeted, the US military failed to capture or kill bin Laden. Nonetheless, the operation received widespread support in the US and abroad. Additionally, President Bush established the federal Office of Homeland Security.

As the war in Afghanistan progressed, President Bush's approval rating in the United States soared. However, America had also entered an economic recession at this time, and critics of the Bush administration began to accuse the White House of violating civil rights in implementing certain antiterrorism measures.

Beginning in 2002, the Bush administration began to turn its attention to the nation of Iraq, which was led at the time by dictator Saddam Hussein. For over a year, President Bush and administration officials presented pieces of evidence that they claimed proved that Hussein was developing and producing biological and chemical weapons in Iraq, also known as weapons of mass destruction (WMD).

The Bush administration's accusations regarding Iraq's weapons of mass destruction resulted in a series of United Nations (UN) resolutions aimed at establishing a rigorous schedule of weapons inspections in the country. However, Saddam Hussein continued to wrangle with inspections, eventually rejecting their entry into the country, and continued to deny the existence of WMD.

In February 2003, US Secretary of State Colin Powell addressed the UN Security Council, presenting the Bush administration's evidence of WMD in Iraq and urging the organization to support an American-led invasion. Powell's request was not approved by a majority of the council, and UN Security

Council approval of military action against Iraq was not granted. The governments of France and Germany publicly stated their opposition to any unsanctioned military invasion of Iraq.

Nonetheless, an American-led full-scale military invasion of Iraq began on March 20, 2003. Hussein was captured by US forces in December of 2003, and after being convicted of war crimes, he was subsequently executed by the newly established Iraq government.

Although the Hussein government was swiftly toppled, the invasion of Iraq resulted in a power vacuum in the country that pitted Sunni Muslim militias against Shiite militias. In addition, forces loyal to the Hussein government implemented numerous guerilla warfare tactics against US and coalition forces. Over four thousand American troops and hundreds of coalition forces have been killed in Iraq. Military activity in the country and the subsequent civil strife that followed has resulted in the deaths of forty thousand Iraqi civilians and resulted in the exile of hundreds of thousands of civilians who fled the violence.

Bush's Second Term

President Bush was re-elected in 2004, defeating Democratic candidate Senator John Kerry. Unlike the 2000 presidential election, Bush won 3.5 million more popular votes than his opposing candidate.

During his second term as president, Bush would come under intense political pressure and national and international scrutiny resulting from the fact that no weapons of mass destruction were ever uncovered in Iraq. In 2004, Secretary of State Colin Powell testified before the Senate Governmental Affairs Committee and stated that the United States received faulty intelligence regarding Iraq's possession of WMD. Powell resigned the same year and was replaced by National Security Advisor Condoleezza Rice. The Bush administration sustained further political damage as a result of the Abu Ghraib prison scandal, which involved internationally published photographs of US military personnel abusing Iraqi inmates at prison facilities in Iraq. This scandal, combined with the raging civil violence that occurred in the country in the years following the invasion, resulted in the resignation of Secretary of Defense Donald Rumsfeld in December of 2006.

In January 2007, President Bush ordered an additional twenty thousand US troops to Iraq in an effort to quell the widespread violence in the country. The so-called "troop surge" was aimed at putting an end to the ongoing military conflict taking place against various sectarian militias. As a result of the surge and an increased effort on the part of US officials to make diplomatic arrangements with various militia groups, violence in Iraq and in major Iraqi cities began to subside from previous levels in the later months of 2007 and early months of 2008. Although improvements on the ground in Iraq resulted in few civilian and military deaths, the controversial nature of the planning and execution of the Iraq War continued.

President Bush's nationwide approval ratings would begin to decrease in the years following his re-election, as a result of the ongoing problems in Iraq. The Bush administration also began to come under intense criticism as the subprime mortgage crisis in the United States slowly evolved into the global financial crisis of 2008. The subprime mortgage crisis came about after US financial organizations had granted housing loans to customers that could not meet the terms of their mortgages. Hundreds of thousands of homeowners nationwide began to default, or fail to make payments, on their mortgages. Subsequently, evidence that major banking institutions had made risky bets on extremely complex financial products began to be uncovered. Critics of the Bush administration cited the White House's history of deregulating the financial industry as one of the causes of this problem. For the first time in several decades, the federal government had to take major steps to bail out some of the nation's largest financial institutions to prevent them from collapse, an event that would have destroyed the US economy and one that would have had untold repercussions worldwide.

Impact

Bush's second term in office ended in January of 2009. It is likely that his response to the September 11 terrorist attacks, the controversial initiation and execution of the Iraq War, and the 2008 global financial crisis will remain the most significant and influential legacies of Bush's presidency. His policies and their impact were central issues of the 2008 presidential race.

Further Reading

Coe, Kevin. "George W. Bush, Television News, And Rationales For The Iraq War." *Journal Of Broadcasting & Electronic Media* 55.3 (2011): 307–24. Print.

Den Dulk, Kevin R., and Mark J. Rozell. "George W. Bush, Religion, and Foreign Policy: Personal, Global, and Domestic Contexts." *Review of Faith & International Affairs* 9.4 (2011): 71–82. Print.

Gellman, Barton, and Jo Becker. "Pushing the Envelope on Presidential Power." *Washington Post.* Washington Post Company 25 June 2007. Web. 12 Nov. 2012.

Harrington, Walt. "Dubya and Me: Over the Course of a Quarter-Century, A Journalist Witnessed the Transformation of George W. Bush." *American Scholar* 80.4 (2011): 20–34. Print.

Lindsay, James M. "George W. Bush, Barack Obama and the Future of US Global Leadership." *International Affairs* 87.4 (2011): 765–79. Print.

Keira Stevenson and Joshua Pritchard

Laura Bush. (Courtesy Westbank Library District/Photograph by Nimai Malle)

■ Bush, Laura

Identification: First Lady of the United States from 2001 to 2009

Born: November 4, 1946; Midland, Texas

Long before she married the man who would become the forty-third president of the United States, former first lady Laura Bush fell in love with reading. Her passion for books and education encouraged her to become both a teacher and a librarian, and remained the focus of her public life as first lady of Texas and then the White House.

Laura Welch was born on November 4, 1946, in Midland, Texas. She was the only child of Harold Welch, who owned his own construction business, and his wife Jenna, a bookkeeper. Welch's mother instilled in her a lifelong love of reading at an early age. During the summer of 1977, Welch attended a friend's backyard barbecue and was introduced to George W. Bush, a member of the wealthy and influential Bush political dynasty. The pair seemed quite different: she was described as quiet and bookish, while Bush was the life of the party. Just three months after they met, Laura Welch became Laura Bush, but only after her husband-to-be promised she would never have to give a political speech.

In 1999, just four years after becoming governor of Texas, George W. Bush decided to run for the Republican presidential nomination. Despite her husband's promise, Bush agreed to give public speeches for her husband, including one at the Republican National Convention in 2000. Once the nomination was in hand, she remained at his side at nearly every campaign stop, and reportedly took part in many campaign decisions. Laura Bush stood next to her husband at his presidential inauguration in January 2001, and thus assumed her new role as first lady of the United States. She pledged to continue her role as a quiet and supportive wife, and not participate in policy making.

Bush did bring her literacy agenda to Washington, however. Similar to her early activities in Texas, she organized the National Book Festival, and began promoting the Ready to Read, Ready to Learn program, which is designed to educate parents about the benefits of reading to children and to improve teacher quality across the country. Bush also advocates the Reach Out and Read program, in which doctors "prescribe" reading by providing children's books and literacy guidance to the parents of young children. Bush was also involved in the publication and nationwide distribution of *Healthy Start, Grow Smart*, a magazine mailed to new parents through state health and human service agencies, providing information and guidance regarding early childhood development, health, and nutrition. In November 2001, Laura Bush became the first US first lady to record a complete presidential radio address, in which she discussed the plight of women and children in Afghanistan, in light of the US military invasion of that country. In February 2003, First Lady Bush planned to host a conference, called "Poetry and the American Voice," at the White House. Despite her professed love and concern for literature, the conference was cancelled when poet and editor Sam Hamill responded to his invitation by soliciting poems from his colleagues protesting the recent US invasion of Iraq. Later that year, the poems were collected and published in an anthology entitled *Poets against the War*, edited by Hamill and featuring the work of many prominent American poets, including former poet laureate Rita Dove. In the wake of the controversy, Bush's bewildering 2002 statement that "there is nothing political about American literature" was widely quoted in the press.

Laura Bush addressed the Republican National Convention in 2004 and spoke on behalf of her husband's bid for a second term in the White House. George W. Bush was reelected in the 2004 election. In 2006, inspired by her mother's battle with breast cancer, Bush became increasingly involved in cancer awareness initiatives, particularly through her work with the Susan G. Komen for the Cure Foundation. She also supported the establishment of the Laura W. Bush Institute for Women's Health at Texas Tech University Health Science Center, which conducts research and offers educational and outreach programs on women's health issues. During her husband's second presidential term, Bush took several trips to Africa and the Caribbean to promote awareness about HIV and AIDS.

Impact

Bush's literacy and reading initiatives remained the hallmark of her time as first lady of the United States. In addition to her reading and library related programs, Bush has made women's health issues a priority, both in the United States as well as overseas. While President Bush was facing low approval ratings across the country in 2006, Laura Bush enjoyed one of the highest approval ratings for a first lady in history, leading her to take her husband's place in

campaigning for other Republican candidates. Bush and her husband returned to Texas following the end of President Bush's second term in January 2009.

Further Reading

Farrell, John Aloysius. "Farrell: A Nod to Laura Bush." *US News Digital Weekly* 1 May 2009: 21. Print.

Kniffel, Leonard. "8 Years Later Laura Bush Librarian in the White House." *American Libraries* 39.11 (2008): 42–47. Print.

Westfall, Sandra Sobieraj. "I Didn't Realize the Impact the First Lady Can Have." *People* 19 Jan. 2009: 60–66. Print.

Jennifer Monroe

■ Business and economy in Canada

Definition: The link between Canadian industries and the health of the nation's economy during the 2000s

As is the case with most industrialized nations, Canada's economic health relies on the vibrancy of its business enterprises. Whether these businesses are small stores or multinational corporations, Canadian businesses are invaluable contributors to the economy. The government, recognizing the importance of this link, continued to regulate the country's industries during the 2000s, working to protect the environment, promote corporate responsibility, and protect against the tumultuous economic periods that marked the decade.

The Canadian economy relies heavily on the strength of its myriad industries. Canadian businesses, from small- to large-scale corporations, contribute the lion's share of Canada's tax revenues, and their employees in turn contribute a substantial amount of personal taxes to the economy. During the 2000s, the Canadian economy largely thrived because of the health of its business enterprises. Although the Canadian economy shares similarities with that of the United States, its largest trading partner, there were certain characteristics and trends that distinguished it from the US system and, to some degree, protected it from the tumultuous conditions of the 2000s.

Toronto, Canada. (Courtesy of Toni Almodóvar Escuder)

Canada's Leading Industries

Canada features a diverse set of major industries, which enabled its economy to show consistent strength during the 2000s. Canada's manufacturing sector, for example, demonstrated great vibrancy during the first half of the 2000s. The country's automobile parts manufacturing industry, made strong by Canada's participation in the North American Free Trade Agreement (NAFTA), was one of world's leading producers. The nation's oil machinery manufacturing industry was also thriving, as North American demand for such equipment was on the rise.

When the global recession began in the United States in 2006, this industry was particularly hard-hit, however. The main culprits behind the downturn were environmental. For example, when the economy of Canada's biggest trade partner, the United States, began to falter and slow, the Canadian dollar—or "loonie," as the Canadian one dollar coin is called—began to surge. This trend created a significant imbalance, with reports of Canadian businesses heading south of the border to save costs.

To be sure, the loonie was enjoying an increase in value since 2002, thanks initially to the rising interest in Canada's leading energy resources, oil and natural gas, which provided North Americans with an alternative to oil from the Middle East. Over time, however, the loonie was buttressed by the strength of other Canadian commodities, such as gold and agricultural products. Wheat, corn, and canola in particular saw strong returns, as international interest in alternative fuel sources like ethanol rose dramatically during the 2000s.

The strengthening loonie caused problems for leading Canadian business industries. When the global recession began in the latter half of the 2000s, the weakness of the US dollar against the loonie, coupled with rising oil prices and the increasing cost of doing business, triggered a slowdown in the Canadian economy's growth. Even small businesses—one of the leading economic contributors in the country—were affected, forcing layoffs and operational reductions in the face of rising costs and reduced business.

Still, many of Canada's major industries were able to avoiding feeling the full brunt of the global recession. Although Canadian businesses were hit hard by the sudden drop in commerce with the country's largest trading partner to the south, the financial industry was able to steer clear from the growing real estate and credit crisis in the United States. This fortune was primarily due to most major Canadian multinational banks not being heavily invested in the US real estate market. Canadian banks were therefore able to retain some of their reserves and continue to provide credit and other support services to Canadian businesses during the recession.

Regulation

A persistent theme in the relationship between Canadian business and the economy is the role of government, both on the federal and provincial levels. Unlike the United States, wherein the federal government over the last several decades has moved away from a strong regulatory presence, Canada's government in Ottawa and the country's provinces and territories during the 2000s maintained partnerships with a wide range of industries.

The Canadian regulatory environment is multi-faceted. The Office of the Superintendent of Financial Institutions Canada (OSFI), for example, regulates all banks doing business in Canada as well as the country's insurance and mortgage lending industries. In 2007, this agency was responsible for issuing new regulations in the wake of the global financial crisis, stressing the need for financial institutions to demonstrate positive financial and business ethics—a lack of which may have facilitated the subprime lending issue that led to the US housing bubble's collapse.

Manufacturers and other industries are also subjected to strict regulations governed by Environment Canada. These regulatory areas include air emissions, water protection, and wildlife. During the 2000s, Canada remained committed to the Kyoto Protocol of 1997, which required participants to significantly lower their collective industries' airborne emissions. Canadian businesses that failed to adhere to the protocol's regulations would pay a substantial fine. By the end of the decade, however, it became clear that Canada could not reach the emissions benchmarks to which it had become committed and that its industries were paying a hefty sum to comply, even during the global recession.

The business regulatory environment has been seen by some Canadian business advocates as onerous. This argument seemed particularly relevant during the late 2000s, when taxes and other expenditures required of businesses continued to eat away at budgets during an unpredictable economic period. Small business in particular was demonstrative of this issue—in fact, by 2007, Canada's Revenue Agency had formed a task force to identify ways that the regulatory compliance burden for small businesses could be lowered in the face of the growing recession.

Impact

Like other industrialized nations, Canada has placed a high priority on creating an environment in which its diverse industrial base can thrive and can continue to support the country's economic health. During the early to mid-2000s, these industries showed a great deal of vibrancy despite the relatively high cost of operating in Canada. In many ways, Canada's businesses were able to survive the global recession of the latter half of the decade, having been insulated somewhat from the sources of that economic downturn. Canada's businesses could not completely avoid being impacted, however, in light of the downturn in international business and the increasing cost of oil and other operational necessities.

Since industries are heavily regulated by Ottawa and the provincial governments, this both helped and worsened conditions for Canadian businesses during the 2000s. The success of Canada's leading industries (including commodities and manufacturing) generated significant tax revenues for the economy. At the same time, the wide range of regulatory requirements made conditions worse for businesses, especially small businesses, hit hard by the economic downturn. Still, the ability of Canada's economy to withstand the tumultuous events of the 2000s added to the prevailing notion that it will remain healthy well into the next decade.

Further Reading

Cross, Philip. "Turbulent Stability: Canada's Economy in 2007." *Canadian Economic Observer* 21.4 (2008): 3.1–3.21. *Statistics Canada.* Web. 5 Dec. 2012. Provides a review of the Canadian economy (including its major industries) and the issues that undermined it during the global recession.

Doern, G. Bruce, and Edward J. Reed, eds. *Risky Business: Canada's Changing Science-Based Policy and Regulatory Regime.* Toronto: U of Toronto P, 2000. Print. Describes how Canada's regulatory agencies have managed several leading industries.

Hale, Geoffrey E. *Uneasy Partnership: The Politics of Business and Government in Canada.* Toronto: U of Toronto P, 2009. Print. Describes the relationship between the Canadian government and business and how this relationship, though sometimes strained, has created mutual benefits for the two parties.

Howlett, Michael, Alex Netherton, and M. Ramesh. *The Political Economy of Canada: An Introduction.* 2nd ed. New York: Oxford UP, 1999. Print. Focuses on the Canadian government's relationship with business, including discussions of the economy and the issues that played a role in Canada's economic performance in the 2000s.

Rollin, Anne-Marie. "Firm Dynamics: Employment Dynamics Arising from Firm Growth and Contraction in Canada, 2001 to 2009." *Canadian Economy in Transition.* Statistics Canada, 27 June 2012. Web. 5 Dec. 2012. Identifies areas in which Canadian businesses have grown and contracted during the decade, including the expansion of 2001 to 2008 and the recession that hit Canada in 2008.

Scott-Clarke, April. "Between a Rock and a Hard Place." *Benefits Canada* 33.3 (2009): 12–19. *Benefits Canada*, 1 Mar. 2009. Web. 5 Dec. 2012. Discusses the issues affecting Canadian small businesses during the economic tumult of the 2000s.

Michael P. Auerbach, MA

■ Business and economy in the United States

Definition: The link between American business and the health of the nation's economy during the 2000s

Business is the lifeblood of a healthy American economy. At the same time, the economy plays a major role in the shape of American business. During the 2000s, this symbiotic relationship was evident, as the successes and failures of a number of industries contributed to the nation's economic health. On the other side, the periods of economic strength and recession that occurred during this decade helped reshape the business landscape.

The American economy relies on the strength of the myriad industries operating on its shores. At the start of the 2000s, many of these industries featured large-scale, multinational corporations that employed hundreds, if not thousands, of employees on a full-time basis. Many such companies were software and technology manufacturers, contributing to what became a technology boom. These corporations thrived on global demand for their products and services. In turn, they paid millions of dollars each year in federal and state corporate taxes, with their employees doing the same. Put simply, these large-scale corporations were major drivers of the US economy.

In 2001, however, the technology boom came to a close with the sudden collapse of many Internet-based companies (the burst of the so-called "dot-com bubble"). Although many of these dot-com companies were profitable in the short term, they had little long-term durability. When a significant number of major Internet companies folded, their dissolution sent shockwaves through the NASDAQ, the US stock exchange where most technology stocks were traded, causing a retreat in the technology sector. Meanwhile, the terrorist attacks of September 11, 2001, worsened matters by causing a major disruption in the Dow Jones Industrial Average, triggering a full-scale recession.

With the technology sector sputtering along with the economy, US business needed to change its approach as well as its profile. This evolution occurred during this recession and continued through the recovery period of the mid-2000s and into the late-2000s recession. Some of the features of this evolu-

tion, and their impact on the US economy, include changes in the corporate work force, investments in global markets, increases in small business and entrepreneurship, and increases in government involvement in the economy.

Layoffs and Outsourcing

When the tech boom came to a close after the dot-com bubble collapsed, employers saw the need to reduce their costs. Employee layoffs were one of the most common cost-cutting measures, saving tens of thousands of salary dollars per employee—not including additional costs for health care, 401(k) contributions, and other benefits. Immediately following the September 11 terrorist attacks, and as the 2001 recession took hold, there was a nationwide spike in layoff events, periods in which layoffs occurred in clusters, which lasted throughout and following the recession. Meanwhile, periods of job creation were significantly less frequent, even after the recession came to an official close. This latter trend indicated that even though the economy was improving, many employers were not willing to return their employee bases to pre-recession numbers.

Employee layoffs during the 2000s were typically seen as a last resort for employers seeking to cut costs. A large percentage of corporate controllers linked production (such as sales) to resources (employees and the tools they utilized to perform); when the money generated from operations dwindled, controllers appreciated that cost-cutting was necessary. However, even layoffs cost money: employers would need to pay out severance packages and unemployment for the employees with whom they separated. Once the economy recovered, employers would need to re-hire employees to meet increasing consumer demand or else risk a reduction in their companies' health over the long term. For this reason, businesses in a downturned economy were reluctant to lay off employees unless it was clear that the recession in question was going to continue having a negative impact on business.

The global recession that began in 2006 was one that lingered in this way. What economists cited as the worst recession to impact the US economy since the Great Depression was so extensive that even global markets staggered. Businesses suffered over several years, losing revenues and lacking the ability to sustain their operations. In these situations, layoffs

Opening bell at the Chicago Board of Options Exchange. (Courtesy Richard Yuan)

may have been a last resort, but most of the businesses that made them had already exhausted all other cost-cutting options.

In some cases, however, there was another option that enabled businesses to retain workers without paying for benefits and unemployment. As the recession continued, many major corporations turned to external vendors to perform many employee tasks (such as information technology and marketing), a practice known as outsourcing. In some cases, outsourcing was even practiced using foreign consultants, saving not only on employee salaries but also on taxes and the cost of manufacturing facility operations. For these reasons, many businesses opted not to rehire some employees after the recessions of the 2000s, and instead continued to outsource many of their operations.

Staying Global

An important aspect of the 2000s was that businesses had greater access to global markets. The

Internet was the main reason for this evolution. To be sure, the Internet was already forging a global community. During the 2000s, however, the Internet became a vibrant marketplace. Business opportunities abounded for corporations and small businesses alike, enabling all types of businesses to gain access to clientele around the globe. With the exception of the recession that began in 2006—which was itself a global recession, with markets all over the industrialized world as frozen as they were in the United States—the Internet offered the chance to earn increased profits.

Toward the mid- to late 2000s, the Internet also began to offer resources that were budget friendly. The various types of available hardware and software (including Internet-based networks and programs) helped save money as more businesses could afford to go global. This development created an Internet middle class in which a growing number of US businesses could tap into the global marketplace by conducting business completely via the Internet. In this

Memorable 2000s Advertising Slogans and Jingles

Product	Slogan or Jingle
McDonalds	I'm lovin' it. We love to see you smile Give me that filet o fish
Apple	There's an app for that
Geico	So easy a caveman could do it
Anheuser-Busch Budweiser Beer	Whassup?
L'Oréal	Because you're worth it
Pepto Bismol	Nausea, heartburn, indigestion, upset stomach, diarrhea, Hey, Pepto Bismol!
Skittles	Taste the rainbow
Taco Bell	Think Outside the Bun
MasterCard	There's some things money can't buy. For everything else, there's MasterCard
AT&T	Your World. Delivered
Bounty	The quicker picker-upper
Meow Mix	I like chicken, I like liver, Meow Mix Meow Mix please deliver!
Subway	Five. Five dollar. Five dollar footlong
Quiznos	We Love the Subs!
NyQuil	The nighttime sniffling sneezing coughing aching stuffy head fever so you can rest medicine.
V-8	Coulda had a V-8!
Dos Equis	He is the Most Interesting Man in the World
Orbit	Dirty Mouth? Clean it up
Microsoft	Be What's Next
Kay Jewelers	Every Kiss Begins with Kay
Metropolitan Life	Have you met life today?
Coca Cola	Open Happiness Enjoy Live on the Coke Side of Life
U.S Army	Army Strong
FreeCreditReport.com	F-R-E-E, that spells "free," credit report dot com baby
Electronic Arts	EA Sports, It's in the game Challenge Everything
Gatorade	Is it in you?
Verizon Wireless	"Can you hear me now?"
Google	Don't Be Evil
Snickers	You're not you when you're hungry
Dunkin' Donuts	America runs on Dunkin'
East West Mortgage	Call 1-800 East West

regard, the global marketplace was also evolving into a virtual economy during the 2000s.

While this development generated tremendous returns for American businesses, and as a result, the American economy, it also posed significant risks. Businesses that invested their resources into the virtual global economy were subject to the same type of market fluctuations that impact US markets. Nowhere was this more manifest than during the global recession that began in 2006. This recession began in the United States, but United States–based banks were invested heavily in global markets—and foreign-based businesses were in turn invested in US banks in those same markets—which facilitated the spread of the economic malaise to an international scale. This economic contagion was worsened by foreign banks invested in the American real estate market and US banks, meaning that they lost their own reserves and capital. In addition to the US economy, other powerhouse economies like the European Union and Japan suffered greatly. For American businesses invested in global markets, there were few opportunities left during this recession, causing a severe impact on those companies.

Entrepreneurship and Small Business

As stated earlier, the business landscape in the United States changed considerably due to the economic recessions of the 2000s. Many businesses significantly reduced their operations by laying off employees, outsourcing activities to external vendors and consultants, and even merging with other businesses and consolidating resources. Another important change that occurred during this period, however, was an increase in small businesses and entrepreneurship. This trend proved to be an important factor in stimulating the US economy.

Small businesses—companies that employ five hundred or fewer workers—are some of the biggest contributors to the US economy, employing most Americans and generating the most business. In light of this, small business entrepreneurs would play a pivotal role not only in maintaining a healthy economy but in stimulating it during periods of recession. Small businesses could quickly adapt to changing market needs, applying innovative approaches and even taking more risks than larger cor-

porations. This is due to small businesses having smaller infrastructures, organizations, and employee bases. They are also powered by entrepreneurs—business owners who are willing to take financial risks to see their business ideas come to fruition. These businesses can quickly adapt to meet client needs. Furthermore, small businesses can offer cost-effective services for clients due to relatively low overhead costs.

Because of their adaptability, innovation, and cost-effectiveness, small businesses helped reinvigorate the economy during the 2000s. This task was not easily accomplished, however. The banking crisis that spurred the 2006 recession forced lenders to curtail extending lines of credit to small business entrepreneurs. Without sources of capital, many small businesses were forced to close their doors. In order to facilitate the economically reinvigorating effects of small business entrepreneurship, therefore, Congress ensured that when a comprehensive stimulus package was passed, it would have special provisions in it to support small businesses and to help them locate new sources of capital. By doing so, Congress made it clear that the economy could not recover without providing assistance to its biggest contributors—small business entrepreneurs.

Business, Government, and the Economy

The 2006 to 2008 recession, it has been argued, was fostered by increasing deregulation of the US banking industry. This lack of government oversight created an environment in which subprime lending—one of the major contributors to the creation and collapse of the housing bubble—and other practices were encouraged to continue. At the start of the recession, the US Federal Reserve lowered interest rates in an attempt to spur economic growth. However, when it became clear that the recession was far more extensive than previously believed, many Americans believed that it was time for the government to become more engaged in helping businesses and the economy.

The US government therefore became an active partner with American businesses. The government invested billions in the US banking system via 2008's Troubled Asset Relief Program (TARP), propping up several large institutions that it deemed "too big to fail" (as their collapse would produce globally devastating effects). These "bailouts" were not handouts—in order to receive an infusion of government cash, banks needed to perform major overhauls of their policies and infrastructures to ensure responsible and efficient operations.

The banking industry was not the only sector to see government intervention during the recession. The US automobile industry, which had long been suffering from the cost of manufacturing, the rising cost of oil, and the recession, was in jeopardy of issuing nationwide layoffs at its plants and facilities. Congress and newly elected President Barack Obama in 2008 deemed that the auto industry needed an infusion of cash to restructure and avoid completely shutting its doors. The infusion, which amounted to about $25 billion, was a loan, to be paid back once the industry returned to a position of profitability. The auto industry and banking bailouts that occurred during the latter years of the 2000s demonstrated the government's increasing interest in becoming more engaged with business to ensure the nation's economic health.

Impact

During the 2000s, American businesses experienced a great deal of change as a result of the economy. The recessions that began in 2001 and 2006 played a major role in this evolution, forcing the need for layoffs and cost-cutting measures, which included outsourcing. The reducing operations and cutting staff at large-scale corporations, however, helped foster entrepreneurship, especially through the economy's biggest contributor, small business. In this regard, small business became a major source of economic stimulus, helping the economy out of its slump.

Two major trends were evident during the 2000s. One was the continuing development of the global economy, which was facilitated by the Internet. American businesses were able to tap into new markets and client bases as well as network with foreign partners. Furthermore, the virtual economy could be accessed not just by major multinational corporations but by all levels of business enterprise, from large- to small-scale businesses.

The second trend was the return to government oversight in business. The severe recession that began in 2006 was at least partly triggered by a lack of government regulation in several areas of the banking and finance sector. Government, which to a large part avoided intervening in business, recognized that the economy would continue to suffer if it continued to stay on the sidelines. By the end of the decade, it was unknown if this trend was a long-term policy or simply an immediate intervention to offset the severe recession at hand. Nevertheless, the government's renewed interest in regulating the business and economy link was an important development during the 2000s.

Further Reading

"Entrepreneurship and the US Economy." *US Bureau of Labor Statistics.* United States Department of Labor, Mar. 2010. Web. 5 Dec. 2012. Overview that provides statistics on the development of new business establishments during the 2000s.

Faktor, Steve. *Econovation: The Red, White, and Blue Pill for Arousing Innovation.* New York: Wiley, 2011. Print. Describes the evolution of entrepreneurship in the global economy that dominated the 2000s. Includes a discussion on the use of social media and other Internet-based innovations to generate global business.

Geho, Patrick R., and Jennifer Dangelo. "The Evolution of Social Media as a Marketing Tool for Entrepreneurs." *Entrepreneurial Executive* 17 (2012): 61–68. Print. Describes how an increasing number of businesses used social media, starting during the latter 2000s, to expand their business marketing efforts.

Lehne, Richard. *Government and Business: American Political Economy in Comparative Perspective.* 2nd ed. Washington, DC: CQ Press, 2005. Print. Discusses the relationship between government and business in the United States. Analyzes government regulations and interventions during times in which the economy is at risk of negative growth.

Rapp, Donald. *Bubbles, Booms, and Busts: The Rise and Fall of Financial Assets.* New York: Springer, 2009. Print. Describes the cyclical nature of financial markets, including the collapses of the dot-com and real estate bubbles during the 2000s.

Valadez, Ray M. "The Value Proposition of Small Businesses: Economic Engines for Job Creation." *Journal of Management and Marketing Research* 9 (2011): 1–11. Print. Describes how small business served as a catalyst for economic reinvigoration after the recessions of the 2000s.

Westervelt, Robert. "DuPont Plants $900-Million Cost Reduction by 2005." *Chemical Week* 165.44 (2003): 8. *Academic Search Complete.* Web. 5. Dec. 2012. Describes how one of the largest employers in Pennsylvania began a major consolidation of its operations (including employee layoffs) as a result of the recession of the early 2000s.

Michael P. Auerbach, MA

C

■ California electricity crisis

The Event: A period of energy shortages and rolling blackouts in California
Date: 2000–2001
Place: California

Between 2000 and 2001, California experienced a widespread electricity crisis, during which severe power shortages led to extended periods of rolling blackouts. While the crisis was attributable to a number of different causes, it was eventually revealed that the crisis was primarily the result of market manipulation on the part of power companies and energy traders.

The roots of the California electricity crisis can be traced back to 1996, when the state passed California Assembly Bill 1890 (AB 1890). This deregulation bill was designed to help restructure the state's energy system, which many regarded as inefficient, overly expensive, and lacking the proper incentives to encourage the establishment of new generating facilities. AB 1890 created new markets for wholesale electricity transactions and established the California Independent System Operator (CAISO) and the California Power Exchange (CalPX) to control these wholesale markets. In addition to these changes, the California Public Utilities Commission (CPUC) introduced retail price controls that placed a cap on how much consumers could be charged, regardless of the costs faced by producers. Although this new system was a necessary step toward deregulation, its implementation proved to be problematic.

Under the rules of the new system, CAISO and CalPX were allowed to operate independently of one another. This arrangement created a potentially volatile energy market that could lead to serious consequences, particularly when combined with retail price controls. While the system was initially successful, the conditions it created left California in a vulnerable position.

After several successful years under its newly deregulated energy system, California faced a series of difficult circumstances that placed significant strain on its energy resources. Strong economic growth in the region had led to significantly increased demand for electricity. From the outset, California was unable to meet its own energy demands, having too few generation facilities to provide adequate energy to meet the growing demands of its population. This, in turn, led the state to become dependent on generation facilities located in neighboring states, primarily hydroelectric plants in the northwestern United States.

The Crisis
In 2000, much of the Northwest was subject to severe droughts that hindered energy production at the region's hydroelectric plants. Faced with staggeringly high demand and virtually no support from power facilities outside the state, some of California's aging power plants experienced outages that left customers without power. While some of these outages were likely legitimate, others, it was later discovered, were part of a plan by power companies to manipulate the market.

The market system established by AB 1890 only made the situation worse. While the ongoing conditions continually increased the cost of energy for suppliers, the retail price controls they were forced to abide by prevented them from passing those costs on to the customers. In April 2000, prior to the onset of the crisis, the wholesale price of electricity was about $30 per megawatt hour. Within six months, prices rose as high as $450 per megawatt hour. As wholesale prices grew and retail prices remained the same, the financial disparity surrounding the energy crisis in California deepened.

Market Manipulation and Resolution
The imbalance between wholesale and retail energy prices led many power companies to become financially unstable. In an effort to offset their losses, some

of these companies attempted to manipulate the market by staging intentional blackouts at critical times to increase their profits. Using this tactic, energy traders, such as Enron Corporation, were able to take advantage of the situation and sell power at significantly higher than normal prices for enormous profit.

Eventually, the state government was forced to step in and address the crisis. Actions were taken to help return California's energy system to normal operation. Most notably, in May 2001, CPUC conceded to a restructuring of the state's retail pricing plan, raising rates for customers based on their individual financial situations. This and other government actions, combined with mild weather and concerted conservation efforts, helped to slowly alleviate the crisis. By the summer of 2001, prices returned to a normal level.

Impact

The California electricity crisis continues to serve as an important lesson on the potential difficulties of electrical deregulation. The crisis illustrated that the deregulation of the electrical energy industry is a more complicated and potentially more problematic endeavor than the deregulation of other, similar industries. The crisis is not, however, a complete indictment of deregulation. Rather, it is a reminder that, while deregulation may indeed be worthwhile, it is an extremely delicate process requiring close attention to detail and careful monitoring.

Further Reading

Borenstein, Severin. "The Trouble with Electricity Markets: Understanding California's Restructuring Disaster." *Journal of Economic Perspectives* 16.1 (2002): 191–211. PDF file. Examines the challenge of deregulation in the energy industry using the California electricity crisis as an example.

Cosgrove-Mather, Bootie. "California Energy Crisis a Sham." *CBS News.* CBS Interactive, 11 Feb. 2009. Web. 10 Sept. 2012. Reveals the role that power companies and energy traders played in the California energy crisis.

Goyette, Martin. "The California Energy Crisis 2000–2001: Update on Post-Crisis Developments." *Office of the Attorney General.* California Department of Justice, 26 Sept. 2011. Web. 10 Sept. 2012. A presentation on the California electricity crisis, created by the state's attorney general's office.

"Subsequent Events—California's Energy Crisis." *EIA.* US Energy Information Administration, 8 June 2005. Web. 10 Sept. 2012. An official US Energy Information Administration report on the California electricity crisis.

Sweeney, James L. *The California Electricity Crisis.* Stanford: Hoover Inst. P, 2002. Print. Provides a detailed review of the California electricity crisis, the history of the state's deregulation efforts, and more.

—. "The California Electricity Crisis: Lessons for the Future." *Stanford University.* Stanford University, 12 May 2002. Web. 10 Sept. 2012. Provides an overview of the California electricity crisis and what it can teach about deregulation of the energy industry.

"The Western Energy Crisis, the Enron Bankruptcy, and FERC's Response." *FERC.* Federal Energy Regulatory Commission, 2005. Web. 10 Sept. 2012. The official Federal Energy Regulatory Commission chronology of the California electricity crisis.

Jack Lasky

■ Cameron, James

Identification: Canadian film director and producer
Born: August 16, 1954; Kapuskasing, Ontario

Canadian filmmaker and producer James Cameron is known for his box office hits and his cutting-edge special effects. His credits include the groundbreaking films Titanic and Avatar. His push for advancement in film technology has innovated the way movies are made.

Academy Award–winning filmmaker James Francis Cameron established his reputation as a creator box office hits in the 1980s and 1990s with *The Terminator* (1984) and *Terminator 2: Judgment Day* (1991), *Aliens* (1986), *The Abyss* (1986), and *Titanic* (1997), which won eleven Oscars, including best picture, best director, and best visual effects. Through these films, Cameron became known for his innovative use of special effects and his heroine-driven storylines.

He continued his critically and commercially successful work during the 2000s starting with the award-winning television series *Dark Angel* (2000–2002). The series stars Jessica Alba as Max, a fugitive who was genetically modified as a child and who lives in a postapocalyptic Pacific Northwest as a young adult.

James Cameron. (Courtesy Steve Jurvetson)

Cameron's other projects during the early part of the 2000s include the science-fiction drama *Solaris* (2002); *Expedition: Bismarck* (2002), an Emmy-winning documentary about the sinking of a German battleship which Cameron wrote, directed (with Gary Johnstone), and produced (with Andrew Wight) for the Discovery Channel; *Ghosts of the Abyss* (2003), a post-*Titanic* 3-D documentary for Disney in which Cameron and a group of scientists explore the wreck of the RMS *Titanic.* Cameron received character-writing credits for two sequels in the Terminator franchise, *Terminator 3: Rise of the Machines* (2003) and *Terminator Salvation* (2009), which were also released during the decade.

According to Cameron, although he first wrote the script for *Avatar* (2009) in 1994, he had to wait until technology had caught up to his vision before he could start filming. He didn't begin working on the film full time until 2005, using camera systems he developed himself. (Cameron had already developed cutting-edge technology for previous films such as *The Abyss.*) The film was vintage Cameron—an emotional storyline wrapped up with pioneering visual effects, with estimates putting the cost of the film close to $300 million. Shortly after its release, *Avatar* became the highest-grossing motion picture. For his

achievement, Cameron received the Golden Globe for best director in 2010.

Impact

As of 2010, Cameron's film *Avatar* (2009) was the highest grossing film of all time, beating the record Cameron himself had set with the 1997 epic *Titanic.* In all, Cameron's directorial efforts, which also include the Academy Award–winning *Aliens* (1986) and *Terminator 2: Judgment Day* (1991), have grossed over $4.6 billion worldwide. Cameron is also a driving force in the advancement of film technology, particularly in the areas of visual effects and underwater filming.

Further Reading

Hedegaard, Erik. "The Impossible Reality Of James Cameron." *Rolling Stone* 1094/1095 (2009): 68–95. Print.

Kluger, Jeffrey. "James Cameron." *Time* 179.14 (2012): 20. Print.

Setoodeh, Ramin. "James Cameron-Peter Jackson." *Newsweek* 154.26 (2009): 88–91. Print.

Bill Rickards

■ Canada and the United States

Definition: An overview of the domestic and foreign-policy issues that define relations between Canada and the United States

The trade between Canada and the United States amounts to approximately $1.5 billion per day, and while both nations have many common interests, their basic economies and constitutional systems are different. This has led to numerous agreements and disagreements dominated by the 5,526-mile border between the two nations and its security.

Throughout the 2000s, following the terrorist attacks on the World Trade Center and the Pentagon on September 11, 2001, security issues involving the border between Canada and the United States were perhaps the most contentious of the issues affecting US-Canadian relations. Border security plays a central role in all cross-border trade agreements, and the necessity of ensuring border security acquired enhanced importance in US-Canada trade and immigration agreements.

Security Issues

Major concerns regarding border security during the 2000s derived from the apparent ease with which foreign nationals could use the Canadian system to gain access to mainland United States at both mainstream border crossings and in areas where the border stretches across miles of open or heavily wooded territory. In many places, it is quite possible to walk undetected from one country into the other across a mere hundred yards of open space, and while it is unknown whether or not this has been done by terrorists, the fact that it could be done became an issue of great concern. Other points of contention involved the massive number of transport trucks that crossed the border from Canada to the United States, about one every two seconds, ferrying close to $2 billion worth of trade between the two nations each day. The trade included everything from basic food goods and raw materials to trash and garbage for landfill and recycling. At issue was ensuring that truck traffic was not being utilized to smuggle people and illicit goods for the purposes of terrorism. The logistics of this latter point, in combination with other factors, led to the termination of some arrangements, such as the movement of municipal trash from Ontario to Michigan, and the negotiation of new agreements, such as the United States–Canada Shared Border Management Pilot Project, which would entail land preclearance by joint US and Canadian customs-agent teams at locations away from the border. Negotiations for the latter were discontinued in 2007 as questions and disagreements arose over the authority of US border agents to make arrests, the constitutional legality of US fingerprinting practices, and the right of individuals to withdraw an application to enter the United States while at a preclearance station in Canada.

Trade and Economic Issues

Canada is the United States' most significant economic trade partner and vice versa. The trade between the two nations amounts to some $1.9 billion per day, with about 80 percent of that trade being carried cross-border by transport trucks. In December 2001, Canada and the United States signed the Smart Border Declaration, which included a thirty-point action plan for ensuring and securing cross-border trade. Two of the initiatives instituted at border crossings since that time are the NEXUS and FAST programs. The former includes a set of border-crossing lanes dedicated for preapproved and low-risk travelers at land crossings, and the latter is a program of expedited clearance processes for preauthorized shipments of material goods.

Other cross-border trade agreements focus on energy, as both the United States and Canada supply the vast majority of each other's electricity imports. In addition, by the end of the 2000s, Canada was supplying some 88 percent of the natural gas imported by the United States, along with over 1.9 million barrels of crude oil per day. According to Canadian government figures, total energy exports to the United States were valued at $76.27 billion in 2009, and by the end of the decade, almost one thousand companies throughout the United States from every sector of the economy were directly supplying goods and services to the oil-production industry in Canada.

A significant proportion of the bilateral trade between Canada and the United States throughout the 2000s supported the North American automobile-manufacturing industry, with component parts produced in one country being transported to assembly plants in the other, typically on a "just-in-time" (JIT) basis. The greatest part of this trade involved the province of Ontario and the states of Michigan, Ohio, Illinois, Indiana, North Carolina, Kentucky, and Alabama.

International Defense Initiatives

Canadian and American military forces regularly functioned in cooperation with each other throughout the 2000s, both internally and abroad through their active involvement in the efforts of the United Nations to mitigate circumstances around the world. While Canada did not fully support the US-led invasion of Iraq that led to the ouster of Saddam Hussein's regime, its forces played a primary role in the effort to remove the Taliban from Afghanistan in favor of a democratic government. Canadian and US forces worked cooperatively in Afghanistan throughout the decade, and well into the next, against the persistent insurgence of Taliban forces intent on maintaining their hold over the Afghan people.

Other strategic defense initiatives that developed throughout the 2000s arose around the Royal Canadian Air Force's existing fleets of CF-18 fighter jets, based on the US military's F/A-18 jets. Though still functional, these aircraft inevitably approached the end of their viable lifetimes and began to exhibit increasing mechanical failures due to age, requiring that ever-increasing amounts be spent on their maintenance. Alternatives were therefore brought into development, including unmanned drone aircraft and the F-35 Joint Strike Fighter program. While Canada had initially agreed to replace its CF-18 aircraft with a fleet of F-35s, by the end of the decade, cost overruns and a furor of public opinion in Canada delayed such action, and the CF-18s continued in service well into the next decade. High-level Canadian military advisers indicated that the F-35 was not an appropriate aircraft for the conditions it would see in Canadian service, and a significant proportion of Canadian citizens felt that for the C\$25 billion cost of the F-35 fleet, it would be more appropriate to develop a "home-grown" Canadian fighter jet, reminiscent of the Avro Canada CF-105 Arrow that was successfully developed and flown in Canada in the late 1950s. By the end of 2010, the issue remained unresolved and highly contentious in both Canada and the United States.

Impact

Events in the decade of the 2000s placed considerable strain on relations between Canada and the United States, mostly centered on issues relating to the security of the US-Canada border, especially following the events of September 11, 2001. While the two nations maintained their cordial diplomatic bonds throughout this period, different attitudes toward immigration and border security served to reinforce the independence of each from the other rather than bring them closer together. As a result, trade between the two nations was affected as various cross-border agreements were ended in some segments of the economy and new agreements were fashioned in others.

Further Reading

Anderson, Greg, and Christopher Sands. *Forgotten Partnership Redux: Canada-US Relations in the 21st Century.* Amherst: Cambria, 2011. Print. Presents a series of analytical essays examining the current state of relations between Canada and the United States, with projections of future relations.

"Canada-US Relations." *Canada International.* Government of Canada, 8 June 2012. Web. 6 Dec. 2012. Provides the Canadian government's perspective of relations with the United States, with links to specific individual areas of application

such as energy, trade and investment, security, and the environment.

Ek, Carl, et al. *Canada-US Relations in Focus.* New York: Nova Sci., 2008. Print. Reviews the relationship between Canada and the United States over the past two hundred years, from their common origins as British colonies to the present day, with extensive analysis of agreements and disagreements between the two nations.

Ek, Carl, and Ian F. Ferguson. *Canada-US Relations.* Cong. Research Service. N.p.: n.p., 5 Apr. 2012. PDF file. Provides a thorough overview of US-Canadian relations from an American point of view, with a historical context from the 1990s through the end of 2010, providing numerous points for consideration.

Lennox, Patrick. *At Home and Abroad: The Canada-US Relationship and Canada's Place in the World.* Vancouver: UBC P, 2009. Print. Presents an analysis of six key events in the history of relations between Canada and the United States that serve to outline and define Canada's role in world politics.

Richard M. Renneboog, MSc

■ Cancer research

Definition: Studies that attempt to determine the underlying causes of cancer, including molecular changes in the cell, and work toward improved methods to cure or control the disease

Twenty-first century research into the causes of cancer resulted in improved understanding of the genetic and molecular changes that take place during the transformation of normal cells into malignant ones. Applications of this knowledge resulted in further development of therapies that focus on characteristics specific to the cancer.

Beginning in the 1970s, the identification of genes that regulate cell division began the process of understanding the molecular biology of cancer. Because aberrant regulation by these genes may result in cancer formation, they became known as oncogenes. By the 2000s, over one hundred such genes had been identified. Many function as either cell surface receptors, stimulating cell division, or as intermediates in pathways that activate genetic elements of DNA, regulating cell division. Because some of these pathways are unique to certain cancer cells, they have become targets of new generations of anticancer drugs, reducing the dangerous side effects often associated with chemotherapy.

Targeting Specific Cancers

Imatinib, the first of the anticancer drugs to specifically target a form of leukemia, was approved by the Food and Drug Administration (FDA) in 2001 to combat chronic myelogenous leukemia (CML). CML is characterized by the "Philadelphia chromosome," a translocation of an oncogene from chromosome 9 to chromosome 22. The result is uncontrolled regulation of an enzyme known as tyrosine kinase, which functions in the regulation of cell growth. Imatinib specifically inhibits the enzyme, preventing replication of CML cells. Imatinib was subsequently found to target a second form of cancer, gastrointestinal stroma tumor.

In 2003, the FDA approved two drugs targeting certain forms of lung cancer: gefitinib and erlotinib, each of which inhibits a cell surface protein (a growth factor receptor) on lung cancer cells. While results with gefitinib have been mixed—it remains unclear whether its use extends life expectancy—erlotinib use has been extended to treat pancreatic cancers.

Since tumor growth requires a blood supply, cancer cells produce angiogenic agents, molecules that stimulate the formation of blood vessels. In 2004, the FDA approved the first drug that targets angiogenesis, bevacizumab, which blocks blood vessel formation. The drug has proven useful in treating a variety of cancers, including those of the colon or rectum, lungs, ovaries, and brain. Additional drugs targeting colorectal cancer were also approved in the 2000s, such as panitumumad (2006). In a manner similar to that of erlotinib, these drugs target the growth factor receptor on the surface of cancer cells.

Earlier Detection of Cancer

In the 2000s, lung cancer superseded breast cancer as the most common cause of cancer deaths in women, and has remained the highest cause of cancer mortality in men, with nearly 160,000 persons dying from the disease each year. Since smoking is the primary cause of most lung cancers in both men and women, improved screening methods have been used for earlier diagnosis. In 2010, a trial funded by the National Cancer Insti-

tute determined that low-dose spiral CT scans (LDCT) of persons at greatest risk for lung cancer reduced cancer mortality by 20 percent over the course of the study. Longer-term observations will be necessary to determine whether earlier diagnosis translates into a longer life expectancy.

Since surgery remains the primary means of treating lung cancer, several methods were introduced during the decade to make surgery less invasive. Often lobectomy, the removal of an entire lobe—in this case of the lung—is the method of choice to better ensure that the cancer has been removed. Studies began comparing the efficacy of lobectomy with the less radical surgery of removing only the tumor and some of the surrounding tissue. Other surgical procedures attempt to avoid the necessity of opening the entire chest. The technique of video-assisted thoracoscopic surgery (VATS), which allows the surgeon to enter the chest through a significantly narrower opening, also began to be tested during the 2000s. Prevention of lung cancer remains the primary goal. Since smoking is the most important environmental factor and can be controlled, education on the dangers of smoking was increasingly emphasized.

Prostate cancer remained the second leading cause of cancer deaths among men, with the American Cancer Society estimating that over 25,000 men will die each year from the disease. Early detection has historically relied on a test that measures prostate specific antigen (PSA), a protein found in association with prostate cells. The PSA test has proven controversial, often missing some forms of prostate cancer while producing frequent false positive results, leading to unnecessary biopsies. The efficacy of yearly PSA testing for most men remains uncertain. A test called PCA3, developed in the 2000s and approved by the FDA in 2012, screens for the presence of a mutation common in most forms of prostate cancer. Though more difficult to run in the laboratory, the increased accuracy of the PCA3 test may result in its replacing that of the PSA screening.

Cancer Vaccines

The National Cancer Institute has defined two categories of anticancer vaccines: (1) those that prevent cancer through immunization of persons against the etiological (causative) agent of the disease, and (2) vaccines that can treat cancers that have already developed, harnessing the immune system in the attack. The hepatitis B vaccines introduced in the 1980s, while indirectly protecting against development of hepatocarcinoma (a type of liver cancer), were targeting hepatitis B virus infections in general. The first vaccine that focused specifically on a type of cancer was Gardasil, approved by the FDA in 2006 to immunize women against cervical cancer. The vaccine contains protein subunits from the four most common types of human papilloma virus (HPV 6, 11, 16, and 18), the etiological agent of the disease. A similar vaccine, Cervarix, directed against HPV 16 and 18, was approved by the FDA in 2009. While initial studies focused on immunizing women against HPV, the recognition that the same virus may cause anal, penile, and oropharyngeal cancer in men has resulted in recommendations that men also receive HPV immunization.

In 2010, the FDA approved the first vaccine for treatment of an existing cancer, that of the prostate. The development of Sipuleucel-T is an example of the application of new techniques in molecular medicine. The vaccine is directed against a specific protein—prostatic acid phosphatase (PAP)—an enzyme located on the surface of prostate cancer cells. The procedure involves the isolation of a subset of immune cells, antigen-presenting cells (APCs), from the patient and incubating them with purified PAP. Once the APCs have been stimulated, they are reinfused into the patient, resulting in a significant increase in the immune response against the cancer.

Impact

Gardasil and Cervarix have proven effective in preventing precancerous lesions associated with HPV infection; few significant side effects have been reported. Field trials that included placebos were so definitive that testing was terminated, with recipients of the placebo allowed to receive the actual vaccines. Long-term studies remain necessary to determine the precise impact on the yearly incidence of cervical cancer. Politics has, however, played a role in the decision as to whether the HPV vaccine should be required for women prior to puberty; some conservative groups have argued that doing so would send a message encouraging premarital intercourse.

The long-term efficacy of targeted treatments of cancer remains to be determined. Nevertheless, through the first decade of the twenty-first century, some 12 million people became cancer survivors, a number up by 20 percent since the beginning of the decade.

Further Reading

Hesketh, Robin. *Introduction to Cancer Biology*. New York: Cambridge UP, 2012. Print. The story of cancer for the nonscientist, included the role played by molecular pathways in the cell that normally regulate cell growth.

Mukherjee, Siddhartha. *The Emperor of All Maladies: A Biography of Cancer*. New York: Scribner, 2011. Print. Covers the disease's first recognition in ancient Egypt through modern understanding and treatment.

Olson, James. *Bathsheba's Breast: Women, Cancer, and History*. Baltimore: Johns Hopkins, 2002. Print. The title originates from the observation that the image of Bathsheba in Rembrandt's painting *Bathsheba at her Bath* shows evidence of breast cancer. Rembrandt's model had in fact died from that disease. The author, who also suffered from cancer, describes how a number of prominent women dealt with their own diagnosis of the disease.

Skloot, Rebecca. *The Immortal Life of Henrietta Lacks*. New York: Crown, 2010. Print. Story of the woman behind HeLa cells, which were used for decades in cellular research. Henrietta Lacks was an African American woman who died from cervical cancer in the early 1950s; samples of her cancer were removed and by chance proved relatively easy to grow in the laboratory. The author addresses both the biology of HeLa cells and the ethical dilemma involved.

Stockwell, Brent. *The Quest for the Cure: The Science and Stories Behind the Next Generation of Medicines*. New York: Columbia UP, 2011. Print. The history of chemotherapy as a treatment for diseases like cancer. Describes the challenges involved in the development of new generations of drugs as well as the future of personalized therapy.

Richard Adler, PhD

■ Chabon, Michael

Identification: American novelist
Born: May 24, 1963; Washington, DC

Michael Chabon is an American novelist who is considered to be one of the best writers of his generation. His work in-

cludes the critically acclaimed novels Wonder Boys and The Yiddish Policeman's Union. He writes in a variety of literary genres, addressing such themes as escapism, superheroes, and the powerful force of history.

Michael Chabon (SHAY-bon)'s best-selling second novel, *Wonder Boys* (1995) was made into a film in 2000, featuring Tobey Maguire and Michael Douglas. Shortly after publishing the novel, Chabon discovered a box of old comic books from his youth and began working on his third novel, which would mark a turn in his work toward an exploration of the themes of escapism and fantasy. In 2000, Chabon published *The Amazing Adventures of Kavalier and Clay*, which won the Pulitzer Prize in fiction. It was also a finalist for both the National Book Critics Circle Award and the PEN/Faulkner Award. *The Amazing Adventures of Kavalier and Clay* harkens back to the work of other great Jewish comics creators, such as Will Eisner, and follows the characters Sammy Clay and Joe Kavalier, two Jewish cousins who create comic books in the early 1940s, the years leading up to the United States' entry into World War II. The novel tracks the rise of the modern superhero and connects it to the ancient story of the golem.

Chabon does not deal directly with the events of World War II, but his 2005 novella, *The Final Solution*, winner of the National Jewish Book Award, tells the story of Linus Steinman, a mute nine-year-old boy who has escaped Nazi Germany with his sole companion, an African parrot. This book deals indirectly with the aftermath of what was arguably the twentieth century's most horrific tragedy: the Holocaust. Devoid of typical images of corpses, camps, and gas chambers, *The Final Solution* is an unusual book because the Holocaust is not mentioned directly except for a few oblique allusions. Instead, the reader wonders who has stolen the child's parrot and is forced to consider the tragedy that hovers darkly over the story.

Chabon has written two collections of short stories, *A Model World and Other Stories* (1990) and *Werewolves in Their Youth* (1999). His first young adult novel, *Summerland*, was published in 2002, and he has written articles and essays, screenplays (sharing story credit for the 2004 film *Spider-Man 2*), and edited the collection *The Best American Short Stories 2005*. His 2007 novel, *The Yiddish Policemen's Union*, is a hardboiled detective novel set in an alternate world in which the state of Israel failed to come into existence.

Michael Chabon. (Courtesy Ken Conley)

Chabon offers readers a counterhistory in which millions of European Jewish refugees take shelter in Alaska, creating a Yiddish colony. *Gentlemen of the Road*, a fifteen-part serial novel about two ancient Khazar bandits that ran in the *New York Times Magazine*, was published in 2007. Chabon published two collections of essays: *Maps and Legends* (2008) and *Manhood for Amateurs: The Pleasures and Regrets of a Husband, Father, and Son* (2009).

Impact

Chabon is skilled in many literary genres, and he is the rare artist whose works appeal to many different types of readers. His novel's, including the critically adored *Wonder Boys*, are beloved by avid readers of comic books, of detective stories, of gangster mob tales, and of alternate histories. One of his common themes is redemption, and another is the overwhelming power of historical forces. Chabon creates characters that come alive, reflecting readers' desires for fantasy and for escape.

Further Reading

Behlman, Lee. "The Escapist: Fantasy, Folklore, and the Pleasures of the Comic Book in Recent Jewish American Holocaust Fiction." *Shofar* 22.3 (2003): 56–71. Print.

Myers, D. G. "Michael Chabon's Imaginary Jews." *Sewanee Review* 16.4 (2008): 572–88. Print.

Straub, Peter, ed. *American Fantastic Tales: Terror and the Uncanny from the 1940's to Now.* New York: Lib. of America, 2009. Print.

Monica Osborne

■ Cheney, Dick

Identification: American vice president, 2001–09
Born: January 30, 1941; Lincoln, Nebraska

Richard Bruce "Dick" Cheney, forty-sixth vice president of the United States, had a career in government that lasted over three decades. Formerly a US representative and secretary of state, many saw Cheney as the ideal running mate for George W. Bush in the 2000 presidential election.

Dick Cheney. (Official White House Photo/Photograph by Karen Ballard)

In 1995, there were rumors that Dick Cheney would seek the Republican Party's presidential nomination in the 1996 election. Instead, he withdrew from politics and became the chief executive of Halliburton Company, a Texas-based oil field services business. After five years at Halliburton, Cheney resigned in 2000 to help Texas Governor and Republican presidential nominee George W. Bush search for a running mate. That summer, Cheney himself accepted the party's nomination as the vice presidential candidate. The choice surprised many observers, since Cheney had resisted running for higher office on several previous occasions. He was only five years older than Bush, but his wealth of political experience, as well as his greater gravitas and seriousness, were seen as assets to the Republican campaign.

The Vice Presidency

The 2000 presidential election proved to be one of the closest elections in American history. Although election night brought calls from various media outlets declaring victory for each party, it was eventually determined in the days following the election that the majority of electoral college votes needed to win the presidency would be decided by the winner of the state of Florida. A month-long legal and political dispute over voting irregularities and recounts in Florida ensued. The battle over which candidate would lay claim to Florida's twenty-five electoral votes, and thus the presidency, eventually reached the Supreme Court. The court ruled in a 5–4 decision to officially end all recounts of the Florida presidential ballots. The decision made official previous vote counts that determined the Bush/Cheney ticket as the winner in Florida and served to officially and legally determine them as the winners of the presidential election. Critics of Bush and supporters of the Gore/Lieberman ticket were bitter about the Supreme Court ruling and noted the fact that Bush/Cheney had lost the popular vote.

In March 2001, not long after being inaugurated as vice president, Cheney complained of chest pains and was admitted to the hospital. Many feared that his history of coronary artery disease would interfere with his ability to serve as vice president. However, after a procedure to re-open a partially blocked artery, Cheney was once again declared fit to return to his duties. After the September 2001 terrorist attacks on New York City and Washington, DC, Cheney was instrumental in organizing the US military offensive against terrorist targets in Afghanistan. His experience as secretary of defense made him uniquely suited to the task.

Enron Scandal

Early in 2002, Cheney found himself at the center of an investigation into the bankruptcy of the Enron Corporation, an energy trading company. The previous year, Cheney headed a presidential task force to draft a proposal for a national energy plan. In a series of discussions, several cabinet members met with representatives from the energy industry (as well as labor, consumer, and environmental groups) in an effort to form a coherent energy policy for the Bush administration.

During the course of the meetings, executives from Enron, at the time one of the largest energy traders in the world, as well as a financial supporter of the Republican Party and the Bush/Cheney campaign, met personally with the vice president. When the company went bankrupt as a result of accounting fraud, questions surfaced regarding Enron's possible influence on the Bush administration's energy recommendations and whether the White House had any advance knowledge of the company's financial difficulties. Thousands of people lost their jobs as a result of the bankruptcy.

In January 2002, the collapse of Enron was being probed by a number of government agencies trying to determine what led to the company's collapse. The US General Accounting Office (GAO), the investigative branch of Congress, asked Cheney for his notes from the energy task force meetings, hoping they would shed some light on the relationship between the administration and Enron. Cheney refused, however, and legal action regarding the documents ensued.

Iraq War

Beginning in 2002, the Bush administration began to turn its attention to the nation of Iraq, led at the time by dictator Saddam Hussein. For over a year, President Bush and administration officials presented pieces of evidence it claimed proved that Hussein was developing and producing biological and chemical weapons in Iraq, also known as weapons of mass destruction (WMD). Vice Presi-

dent Cheney played a significant role in stressing the importance of ridding Iraq and the Hussein regime of such weapons.

In February 2003, US Secretary of State Colin Powell addressed the UN Security Council, presenting the Bush administration's evidence of WMD in Iraq and urging the organization to support a US-led invasion. Powell's request was not approved by a majority of the council, and UN Security Council approval of military action against Iraq was not granted. The governments of France and Germany publicly stated their opposition to any unsanctioned military invasion of Iraq.

Nonetheless, an American-led military invasion of Iraq began on March 20, 2003. Hussein was captured by US forces in December of 2003, and after being convicted of war crimes, he was subsequently executed by the newly established Iraq government.

Although the Hussein government was swiftly toppled, the invasion of Iraq resulted in a power vacuum in the country that pitted Sunni Muslim militias against Shiite militias. In addition, forces loyal to the Hussein government implemented numerous guerilla warfare tactics against US and coalition forces. Over four thousand American troops and hundreds of coalition forces have been killed in Iraq. Military activity in the country and the subsequent civil strife that followed has resulted in the deaths of 40,000 Iraqi civilians and resulted in the exile of hundreds of thousands of civilians who fled the violence.

Cheney's Second Term

President Bush and Vice President Cheney were re-elected in 2004, defeating Democratic Party candidate Senator John Kerry. Unlike the 2000 presidential election, the Bush/Cheney ticket won 3.5 million more popular votes than his opposing candidate.

During its second term, the Bush administration would come under intense political pressure and national and international scrutiny resulting from the fact that no weapons of mass destruction were ever uncovered in Iraq. In 2004, Secretary of State Colin Powell testified before the Senate Governmental Affairs Committee and stated that the United States received faulty intelligence regarding Iraq's possession of WMD. Powell resigned the same year and was replaced by National Security

Advisor Condoleezza Rice. The Bush administration sustained further political damage as a result of the Abu Ghraib prison scandal, which involved internationally published photographs of US military personnel abusing Iraqi inmates at prison facilities in Iraq. This scandal, combined with the raging civil violence that occurred in Iraq in the years following the invasion, resulted in the resignation of Secretary of Defense Donald Rumsfeld in December of 2006. Vice President Cheney continued to defend the decision to invade Iraq, stating that it served to prevent further terrorist attacks on the United States.

In January 2007, President Bush ordered an additional twenty thousand US troops to Iraq in an effort to quell the widespread violence in the country. The so-called "troop surge" was aimed at putting an end to the ongoing military conflict taking place against various sectarian militias. As a result of the troop surge and an increased effort on the part of US officials to make diplomatic arrangements with various militia groups, violence in Iraq and in major Iraqi cities began to subside from previous levels in the later months of 2007 and early months of 2008. Although improvements on the ground in Iraq resulted in few civilian and military deaths, the controversial nature of the planning and execution of the Iraq War remains.

Vice President Cheney's nationwide approval ratings would begin to decrease in the years following his re-election as a result of the ongoing problems in Iraq. The Bush administration also began to come under intense criticism as the subprime mortgage crisis in the United States slowly evolved into global financial crisis of 2008. The subprime mortgage crisis came about after US financial organizations had granted housing loans to customers that could not meet the terms of their mortgages. Hundreds of thousands of homeowners nationwide began to default, or fail to make payments, on their mortgages. Subsequently, evidence that major banking institutions had made risky bets on extremely complex financial products began to be uncovered. Critics of the Bush administration cited the White House's history of deregulating the financial industry as one of the causes of this problem. For the first time in decades, the federal government had to take major steps to bail out some of the nation's largest financial institutions to prevent them from collapse, an event that would have destroyed the US economy.

Impact
US Vice President Dick Cheney's second term in office ended in January of 2009. Few doubt that his support of the controversial initiation and execution of the Iraq War and the 2008 global financial crisis will remain the most significant and influential legacies of his vice presidency.

Further Reading
Bolton, John. "Dick Cheney: Conservative of the Year. (Cover Story)." *Human Events* 65.44 (2009): 1–9. Print.

Cheney, Dick, and Liz Cheney. *In My Time: A Personal and Political Memoir.* New York: Simon & Schuster, 2011. Print.

Donnelly, Sally B. et al. "7 Clues to Understanding Dick Cheney." *Time* 160.27/1 (2002): 98. Print.

Duss, Matthew. "Attack of the Cheneys." *Nation* 290.13 (2010): 11–17. Print.

Gellman, Barton. *Angler: The Cheney Vice Presidency.* New York: Penguin. 2008. Print.

Morris, Kieran. "The Other Side of Dick Cheney." *Quadrant Magazine* 56.1/2 (2012): 31–33. Print.

Eric Badertscher

■ Children on the Internet

Definition: Children's access to the Internet drastically increased during the 2000s at both home and in school, which increased concerns over censorship, cyberbullying, and developmental issues.

The sharp increase of social media and Internet access via mobile devices in the 2000s greatly transformed the lives of children, both at home and in school. Research found that children as young as two had some kind of online interaction on a home computer, smartphone, or tablet. It was typical for a middle school student to own a cell phone, with which they frequently communicated to their peers during the day. These online interactions raised several concerns over the physical and emotional development of children, the rise of cyberbullying, and desensitization.

How Children Use the Internet
The amount of content and interaction children and adults can access via the Internet is staggering. Children typically use the Internet in schools as a resource for information related to current events,

encyclopedias, and other library-related sources. However, both at school and at home children also use the Internet for communicating with friends on social networking applications such as Facebook. Although Facebook's policies require a user to be thirteen years old or over, children younger than that can simply lie about their age while signing up. Children also play games and watch movies and television shows online. The Internet allows children to click spontaneously through different content, which caters to a child's impulsive and inquisitive behavior.

The rise of mobile Internet technology during the 2000s further increased children's access to online resources and entertainment. Developments in mobile technology led to cell phones, music players, and other portable devices that were capable of connecting to the Internet. Without proper parental supervision or restrictions, a child could easily access parts of the Internet that could be inappropriate or harmful to their development. A child with an Internet-capable cell phone or smartphone could effortlessly gain access to graphic images of violence.

Concerns

Typically, there is no supervision by online moderators in chat rooms or on social networking applications. Due to the level of anonymity in chat rooms, there is no way to tell if children are communicating with others their age or with a child predator pretending to be a young person. There were several cases in the 2000s of child predators using the Internet to prey on children throughout the United States and convincing them to meet in person. Some children could also be persuaded to disclose personal information such as passwords and home addresses. Unless a parent diligently monitors all Internet activity of their children, it is extremely difficult to prevent them from talking with potentially dangerous individuals.

Impulsively clicking through the Internet can also lead children to online areas that promote hate and racism toward others. Hate groups are allowed to have their own websites just like any other organization, and they can detrimentally mislead children who do not know any better. Pornography that can cause harmful effects on a child's psyche can also be easily accessed. Video streaming websites that became popular during the 2000s, such as YouTube

and Netflix, have very loose age restrictions, so it is simple for a child to view an R-rated film without a parent knowing. Consuming this type of content at a young age can affect a child's understanding of violence and human sexuality.

The increasing amount of time children spent online during the 2000s also raised concerns that it would impede their physical and social development. While online applications such as Facebook gave children the feeling of belonging to a community, it also distanced them from actual human interaction. This raised several questions about excessive Internet and cell phone use. A study in a 2009 issue of the *Journal of Adolescent Health* found that heavy Internet use increased aggressive behavior in children. Researchers found that being away from the Internet can make children go through withdrawal symptoms such as irritability and mood swings. Studies also found connections between Internet use and depression.

A Pew Research Center study released in 2010 found that approximately 75 percent of teenagers ages twelve to seventeen owned cell phones, and on average they sent sixty text messages a day. Fifteen percent of teenage cell phone owners sent more than two hundred texts a day. Researchers stated that this affects a child's ability to focus and live in the moment, since they are always being called away by their cell phones.

Excessive use of the Internet also limits a child's time spent being physically active. Some studies found links between Internet usage and childhood obesity, which was something that became a nationwide issue during the 2000s.

Cyberbullying

The increase in accessibility to the Internet and the popularity of social networking applications such as Facebook led to a drastic rise in cyberbullying between children. Cyberbullying is the act of using various online communication devices to intentionally cause emotional harm. Throughout the decade, reports of cyberbullying became more prevalent. Because messages can be shared so easily on social networks and cell phones, it was not uncommon for the author of a harmful message to spread it throughout various online applications for a large number of their peers to see. Another form of cyberbullying—in addition to spreading rumors and inflammatory messages—is stealing the passwords of a classmate, locking the child out of his or her accounts, and posting potentially harmful messages while posing as that child.

Experts have stated that the effects of cyberbullying are similar to the emotional and psychological effects of physical bullying. Oftentimes, it is much worse, since the Internet is available every hour of the day, not just during school hours. While it is possible for a teacher or authority figure to intervene at school, research has found that most victims of cyberbullying do not report it to parents.

On October 17, 2006, thirteen-year-old Megan Meier committed suicide. Soon afterward, an investigation concluded that her death was attributed to cyberbullying on the social networking website MySpace. This tragic case led to several jurisdictions concerned with electronic harassment, and it also raised awareness of cyberbullying throughout the nation.

Controlling Access

In 2000, the US Congress enacted the Children's Internet Protection Act (CIPA). This act was created to address concerns about the exposure of children to obscene or harmful online content. The act requires schools and libraries that receive discounts for their Internet access through the Federal Communications Commission (FCC) to certify that they have an Internet safety policy. These policies must block or filter Internet access to obscene, pornographic, or any other content that could be harmful to children.

The easiest way parents can protect children from harmful content and communication on the Internet is to monitor their use and educate them on possibly negative areas. They can also teach their children to never distribute personal information, such as home addresses and passwords, no matter who the person they are communicating with claims to be. Limiting the time a child can spend online is a good way to make sure they spend more time being physically active.

The use of web filters and censorship programs became popular in the 2000s as a way to protect children online. Web filters screen websites to determine whether they are suitable to be viewed by children. They work by checking the origin or content of the website and then comparing it to the set-

tings chosen by the user. Parents typically determine these setting. Web filters can block websites containing pornographic material, objectionable advertising, and viruses. Parents can also use the web filter to look at what websites their children are visiting. Popular web filters during the 2000s included Net Nanny and CYBERsitter.

Impact

The excessive use of the Internet by children in the 2000s raised a broad range of concerns relating to physical, psychological, and emotional development. While there were many benefits of using the Internet for educational and communications purposes, many parents worried about the easy accessibility to possible harmful content. The rise in Internet use among children also saw a decline in the use of books as a source for information.

Further Reading

Good, R. Stephanie. *Exposed: The Harrowing Story of a Mother's Undercover Work with the FBI to Save Children from Internet Sex Predators.* Nashville: Nelson, 2007. Print. This book, written by a woman who, with the help of the FBI, posed as a young girl online to bait sexual predators, discusses the use of the Internet by sexual predators.

Kirsch, Steven J. *Media and Youth: A Developmental Perspective.* Malden: Wiley, 2009. Print. This Examines and critiques the research done on how media affects children's development.

Livingstone, Sonia M.. *Children and the Internet: Great Expectations, Challenging Realities.* Malden: Polity, 2009. Print. Looks at the daily use of the Internet by children in relation to the modern conditions of childhood.

MacDonald, Gregg. "Cyber-bullying Defies Traditional Stereotype." *Washington Post.* Washington Post, 2 Sept. 2010. Web. 7 Dec. 2012. Examines the rise of cyberbullying and looks at research that suggests females are more likely to cyberbully than males.

Pogue, David. "How Dangerous Is the Internet for Children?" *New York Times.* New York Times Co., 28 Feb. 2008. Web. 7 Dec. 2012. Examines whether the dangers and effects of the Internet on children are being overhyped.

Patrick G. Cooper

■ Children's Internet Protection Act of 2000

The Law: Federal law requiring public schools and libraries to use Internet content filters to qualify for discounts on the cost of Internet access

Date: December 21, 2000

Also known as: Children's Internet Protection Act; CIPA

The Children's Internet Protection Act of 2000 was designed to help provide student minors with the opportunity to conduct research on the Internet in public schools and libraries without risk of exposure to indecent material. CIPA made this possible by requiring public schools and libraries to install Internet filtering software, for which they would qualify for discounts on the cost of Internet service.

In the 1990s, as interest in and use of the Internet expanded, many public schools and libraries began to offer free Internet access to students and other users. At the same time, the amount of explicit content available online increased as well. In response, many activists called for the federal government to enact some form of legislation that would protect children from exposure to explicit content while using public computers to access the Internet.

Prior to the 2000s, Congress twice tried to enact legislation intended to address this issue. In 1996 and 1998, respectively, Congress passed the Communications Decency Act (CDA) and the Child Online Protection Act (COPA), but both of these laws were eventually struck down by the Supreme Court after they were deemed in violation of the First Amendment. The Children's Internet Protection Act, first introduced in 1999, was designed to protect young Internet users while respecting the constitutional rights of users in general.

While earlier legislation tried to criminalize the transmission of inappropriate materials via the Internet, CIPA provides an incentive for public schools and libraries to use filtering software on their computers. Specifically, CIPA states that public schools and libraries can only be eligible for federal discounts on Internet access if they employ filtering software that blocks any material that is obscene, pornographic, or otherwise inappropriate for children.

While CIPA was enacted successfully and survived the scrutiny of the Supreme Court, it had detractors. Some argued that CIPA violates the First Amendment in that it interferes with users' access to legitimate information. CIPA's opponents argued that the use of filtering software is an ineffective means of protecting children, because it often either under-blocks or over-blocks content, meaning that it may allow some explicit content to be viewable while blocking other appropriate content that it mistakenly deems inappropriate.

Impact

Though debate over the constitutionality of CIPA continued throughout the 2000s, the law remained in force. Its supporters held that it is an important tool in the effort to protect children from explicit content and provide them with a safe online environment for learning. As one of the earliest successful pieces of Web-related legislation, CIPA stood as one of the landmark achievements of Internet law.

Further Reading

Gottschalk, Lana. "Internet Filters in Public Libraries: Do They Belong?" *Library Student Journal.* Library Student Journal, Sept. 2006. Web. 7 Dec. 2012.

Rodden, Kelly. "The Children's Internet Protection Act in Public Schools: The Government Stepping on Parents' Toes?" *Fordham Law Review* 71.5 (2003): 2141–75. Print.

United States. Cong. Senate. Children's Internet Protection Act of 2000. 106th Cong. 1st sess. S 97. Washington: GPO, 1999. Print.

Jack Lasky

■ Children's literature

Definition: Also referred to as juvenile literature, children's literature is any written work—whether fiction, nonfiction, or poetry—for which the intended audience is children to the age of eighteen

Children's literature can be studied as a body of literature and as an educational tool that can support and direct learning, whether through enhancing vocabulary, teaching ethics, or establishing cultural norms. Publishers of children's literature in the first decade of the twenty-first century

utilized both of these aspects, capitalizing on educating and entertaining readers, especially through the use of technology.

Traditionally, children's literature is divided by genre and into several specific age groupings. Picture books and early readers are written for children through age seven, while chapter books are written for readers between the ages of seven and twelve. For children who are thirteen to eighteen years old, literature is typically classified as young adult (YA) fiction. While these divisions suggest an intended audience and targeted learning objectives, there is often an overlap among readers, which has become increasingly noticeable with the popularity of YA fiction among adults.

Bilingual Literature

The Spanish language has become a noticeable facet of American culture, and children's literature has been swept up in this movement. Because young minds tend to learn language quickly and easily, the push in the publishing industry to create bilingual children's books serves the educational needs of American children while acknowledging increased globalization nationwide and capitalizing on the growing population of young Spanish speakers.

Bilingual children's books are often developed in response to popular television programming that incorporates English and Spanish in its storyline. The children's television network Nickelodeon, for example, launched the cartoon *Dora the Explorer* in 2000. The title character is bilingual and taught viewers Spanish words and phrases as she maneuvered through her various adventures. *Go, Diego, Go!*, which aired on Nickelodeon from 2005 through 2011 and was a spin-off from the *Dora* series, also taught Spanish to children by incorporating the language into Diego's animal rescue missions. The Disney Channel launched *Handy Manny* in 2006, which is aimed at preschoolers and centers around the bilingual handyman Manny and his bilingual tools. Additionally, PBS television aired *Maya & Miguel* from 2004 to 2007, which followed preteen Spanish-speaking twins. Books created from children's television programs were initially part of the show's overall marketing package, but they also encouraged further learning through reading and provided bilingual education and a valuable cultural

Pam Alexander, illustrator for the Yumion series of children's books, visits the students of Berrien Elementary School. (Courtesy Judy Baxter)

reference point in an increasingly multicultural nation.

Movie Adaptations of YA Fiction

The film industry in the early 2000s was a key player in expanding the audience for children's literature. The first decade of the century witnessed trends in movie adaptations, particularly in the adaptations of serial books.

Early in 2001, New Line Cinema released *The Lord of the Rings* trilogy, based on the popular series by J. R. R. Tolkien. Although the books were first published in 1954 and 1955, the movies, which were released in 2001, 2002, and 2003, are attributed to reinvigorating book sales and cultivating an interest among readers in other science fiction and fantasy novels.

The massively popular Harry Potter series, which chronicles the lives and adventures of middle and high school witches and wizards, was published in

Newbery Medal Awards 2000–2009

2000	*Bud, Not Buddy* by Christopher Paul Curtis
2001	*A Year Down Yonder* by Richard Peck
2002	*A Single Shard* by Linda Sue Park
2003	*Crispin: The Cross of Lead* by Avi
2004	*The Tale of Despereaux: Being the Story of a Mouse, a Princess, Some Soup, and a Spool of Thread* by Kate DiCamillo
2005	*Kira-Kira* by Cynthia Kadohata
2006	*Criss Cross* by Lynne Rae Perkins
2007	*The Higher Power of Lucky* by Susan Patron
2008	*Good Masters! Sweet Ladies! Voices from a Medieval Village* by Laura Amy Schlitz
2009	*The Graveyard Book* by Neil Gaiman

Source: Carnegie Library of Pittsburgh

the US in 1998 by Scholastic. First published in the United Kingdom in 1997 by British author J. K. Rowling, the books quickly gained popularity around the world. The seven-book series continued to be published throughout the 2000s. The first movie adaptation opened in 2001, and each new release of a Harry Potter book or movie drew huge crowds. Copies of the books were preordered by the tens of thousands, and fans often costumed themselves as their favorite character when attending a book release or a movie's premier. The Harry Potter series has also been credited with inspiring and fostering an appetite for reading among readers and non-readers alike.

The Twilight Saga by Stephanie Meyer was published from 2005 through 2008. Much like the Harry Potter series, the *Twilight* fantasy books, which revel in vampire life and love, were further popularized by movie adaptations. Although the books did not cultivate a fan base as extensive as Harry Potter's, the excitement surrounding the *Twilight* movies still renewed interest in reading.

Not all movie adaptations of YA fiction were as commercially successful. In 2004, Brad Silberling directed an adaptation of Lemony Snicket's *A Series of Unfortunate Events* books. Although the book series

was popular among children and critics alike, the adaptation enjoyed mediocre success.

The relationship between films and books has been constant for decades. Yet, while previous eras of filmmaking have emphasized fairy tales, crime novels, or other genres, the 2000s captured the energy of serial stories that were geared toward teens. In targeting this group, film producers and book publishers were able to benefit from each other while simultaneously expanding their audience to include younger children and adults.

Expanding the Audience for Children's Literature

Adult interest in children's literature, particularly in YA fiction, grew dramatically during the early years of the twenty-first century. Book club members, for instance, began reading and discussing books originally written for a teen audience. The line that previously determined a book's targeted age range began to blur, and debates ensued surrounding what the general public versus what the publishing industry considered appropriate content for younger readers. Discussions of appropriateness in literature often focused on the moral legitimacy of denying adult content to younger readers as opposed to the marketing potential of YA fiction with added content adults could relate to. Another debate has centered on whether adults are limiting themselves and their potential for intellectual growth by reading YA fiction and whether publishers are more concerned with profits than they are in producing quality books with age-appropriate content and writing style.

While adults have been drawn to the Harry Potter books and *The Twilight Saga*, book clubs for adults have also received considerable attention for their interest in *The Hunger Games* by Suzanne Collins. Published in 2008, the book leans heavily on the mature topics of war and poverty, but its simple style, language, and sentence structure placed it in the YA fiction genre. As long as books like *The Hunger Games* are shelved in libraries and bookstores in both the YA and adult fiction sections, concerns will continue as to what qualifies a book to be more appropriate for children or adults.

Impact

While television and film have expanded the audience for children's literature, the legacy of the 2000s continues in electronic books, or e-books. Publishers tend to favor e-books for their cost efficiency, which also allows any individual or company to produce an e-book without relying on the publishing industry to create and distribute printed material. Additionally, by providing access to books in new formats, e-books can enhance the reading experience through links to activities to further learning or to other books. On the other hand, e-books cannot replicate the tactile quality of printed books, which many educators believe is vitally important to early reading development.

The increased interplay between reading and technology defines literature of the early twenty-first century. While offering access to stories in new formats and in various media serves to expand the size and age range of the audience, many argue that quality of content is compromised. Critics of e-books for children cite enhancements to books as distractions that inhibit adult/child interaction in reading and thus inhibit language development. Furthermore, readers themselves often criticize movie adaptations of their favorite books for neglecting to include plot points and characters and for providing a much less rewarding experience. While the early 2000s have confirmed the symbiotic relationship between children's literature and technology, the ultimate benefactor of this convergence remains to be seen.

Further Reading

Donahoo, Daniel. "Improving Children's Literature in Digital Spaces." *Huffington Post*. TheHuffingtonPost.com, Inc., 17 July 2012. Web. 26 Nov. 2012. Discusses the challenges posed by creating and distributing children's literature in digital formats. Focuses on the quality of content.

Lerer, Seth. *Children's Literature: A Reader's History from Aesop to Harry Potter*. Chicago: U of Chicago P, 2008. Print. Chronicles the historical shaping of children's literature from some of its earliest records through the 2000s.

Nikolajeva, Maria. *Aesthetic Approaches to Children's Literature: An Introduction*. Lanham: Scarecrow, 2005. Print. Acknowledges the shift in studying children's literature from the context of education to literary studies. Offers an examination of children's literature through the eyes of adults using literary theory and aesthetics.

"The Power of Young Adult Fiction." *New York Times* 28 Mar. 2012. Web. 26 Nov. 2012. Several published writers debate the merits and detractions of adults reading young adult fiction.

Reynolds, Kimberly. *Children's Literature: A Very Short Introduction*. New York: Oxford UP, 2011. Print. Provides context for the study of children's literature, highlighting the topics of publishing, genre, and ethics.

Zipes, Jack. *The Enchanted Screen: The Unknown History of Fairy-Tale Films*. New York: Routledge, 2011. Print. Examines the growth of film adaptations of classic fairy tales from the early 1900s through the early 2000s.

Lucia Pizzo

■ Chrétien, Jean

Identification: Canadian politician and prime minister of Canada, 1993–2003
Born: January 11, 1934; Shawinigan, Quebec, Canada

Jean Chrétien was the twentieth prime minister of Canada. As a member of the Liberal Party and an anti-separatist, he was instrumental in preventing the secession of Quebec from mainland Canada.

Jean Chrétien, the successful and popular leader of Canada's Liberal Party, helped the Liberals win a resounding majority over the Progressive Conservative Party in 1993. Shortly thereafter, Chrétien defeated Brian Mulroney to become Canada's twentieth prime minister. The Liberal Party remained in power throughout most of Chrétien's term, mostly because the Progressive Conservative Party had weakened and no other parties posed a legitimate threat. At the end of the 1990s, the Canadian Alliance Party became a realistic opponent of the dominant Liberal Party.

Chrétien called for a surprise election in 2000, giving the Canadian Alliance little time to prepare a campaign. In these elections, Chrétien and the Liberals won by a landslide, and he became the first prime minister since 1945 to win a third consecutive majority.

Jean Chrétien. (Courtesy Tourisme Mauricie)

The last years of Chrétien's term, however, were marked by government scandals and bad publicity. A series of allegations regarding the misappropriation of funds were made against the Liberal Party. It was eventually uncovered that Chrétien's minister of finance, Alfonse Gagliano, was at the center of two major financial scandals.

Rumors of Chrétien's intended retirement began to circulate and numerous members of the Liberal Party announced that they would run for prime minister. By 2002, excitement within the party began to impede government business. Chrétien became frustrated with his colleagues, and demanded they set aside their personal campaigns.

When the United States invaded Iraq in 2003, President George W. Bush encouraged Chrétien to provide Canadian troops. Chrétien refused to involve Canada in the Iraq War, on the grounds that the United Nations Security Council would not authorize the war. Although Canadian citizens generally supported Chrétien's decision not to enlist Canadian troops, Chrétien became unpopular with the US government.

With his support dwindling, his international reputation damaged, and his peers anxious to take his job, Chrétien announced that he would retire as prime minister at the end of 2003. Voters elected Paul Martin, his one-time collaborator and long-time rival, in his place. On December 12, 2003, Chrétien officially resigned.

After leaving public office, Chrétien took a position at a law firm, Heenan Blaikie. In 2005 the Gomery Commission investigated the federal sponsorship scandal that allegedly took place between 1996 and 2004. The commission reported that although the former prime minister was not guilty of direct wrongdoing, he and his staff were responsible for misspending public funds and fraud. A later Federal Court ruling in 2008 found that the Gomery Commission may have been biased against Chrétien and he was able to recoup some of his legal expenses. Chrétien published his memoir, *My Years as Prime Minister*, in 2007.

Impact

Though Chrétien left office in the midst of a period marked by scandal and waning public approval of his administration, the former prime minister left a legacy of successful political ventures His early years as prime minister were marked by fiscal accomplishments like eliminating the deficit and lowering the federal debt. His efforts to prevent the secession of Quebec resulted in the passing of important legislation for managing future referendums on Quebec's sovereignty.

Further Reading

Barry, Donald. "Chrétien, Bush, And The War In Iraq." *American Review Of Canadian Studies* 35.2 (2005): 215–45. Print.

Chrétien, Jean. *My Years as Prime Minister*. Toronto: Knopf, 2007. Print.

"Jean Chrétien." *CBC News Canada*. CBC, 13 July 2009. Web. 29 Oct. 2012.

Richard Means

■ Cincinnati riots of 2001

The Event: Four days of riots stemming from years of racial tensions between Cincinnati police officers and community members
Date: April 9–12, 2001
Place: Cincinnati, Ohio

The Cincinnati riots of 2001 turned the city upside down and pitted city officials and police officers against community members. After four days of riots and millions of dollars in damages, the city tried to put its community back together. However, violence and crime continued to plague the city for some time afterward.

On April 7, 2001, white Cincinnati police officer Stephen Roach shot and killed African American suspect Timothy Thomas. The nineteen-year-old, who had fourteen warrants, fled from police officers. When Roach caught Thomas in an alley, he claimed that the suspect reached for a gun, which resulted in Roach shooting him. Thomas later died, and police discovered that the teenager was unarmed and that the warrants were for traffic violations. He was the fifteenth African American killed by the Cincinnati police department in six years.

A month before this incident, the Cincinnati Police Division was accused of racial profiling in a lawsuit filed by more than thirty African Americans. They accused the department of years of abuse and mistreatment, dating back to the 1960s. On April 9, 2001, protesters, angered by Thomas's death, packed a council meeting. The crowd then continued their protest in the streets. Soon afterward, calls came in for police assistance as the protest turned into a riot.

Two days passed, and the violence continued. By April 11, hundreds were jailed and hundreds more were injured. Fires continued to burn while looting and property damage increased. The riots attracted the attention of the media, which warned people to avoid Cincinnati. After rioters shot a police officer on the night of April 11, Mayor Charles Luken issued a state of emergency and imposed a curfew. The violence stopped by April 13, enabling city officials to begin assessing the damage.

Impact

Fear of another riot caused Cincinnati police to withdraw from problematic areas of the city after the 2001 riots; crime and violence overtook those neighborhoods. Daytime shootings and drug deals increased as the police ignored criminal activities. Another shooting and other incidents threatened the city during the following months.

Although the city remained divided in many ways, officials focused on improving police training and updating equipment to prevent similar situations and to repair the relationship between government officials and residents. In addition, the Citizens Complaint Authority was created in 2002 to review serious uses of force by police officers. Data from the organization showed a decrease in the number of complaints against officers in the years following the riots.

Further Reading

Horn, Dan. "Cincinnati: 2001 Year of Unrest." *Cincinnati Enquirer.* Gannett Co. Inc., 30 Dec. 2001. Web. 15 Aug. 2012.

Moore, Dan P. *Mark Twain Was Right: The 2001 Cincinnati Riots.* Lansing, KS: Microcosm, 2012. Print.

Predergast, Jane. "2001 Riots Led to Top-Down Change for Cincinnati Police." *USA Today.* Gannett Co. Inc., 3 Apr. 2011. Web. 15 Aug. 2012.

Angela Harmon

■ Clarkson, Kelly

Identification: American singer and songwriter
Born: April 24, 1982; Fort Worth, Texas

Clarkson won the first American Idol *reality-television singing competition in 2002, and has since become of one of the world's leading pop singers.*

Kelly Clarkson came to national prominence when she won the first season of the reality television singing competition *American Idol* in 2002. The song Clarkson sang on the show's season finale, "A Moment Like This," moved fifty-one spots on the Billboard Hot 100 chart to reach number one. The song broke a Billboard Hot 100 record set by the Beatles' song, "Can't Buy Me Love," which moved twenty-six spots to number one in 1964.

"A Moment Like This" was a featured track on Clarkson's first album, *Thankful,* which was released in 2003. The album went double platinum, selling more than two million copies. Clarkson's next album, *Breakaway* (2004), sold more than twelve million copies worldwide. The album remained at number one on the Billboard chart for more than two years, and produced five Top 10 songs, including "Since U Been Gone" and "Because of You."

In 2006, Clarkson won two Grammy Awards: Best Female Pop Vocal Performance and Best Pop Vocal Album. Later that year, she won Best Female Video at the MTV Video Music Awards for "Because of You," which was inspired by her parents' divorce when she was sixteen. Clarkson's 2007 album, titled *My December*, sold more than one million copies.

In 2009, Clarkson's album *All I Ever Wanted* debuted at the top spot on Billboard's Top 200 chart. She returned to *American Idol* in January of that year to perform her single "My Life Would Suck Without You," which reached the number-one spot on Billboard's Hot 100 chart in February 2009.

Impact

Clarkson's win on the first season of *American Idol* and subsequent chart-topping music sales helped establish the viability of the reality television talent competition format in the United States. Although some industry analysts have criticized the accuracy of show's voting process, and the contractual details of music deals earned by its winners, which require that the show's producers receive a share of sales revenue, *American Idol* has had a significant impact on the popular music industry, establishing a new platform through which aspiring musical artists earn exposure to larger audiences. While the show's viewing audiences have decreased since its prime in the 2000s, its impact on popular culture, television programming, and the music industry continues to be felt.

Further Reading

Bronson, Fred. "American Idol's Tenth Anniversary: Kelly Clarkson's Journey to 73 Billboard Chart Toppers." *Billboard* 11 June 2012. Web. 6 July 2012.

Hinkley, David. "'American Idol' Impact: More Pop Hits." *New York Daily News* 24 Jan. 2008. Web. 11 July 2012.

Tracy, Kathleen. *Kelly Clarkson*. Hockessin: Mitchell, 2007. Print.

Gina Kuchta

■ Classical music

Definition: Western sacred and secular music from the medieval period onward, including modern music rooted in a classical-music style

As with the music industry in general, the classical-music industry was thrust into turmoil by the transition to online digital music and, to a lesser extent, the economic recession that began in 2008. While recovering, the industry expanded in new directions with technology-based projects and an abundance of American ingenuity and talent.

The first decade of the twenty-first century represented an unsettling time for the classical-music industry, as the transition to MP3s and online file sharing weakened CD sales and caused the demise of many traditional music retailers. The economic recession hurt school music programs and orchestras as tax dollars to fund the arts fell short. The bright side, however, was that the shift to MP3s, the development of music streaming and downloading sites such as iTunes, and the expansion of online social networking and music resources attracted a new and relatively young audience of classical music fans. One highlight of the digital transformation was the first YouTube collaborative online orchestra, founded in 2009. The entertainment site brought together ninety-six youthful (or young at heart) musicians from thirty countries to perform at Carnegie Hall in New York City. The event was the first time a symphony orchestra recruited musicians from online auditions, and it inspired Tan Dun's Internet Symphony no. 1 (*Eroica*) a piece performed at the concert.

American composers responded to defining events of the decade. John Adams wrote the moving composition *On the Transmigration of Souls* to commemorate the September 11, 2001, attacks on the World Trade Center. Adams's original opera, *Doctor*

Yo-Yo Ma (right) and Itzhak Perlman. (Courtesy Penn State News)

Atomic, represented a compositional trend toward operas about historic American events or important cultural works and helped rejuvenate opera.

Other musicians who made lasting contributions during the decade included cellist Yo-Yo Ma, known especially for his many crossover collaborations and as the founder of the Silk Road Ensemble, a collective of musicians from more than twenty countries, and Steve Reich, winner of the 2009 Pulitzer Prize for Music for *Double Sextet.*

The 2000s can also be viewed as a significant decade for women in classical music, with lasting contributions made by composers Jennifer Higdon (*City Scape*, Concerto for Orchestra, and Violin Concerto) and Joan Tower (*Made in America*), soprano Renée Fleming, and violinist Hilary Hahn. The latter two are known for their stunning interpretations of classical music.

Impact

The shift to online digital music and the many related technological advancements in audio and electronics during the decade changed the way classical music was composed, recorded, and listened to. This transformation resulted in new talent, innovative compositions, and pioneering collaborations such as the Silk Road Ensemble, one of the most significant examples of multicultural collaboration in the history of music. While the canon of European music remains popular, rich new sounds emerged during the decade that diluted the emphasis on music from the baroque or romantic periods and inspired musicians throughout the world to contribute to the heritage of classical music.

Further Reading

Lebrecht, Norman. "Post Mortem." *The Life and Death of Classical Music.* New York: Anchor, 2007. Print.

Midgette, Anne. "Best of the Decade: Classical Music." *Washington Post* 27 Dec. 2009. Web. 9 Oct. 2012.

Sally Driscoll

■ Clinton, Hillary Rodham

Identification: The sixty-seventh secretary of state of the United States

Born: October 26, 1947; Chicago, Illinois

Hillary Rodham Clinton served as the secretary of state of the United States from January 2009 through January 2013. Clinton served as a Democratic senator from 2001 until 2009, representing New York. After winning a senate seat, she became the first former first lady of the United States to be elected to national office.

Hillary Diane Rodham was born in Chicago, Illinois, on October 26, 1947. In 1965, Rodham enrolled in Wellesley College, where she majored in political science with a minor in psychology. She graduated in 1969 with high honors. Rodham went on to Yale Law School, where she began to identify more strongly with the Democratic Party. During her time at Yale, Rodham met Bill Clinton, a fellow student from Arkansas. Although the two dated as students, they went their separate ways after graduating in 1973: Rodham to Washington, DC, and Clinton to Arkansas. But in 1974, Rodham accepted a teaching position at the University of Arkansas Law School.

Hillary Rodham married Bill Clinton on October 11, 1975. They relocated to Little Rock when Bill Clinton became the Arkansas attorney general, and Hillary Clinton was made a partner in the Rose Law Firm. She became first lady of Arkansas when her husband was elected to his first term as governor in 1978. She gave birth to the couple's daughter, Chelsea, in 1980. Then, in 1992, she became first lady of the United States when Bill Clinton was elected president, defeating incumbent George H. W. Bush.

Senator of New York

In 1999, as her husband's second term as president was about to expire, Clinton announced her candidacy for the US Senate, representing the state of New York. In January 2000, she moved from Washington, DC, in order to meet the residency requirement for the position. The Clintons bought a home in Chappaqua, New York. Although she was criticized by some for not being a New York native, Clinton went on to win the general election, after facing off against Rudolph Giuliani, the former mayor of New York City, and Republican representative Rick Lazio. Clinton was sworn in as senator on January 3, 2001.

During Senator Clinton's first term in office, she focused on serving the people of New York City in the wake of the economic and emotional damage caused by the September 11 terrorist attacks of

*Secretary of State Hillary Rodham Clinton and President Mintimer Sharipo-
vich Shaimiev of Tatarstan at the Presidential Palace in Kazan, October 2009.*
(U.S. Department of State)

2001. In December 2001, Clinton worked to guide a
bill through the Senate allowing a one-time, thir-
teen-week extension on unemployment benefits. In
June 2003, Clinton published *Living History*, a
memoir of her life and career. The book became an
instant bestseller, with sales of more than one million copies in its first month of release. During the
Thanksgiving season of 2003, Senator Clinton visited US troops that were stationed in Iraq and Afghanistan. Senator Clinton also stood by her husband Bill Clinton as he underwent successful bypass
surgery in 2004. In 2005, Senator Clinton was in-
ducted into the National Women's Hall of Fame.
She was reelected to the Senate in 2006.

2008 Democratic Presidential Primaries

In January 2007, Clinton officially announced her
candidacy for the 2008 presidential election. She
hoped to become the first woman in US history to
gain the nomination of a major political party. As a
candidate, Clinton touted her experience in the
White House as first lady for eight years and as a
senator over the last seven years. In the beginning
of the contest for the 2008 Democratic Party nomination, it was viewed to be a race between three politicians: Clinton, Senator Barack Obama of Illinois,
and former senator John Edwards of North Caro-

lina. Clinton placed third in the 2008
Democratic Party caucus in Iowa, earning
approximately 29.5 percent of the vote.
She won the 2008 New Hampshire Democratic primary, earning 39 percent of the
vote. Clinton also placed first in the Nevada caucus, earning just over 50 percent
of the vote. Clinton earned another victory in the Florida primary.

The 2008 "Super Tuesday" primaries
and caucuses were held on February 5, in
which twenty-two states voted. Clinton
won Arkansas, Arizona, California, Massachusetts, New Jersey, New Mexico, New
York, Oklahoma, and Tennessee. Victories in these states resulted in Clinton
pulling ahead in the overall delegate
count. Barack Obama won several states
on February 5th as well, however. Clinton
placed second behind Obama in the primaries held mid-February in Louisiana,
the District of Columbia, Maryland, and
Virginia. Victories in these contests put
Obama ahead in the overall delegate count. In
Democratic Party primaries held on March 4,
Clinton won Texas, Ohio, and Rhode Island. Obama
won in Vermont. Although Obama retained his lead
in the overall delegate count, these victories were
significant for the Clinton campaign. Many analysts
suggested that without victories in Ohio and Texas,
her campaign would have to end.

Clinton and Obama remained locked in a close
race for the 2008 Democratic Party presidential nomination after Edwards left the race. Despite the fact
that some analysts had begun to call for Clinton to
leave the race, stressing the importance of party unity,
she won the Pennsylvania primary held on April 22 by
more than 9 percentage points. Clinton also won the
May 6 primary in Indiana. However, Obama won the
May 6 primary in North Carolina. Many analysts
began to speculate that Obama had become the likely
Democratic Party nominee given the number of delegates he had earned through May. Nonetheless,
Clinton pledged to continue fighting on. Regardless
of the speculation, it became clear that Democratic
Party "superdelegates"—or party officials who hold a
vote for the nomination—would be crucial in the
process of selecting the final candidate.

Clinton won the May 13 primary in West Virginia
and the May 20 primary in Kentucky. However, she

lost the Oregon primary to Obama, which was also held on May 20. Obama's campaign stated that their victory in Oregon clinched the number of necessary delegates needed to win the Democratic nomination. Many media analysts stated that despite the Clinton campaign's persistency, the nomination was at that point all but decided. However, Puerto Rico, Montana, and South Dakota had yet to hold their primaries. Clinton vowed to stay in the race for the nomination until every primary election was held.

Controversy remained over whether or not the Democratic Party would opt to include voting results from Florida and Michigan, the states that went against party rules and voted at a date earlier than scheduled. Clinton, who won both states, continued to ask that those votes be counted instead of dismissed, though Obama was not listed as a candidate on Michigan's ballot and refrained from campaigning in Florida altogether.

On May 31, 2008, Democratic Party officials met to vote on how the results of the Florida and Michigan primaries would be tallied. It was decided at that meeting that delegates from each state would be counted, but would count for only a half vote each at the nominating convention. The decision was widely viewed as a heavy blow to the Clinton campaign, because it essentially finalized the determination that Obama would earn the majority of delegates nationwide.

On June 1, 2008, Clinton won the Democratic primary in Puerto Rico. On June 3, in the final two primaries of the 2008 nominating season, Obama won Montana while Clinton won in South Dakota. Nonetheless, Obama's victory in Montana helped to further establish his lead in the overall delegate count. Obama publicly announced that he had secured the nomination on June 3, 2008. Despite Obama's announcement, the Clinton campaign did not immediately announce its withdrawal from the race for the nomination, nor did it recognize Obama's claim to victory. However, with no more primaries scheduled and the official decision on Florida and Michigan made, few options remained for the Clinton campaign. On June 7, Clinton officially ended her campaign for the 2008 Democratic Party presidential nomination. In a speech delivered in Washington, DC, Clinton paid tribute to her supporters and stated that her historic campaign had helped make the idea of a woman as a serious presidential contender a reality. In addition, Clinton congratulated Barack Obama and campaigned nationwide prior to his election as president on November 4, 2008.

Secretary of State

President-elect Barack Obama nominated Clinton as his secretary of state on December 1, 2008. She officially assumed the role on January 21, 2009, and made her first diplomatic tour in Asia in February. Secretary of State Clinton has maintained vocal criticism of North Korea's and Iran's aims to further develop their nuclear technology.

In August 2009, Secretary of State Clinton embarked on a multinational tour of Africa. She met President Sharif Sheikh Ahmed of Somalia and stressed the importance of stabilizing that country in the effort to prevent the development of terrorist organizations. Clinton also visited Kenya, Liberia, and the Democratic Republic of Congo. Among the issues she discussed in public during her tour of Africa was the need to maintain the supply of humanitarian and economic aid to the continent. Clinton was also active in efforts to address global food shortages. She was largely responsible for advancing the Quadrennial Diplomacy and Development Review to regularly review US foreign policy initiatives.

Impact

At odds with conservative critics since her days as first lady of Arkansas, Clinton's determination to retain her own identity while sharing the spotlight with her husband, former President Bill Clinton, has earned her both respect and criticism. As an experienced attorney and legislator, Clinton has been a staunch proponent of women's and children's rights. Her work in the Senate, on the presidential campaign trail, and as secretary of state has inspired many women to pursue politics. In 2009, for the fifth time in her career, Clinton was listed among the one hundred most influential people in the world by *Time* magazine.

Further Reading

Gates, Robert. "Hillary Clinton." *Time* 179.17 (2012): 155–57. Print.

Sklar, Kathryn Kish. "A Women's History Report Card on Hillary Rodham Clinton's Presidential Primary Campaign, 2008." *Feminist Studies* 34.1/2 (2008): 315–22. Print.

Westfall, Sandra Sobieraj. "Hillary Rodham Clinton: On the Road Again . . . and Again." *People* 4 Apr. 2011: 84–88. Print.

Donna Norman

■ Clooney, George

Identification: American actor, director, producer, and activist
Born: May 6, 1961; Lexington, Kentucky

Though Clooney made a big impression as Dr. Doug Ross in the television series ER *during the 1990s, he shifted the focus of his career to films in the 2000s. His success at the box office made him a Hollywood icon. In addition to his work as an actor, Clooney has also worked as a producer and director. Clooney has also leveraged his celebrity status to bring attention to various political issues and humanitarian causes.*

Film Career

As an actor, George Clooney has played a variety of roles, including a superhero, fisherman, and escaped convict. His 2000 performance in the musical comedy *O Brother, Where Art Thou?* was a commercial and critical success. Written and directed by Joel and Ethan Coen, the film is a Depression-era adaptation of Homer's *Odyssey*. Clooney plays a convict who leads a group of fellow escapees to his hidden loot. His performance earned him a Golden Globe Award for Best Actor.

In 2001, Clooney starred with Matt Damon, Brad Pitt, and Julia Roberts in the blockbuster film *Ocean's Eleven*, a remake of a film originally released in 1960. Clooney plays Danny Ocean, who helps organize a casino heist. Clooney also stars in the film's two sequels, *Ocean's Twelve* (2004) and *Ocean's Thirteen* (2007). Clooney received praise for his role as the captain of a doomed fishing boat in *The Perfect Storm* (2000), which costarred Mark Wahlberg and Diane Lane.

Clooney won the Academy Award for best supporting actor for his work in the thriller *Syriana* (2004), his first high-profile success as an executive producer. He suffered a serious head injury during filming, however, and underwent surgery to relieve excruciating headaches. In 2005, Clooney received Oscar nominations for best director and best original

George Clooney. (©iStockphoto.com/Jason Merritt)

screenplay for *Good Night, and Good Luck*. He also acted in the film. Clooney received an Academy Award nomination for best actor for his work in *Michael Clayton* in 2007, and was nominated again in 2009 for *Up in the Air*. As one of the best-known actors in Hollywood, Clooney has made numerous television appearances, and appeared regularly on the cover of entertainment and fashion magazines. In addition to media interest in his romantic involvements, his name has been included several times on *People* magazine lists of top bachelors and sexiest men. From 1989 to 1993, he was married to actress Talia Balsam; he has no children.

Humanitarian Works

Since becoming a successful actor, Clooney has been a vocal supporter of various political and social issues and humanitarian efforts. Clooney helped organize the benefit concert and telethon *America: A Tribute to Heroes* following the September 11, 2001, terrorist attacks in the United States. The telethon raised more than $150 million for victims.

In 2006, the actor and his father, journalist Nick Clooney, made the documentary film *A Journey to Darfur*. During a dangerous nine-day trip to the Darfur region of Sudan, the pair filmed victims of the country's civil war who were living without food, water, or shelter. The film tells the story of villages where wells were poisoned and women were raped by members of the militia fighting against the government. *A Journey to Darfur*, which also detailed the efforts of humanitarian aid workers, aired in 2007 on the AmericanLife TV Network.

Clooney and his father donated money for several projects in the Sudan, including projects designed to dig new wells and provide housing. Clooney has continued to use his celebrity status to bring attention to humanitarian crises and encourage politicians to commit resources to such causes.

With Don Cheadle, Matt Damon, Brad Pitt, David Pressman, and Jerry Weintraub, he cofounded Not On Our Watch (NOOW) in 2007. The nonprofit organization works to stop genocide and support human rights in such places as Burma, Darfur, and Zimbabwe. NOOW has provided humanitarian aid to Darfur, working with the United Nations (UN) World Food Programme; before NOOW provided funds for helicopters and planes, the UN aid program in Darfur was nearly shut down because trucks were being hijacked on the region's unsecure roads. Clooney has also visited Darfur and Chad with UN representatives to draw attention to the plight of millions of people killed or displaced by the region's civil war. In 2010, he cofounded the Satellite Sentinel Project, aimed at using satellite images to detect and draw attention to atrocities in Sudan as they arise.

Impact
Once a well-known and popular television actor, Clooney has become one of the most famous and successful movie stars of his generation. He has become as well known for his films as for his work with politicians and aid organizations on the problems of violence and development in the Darfur region of Sudan. In 2011, he received an Academy Award nomination for best actor for his role in the *The Descendants*.

Further Reading
Avlon, John. "Clooney's Not Kidding: Actor Adds 'Arrested Activist' to Credit Roll." *Daily Beast.* Newsweek/Daily Beast, 20 Feb. 2011. Web. 11 July 2012.
"Our Story." *Satellite Sentinel Project.* Center for American Progress, 2012. Web. 11 July 2012.
Potts, Kimberly. *George Clooney: The Last Great Movie Star.* Rev. ed. New York, Applause, 2011. Print.
Thomson, Katherine. "George Clooney, Brad Pitt, Pax and Maddox at Venice Film Festival." *Huffington Post.* TheHuffingtonPost.com, 26 Aug. 2008. Web. 11 July 2012.
"Who We Are." *Not On Our Watch.* Not On Our Watch, n.d. Web. 11 July 2012.

Josephine Campbell

■ Cloud computing

Definition: The ability to access shared content and computing resources from anywhere via the Internet

Cloud computing enables computing resources to be accessed from anywhere and on any compatible device. The practice became popular during the 2000s due to widespread Internet access and the rise in popularity of mobile devices such as smartphones.

Cloud computing represents a shift away from the need to install software applications on local machines. At its most basic level, cloud computing uses the Internet to share computing resources—such as memory, storage, and processing power—and provide access to applications, data, and services from anywhere, on any device. The defining characteristics of cloud computing are: Internet accessibility, resource configurability, multitenancy (one software instance serving many users), broad authentication, subscription options, self-service features, and accessibility from anywhere.

Internet retailer Amazon helped popularize the use of cloud-based infrastructure as a service (IaaS). After realizing that its data centers had significant unused capacity, the company developed a system to distribute the processing power of its servers, allowing for usage-based scaling. In 2004, Amazon released a version of this system—called Amazon Web Services, or AWS—to the public, making it possible for anyone to establish a cloud network. By June 2007, Amazon reported that 330,000 users had signed up for AWS. IaaS enables companies to create clouds of their own, while platform as a service (PaaS) offerings like the Google App Engine (GAE, released 2008) simplify the process of deploying cloud applications.

The most common conception of cloud computing is software as a service (SaaS), which refers to the cloud applications that end users access. SaaS includes web-based e-mail services such as Microsoft's Hotmail (released in 1996) and Google's Gmail (2004); distributed customer relationship management (CRM) systems such as NetSuite (1998) and Salesforce (1999); web-based content development and sharing applications such as Google Apps (2004); and media streaming services such as Hulu, Netflix, and Pandora. Another popular use for the cloud is as a data backup service, enabled by SaaS applications such as Dropbox (2007) and Microsoft SkyDrive (2007).

Although many cloud applications achieved notable consumer popularity, gaining millions of users, businesses were slower to adopt cloud models. Only 2 percent of companies used PaaS in 2009. However, another survey found that 57 percent of companies were planning to make strategic cloud investments in 2009, demonstrating interest if not active usage.

Despite its uses and popularity, people have expressed concerns about cloud computing adoption. One concern is the lack of control over the infrastructure, particularly in terms of data ownership and security. Another concern regards the openness and interoperability of cloud services developed by various corporations.

Impact

Cloud computing made accessing data and services from any device faster, easier, and better synchronized, improving personal and professional computing for millions of people and allowing the rapid launch of new software companies in the 2000s. As a result, the ability to access personal information and services from anywhere became an expectation for many Americans.

Further Reading

Benioff, Marc, and Carlye Adler *Behind the Cloud: The Untold Story of How Salesforce.com Went from Idea to Billion-Dollar Company—and Revolutionized an Industry*. San Francisco: Wiley, 2009. Print.

Koulopoulos, Thomas M. *Cloud Surfing: A New Way to Think About Risk, Innovation, Scale and Success*. Brookline, MA: Bibliomotion, 2012. Print.

Nielsen, Lars. *The Little Book of Cloud Computing*. 2012 ed. Wickford, RI: New Street Communications, 2012. eBook.

Kerry Skemp, MA

■ The Colbert Report

Identification: Satirical news program hosted by faux conservative Stephen Colbert
Executive Producer: Stephen Colbert (b. 1964)
Date: Premiered on October 17, 2005

The Colbert Report, *a spin-off of the popular comedy news program* The Daily Show with Jon Stewart, *includes interviews with politicians and celebrity guests as well as commentary from faux-conservative host Stephen Colbert.*

After developing his character on *The Daily Show*, Colbert got his chance to host his own comedy news program in 2005 when Comedy Central started airing *The Colbert Report*. While creating his on-air persona—an extremely patriotic, right-wing conservative—Colbert and his staff looked to popular cable news hosts for inspiration. The television personality that had the most influence on Colbert was Bill O'Reilly, the conservative Fox News host of *The O'Reilly Factor*.

While news and politics were the main focus of the show, Colbert also discussed cultural and entertainment headlines. The show, which was a companion to the popular *Daily Show*, quickly became a hit with critics and fans, the latter of which became referred to as the Colbert Nation. Colbert also managed to attract many high-profile guests from various fields. His political guests have included Barney Frank, Madeline Albright, Nancy Pelosi, and even President Barack Obama. Colbert has also interviewed legendary newscasters, such as Tom Brokaw and Charlie Rose, as well as many celebrities, including Jane Fonda and Conan O'Brien. Even the man who inspired Colbert's character, Bill O'Reilly, appeared on the show. Although the show is a satire, Colbert and his team received several major awards during the 2000s, including an Emmy Award and a Peabody Award in 2008.

Stephen Colbert (left) and Jeff Tweedy perform at the Comedy Central "Rally to Restore Sanity And/Or Fear," (©iStockphoto.com/Chip Somodevilla)

Impact

The Colbert Report had a real impact on American culture and politics during the decade. Colbert ran a fake campaign for the 2008 presidential nomination in 2007, but it only lasted a few weeks. Still, the satirical show's influence was felt in many arenas. Colbert found success in the literary world when his book *I Am America (And So Can You!)* spent thirteen weeks at the top of the New York Times Best Sellers list in 2007. The show and its host have been the subjects of multiple scholarly essays, and *The Colbert Report* has even been credited with encouraging young people to take an interest in politics.

Further Reading

Colbert, Stephen. *I Am America (And So Can You!)*. New York: Grand Central, 2007. Print.

Daly, Steven. "Stephen Colbert: The Second Most Powerful Idiot in America." *Telegraph* [London]. Telegraph Media Group Ltd., 18 May 2008. Web. 10 Aug. 2012.

Kain, Ed. "Stephen Colbert's Real Advantage: Free Air Time." *The Atlantic.* The Atlantic Monthly Group, 17 Jan. 2012. Web. 7 Aug. 2012.

Rebecca Sparling

■ Coldplay

Definition: British alternative rock band

Coldplay was one of the first alternative rock bands to reach worldwide commercial success in the new millennium. The group's distinctive yet accessible sound has garnered its members a massive fan base. Paired with its commercial success, the group's popularity has been compared to that of longtime rock-n-roll heavyweights U2 and Radiohead.

Newly signed to the music label Parlophone, Coldplay finished recording their debut album, *Parachutes,* in early 2000 at Parr Street Studios in

Liverpool, England. The single "Yellow" was released soon after and quickly climbed the charts in both the United Kingdom and the United States. The full album was released in July of 2000 in the United Kingdom and was an instant hit. The album was also a commercial success in the United States and won the Grammy Award for Best Alternative Music Album in 2001.

The band followed *Parachutes* with *A Rush of Blood to the Head* in August of 2002. Songs like "Clocks" and "The Scientist" were played consistently on radio stations around the globe. The album won the group its second Grammy Award for Best Alternative Music Album. "In My Place," a hit single from the album, won a Grammy Award for Best Rock Performance, while the song "Clocks" won a Grammy for Record of the Year in 2003.

After releasing *A Rush of Blood to the Head*, the band embarked on a global tour, releasing a live recording titled *Live 2003* later that year. In December of 2003, front man Chris Martin married actress Gwyneth Paltrow, giving the band an unexpected boost in publicity.

Soon after the birth of Martin and Paltrow's daughter, Apple, the band started recording their third album in the spring of 2004. They released the hit single "Speed of Sound" a year later, and the full album, titled *X&Y*, was released in June of 2005. The record produced several hits including "Fix You" and "Talk," and it sold more than eight million copies in its first year.

It took Coldplay another three years to complete their fourth record, *Viva la Vida*, which released in June of 2008. They began recording in late 2006, collaborating with unconventional producer Brian Eno. The album was their most experimental to date. Despite the divergence, the album sold more than six million copies in five months and won the Grammy Award for Best Rock Album in 2008. The title track hit number one on the charts and also won a Grammy Award for Song of the Year in 2009. Coldplay went on another worldwide tour after the album's release. When the tour ended, they returned to England and began recording their fifth album.

Impact

Despite their highly lucrative career, the members of Coldplay never adopted the explosive persona typically associated with rock stardom. The band members instead project a down-to-earth attitude and

involve themselves in various activist issues. Ten percent of the group's profits go to charity.

Further Reading

Leahey, Andrew. "Coldplay: Biography." *Allmusic.* Rovi Corp., 2012. Web. 14 Nov. 2012.

Macnie, Jim. "Coldplay." *Rolling Stone.* Wenner Media, n.d. Web. 14 Nov. 2012.

Roach, Martin. *Coldplay: Nobody Said It Was Easy.* London: Omnibus, 2003. Print.

Cait Caffrey

■ Commodity Futures Modernization Act of 2000

The Law: Federal law that changed the regulation of complex financial products called "derivatives"
Date: December 21, 2000
Also known as: CFMA

The Commodity Futures Modernization Act of 2000 dramatically changed the way that certain financial instruments collectively known as "over-the-counter derivatives" are regulated. It stated that so-called sophisticated parties were free to engage in derivatives trades without adherence to existing laws such as the Commodities Exchange Act of 1936 or to the Securities and Exchange Commission. Although it received almost no public attention at the time, the new law was a factor in the economic bubble of the early 2000s and the recession that began in 2008.

Over-the-counter derivatives are a diverse set of complicated financial instruments, all of which derive value from underlying assets. They are essentially contracts between buyers and sellers, not traded on public securities exchanges. This wide set of financial instruments has several subsets. Futures are agreements to buy or sell something at a later date for a price set in the present. Options are agreements to allow the choice of whether or not to buy something in the future for a set price. Swaps are agreements to make payments based on the underlying or estimated future value of an asset.

Since the 1980s, derivatives grew in importance to financial markets. They provided ways for investment firms to make small adjustments, often called hedges, to their investment positions. In theory, this meant that derivatives could be used to reduce downside, or risk, for large financial transactions. However, the risks of derivatives themselves have never been fully understood. What the CFMA did was to say that the traditional regulatory agencies should not be responsible for understanding these inherent risks, since this was best left to the presumably sophisticated parties that trade them.

Impact

The CMFA effectively removed the last major regulatory barrier to the free use of derivatives. At the same time, new players such as investment banks were allowed to participate in derivatives trading due to contemporary legislation, such as the Financial Services Modernization Act of 1999. As a result, the use of derivatives increased exponentially and took on innovative forms. In the short term, this led to record profits for investment banks and hedge funds that traded them.

However, some of the new uses for derivatives proved to be extremely risky. For instance, the recession that began in 2007 was triggered by a fast downturn in real estate prices and by record levels of mortgage defaults. Credit default swaps, derivatives in which sellers agree to pay buyers in case of bond or loan defaults, had become common and lucrative products for investment banks. Their hugely expanded use wreaked havoc on the financial sector when the real estate market plummeted. Many analysts consider the widespread use of under-regulated derivatives to have been a key factor in the crisis.

Further Reading

Butler, Brian, David Butler, and Alan Isaacs. *A Dictionary of Finance and Banking.* Oxford: Oxford UP, 1997. Print.

Greenberger, Michael. "The Role of Derivatives in the Financial Crisis: Testimony of Michael Greenberger, Law School Professor, University of Maryland School of Law." Financial Crisis Inquiry Crisis Commission Hearing. Washington, DC: US Senate, 30 June 2010. PDF file.

Leising, Matthew. "Credit Markets Safest Since 2008 as Derivatives Migrate to Clearinghouses." *Bloomberg.* Bloomberg, 5 Aug. 2011. Web. 7 Dec. 2012.

Adam J. Berger, PhD

■ Computer worms and viruses

Definition: Damaging, self-replicating computer codes that can access, modify, or destroy programs and information on a computer

Beginning in the late 1990s, Internet access rapidly expanded, as did the prevalence of computer viruses and worms. In May 2000, the ILOVEYOU worm, a VBScript program embedded in e-mail attachments, infected tens of millions of Windows computers, highlighting the dangers of using the Internet without an efficient antivirus program. Throughout the 2000s, worms and viruses found new and more esoteric ways to attack computers connected to the Internet, but increasingly sophisticated protection software was developed to counter these threats.

In 1966, mathematician John von Neumann published the book *Theory of Self-Reproducing Automata*, one of the earliest publications to describe the nature of computer viruses and worms. In 1971, American computer programmer Bob Thomas developed a program called the Creeper to demonstrate the ease with which a self-replicating program could be written. The Creeper did no damage, it just displayed the message "I'm the Creeper. Catch me if you can!" But when the program spread to a number of computers connected to the ARPANET, the forerunner of today's Internet, it demonstrated the potential danger of worms. Shortly after that, Ray Tomlinson, a colleague of Thomas, wrote the first antivirus program, the Reaper, to remove the Creeper from infected systems.

By the late 1990s, most computers were connected to corporate networks or modems, so virus and worm attacks on networked computers became more common. By the 2000s, most virus and worm attacks were launched against computers connected to the Internet, especially through e-mail attachments.

Much of the malware produced during the 2000s contained a virus or worm as part of a complicated blended attack. For example, most Trojan horse attacks, which trick users into downloading malware by presenting a seemingly legitimate file or program, work by loading a virus to a browser helper object, such as a toolbar or web application, which then loads a virus or worm to the temporary Internet files, causing the main damage. These types of attacks can give hackers access to infected computers, who may

ILOVEYOU Virus

On May 4, 2000, computer users around the world were greeted with an email enticingly titled "ILOVEYOU." The text of the email message read, "Please look at this love note that I've sent you," and contained an attachment labeled "LOVE-LETTER-FOR-YOU.TXT.vbs." Upon opening the attachment, computer users did not receive a love message but unwittingly activated a program that renamed or destroyed a variety of files on their hard drives—including multimedia images and audio files. The Rogue program, or virus, also created a backdoor on the user's computer, allowing hackers to surreptitiously access data and passwords. The virus then created further havoc by automatically forwarding the original email message to every address in the user's address book. In addition to the file damage and breach of security to the user's computer, the almost endless replication of email messages immediately overloaded and disabled network servers around the world. Institutions ranging from the Ford Motor Company to the British House of Commons were forced to shut down servers temporarily in response to the flood of electronic messages.

The ILOVEYOU virus (sometimes called the LOVE bug or Love Letter), which operated by means of the attachment written in Visual Basic Software (vbs) code, was determined to have been created by a Filipino student. Although the computer virus did an estimated $5.5 billion in damages to computer systems worldwide, the suspected student (as well as another young Filipino computer programmer) was not prosecuted for lack of applicable computer crime laws. Because of the virus, many users took responsibility for their own antivirus protection, and antivirus programs such as McAfee Virus Scan became the most-downloaded programs in the wake of the ILOVEYOU virus.

to the Storm botnet launched a distributed DoS attack on a number of antispam websites at a predetermined signal, causing the sites to slow or crash.

Viruses and Worms Attack in Many Ways

USB portable storage devices (key drives) have become very popular as a way to backup work offline or transfer files from one computer to another, but they are vulnerable to virus and worm attacks. Since most operating systems support booting from a key drive, the technique of embedding a virus or worm in the boot sector of the key drive (which copies itself to the hard drive when inserted into a computer and can then infect the next key drive inserted into the system) works effectively as a Trojan. For example, in 2009, more than nine million computers running on Windows were attacked by the Conficker worm, making this one of the most widespread worm attacks of all time. A major component of the Conficker's attack spread from infected key drives to corporate servers. Once a computer was infected by the Conficker worm, the attacker could remotely download and install additional malware to the computer. In 2007, the W32/LiarVB-A worm found a different way for a key drive to infect a computer. W32/LiarVB-A placed a file, autorun.inf, on a key drive. When the key drive was inserted on a Windows system, the file automatically ran and infected the computer, which then infected both new key drives and shared network drives.

Files have always been used to spread viruses and worms. Some files, like Microsoft Word, contain an execution engine which runs embedded scripts called macros. Hackers quickly learned how to write malicious scripts, called macro viruses, into such files. For example, in the early 2000s, the Melissa virus used both Word document files and Outlook Express e-mail messages to trigger mass mailings from infected computers, causing congestion for a number of e-mail servers.

Infected HTML pages on web servers are also used to spread viruses and worms. For example, in

then steal data, modify files or codes, record keystrokes, cause system crashes, or launch automated spam or denial-of-service (DoS) attacks.

DoS attacks work in a number of different ways to prevent users from accessing a particular program or network, most commonly by overwhelming or "flooding" the targeted network or program with information. In 2007, millions of computers were linked to the Storm botnet through infected e-mail attachments. A botnet is a group of infected computers that can be controlled remotely by the attacker. In January 2007, all the computers connected

The U.S delegation meets at the Cooperative Cyber Defense Center of Excellence in Tallinn, Estonia. (Courtesy U.S. Helsinki Commission)

2001, the Code Red worm infected thousands of computers (using a vulnerability in Microsoft's IIS web server) and subsequently mounted DoS attacks on a number of sites, including WhitcHouse.gov. In 2003, the SQL Slammer worm used a buffer overflow vulnerability of Microsoft's SQLServer database to mount a DoS attack on a large number of routers. Slammer was notable for the speed with which it spread and the damage it incurred. The Slammcr worm was responsible for a number of airline-flight cancellations and several ATM failures.

Social-media websites became common targets for worm and virus attacks in the late 2000s. The viral nature of social-media networks makes them an ideal way to rapidly spread a worm or virus. At the end of the decade, the Ramnit worm was responsible for stealing tens of thousands login credentials from Facebook users. Most antivirus software vendors now place a special emphasis on addressing the security issues related to social media, but more work needs to be done.

Smart mobile devices all have a standard operating system, as well as the same e-mail and browser capability, making them susceptible to viruses and worms. During the 2000s, mobile devices and smartphones proved to be relatively safe from these attacks due to their relative newness. Some mobile operating systems are open (like Android and Windows), while others are closed (like Apple's iOS). Although there are arguments as to the security of each type of system, there have been successful malicious code attacks on both types of operating systems. For example, in 2009, iKee appeared as the first iPhone worm. Since the late 2000s, several smartphone antivirus programs and special software written to protect Facebook users have been developed.

Cyberwarfare

In cyberwarfare, one nation attacks another to destroy, degrade, or compromise its data, communications, or critical infrastructures. During the 2000s, cyberwarfare capability was developed in a number of countries, including the United States.

In May 2007, web servers supporting the electrical grid in Estonia were subjected to a powerful DoS attack, which was launched in protest against the removal of a Soviet-era monument. The attack appears to have been a worm-based attack that originated in Russia, and may have even been initiated by the government. The attack lasted more than a month, severely damaging the ability of Estonia to deliver electricity to its citizens, and it appears that the United States and Israel assisted in stopping the attack. This attack made it clear that all countries needed to develop their cyberwarfare capabilities and cybersecurity efforts. For example, NATO established the Cooperative Cyber Defense Centre of Excellence in Estonia in 2008 to improve its cyberwarfare capability.

Impact

The 2000s saw rapid growth in using the Internet to communicate, transact business, access entertainment, and obtain information. Virus and worm attacks launched through e-mail and web browsing increased throughout the 2000s, but improved antivirus software largely succeeded in combating these attacks. Throughout the decade, virus and worm attacks became increasingly clandestine, as hackers became more interested in using worms and viruses to steal personal or financial information from infected computers than in gaining fame or notoriety. In addition, many new uses of the Internet were developed during the 2000s, including social media, cloud computing applications, and mobile applications, but they all proved to be vulnerable to virus and worn attacks. Cyberwarfare also developed during the 2000s and made considerable use of virus and worm attacks. Improved antivirus software, intrusion-detection systems, and strong authentication techniques provided considerable protection against these attacks, but the cat-and-mouse game of new attacks and better defenses continues.

Further Reading

Aycock, John. *Computer Viruses and Malware.* New York: Springer, 2006. Print. Compares and contrasts viruses and worms, with several complete examples.

Bisong, Anthony, and Syed Rahman. "An Overview of the Security Concerns in Enterprise Cloud Computing." *International Journal of Network Security & Its Applications* 3.1 (2011): 30–45. Print. Contains a good overview of the viruses and worm vulnerabilities in cloud computing.

Leavitt, Neal. "Mobile phones: The next frontier for hackers?" *IEEE Computer* 38.4 (2005): 20–23. Print. Presents a discussion of viruses on smartphones, including several specific examples.

Pope, Clark, and Khushpreet Kaur. "Is it Human or Computer? Defending e-commerce with Captchas." *IEEE Computer* 7.2 (2005): 43–49. Print. Discusses a secure method of authentication in ecommerce.

Szor, Peter. *The Art of Computer Virus Research and Defense.* Upper Saddle River: Addison, 2005. Print. Contains a complete coverage of the theory of detecting and controlling worms.

George Whitson, PhD

■ Concussions in sports

Definition: Traumatic brain injuries often suffered by athletes in contact sports

Concussions represent damage to brain tissue itself, typically from being shaken within its protective cavity. These brain injuries occur after jolts that cause nerve, blood vessel, or metabolic damage to parts of the brain. Symptoms can be immediate or delayed and include blurred vision, slurred speech, dizziness, balance impairment, light and noise irritation, and sluggishness.

Although the true number of concussions in professional or youth sports is difficult to quantify, the US Centers for Disease Control and Prevention (CDC) estimates that concussions account for approximately 15 percent of sports-related high school injuries, with a total of 3.8 million sports- and recreation-related concussions each year in the United States. Although male-dominated football and hockey have been consistently associated with the greatest incidence, concussions have also been reported in lacrosse and soccer, played in both genders.

Changing Symptoms and Grading

Concussions were once thought to be simple injuries with no long-term consequences. In fact, symptoms of concussions and their timing vary among people and incidences. As more is learned about concussions, the true effect of additive concussive damage in youth is better described. Because of the limited neck strength and the disproportionate head-to-body ratio in youth eighteen years and younger, this population is at particular risk of lasting damage from brain injuries.

Although symptoms were first defined in 1966 and the functional concerns of injury were reiterated in 2001, headache and nausea were added to the symptom list only by 2004. The 2004 and 2008 International Conference on Concussion in Sport guidelines also emphasized that delayed symptoms can be as frequent and important but less noticeable as common initial ones. Postconcussion symptoms recognized in the 2000s include reduced processing ability, poor short-term memory, poor concentration, and fatigue.

Symptoms are best evaluated by an onsite trainer, with possible referral to a physician or professional versed in brain injury presentation. Following professional athletic organizations, school sports trainers started becoming prevalent; still, fewer than half of US high schools employed full-time athletic trainers in 2009. Multiple symptom evaluation tools, including the Standard Assessment of Concussion and the Immediate Post-Concussion Assessment and Cognitive Testing, were available for trainers by the early 2000s. Regardless of the scale used, stepwise symptom-based care became standard and generous return-to-play delays recommended, because younger athletes recover more slowly from injury than adults. Guidelines also advised that student cognition and balance, at minimum, should return to normal before sport reentry participation.

Public and Private Initiatives

Efforts to protect youth athletes in particular have grown in the 2000s. Concussion rates increased by more than 16 percent each year in both genders starting in 2005, likely attributed to better identification by full-time trainers.

In 2004, the National Athletic Trainers' Association (NATA) released a position statement to increase the awareness of youth concussions, as a trickle-down result of professional high-profile deaths and injuries. At the time, injury evaluation and return-to-play decisions remained nonstandardized. NATA encouraged consistent application of injury evaluation tools and suggested baseline testing

that provides an active comparison when injury has occurred. A longer interim period before returning to athletic activity was highly suggested as well, because damage in younger patients can leave more lasting impairment.

The CDC, individually and through promotion by the National Council of Youth Sports, similarly emphasized education of students, trainers, and other responsible adults in the care and prevention of traumatic brain injury. Their National Center for Injury Prevention and Control's "Heads Up: Concussions in Youth Sports" initiative provided toolkits and an online training course to educate parents, health professionals, trainers, and school administrators about concussion risks, safety evaluations, and appropriate treatment considerations after an injury.

Similarly, the nonprofit Sports Legacy Institute (SLI) was started in 2007 to bring attention in particular to the long-term and cumulative effects of concussions in youth sports. SLI formed a concussion checklist to identify a consensus action plan to include preseason education, baseline testing to compare with function after an injury, respectful awareness of the dangers of head injuries, and sports removal and return-to-play clearance by professionals.

Professional Sports

Concussions are also prevalent and dangerous in professional sports. Acknowledgement of this by a professional sports league has itself been a contentious issue—only in 2009 did the National Football League (NFL) admit the dangerous long-term effects of concussion, becoming the first professional sports league to publicly do so. Before doing so, the NFL's disability system denied benefits to retired players suffering the effects of multiple concussions, an issue that prompted a congressional warning in 2007. As high-profile concussion cases came to light—such as the one involving former NFL player Andre Waters who, after committing suicide at forty-four, was autopsied and found to have a brain similar to that of an eighty-five-year-old—did the need for a culture change in sports definitively materialize. After his death from a drug overdose in 2008, former NFL player Tom McHale showed signs of chronic traumatic encephalopathy, a progressive degenerative disease. Another football player, Terry Long, committed suicide in 2005, and postmortem examinations indicated similar brain damage that contributed to depression and suicide. The book *Head Games: Football's Concussion Crisis* (2006), by Christopher Nowinski, addressed the long-term effects of head injuries and brought this issue to mainstream attention. NASCAR and Major League Baseball also implemented concussion policy in the 2000s.

Impact

The better identification of concussion effects in professional and youth athletes continues to lead to better understanding of the short- and long-term risks of this brain injury. A battle cry of the early twenty-first century is best indicated by the CDC motto, "It's better to miss one game than the whole season." The Youth Sports Safety Alliance, a division of NATA, ensures that high school athletes receive the most appropriate preventive and therapeutic care during any sports venture.

Further Reading

Cantu, Robert, and Mark Hyman. *Concussions and Our Kids: America's Leading Expert on How to Protect Young Athletes and Keep Sports Safe.* New York: Houghton, 2012. Print. Consumer-friendly resource for concussion statistics and evaluation approaches.

"Heads Up to Schools: Know Your Concussion ABCs." *Centers for Disease Control and Prevention.* Centers for Disease Control and Prevention, 23 Mar. 2012. Web. 10 Dec. 2012. Initiative materials to enhance education of trainers, teachers, and parents who supervise youth at risk of sports-related concussions.

Keatley, Mary Ann, and Laura L. Whittemore. *Understanding Mild Traumatic Brain Injury (MTBI): An Insightful Guide to Symptoms, Treatments, and Redefining Recovery.* Boulder: Brain Injury Hope Foundation, 2010. Print. Explains the short- and long-term impacts of concussions.

Moser, Rosemarie Scolaro, and Bill Pascrell Jr. *Ahead of the Game: The Parents' Guide to Youth Sports Concussion.* Lebanon: Dartmouth College P, 2012. Print. Explains the serious impact of concussion on children, complemented by caregiver considerations for safety and health.

Nicole Van Hoey, PharmD

■ Cooper, Anderson

Identification: Television host, news anchor, journalist
Born: June 3, 1967; New York, New York

As CNN's prime-time news anchor, host of Anderson Cooper 360°, and a frequent field reporter, Anderson Cooper covered major events such as the wars in Iraq and Afghanistan, Hurricane Katrina, and the 2011 Egyptian revolution.

After a successful start with ABC News in the latter 1990s, Anderson Cooper's budding career as a reporter and news anchor was briefly sidetracked in 2001, when he hosted ABC's reality game show *The Mole.* After two seasons, he returned to CNN to co-host *American Morning with Paula Zahn.* As his popularity grew, especially among young people who

Anderson Cooper. (©iStockphoto.com/Brad Barket)

related to his youthful demeanor, CNN hired him to anchor their prime-time weekend news shows. On September 8, 2003, CNN premiered his hour-long prime-time news show, *Anderson Cooper 360°*, an opportunity for Cooper to offer in-depth coverage of select news topics. He also began coanchoring *NewsNight with Aaron Brown*. In November 2005, CNN replaced *NewsNight* with *Anderson Cooper 360°* and doubled the time slot. The show became known for presenting multiple viewpoints on controversial issues, including gay and lesbian parenting, bullying in schools, and stem cell research. In 2006, he won an Emmy Award for the episode "Starving in Plain Sight," and was nominated for "The Children: Part One and Part Two." In 2006, Cooper was hired as a contributor for CBS's *60 Minutes*. During the following year, he also began cohosting CNN's *Planet in Peril* and *CNN Heroes: An All-Star Tribute*.

Cooper's *New York Times* best-selling memoir, *Dispatches from the Edge: A Memoir of War, Disasters, and Survival* (2005), recounts his experiences being on the front line as a journalist in Iraq, Niger, Sri Lanka, and New Orleans, while connecting the events to his personal life. The work also discusses the suicide of Anderson's older brother, his upbringing, and his famous mother, artist and fashion designer Gloria Vanderbilt.

Impact

Often appearing in his signature black t-shirt or a designer suit, Anderson Cooper has become one of the world's most-recognized television personalities for his provocative coverage of prominent social issues and events, as well as his advocacy for environmental causes. Although he has kept his private life separate from his life as a public figure, Cooper publically confirmed in July 2012 that he is gay. Cooper has received numerous rewards for his work as a journalist, including a Peabody Award and several Emmy Awards.

Further Reading

Cooper, Anderson. *Dispatches from the Edge: A Memoir of War, Disasters, and Survival.* New York: HarperCollins, 2006.

George, Lianne. "Anderson Cooper Feels Your Pain." *Maclean's* June 5, 2006: 66–8.

Goldfarb, Brad. An Interview with Anderson Cooper. *Interview* 34.9 (October 2004): 122–29.

Sally Driscoll

■ Couric, Katie

Identification: American television journalist and news anchor
Born: January 7, 1957; Arlington, Virginia

Couric is an award-winning journalist, best-selling author, and spokesperson and advocate for colorectal cancer research and prevention.

Katie Couric became a household name in the United States after becoming a coanchor on the *Today* show in 1991. In many ways, Couric's name became synonymous with *Today*, where she remained for the next fifteen years. During her career as a journalist, Couric has interviewed five US presidents.

After her husband, Jay Monahan, died of colon cancer in January 1998 at the age of forty-two, Couric set out to raise both awareness of colon cancer and began working as a fundraiser for colon cancer research and testing. In March 2000, Couric underwent a colonoscopy, a visual screening of the colon, on live television, as a way to increase colorectal cancer awareness. Her efforts raised more than $10 million dollars by the end of 2000. During this time, Couric also published a *New York Times* best-selling children's picture book, *The Brand New Kid*, which ranked highly on the best sellers list for three weeks.

While writing and raising money for colorectal cancer research, Couric continued as a morning talk show cohost with *Today* on NBC. In 2002, Couric signed a contract that made her one of the highest paid television personalities in history. The four-and-half-year contract earned her more than $65 million.

In 2004, Couric published her second children's book, *Blue Ribbon Day*. In 2006, Couric left *Today* to anchor the *CBS Evening News*, making her the first woman to anchor an evening news show on her own. Her presence drew the show's largest audience since 1998. She also began appearing regularly as a correspondent on the television news program *60 Minutes*. Couric's 2008 television interviews with Republican Vice Presidential candidate Governor Sarah Palin received widespread notoriety. While Palin's supporters criticized Couric as vindictive, others praised Couric for conducting a professional interview that challenged Palin's political credentials.

Katie Couric talks with Governor Howard Dean. (©iStockphoto.com/Mark Wilson)

Impact

Since the death of her husband, Couric has become a dedicated advocate for colorectal cancer awareness. She is cofounder of Stand Up to Cancer (SU2C) and the National Colorectal Cancer Research Alliance (NCCRA). She is founder of the Jay Monahan Center for Gastrointestinal Health, a clinical center in New York-Presbyterian Hospital and the Weill Medical College of Cornell University. When Couric broadcast her own colon screening in 2000, the sign-up rate for individual screenings across the country increased by more than 20 percent. Researchers refer to this phenomenon as "the Katie Couric effect."

Further Reading

Couric, Katherine. *The Best Advice I Ever Got: Lessons from Extraordinary Lives.* New York: Random House, 2012. Print.

Gorman, Christine, David S. Jackson, Alice Park, and Dick Thompson. "Katie's Crusade." *Time,* 13 Mar. 2000. Web. 9 July 2012.

Klein, Edward. *Katie: The Real Story.* New York: Three Rivers, 2007. Print.

Gina Kuchta

■ Craigslist

Definition: Craigslist is the world's largest online "bulletin board," featuring community-moderated classified and personal ads, no-frills social networking, and discussion forums on a variety of topics

Craigslist's innovative business model as a community-oriented online bulletin board made it the premier site for advertising goods, real estate, employment opportunities, and services during the 2000s. Though originally based in San Francisco, the company expanded both domestically and internationally during the decade, generating tens of millions of users worldwide.

Craigslist is named for its founder, Craig Newmark, who began to maintain an email list of events for the San Francisco community in the mid-1990s. As "Craig's list" became unwieldy, he created a website on which to host the listings. To pay for the service, Newmark began to charge a minimal fee to post certain employment and real estate listings. In 1999, Newmark decided to incorporate and hired Jim Buckmaster as a programmer. Soon after, he named Buckmaster chief executive officer (CEO), which freed Newmark to handle customer service and other behind-the-scenes tasks.

The company began to expand within the United States in 2000, creating individual web pages for cities such as New York, Los Angeles, and Chicago. Craigslist became an international company in 2001 with the creation of a site for Vancouver, Canada. By the end of the decade, Craigslist had grown into a worldwide phenomenon, generating billions of hits each month and earning tens of millions of dollars.

Services

In addition to event listings, Craigslist offered free classified advertisements for jobs, cars, apartments, and household and other items as well as advertisements for professional and personal services. Bartering was common, as were listings for free items.

Craigslist's popularity has been attributed especially to the speed and ease of publishing such advertisements online, as opposed to in traditional print magazines and newspapers, as well as the tendency to receive faster responses.

Craigslist also offered social networking opportunities, personal ads for users seeking romantic or sexual partners, and forums in which users could discuss politics, the arts, or dozens of other topics. New discussion forums opened regularly upon popular request, focusing on heated topics such as taxes and politics as well more innocuous topics such as diets and shopping. After Hurricane Katrina devastated the United States' Gulf Coast in 2005, Craigslist set up a hurricane forum to aid with relief and offer an outlet for those affected by the storm.

The virtual lack of a maximum word count for listings on Craigslist encouraged users to create imaginative sales pitches, and advertisements for such ordinary items as used cars or pieces of furniture at times became quirky short stories, humorous autobiographical narratives, or pitches for romance. In 2000 Craigslist introduced the "best of Craigslist" section, which collected posts that users flagged as particularly humorous, insightful, or bizarre. Many of the listings in this section were culled from craigslist's "missed connections" category, in which users posted messages in the hope of connecting with strangers they had encountered on public transportation, at events, or in other public venues.

Controversies

As the volume of postings increased at an exponential rate, Newmark, Buckmaster, and their small workforce were unable to read each listing to ensure that it did not violate the law or craigslist's policies. Instead, they began to rely on users to flag illegal or especially offensive listings. They also posted detailed user guidelines and warnings about adult content or scams as relevant to each area of the site. Nevertheless, illegal postings at times remained online too long. Some housing ads violated the federal Fair Housing Act by specifying the preferred racial background, gender, or sexual orientation of prospective tenants. Some users tried to sell illegal items, such as fireworks, stolen property, or jammers intended to block cell phone calls or GPS systems, or other items specifically listed as off-limits by Craigslist. Scammers paying with counterfeit money orders or checks or phishing for personal information that could be used for identity theft also became a significant concern.

Craigslist also became known for attracting sexual predators, prostitutes, and drug dealers and for hosting ads for human trafficking, child pornography, and other illegal behavior, which led to a number of high-profile lawsuits. The "erotic services" category, in which users could advertise for escorts, phone sex, and other legal adult services, came under special scrutiny. In 2009, in response to a lawsuit filed by multiple state attorneys general over charges of abetting prostitution, Craigslist dropped erotic services in favor of "adult services." They also began charging for adult services ads and accepting payment by credit card only, employed attorneys to screen the ads for illegal behavior, and implemented a phone verification system. After facing additional complaints and lawsuits, the company took down the adult services section completely.

A few highly publicized murder cases also tainted Craigslist's image. In October of 2007, nineteen-year-old Michael John Anderson lured twenty-four-year-old Katherine Ann Olson to his home and shot her to death after she responded to a fake ad for a nanny. In 2009, twenty-three-year-old Philip Markoff, a student at Boston University, robbed three women who had placed advertisements for adult services and murdered one of them, twenty-six-year-old Julissa Brisman.

As an easy-to-use site allowing users to post free or inexpensive classified ads of unlimited length and receive nearly instant results, Craigslist proved to be a major source of competition for local and independent newspapers that provided similar services. By the end of the decade, some newspapers claimed to have lost millions of dollars in classified advertising revenue to the site at a time in which that income was needed to offset declining subscription numbers. In light of this effect, some newspaper publishers accused Craigslist of contributing to the widespread decline of the industry during this period.

Impact

Although Craigslist generated controversy during the 2000s, the site was one of the most innovative of the decade and served as a prototype for other e-commerce sites. Its success is all the more remarkable in light of its small workforce, with only about thirty employees by the end of the decade, and its utilitarian website design. While remaining focused on its original mission to serve as a community bulletin board, Craigslist continued to expand into the next decade, launching sites dedicated to cities and regions in dozens of countries throughout the world.

Further Reading

LaRosa, Paul, and Maria Cramer. *Seven Days of Rage: The Deadly Crime Spree of the Craigslist Killer.* New York: Pocket, 2009. Print. Pieces together the 2009 crimes committed by Markoff and attempts to uncover his motivation while investigating the policies at Craigslist that allowed him to connect with his victims.

Melnitzer, Julius. "Craigslist Suit Challenges Immunity of Web Operators." *Insidecounsel* Apr. 2006: 88. Print. Details a federal lawsuit filed by the National Fair Housing Alliance against Craigslist for allowing discriminatory housing ads.

Podhoretz, John. "The News Mausoleum." *Commentary* May 2008: 37. Print. Examines Craigslist's business model and its effects on the newspaper industry.

Weiss, Philip. "A Guy Named Craig." *New York* 16 Jan. 2006: 8. Print. Provides a profile of Newmark and assesses the effects of Craigslist on print journalism.

Wolf, Gary. "Why Craigslist is Such a Mess." *Wired.* Condé Nast, 24 Aug. 2009. Web. 6 Nov. 2012. Profiles Newmark and Buckmaster in light of the general history of Craigslist.

Sally Driscoll

■ Crimes and scandals

Definition: A number of significant political scandals and criminal acts that took place during the 2000s

*The United States saw a number of high-profile crimes and political scandals during the first decade of the twenty-first century. Many of these incidents were part of broader events and trends, while others were reflective of the changing international economy. Still others captured the public attention simply because of the unusual nature of the crimes, scandals, or figures involved. Among these well-publicized crimes and scandals were political sex scandals, large-scale corporate acts (including so-called white collar crimes), and inappropriate political activi-*ties. *These crimes and scandals had broader implications for the American economy, political environment, and media.*

During the 2000s, the United States saw many high-profile criminal acts as well as scandals that spoke to the new social, political, and economic environment of the twenty-first century. Because of the extensive nature of the news media, many of these incidents were given considerable coverage and, therefore, were presented to the public in comprehensive fashion, even if they did not reach a significant conclusion. Others were confirmed by the very people who committed them or in a court of law. Still other incidents had implications for the American political landscape, economy, or culture.

White-Collar Crimes

The term given to nonviolent crimes such as embezzlement, accounting fraud, and price-fixing, white-collar crimes often suggests that the crimes in question do not have broad implications for the rest of society. This misconception is further bolstered by the fact that most convicted white-collar criminals are sent to minimum-security prisons, where they are allowed a greater degree of personal liberty than the populations of medium- or maximum-security correctional facilities.

Several criminal acts and scandals that took place during the 2000s did a great deal to undo this perception. The Enron scandal, for example, had tremendous impact on investors and the general public alike (particularly the thousands of Enron employees who suddenly lost their jobs once the scandal became apparent). By the end of the 1990s, this energy company was viewed as one of the most dynamic and cutting-edge corporations on the stock market, trading as high as $90 per share and boasting a market value of $70 billion. In 2001, however, the situation at Enron was revealed to be far less stellar—the company suddenly reported a nearly $640 million income loss and a $1.2 billion debt. This dramatic change necessitated a major investigation into Enron's accounting practices. It was revealed that the company's leaders had engaged in misleading accounting policies, inflating its income based on anticipated (and not actual) profits when reporting its earnings from natural gas contracts. Enron officials also hid the company's debts in special purpose entities—partnerships with other companies that Enron

Tom Delay. (©iStockphoto.com/Ben Sklar)

created to absorb the debts from the corporate headquarters. The result was unreported corporate debt, which helped the company continue its performance surge.

When Enron was no longer able to hide the reality of its condition, the corporation quickly declared bankruptcy as its stock plummeted. Enron's corporate leaders were indicted and found guilty, having earned millions of dollars from the corporation's illegal accounting practices through fraud, insider trading, and other criminal actions. Meanwhile, thousands of Enron employees suddenly lost the entirety of their retirement pensions and health coverage when the company quickly closed its doors. The budget-strapped state of California, which had purchased energy from Enron at inflated rates, lost enormous sums from their relationship with the company, as well as more money lost from pensions invested in the company. Enron's extensive corporate reach, created because of its presumed success during the 1990s, meant that the scandal had implications throughout the economy. The scandal also prompted the government to apply greater scrutiny to corporate accounting practices, which meant that other corporations needed to ensure that their ac-

counting practices were reasonable or else face possible prosecution themselves.

In late 2008, one man's scandalous actions were nearly as impactful as actions of the entire Enron corporate leadership. Investment consultant Bernard L. Madoff had a reputation across a wide range of industries (including the nonprofit world) that had given him myriad clients over decades. His fund, Bernard L. Madoff Investment Securities LLC, provided respectable and consistent profits for those clients. What those clients did not realize was that Madoff's fund was in fact a criminal enterprise known as a Ponzi scheme. In the simplest of terms, Madoff would acquire new clients and use their money to pay returns to Madoff's older clients. His scheme was helped by the fact that most investors viewed his fund as a long-term investment—they were not likely to take out money from their accounts, preferring to keep them intact, but inadvertently allowing the Ponzi scheme to continue.

It was only when the number and quantity of new client investments could not cover the expected returns to be paid to older clients that Madoff himself confessed to his crime. He had been investigated in the past, but those investigations failed to unearth any improper activity. By the time Madoff confessed to his crimes, he had defrauded countless nonprofit organizations and businesses, costing them nearly $50 billion. In 2009 Madoff was sentenced to 150 years for his crimes, but the impacts of his actions were still being assessed by the end of the decade.

Political Scandals

The 2000s also saw a number of scandals that had significant implications for the nation's political system. That elected officials engaged in scandalous behavior during the 2000s was not a new development. However, some of the scandals involving legislators, executives, and political candidates that occurred were significant because this behavior often involved the officials using their office resources and staff to cover up their activities.

One such scandal involved Illinois Governor Rod Blagojevich. Blagojevich was responsible for appointing a new US Senator to fill the seat vacated in 2008 by Barack Obama, who had won the presidential election. Blagojevich was indicted for using this opening for personal financial gain, offering to give the seat to the highest bidder. Before he was ousted

United States Crime Rates Per 100,000 Inhabitants, 2000-2009

Year	Population	All Crimes	Violent	Property	Murder	Forcible Rape	Robbery	Aggravated Assault	Burglary	Larceny	Vehicle Theft
2000	281,421,906	4,124.8	506.5	3,618.3	5.5	32.0	145.0	324.0	728.8	2,477.3	412.2
2001	285,317,559	4,162.6	504.5	3,658.1	5.6	31.8	148.5	318.6	741.8	2,485.7	430.5
2002	287,973,924	4,125.0	494.4	3,630.6	5.6	33.1	146.1	309.5	747.0	2,450.7	432.9
2003	290,788,976	4,067.0	475.8	3,591.2	5.7	32.3	142.5	295.4	741.0	2,416.5	433.7
2004	293,656,842	3,977.3	463.2	3,514.1	5.5	32.4	136.7	288.6	730.3	2,362.3	421.5
2005	296,507,061	3,900.5	469.0	3,431.5	5.6	31.8	140.8	290.8	726.9	2,287.8	416.8
2006	298,754,819	3,808.1	480.6	3,357.7	5.8	31.7	150.6	292.6	735.2	2,221.4	401.1
2007	301,290,332	3,730.4	472.0	3,276.8	5.7	30.5	148.4	287.4	726.0	2,186.3	364.6
2008	304,374,846	3,669.0	457.5	3,211.5	5.4	29.7	145.7	276.7	732.1	2,164.5	315.0
2009	307,006,550	3,465.5	429.4	3,036.1	5.0	28.7	133.0	262.8	716.3	2,060.9	258.8

Source: Federal Bureau of Investigation Uniform Crime Reports and the Disaster Center.

from office, Blagojevich used his remaining power to appoint Roland Burris to the post. Burris himself was not a controversial figure, but the fact that Blagojevich appointed him led the US Senate to initially deny him a seat, an impasse that lasted for a few weeks before the Senate relented. Blagojevich, meanwhile, awaited a trial on federal corruption charges at the end of the decade, while Congress and other officials used the case to explore new campaign finance laws.

The political scandals of the 2000s also included a series of high-profile sex scandals. Among the number of incidents was the case of Florida Congressman Mark Foley, who in 2006 resigned in disgrace after it was revealed that he sent sexually explicit e-mails and text messages to teenage, male congressional pages. Foley's scandal came less than two months before pivotal midterm elections, which led other Republican Congressional candidates to quickly distance themselves from Foley amid mounting Democratic criticism. A year later, John Edwards—a former US Senator and vice-presidential candidate who was running for the Democratic nomination for President—was revealed to have fathered a child with a mistress. His infidelity was matched by his efforts to conceal the child's birth by attempting to have an aide claim paternity. Edwards later confessed to the affair and

child, but by then his rising star in the Democratic Party had quickly extinguished. In 2008, New York Governor Eliot Spitzer, a former attorney general, was quickly removed from office in 2008 after it was revealed that he frequented a high-end prostitution service.

One of the decade's most damaging political scandals for Congress was not about marital infidelity, but the relationship between congressional leaders and one of Washington's best-known lobbyists. Jack Abramoff was a familiar face in former House Majority Leader Tom DeLay's office, and was also closely linked with a large number of other Republican congressmen and members of the administration of President George W. Bush. In an era of public advocacy for campaign finance reform and reducing the influence of lobbyists on the public policy process, Jack Abramoff was known to hand out luxury tickets to sporting events, purchase expensive dinners, and even host international golf junkets for elected officials and their staffs. Abramoff led a resurgence of this type of approach to lobbying in Washington, as lobbyist spending spiked during the 2000s.

Abramoff's seemingly corrupt approach to lobbying was brought out into the open in 2006, when he was accused of bribing public officials and defrauding his clients. Among the charges was that he took millions in fees from the Coushatta Indian tribe in Louisiana to help them close a rival tribe's casino, only to turn around and take the rival tribe as a client—he claimed to be able to help them reopen it, but Abramoff allegedly pocketed the money without helping the tribe. In fact, Abramoff was accused of taking advantage of a large number of Indian tribes across the country, raking in millions of dollars while continuing a personal campaign of bribery and corruption with his congressional cronies. Abramoff's corruption charges eventually cost DeLay his job and prompted Republicans to distance themselves from Abramoff, who until those charges were leveled was one of the most influential lobbyists in Washington.

Impact

The 2000s saw a wide range of major political and criminal scandals. Some of these scandals affected thousands of people, causing them to lose their jobs, benefits, and great sums of money. Others only affected the perpetrators themselves, costing them their jobs and professional reputations in a very public way. The scandals and crimes described here were high-profile, given full exposure in the public eye by the media. Although scandals and crimes such as these had major negative effects, they did foster a positive reaction—the high level of publicity given to them led the public to call for reforms and regulations that would protect the public, economy, and political system from a recurrence of such illicit behavior.

Further Reading

Abramoff, Jack. *Capitol Punishment: The Hard Truth About Washington Corruption from America's Most Notorious Lobbyist.* Washington, DC: WND, 2011. Print. Presents the memoir of Jack Abramoff, describing his experience as an influential lobbyist.

Arvedlund, Erin, ed. *The Club No One Wanted to Join—Madoff Victims in Their Own Words.* Andover: Doukathsan, 2010. Print. A compilation of comments made by victims of the Ponzi scheme run by Bernard Madoff that counters the perception that Madoff's crime only affected wealthy investors.

Gose, Ben. "In Scandal's Wake." *Chronicle of Philanthropy* 21.6 (2009): 20. Print. Provides a report on the impact of the Madoff scandal on the wide array of philanthropic organizations and its implications for future nonprofit investment policies.

Holt, Andrew, and Timothy Eccles. "Accounting Practices in the Post-Enron Era: The Implications for Financial Statements in the Property Industry." *Briefings in Real Estate Finance* 2.4 (2003): 326–40. Print. Describes the accounting practices that doomed Enron and scandal's implications for other corporations in the future.

Koppel, Nathan. "Corruption Cases Renew Debate on Campaign-Finance Laws." *Wall Street Journal Eastern Edition* 15 Jan. 2009: A12. Print. Discusses the increased calls for reforms to campaign finance laws in the wake of the corruption charges against prominent leaders like Governor Rod Blagojevich.

Young, Andrew, and Kevin Foley. *The Politician: An Insider's Account of John Edwards's Pursuit of the Presidency and the Scandal that Brought Him Down.* Old Saybrook: Tantor, 2010. Print. Written by a close aide to then-Senator John Edwards and describes Edwards's effort to conceal his extramarital affair while running for president in 2008.

Michael P. Auerbach, MA

■ *CSI: Crime Scene Investigation*

Identification: Television drama about forensic investigators working for the Crime Scene Investigations Bureau of the Las Vegas Police Department
Executive Producer: Anthony E. Zuiker (b. 1968)
Date: Premiered October 6, 2000

Following its premier in 2000, the television crime drama CSI: Crime Scene Investigation *became one of the most popular shows of the decade and garnered numerous awards, including four Emmys. The show focuses on a team of Las Vegas investigators who use high-tech forensic science to determine not only who was responsible for committing a crime but also how the crime was committed.*

CSI: Crime Scene Investigation aired on the television network CBS throughout the decade, beginning its tenth season in late 2009. The creation of American television writer Anthony E. Zuiker, *CSI* follows a team of Las Vegas forensic investigators who examine crime scenes to find clues that will help solve cases. The first season introduces viewers to the team, which includes head supervisor Gil Grissom (played by William Petersen) and level-3 investigators Catherine Willows (Marg Helgenberger), Nick Stokes (George Eads), Warrick Brown (Gary Dourdan), and Sara Sidle (Jorja Fox). The team, which underwent several changes in membership over the course of the decade, typically investigates a new crime in each episode. The series also focuses on the professional and personal relationships between the investigators.

Zuiker initially pitched the idea for *CSI* to American producer Jerry Bruckheimer, best known for films such as *Bad Boys* and *Armageddon*, and who became one of the show's executive producers. The two worked together on the show throughout the decade. While developing the series, Zuiker researched the procedures and techniques used by forensic investigators by accompanying a real-life Las Vegas forensics team on investigations. He drew on his experiences with the team when writing the pilot episode.

Impact

The popularity of *CSI: Crime Scene Investigation* has raised concern among some legal experts, who believe that the show misrepresents forensic procedures and leads the public and juries to demand high-tech forensic evidence in legal cases. A number of organizations have also criticized the show for its often-graphic depictions of violence. Nevertheless, *CSI* has remained one of the most popular television shows in the United States, inspiring the creation of spin-offs *CSI: Miami*, which aired from 2002 to 2012, and *CSI: New York*, which premiered in 2004.

Further Reading

Archive of American Television. "Uncovering *CSI*: Creator Anthony E. Zuiker's Interview Is Now Online." *Archive of American Television.* Academy of Television Arts & Sciences Foundation, 20 Sept. 2011. Web. 6 Aug. 2012.

Ramsland, Katherine M. *The Forensic Science of* CSI: New York. Berkley Boulevard, 2001. Print.

Rath, Arun. "Is the '*CSI* Effect' Influencing Courtrooms?" *NPR.* National Public Radio, 6 Feb. 2011. Web. 6 Aug. 2012.

Angela Harmon

■ Cyberbullying

Definition: The act of harassing a person through the use of the Internet and related technologies

Bullying took on a whole new meaning with the widespread use of communications technologies such as the Internet and cell phones. Intimidation that transpired via these technologies was dubbed cyberbullying and was most commonly experienced by young people. Such harassment became especially prevalent in the 2000s with the introduction of social networking websites.

The term "cyberbullying" was first used by educator Bill Belsey in 2004 in an essay detailing the emerging threat of harassment through the use of information and communication technologies. He described cyberbullying as a pervasive form of intentional harassment by a group or individual acting with hostility toward another person, aided by the Internet's invasive capabilities. The act of cyberbullying, however, was present long before it was given a name. When the Internet became a significant source of connectivity near the close of the twentieth century, a new kind of rapport developed between people. Individuals communicating through a computer screen were able to behave and interact differently than they could face to face. Technology allowed for an anonymity that made bullying easier. Paired with the distancing effect many experienced through the use of such devices, bullying had the potential to be even more vicious than it would be in face-to-face situations.

As awareness of cyberbullying increased, researchers began surveying students about the incidence of such harassment among American youth. Teenagers seemed to be the main demographic affected by cyber harassment. In 2000, the Crimes Against Children Research Center interviewed 1,501 young people ages ten to seventeen. The survey found that one in seventeen kids—about 6 percent—had experienced threats or harassment online. This number increased to 9 percent five years later. In 2004, the Internet safety education website i-Safe. com surveyed the same number of students between grades four and eight and found that 42 percent of students had been bullied online; 35 percent of those surveyed had been threatened and many said it had happened more than once.

Legislation against Cyberbullying

In late 2006, thirteen-year-old Megan Meier of Missouri committed suicide after a campaign of harassment over the Internet. After an investigation, Meier's death was attributed to repeated cyberbullying via the social networking website MySpace. There were no laws against cyberbullying at the time, so the offenders—including an adult neighbor—were indicted on charges of "unauthorized access of a computer system with intent to harm another person." The case incited intense public outrage and prompted many states to take legislative action against cyberbullying; soon, many had passed laws criminalizing it.

Schools, too, began taking steps to prevent cyberbullying. Many instituted programs of awareness and established punishments for those found guilty. Some debate was centered on use of school equipment, while others addressed all types of harassment of other students. Numerous organizations also advised victims to document cyberbullying for possible prosecution.

Campaigns against Cyberbullying

To increase awareness of the issue, many American organizations dedicated themselves to the prevention of cyberbullying. The National Crime Prevention Council created a public advertising campaign in 2007 and even initiated a contest challenging entrants to create their own public service announcements. The video-sharing website YouTube created an antibullying channel designed to encourage teens to speak out against harassment. Many more websites committed to fighting cyberbullying continued to crop up on the Internet.

Impact

The rise of cyberbullying in America has led to increased awareness among the public and in the government and has inspired legislation intended to prevent such offenses. By the end of 2009, twenty-seven states had enacted laws against cyberbullying.

Though cyberbullying is predominantly seen among youth, all age groups are affected by this type of harassment. Cyberbullying has had distressing effects on victims and can even be damaging to their physical health. Many experience anxiety, depression, and other related stress disorders. Victims have also been known to become isolated and undergo severe changes in behavior and mood. Some have committed suicide as a result. The campaign against cyberbullying has also raised public awareness of different forms of harassment that occur both online and offline.

Further Reading

Belsey, Bill. "Cyberbullying: An Emerging Threat to the 'Always On' Generation." *Cyberbullying.ca.* Cyberbullying.ca, 2004. Web. 30 Nov. 2012. Presents an essay from Belsey, who is credited with coining the term "cyberbullying," about the growing threat of harassment through technology.

Cloud, John. "Bullied to Death?" *Time* 18 Oct. 2010: 60–63. Print. Discusses bullying and bullying-related suicides among middle school students in the United States, noting a series of student suicides in September 2010.

Donegan, Richard. "Bullying and Cyberbullying: History, Statistics, Law, Prevention and Analysis." *Elon Journal of Undergraduate Research in Communications* 3.1 (2012): 34–36. Print. Examines the history of bullying, the development of cyberbullying, and the effects of online harassment on society.

"Parents: Cyber Bullying Led to Teen's Suicide." *ABC News.* ABC News Internet Ventures, 19 Nov. 2007. Web. 30 Nov. 2012. Discusses the suicide of Megan Meier, the connection to cyberbullying, and online harassment.

Siegel, Lee. "The Kids Aren't Alright." *Newsweek* 15 Oct. 2012: 18–20. Print. Reports on the use of the Internet and social networks among young students and their roles in cyberbullying, while also discussing online privacy.

Cait Caffrey

■ Cybercrime

Definition: A crime that uses a computer, often attached to the Internet, as a target, weapon, or accessory for attacking individuals, groups, or their property.

Criminals exploited computers shortly after their commercialization in the 1950s. The introduction of the Internet in the 1980s led to a marked increase in cybercrime, but the development of the ubiquitous World Wide Web in the 2000s—with access from home, work, and mobile devices—led to exponential growth of all types of cybercrime.

Researchers Doug Johnson and Judy Chiarelli of the Argonne National Laboratory's National Security Information Systems (NSIS) Team. (Courtesy Argonne National Laboratory)

There are many examples of cybercrime—including identity theft, denial-of-service attacks, Internet fraud, online predators, and theft of intellectual property—that have appeared in the media, but none is better known than identity theft. Identity theft is the use of personal identifying information to take actions regarding that person, usually by someone intent on performing an illegal act. While illegally impersonating someone is an old type of crime, the increasing use of the Internet for business and pleasure in the 2000s resulted in the creation of a digital identity, made up of names, social security number, credit card numbers and the like, and identity thieves developed many ways of stealing these digital identities.

One of the most popular digital identity attacks of the 2000s was phishing with e-mail. In a phishing attack, the thief sends an e-mail to an unsuspecting victim, requesting their digital information under false pretenses, such as pretending to be the victim's bank and asking for their social security and back account numbers. Once the thief has the banking information, they then empty the victim's bank account. Thieves also steal identities by placing spyware in a victim's computer to secretly log their private information. Protection from an identity theft attack is tailored to the attack. For example, training has helped reduce phishing attacks, while Internet secu-

rity programs that specialize in antispyware are the best protection against a spyware attack.

Accessing and storing child pornography on a computer is another common type of cybercrime that increased as the web became more popular and accessible. Sites exhibiting a wide range of images and videos of child pornography are easily accessible from a web browser unless some type of blocking software has been installed. Many public libraries and home computers installed blocking software over the course of the 2000s. Social medial sites generally tried to control improper content by carefully monitoring their sites. Law enforcement personnel involved in computer forensics spent much of their time searching computers for child pornography and then testifying in court.

One of the most popular uses of the Internet is to download and listen to music. The 2000s saw the creation of hundreds of sites where one can download all types of music in several formats like MP3, and many artists began marketing their music from their own websites. For example, the Apple iTunes site downloaded millions of recordings and albums to iPhones and personal computers. In spite of the large number of legal websites to download and play music, there were even more illegal sites created. These illegal sites have greatly reduced the profitability of the recording industry. The Recording Industry Association of America (RIAA), initially founded in 1952 to administer standards of frequency during recording, focused in the 2000s on helping to fight the illegal downloading of music. The RIAA became a leader in developing ways to secure the music downloading process, using special formats to protect music files and taking legal action at the discovery of illegal downloading sites.

Illegal downloading of motion pictures is another common form of cybercrime. Some popular films of the 2000s were recorded with cell phones and placed on illegal websites within days of their release. The Motion Picture Association of America (MPAA) is a trade group that has increasingly worked to combat this type of theft, using technology and lawsuits. The theft of music and motion pictures on the Internet is just one example of the theft of intellectual property that became pandemic in the 2000s. Theft of software, images, and even company secrets also became a major problem for industry. To protect against such attacks, companies have implemented expensive network and computer software, conducted massive training programs, and employed many computer security specialists.

Attacks on Computers

The most common form of attack on a computer is an intrusion attack. These have many forms: viruses, codes that can replicate themselves and damage computers; worms, programs that can replicate themselves and damage computers; bots, programs that help attack other computers; and spyware, programs that collect and forward private information. Trojan horses are one of the most dangerous forms of intrusion attack, as they are often launched from a hacker website, masquerading as a useful site. For example, starting in 2007, the Trojan horse ZeuS was used to steal online banking information after infecting a user through a download from a website—whether a malicious site or an infected legitimate site—or by a link in an e-mail to such a site. Almost all intrusion attacks constitute a crime, although some are simply attempts to irritate the attacked user. Training about how to avoid attacks and protecting software—antivirus, antispyware, and intrusion protection systems—provided reasonable protection from intrusion attacks in the 2000s, but hackers still found vulnerabilities to attack.

Another well-known type of attack on computers is a denial-of-service (DoS) attack, during which a hacker sends a massive volume of messages to a server, usually on the Internet, that interfere with the server's ability to function properly. A 2007 attack that interrupted electric service in Estonia is probably the best-known DoS attack of the 2000s, but there were many others. DoS attacks are generally cybercrimes, but they can be hard to prosecute. DoS attacks were also sometimes mounted by nations as a part of cyberwarfare, and in these cases were not technically a crime. A variety of defenses are used to combat DoS attacks. One of the most effective is to employ a honeypot, a computer that appears to be the server under attack, and let it draw the attacking traffic to it; intelligent firewalls and routers have also proven to be effective.

Attacks Using Computers

Fraud has always been a major problem for law enforcement, and in the 2000s it largely migrated to the Internet. Digital identities can be hard to recognize and validate on the Internet. For example, customers can log in to what they think is the rewards site for their credit card and give all their credit card information to a thief who proceeds to buy the maximum amount with their card. In another famous example of Internet fraud during the decade, a criminal or criminals posed as a Nigerian lawyer who solicited victims via e-mail by promising to transfer an inheritance into their bank accounts upon receipt of their account numbers, and instead took all their money. Consumer education is one of the best defenses against Internet fraud, but has needed to be combined with improved authentication techniques. One example is to give each Internet user or site a digital certificate, thus creating a digital identity for all on the Internet, so that cybercriminals intent on committing Internet fraud can be detected and stopped.

Cyberbullying, the use of communications devices or the Internet to verbally abuse or threaten another individual, was recognized as a major problem after the shooting at Columbine High School in 1999. During the 2000s, many laws were passed to limit cyberbullying, but it has continued to be a difficult type of cybercrime to control, especially on social media sites.

Impact

The 2000s saw rapid growth in using the Internet to communicate, transact business, access entertainment, and obtain information. Along with this growth came a proportionate increase in cybercrimes. Initially, most Internet users paid little attention to these cybercrimes. However, publicity about the financial losses incurred by identity theft victims, the physical harm suffered by cyberbullying victims, and damage done to companies and nations by DoS attacks made people aware of the dangers of cybercrime. As a result, by the end of the 2000s, Internet users had developed a healthy fear of cybercrime. Industry, educational institutions, and individuals purchased security software and hardware to protect their systems, greatly increasing the cost of the using the Internet.

Further Reading

Bradbury, David. "When Borders Collide: Legislating Against Cybercrime." *Computer Fraud and Security* 2 (2012): 11–15. Print. Introduction to the problems associated with prosecuting cybercrimes, spanning several countries.

Cilli, Claudio. "Identity Theft: A New Frontier for Hackers and Cybercrime." *Information Systems Control Journal* 6 (2005). 1–4. Print. A description of identity theft, including some statistics of the consequences of a successful attack.

Doyle, Charles. *Cybercrime: An Overview of the Federal Computer Fraud and Abuse Statute and Related Federal Criminal Laws.* Washington: Congressional Research Service, 2010. Print. A discussion of cyberfraud and the laws that work to prevent it.

McLaurin, Joshua. "Making Cyberspace Safe for Democracy: The Challenge Posed by Denial-of-Service Attacks." *Yale Law and Policy Review* 30.1 (2011): 11. Concise analysis of the problems posed by denial of service attacks.

Schell, Bernadette H., and Clemens Martin. *Cybercrime : A Reference Handbook.* Santa Barbara: ABC-CLIO, 2004. Print. An introduction to cybercrime.

Wall, David. *Cybercrimes: The Transformation of Crime in the Information Age.* Cambridge: Polity, 2007. Print. Demonstrates how modern cybercrime evolved from earlier types of crime.

George Whitson, PhD

D

The Da Vinci Code

Identification: Best-selling mystery novel that interweaves a murder investigation with a historical and religious conspiracy
Author: Dan Brown (b. 1964)
Date: Published in 2003

The Da Vinci Code became a cultural phenomenon in the mid-2000s, selling more than eighty million copies over the course of the decade. Focusing on a conspiracy that challenges the central tenets of Christianity, the novel generated a great deal of controversy and drew public attention to subjects such as theology and art history.

The Da Vinci Code was published in the United States by Doubleday in April 2003 and was later published in more than thirty countries. The fourth novel by American writer Dan Brown, the book begins with the murder of the curator of the Louvre, Jacques Saunière. Robert Langdon, a professor of religious symbology and the protagonist of several of Brown's novels, is called upon by police to help decipher some of the bizarre clues left by the dead curator. Working with Saunière's granddaughter, police cryptologist Sophie Neveu, Langdon uncovers a vast conspiracy by the Catholic Church to hide several truths that would destroy the foundation of Christianity.

The novel proposes that Jesus and his follower Mary Magdalene were secretly married and had a child together, thus continuing a royal Jewish bloodline extending from the reigns of biblical kings David and Solomon to the present time. The Priory of Sion, a secret society, is devoted to protecting their descendants. The society also founded the Knights Templar and tasked them with retrieving and preserving a collection of documents that attest to this genealogy as well as to the church's suppression of the feminine sacred. The novel's title refers to Italian Renaissance artist Leonardo da Vinci, who is identified as a member of the Priory of Sion along with such historical figures as Italian painter Sandro Botticelli and English scientist Isaac Newton. Da Vinci's painting *The Last Supper* is said to contain clues that point to the conspiracy.

Impact

The popularity of *The Da Vinci Code* sparked public interest in secret societies, the Knights Templar, and related subjects, prompting the publication of many books and articles discussing the factual and fictional aspects of the work. The novel also inspired a film adaption, released by Columbia Pictures in 2006. Directed by Ron Howard, the film stars Tom Hanks as Langdon and Audrey Tautou as Neveu.

Further Reading

Bock, Darrell L. "Fact, Fiction, and the *Da Vinci Code*." *Human Events* 60.19 (2004): 22. Print.
"Christians Counter *The Da Vinci Code*." *Christian Century* 121.5 (2004): 13–14. Print.
Cowley, Jason. "The Author of the Best Selling *Da Vinci Code* Has Tapped into Our Post–9/11 Anxieties and Fear of Fundamentalism." *New Statesman* 13 Dec. 2004: 18–20. Print.

Sally Driscoll

The Dark Knight

Identification: 2008 film and the second installment in director Christopher Nolan's Batman series, following *Batman Begins* in 2005.
Director: Christopher Nolan (b. 1970)
Date: Released on July 18, 2008

Following the critically acclaimed and financially successful Batman Begins *(2005),* The Dark Knight *continued Christopher Nolan's reimagining of the Batman franchise. The film was interpreted as a commentary on America following the terrorist attacks of September 11, 2001. It was celebrated for its mature approach to the superhero film genre and the performance of Heath Ledger as the villain called the Joker.*

At a time when superhero films were seen as thematically weak and lacking in characterization, Nolan's *Batman Begins* proved that the genre could be used to explore deeper psychological and sociological themes. Although Nolan was not sure he wanted to direct another Batman film after *Batman Begins*, his desire to reinterpret the character of the Joker drew him into the project. Together with writers David S. Goyer and Jonathan Nolan, they developed a film that further explored the psyche of Batman and how his presence affects Gotham City. In their work developing the Joker character, Nolan and his crew were inspired by appearances of the Joker in the *Batman* comic books from the 1940s.

In the film, Batman (Christian Bale) and Lieutenant Jim Gordon (Gary Oldman) team up with district attorney Harvey Dent (Aaron Eckhart) to bring down the mob in Gotham. The Joker kills the leader of the mob and begins a reign of terror in the city that includes mass murder and terrorism. Dent's face becomes disfigured following an explosion planned by the Joker, causing Dent to seek misguided revenge on Batman and Gordon.

Nolan stated that he wanted the Joker to be an element of chaos with no particular motivation or origin story. This made the conflict between chaos and order one of the central themes in the film, with the Joker representing anarchy. Other major themes of the film were revenge and escalation. Nolan explained that the situation in Gotham had to escalate for the worse before they could get better. Several critics opined that the extremes Batman went to in the film to stop the Joker were a commentary on President George W. Bush and his War on Terror following the terrorist attacks of September 11, 2001.

Impact

For his portrayal of the Joker, Heath Ledger won over twenty awards, including the Academy Award for best supporting actor. Ledger passed away before the release of the film and his family accepted the Academy Award at the ceremony. The movie was nominated for several film industry awards and became the highest-grossing film of 2008. Critics praised the film's approach to the superhero genre and its handling of dark and mature themes. Even critics who did not favor the film noted that Ledger's performance was something to be applauded.

Further Reading

Byrne, Craig, Mike Essl, and Alexander Tochilovasky. *The Dark Knight: Featuring Production Art and Full Shooting Script.* New York: Universe, 2008. Print.

Jesser, Jody Duncan, Janine Purroy, and Chip Kidd. *The Art and Making of the Dark Knight Trilogy.* New York: Abrams, 2012. Print.

Patrick G. Cooper

■ Decriminalization of Marijuana

Definition: Classification of marijuana possession as a misdemeanor, typically involving a fine

Although the US federal government has not decriminalized marijuana, decriminalization of marijuana for personal use has gained popularity at the state level. Because some state governments have reduced the penalty for cannabis possession from a criminal offense, involving possible incarceration and a criminal record, to a misdemeanor, law enforcement officials have redirected their resources to fighting more serious crimes.

In 1972, the National Commission on Marihuana and Drug Abuse published its review of cannabis. It claimed that marijuana use did not cause physical or psychological problems, that the drug was instead opposed as "a symbol of the rejection of cherished values" (Lee 122). The group warned against prohibition and recommended that personal use of marijuana be decriminalized. While President Richard M. Nixon rejected the commission's conclusions, in the early 2000s, the statements were embraced by many in the general populace.

Some of the loudest proponents of decriminalization have argued their side on the basis of economics. In 2001, the New Mexico Drug Policy Advisory Group suggested decriminalization as a way to better allocate money for police officers to target serious criminals. The police department of Oakland, California, moved beyond decriminalizing personal use by classifying marijuana possession and distribution as low priorities in 2004. Then, in 2005, hundreds of economists petitioned President George W. Bush to legalize marijuana. While moral issues continued to be part of the marijuana discourse, it became clear that the drug was also a symbol for broader concerns in the United States.

Decriminalization by State

Throughout the early 2000s, many states decriminalized marijuana. Levels of decriminalization varied with regard to the amount of marijuana in possession and whether the drug was for personal use, cultivation, or distribution. By 2010, marijuana had been at least partially decriminalized in Arkansas, California, Colorado, Hawaii, Illinois, Maine, Michigan, Minnesota, Mississippi, Montana, Nebraska, Nevada, New Hampshire, New York, North Carolina, Ohio, Oregon, Washington, and Wisconsin. In Alaska and Massachusetts possessing one ounce of marijuana was deemed legal.

Various groups supported decriminalization and pushed for state reform. These groups included National Organization for the Reform of Marijuana Laws (commonly known as NORML), Americans for Safe Access, and Law Enforcement Against Prohibition. Advocates of the legalization of marijuana argued from the standpoint of freedom of choice, with supporters clamoring against unnecessary government interference. Promoting the therapeutic aspects of cannabis, some groups presented marijuana access as a human-rights issue and proposed that the drug be available for medical purposes. As more states decriminalized marijuana, and as proponents of decriminalization argued widely against prohibition, the argument for protecting "cherished values" began to weaken.

Health and Morality

Initially thought to have adverse health effects, marijuana gained prominence as a natural therapy. It has been shown to revive the appetites of cancer patients undergoing chemotherapy and to provide relief for those with AIDS or other health problems. Representing a state that was an early supporter of medical marijuana, legislators in California passed the Compassionate Use Act (Proposition 215) in 1996, allowing doctors to legally prescribe marijuana to their patients. Promoting medical marijuana access as a means of compassion directly contrasted views of marijuana use as immoral.

Following California's lead, Alaska, Maine, and Oregon legalized medical marijuana in the 1990s. In the 2000s, medical marijuana also became legal in several other states. With legalization came questions of regulation. The cases *United States of America v. Oakland Cannabis Buyers' Cooperative and Jeffrey Jones* (2001) and *Gonzales v. Raich* (2005) assessed the role of the federal government in regulating medical-marijuana distribution. As the federal government became more involved with the economic aspects of medical marijuana, the need for a unified national policy on the drug grew more urgent.

Impact

The trend of decriminalizing marijuana throughout the early 2000s seems likely to continue in subsequent decades. While the United States continues to fight the War on Drugs, states have waged their own battles. By decriminalizing marijuana, states have been able to focus on hard drugs, such as cocaine and heroin, freeing space in crowded prisons for offenders of serious crimes. While some fear that decriminalization communicates an acceptance of drug use and illegal behavior, others cite the health benefits of marijuana.

Further Reading

Campbell, Greg. *Pot, Inc.: Inside Medical Marijuana, America's Most Outlaw Industry.* New York: Sterling, 2012. Print. Investigates American attitudes toward marijuana, highlighting the move toward acceptance as the drug's medical benefits become a part of the societal discourse.

Lee, Martin A. *Smoke Signals: A Social History of Marijuana—Medical, Recreational, and Scientific.* New York: Scribner, 2012. Print. Traces the history of the War on Drugs in the United States, devoting significant attention to legislative, judicial, and medical advances concerning marijuana use in the twenty-first century.

Linden, David J. *The Compass of Pleasure.* New York: Viking, 2011. Print. Explores the brain's pleasure receptors and how they process a range of activities from doing drugs to learning.

Regan, Trish. *Joint Ventures: Inside America's Almost Legal Marijuana Industry.* Hoboken: Wiley, 2011. Print. Provides a balanced inside look at the marijuana industry from an economic standpoint.

Smith, Mark Haskell. *Heart of Dankness: Underground Botanists, Outlaw Farmers, and the Race for the Cannabis Cup.* New York: Random, 2012. Print. Chronicles novelist Smith's experiences, particularly in California, as a medical marijuana user.

The Union: The Business behind Getting High. Dir. Brett Harvey. Phase 4 Films, 2009. DVD. Examines the economic, social, and health aspects of growing, distributing, and using marijuana, focusing on British Columbia.

Lucia Pizzo

■ DeGeneres, Ellen

Identification: American comedian, talk show host, and animal rights activist
Born: January 26, 1958; Metairie, Louisiana

Although DeGeneres is a comedian who is known for her quick wit and dry humor, she is also an advocate for serious issues including gay and lesbian rights, sexual abuse of teenage girls, and animal rights.

After her sitcom, *Ellen* (1994–98) and *The Ellen Show* (2001–2002), Ellen DeGeneres launched *The Ellen DeGeneres Show* in 2003. The show won the Daytime Emmy Award for Outstanding Talk Show in 2004 and 2006–2008. DeGeneres also won People's Choice Awards in 2005–2008 for Favorite Daytime Talk Show Host and Favorite Funny Female Star. The year 2003 was also marked by the release of the popular animated Pixar film *Finding Nemo*, in which DeGeneres voiced Dory the fish, Marlin's friend. She also performed her stand-up comedy routine "Here and Now" in cities across the United States.

In addition to her success as a comedian and television personality, DeGeneres has also found success in 2003 as an author. Her second book, *The Funny Thing Is . . .* , a collection of comedic essays,

Ellen DeGeneres (right) and Michelle Obama dance during a taping of The Ellen DeGeneres Show. *(Official White House Photo/Photograph by Chuck Kennedy)*

became a *New York Times* best seller. Since then she has published a third book, *Seriously . . . I'm Kidding* (2011).

DeGeneres's humorous views about everyday experiences—evident both in her stand-up comedy and in her books—and her experience as a talk show host have helped her land prominent emcee positions, most notably as host of the Emmy Awards (2001) and the Academy Awards (2007). She also judged one season of *American Idol*, the popular reality television–singing competition, in 2009.

DeGeneres has served as a vocal advocate of human and animal rights. In 1997, she publicly announced her sexual orientation. She began dating actress Portia de Rossi in 2004. The couple wed on August 16, 2008, in California, where gay marriage had recently been legalized. During the same year that DeGeneres and de Rossi first became involved, DeGeneres revealed to *Allure* magazine that her stepfather had sexually abused her as a teenager. DeGeneres hoped her revelation would encourage teenage girls caught in the same situation to seek help. Both DeGeneres and de Rossi have worked for the cause of animal rights. In 2009, the couple were jointly awarded the Wyler Award, a Humane Society honor given to public figures who publically support animal rights.

Impact

The *Ellen DeGeneres Show* has received over thirty Daytime Emmy Awards, and maintains an audience of 2.5 million people per episode. Critics have praised DeGeneres for her ability to bring humor to everyday experiences. DeGeneres' honesty and self-awareness around both her sexual orientation and her early experiences as a teenager have helped others facing similar challenges. Additionally, her animal rights advocacy has brought nationwide awareness to the issue.

Further Reading

DeGeneres, Ellen. *Seriously . . . I'm Kidding*. New York: Grand Central, 2011. Print.
"Ellen DeGeneres." *Celebrity Central: Top 25 Celebs. People*. Time, Inc., 2012. Web. 9 July 2012.
"Ellen DeGeneres Molested as Teen." *CBS News*. CBS News Entertainment, 11 Feb. 2009. Web. 6 Aug. 2012.

Gina Kuchta

■ Demographics of Canada

Definition: The distribution of Canada's population according to various defining criteria such as age, ethnicity, sex, income, or geographic location

Demographic changes are reflective of the dynamic nature of Canada's population. During the 2000s, the changes affected and were affected by the enactment of laws, determination of policy directions, and distribution of supports and programs by the government and private businesses.

Population Dynamics and Distribution

The second-largest country in the world by land area, Canada was nevertheless only sparsely populated throughout the 2000s, despite having high population growth relative to other industrialized countries during the decade. In 2006, the population of Canada was 32.6 million persons, up from 12.3 million in 1946. Through the decade, the population increased at a steady rate of approximately 1.0 percent, and by the end of 2010 stood at about 34 million.

The majority of Canadians lived in the southern part of the country, near the border between Canada and the United States. The greatest concentrations were found in the region between Windsor, Ontario, and Quebec City, Quebec; in south coastal British Columbia; in southern Manitoba; and in Alberta between Calgary and Edmonton. The remainder were distributed throughout the vast expanse of the country, localized in various communities.

Throughout the decade, this distribution remained essentially the same, although a significant number of people moved from various locales within Canada to northern Alberta, as the Oil Sands project there expanded and offered ready employment in many fields.

Immigration

Canada's immigration and multiculturalism policies encouraged people from all parts of the world to immigrate throughout the decade. By 2006, immigration accounted for fully two-thirds of the overall population growth. Some 85 percent of immigrants settled in the provinces of Ontario, Quebec, or British Columbia, with half settling in Ontario. The cities of Toronto and Vancouver, being the principal ports of entry for immigrants to Canada, maintained

Toronto's urban diversity in evidence on Church Street during Toronto Pride Week. (Courtesy Andres Musta)

the highest proportion of immigrants in the population, comprising almost half of metropolitan residents in both cities.

Immigration trends of the decade often reflected local situations elsewhere in the world. The largest influxes of immigrants—as of 2006 census data—were from China and other Asian countries (60.5 percent), and from European nations (16.4 percent). Immigrants from Africa and from South and Central America combined to account about equally for another 20 percent of immigrants. Some 2.6 percent of immigrants came to Canada from the United States, and less than 1 percent from Australia and Oceania. More than half of the immigrants were admitted on economic grounds, deemed to be a positive force on the national economy or to integrate readily into the Canadian labor market according to their age, education level, and ability to communicate in one of the official languages of Canada. The proportion of immigrants in 2006 who were admitted as refugees was 12.9 percent. Approximately 250,000 immigrants were admitted to Canada each year.

Sex, Birth Rates, and Life Expectancy

Up until the retirement age of sixty-five, the male population of Canada outnumbered the female population by approximately 1.04 to 1; after retirement, this trend reversed such that the ratio became 0.79 to 1. Over the entire population, the ratio of males to females was 0.98 to 1. Census data showed that in 2006, the median age of the overall population was 38.8 years, with those living in Quebec and the eastern provinces having a higher median age, and the rest of the country having a lower median age. One major aspect of the population's age distribution during the 2000s was a shift in the relative ages of the population as the so-called baby boomer generation progressed through its life expectancy. The result was that an older age group came to represent a significantly larger portion of the population than those of a lesser age. Canadians have had a significantly higher life expectancy than that of most other nations of the world. This steadily increased through the decade, adding about 1.5 years to the life expectancy of women and about three years to that of men. In 2005, life expectancy for Canadian women was 82.7 years, and that of Canadian men was 78.0 years. The disparity between the two decreased continually as well.

As was the case in all industrialized countries, the birth rate in Canada declined over the decade, a trend that is expected to continue past the point at which the death rate would exceed the birth rate. This was attributed to a number of factors observed over course of the decade. The fertility rate of women in Canada, measured as the number of children born, averaged only 1.5 through the 2000s, well below the natural replacement rate of 2.1. During the decade, Canadian women as a group gave birth later in life than they had in previous decades.

Impact

Understanding the dynamics of demography has been essential for Canadian policy administration. Trends observed over the decade of the 2000s have enabled forecasts of conditions likely to exist in the foreseeable future, allowing policymakers to plan for exigencies that could impact social programs such as immigration, medical care, pension and old age security plans, employment insurance, and others. The use of demographic information to prepare and construct viable programs to meet future needs remains an important aspect of the Canadian government's primary constitutional duty of safeguarding the welfare of Canadians.

Further Reading

Bramadat, Paul, and David Seljak, eds. *Religion and Ethnicity in Canada.* Toronto: U of Toronto P, 2009. Print. Discusses in detail the role of religion and ethnicity in public policy and their effects on the education and health care systems in Canada.

"Canadian Demographics at a Glance." *Statistics Canada.* Government of Canada, Jan. 2008. Catalogue no. 91-003-X. PDF file. 26 Dec. 2012. Provides a thorough analysis of Canadian demographic data, with clear explanations and numerous charts.

"A Demographic Profile of Canada." *CCSD's Stats & Facts.* Canadian Council on Social Development, n.d. PDF file. 26 Dec. 2012. Provides a concise account of Canadian demographics.

Peters, Evelyn J. *Urban Aboriginal Policy Making in Canadian Municipalities.* Montreal: McGill–Queen's UP, 2011. Print. As one of the fastest-growing minorities in Canada, the Aboriginal population has presented unique challenges and requirements for policymakers in light of constitutional and treaty rights.

Tindal, C. Richard. *A Citizen's Guide to Government.* 3rd ed. Toronto: McGraw, 2005. Print. Provides a thorough explanation of Canadian government function, with a discussion of the social safety net that demonstrates the need for demographic information and how it is used in determining public policy in Canada.

Richard M. Renneboog, MSc

■ Demographics of the United States

Definition: Demographics can be defined as the statistical characteristics of a group, whether applied to a geographic population or some other subgroup within a larger population. Demographic analysis can be conducted on a large group, such as the US population as a whole, or may be directed toward a more specific subgroup.

A variety of factors commonly measured through demographic analysis, including racial and gender diversity, national origin, and political preference, are used to evaluate evolution and change in a society. By measuring changes in demographics, it is possible to analyze the ways that society and culture are likely to change in the future.

Population Growth and Immigration

Estimates from the US Census Bureau indicated that there were 281,421,906 residents living in the United States in 2000. During the course of the decade, the population grew by more than 9.7 percent to reach 308,745,538 in April of 2010. More detailed breakdowns of population indicated that California was the most populous state in the country, with 37,253,956 residents, while Wyoming was the least populous state, with 563,626 residents in 2010. During the 2000s, the United States had a 2.7 percent birth rate, constituting an average of one birth every eight seconds and one death every twelve seconds.

From 2000 to 2010, the United States experienced the slowest population growth in the nation's history since the Great Depression. The United States was the still the fastest growing industrialized nation and the third most populous nation in the world. Analysts believed that reduced immigration and economic recession were the primary factors leading to reduced population growth. Census Bureau estimates indicated that the nation's population was likely to grow by 13 percent between 2010 and 2025.

Between 2000 and 2010, more than 11.3 million immigrants obtained permanent legal residence in the United States. The largest immigrant contributions to the United States came from Europe, Asia, Mexico, and the Caribbean. Of the 11.3 million immigrants who became residents during the decade, more than two million came from Europe, 3.8 million came from Asia, 1.8 million came from Mexico, and 1.2 million from the Caribbean.

In order for an individual to obtain legal permanent resident status, they must qualify for one of several classes of admission determined by the US government. During the 2000s, those categorized as refugees comprised the largest class of accepted immigrants, accounting for more than 800,000 of the immigrants joining the country during the decade. Another prominent group of US immigrants were those who applied for political asylum, accounting for more than 400,000 of the total number of immigrants. More than one million new immigrants were admitted because of family preferences, many having immediate family who had previously obtained resident status.

Race and Ethnic Diversity

In 2010, more than 97 percent of Americans described themselves as representing "one race."

Domestic Migration, 2000-2009

The 5 Best States		The 5 Worst States	
Florida	+ 1,154,000	New York	− 1,650,000
Texas	+ 838,000	California	− 1,490,000
Arizona	+ 697,000	Illinois	− 614,000
North Carolina	+ 663,000	Michigan	− 537,000
Georgia	+ 550,000	New Jersey	− 451,000

Source: The US Census Bureau

Over the course of the decade, this percentage changed by less than 1 percent of the total population, from 97.6 percent in 2000 to 97.1 percent in 2010. The remaining 2.9 percent of the population described themselves as being of two or more racial backgrounds.

The number of Americans describing themselves as "White" fell 2.7 percent during the decade, from 75.1 percent in 2000 to 72.4 percent in 2010. The nation's largest minority group was comprised of those who described themselves as "Hispanic" or "Latino," accounting for 16.3 percent of the population in 2010, an increase of 3.8 percent since 2000. Americans describing themselves as "Black" or "African American" represented 12.6 percent of the population in 2010, up from 12.3 percent in 2000. Americans of Asian descent increased by 1.2 percent during the decade, from 3.6 percent in 2000 to 4.8 percent in 2010. Other major ethic groups included American Indians or Alaskan Natives (0.9 percent) and Native Hawaiian and Pacific Islanders (0.2 percent). Approximately 6.2 percent of Americans identified as "some other race" in 2010, an increase from 5.5 percent in 2000.

According to Census Bureau analysis, Asian Americans were the fastest growing minority group. The Asian American population increased by more than 43 percent during the period, far outpacing the 9.7 percent growth recorded for the population as a whole. The white population was the only major ethnic group that declined as a percentage of the population, indicating an overall trend toward increased racial diversity continuing from previous generations.

The percentage of Americans identifying as "some other race," increased by 24 percent during the decade, representing over nine million Americans in 2010. A difficulty in determining racial diversity resulted from different opinions by people of Hispanic and Latino descent over the degree to which they saw themselves as representatives of a certain ethnic group. Analyses indicated that eighteen million Americans of Hispanic or Latino ancestries described themselves as "some other race" in 2010. In 2012, the Census Bureau considered further revisions to the racial and ethnic categories used on census forms.

Employment and Income

During the 2000s, income levels declined for most segments of the US population, beginning in 2000 after a peak in median income levels across the country. The Census Bureau estimated a median income of $42,148 in 2000 and $49,445 in 2010. During this same period, the nation experienced 26.6 percent inflation. The annual increase in median income was insufficient to account for inflation and other factors, resulting in a net reduction in income for most American families.

Census data from 2010 indicated that 15.1 percent of the population was living in poverty, as opposed to 11.3 percent in 2000. The most significant changes in poverty levels and median income came during the decade's two recessions. Approximately 31 percent of the population dropped into the "poverty range" for a period of at least two months between 2004 and 2007. Unemployment more than doubled during the decade, from 5.6 million in 2000 to more than 14.8 million in 2010.

Religion in the United States

The religious and spiritual landscape of the United States changed considerably during the decade from 2000 to 2010, largely continuing ongoing trends since the Census Bureau began measuring religious affiliation in the 1940s. More than 78 percent of Americans identified themselves as affiliated with some form of Christianity in 2010. While the United States has been predominantly Protestant since the founding of the nation, Protestant membership accounted for 51 percent of the nation in 2010, a reduction of 3 percent

An interpretive exhibit at Ellis Island captures the history of immigration to the United States by decade and region of origin up to the 2000s. (Courtesy Koen Schepers)

since 2000. The movement away from Protestantism has been ongoing since the 1950s, when the number of Protestants accounted for more than 68 percent of the population.

The numbers of individuals identifying as Muslim in America represented less than 1 percent of the population in 2010. However, estimates of Islamic adherence varied widely from 2003 to 2010, in part due to a preponderance of inaccurate estimates from anti-Islamic groups. The Census Bureau estimated in 2010 that Islam was one of the fastest-growing religions in the nation.

Among the most significant changes to religious affiliation between 2000 and 2010 was an increase in the number of unaffiliated Americans, who are not affiliated with any organized religion but tend to adhere to some form of personal or private spirituality. The number of unaffiliated Americans increased from 8 percent to more than 16 percent between 1990 and 2010. Though more Americans were moving away from organized religion, more than 92 percent of Americans described themselves as believing in a god of some kind.

Marriage and Divorce Rates

According to the Centers for Disease Control and Prevention (CDC), the percentage of Americans choosing to get married declined from 2,315,000

marriages recorded in 2000 to 2,096,000 in 2010. As a percentage of the population, marriage declined by 1.4 percent during the decade, from 8.2 percent in 2000 to 6.8 percent in 2010.

Declining marriage rates during the 2000s were partially attributed to the effects of economic recession and the decision by some couples to delay marriage for financial reasons. In contrast, the number of divorces and annulments decreased during the decade from 944,000 in 2000 (4 percent) to 872,000 in 2010 (3.6 percent). The state with the highest divorce rate in 2010 was Nevada, which recorded a 6.6 percent divorce rate for the year.

A number of researchers stated that data on divorce rates during the decade was inaccurate because a number of key states, including California, Georgia, Hawaii, and Indiana, did not report marriage data to the Census Bureau or the CDC, thereby hindering attempts to accurately calculate marriage and divorce rates. Researcher Paul Amato reported in a 2010 study of marriage and divorce trends in America that approximately 50 percent of all marriages end in divorce and that divorce rates are closely associated with economic and educational attributes. Studies found that divorce is more likely in marriages that occur before the age of twenty-five and between individuals of lower socioeconomic status.

Impact

Demographic data collected on the United States population between 2000 and 2010 indicated significant changes in economic and population characteristics during the decade. Despite increasing unemployment rates and falling income levels, the United States was one of the few industrialized nations to record growing population rates during the decade. In comparison, many Asian and European nations experienced negative growth, leading to some concerns over the potential for a growing age imbalance among the populations of many nations.

During the 2000s, US population growth fell to the lowest levels recorded since the Great Depression. Analysts attributed reduced population growth to economic factors, including the recession of the late 2000s, and to an overall reduction in immigration rates. Immigration fell sharply following the 2001 terrorist attacks and remained lower throughout the decade due to increased regulation. Immigration rates began to return to their pre-2001 levels after the middle of the decade.

As the population of the United States continued to grow throughout the decade, the diversity of the population also increased in terms of both ethnic and racial composition and religious/spiritual affiliation. The increasing diversity of the US population was partially due to immigration from a variety of nations and partially due to the intermixing of racial and ethnic populations. For instance, the number of persons describing themselves as having "mixed racial ancestry" increased as a percentage of the population from 2.4 percent to 2.9 percent between 2000 and 2010, and analyses indicated that this trend would be likely to continue in subsequent decades.

Further Reading

"2010 Yearbook of Immigration Statistics." *Office of Immigration Statistics.* Department of Homeland Security, Aug. 2011. PDF file. 21 Dec. 2012. Provides data on immigration rates and countries of origin for immigrants from 2000 to 2010.

Bok, Derek C. *The Politics of Happiness: What Governments Can Learn from the New Research on Well-Being.* Princeton: Princeton UP, 2010. Print. Discusses marriage and divorce rates in the United States, the difficulty in measuring marriage and divorce trends, and contributing factors.

DeNavas-Walt, Carmen, Bernadette D. Proctor, and Jessica C. Smith. "Income, Poverty, and Health Insurance Coverage in the United States: 2010." *Current Population Reports.* US Census Bureau, Sept. 2011. PDF file. 21 Dec. 2012. Discusses income, poverty levels, and contributing factors within the US population, with comparisons to previous periods in US history.

Klein, Herbert S. *A Population History of the United States.* New York: Cambridge UP, 2012. Print. Provides a historic analysis of population trends in the United States and their significance concerning a variety of sociological issues.

"US Census Bureau Announces 2010 Census Population Counts." *United States Census 2010.* US Census Bureau, 21 Dec. 2010. Web. 21 Dec. 2012. Summary of findings related to the 2010 population census, including data on state census figures.

"US Religious Landscape Survey." *Pew Forum.* Pew Forum on Religion and Public Life, 2010. Web. 21 Dec. 2012. Discusses religious affiliation and developments from the 1950s to 2010. Includes analyses of the growth in unaffiliated Americans and changes in Christian affiliation.

Verdugo, Richard R., ed. *The Demography of the Hispanic Population: Selected Essays.* Charlotte: Information Age Pub, 2012. Print. Provides an analysis of the Hispanic population of the United States from a variety of perspectives, including immigration and naturalization, as well as racial/ethnic identification.

Micah Issitt

■ Department of Homeland Security

Definition: A cabinet department of the federal government tasked with the protection of the county from threats to its security—both human, such as terrorism, and natural disasters, such as hurricanes—since its creation in 2002

The Department of Homeland Security was the congressional response to the September 11, 2001, terrorist attacks on the United States as well as an attempt to prevent future attacks. Strengthened by pieces of many other federal departments and legislation providing it with the power to create a national defense plan, the Department of Homeland Security grew into a powerful entity within the government, even obtaining a presidential cabinet seat.

The Office of Homeland Security was created by President George W. Bush in direct response to the September 11 terrorist attacks on the United States. Bush named Pennsylvania Governor Tom Ridge as the director of the Office of Homeland Security just weeks after the attack. In order to streamline reactions to future threats and attacks, the office was created to funnel information into one department and streamline the response process. The Office of Homeland Security consolidated twenty-two federal departments in order to ensure national security, as well as detect, prevent, and respond to attacks. The departments, or parts of departments, that were folded into the newly created department include the Transportation Security Administration, the Federal Emergency Management Agency (FEMA), the Immigration and Naturalization Service, the Nuclear Incident Response Team, the National Domestic Preparedness Office, the National Communications System, the US Coast Guard, and the US Secret Service.

A police officer asks Virginia National Guard aviators about the civil command and control capabilities of a light utility helicopter. (Virginia Department of Military Affairs/Photograph by Cotton Puryear)

Formation of the Department

The Department of Homeland Security (DHS) was established with the Homeland Security Act of 2002, which made it a cabinet department of the federal government and also created cabinet position for its secretary. Tom Ridge was the first Secretary of Homeland Security, followed by Michael Chertoff in 2005 and Janet Napolitano in 2009. The DHS grew through the decade, eventually becoming the third-largest department after the Department of Defense and the Department of Veterans Affairs.

Many high-profile features were added in the early days of the DHS. One example is the Homeland Security Advisory System—a color-coded scale, from green to red, that indicated the risk of a terrorist attack on the country. The DHS also created systems for emergency preparedness and disaster response. The National Incident Management System and the National Response Plan both came into effect under President Bush.

Modifications to the Department

Once the DHS was established several changes were made to refine its management and operations. After approximately three years under Secretary Michael Chertoff the Second Stage Review was held to assess and its inner workings related to policies and procedures. This review led to a reorganization of the

department—entitled the Department Six-point Agenda—in July 2005. That same year the Domestic Nuclear Detection Office was formed and FEMA became the oversight department of the Radiological Preparedness Program and the Chemical Stockpile Emergency Preparedness Program. This agenda also aimed to make improvements to transportation for people and cargo, deal more effectively with disasters, decrease illegal immigration while increasing border security, expand interdepartmental relations and communication, and generally improve management of the DHS as a whole. Fifteen months later, the department was reformed once again with the passing of the Security Accountability for Every (SAFE) Port Act of 2006. The SAFE Port Act reorganized FEMA at the same time that it removed some of the subdepartments of homeland security.

Hurricane Katrina and Resulting Changes

From August 23 to August 31, 2005, Hurricane Katrina made landfall on the southern coast of North America, moving in a northerly direction from the Gulf of Mexico. The storm caused approximately $125 billion worth of damage, and is one of the most costly hurricanes on record. There was significant outcry concerning the failure of the government to adequately respond to Hurricane Katrina, mainly against FEMA and its slow response to the crisis. FEMA was accused of mismanagement and poor leadership; the DHS was seen as failing in its preparation for the storm which killed over 1,800 citizens, and its aftermath, which left thousands more without food, water, or shelter.

This prompted Congress to pass the Post-Katrina Emergency Management Reform Act of 2006, which revised emergency responses, but kept FEMA part of the DHS. Essentially, this act reformed the infrastructure of both departments so that, in the case of a future emergency, aid will reach those in need effectively and in a timely manner. The following year another act was passed—the Implementing Recommendations of the 9/11 Commission Act of 2007—which made further changes to how FEMA administered its funds and how intelligence at the DHS was handled and implemented. It was also at this time that the DHS incorporated the findings in the official 9/11 Commission Report in order to create a stronger and more effective protective force for the United States.

Impact

The DHS, while still in its infancy during the 2000s, changed the way that terrorism was viewed and handled in the United States. Created out of the chaos and panic of the September 11 attacks, the department now controls how disasters and terrorism is dealt with in America, growing and adapting throughout the decade in order to improve reaction times and protocols. Comprised of pieces of many federal departments, the department was tasked with protecting the nation from threats domestic and international, as well as aiding with natural disasters, which it did with limited efficacy. Through reforms fashioned from previous failures, capitalizing on successes, and a strengthened infrastructure, the DHS became a power part of the federal government and will continue with its stated mission "to secure the nation from the many threats we face."

Further Reading

Brian, Bennett. "The Running Man." *Time* 2 July 2007: 34–35. Print. Discusses Michael Chertoff's work as the secretary of the DHS and his leadership during Hurricane Katrina.

Bush, George W. "Remarks on the Fifth Anniversary of the Department of Homeland Security." *Weekly Compilation of Presidential Documents* 44.9 (2009): 333–38. Print. Contains the text of Bush's speech on the five-year anniversary of the DHS in which he discusses September 11, terrorism, Hurricane Katrina, and the many facets of the department and its duties.

Chertoff, Michael. *Homeland Security: Assessing the First Five Years.* Philadelphia: Pennsylvania UP, 2009. Print. Provides Chertoff's assessment of the DHS, its establishment, and its roles in national security and emergency response.

"Creation of the Department of Homeland Security." *Department of Homeland Security.* USA.gov, n.d. Web. 7 Nov. 2012. A governmental website laying out the creation and modifications made to the Department of Homeland Security and how it tied into other governmental departments and programs.

Flynn, Stephen. "Recalibrating Homeland Security." *Foreign Affairs* 90.3: 130–40. Print. Overview

of the DHS under Presidents Bush and Obama and discusses policies related to border control, law enforcement, and the Transportation Security Administration.

Haulley, Fletcher. *The Department of Homeland Security.* New York: Rosen, 2005. Print. A book devoted to the history and inner-workings of the Department of Homeland Security.

Anna Accettola, MA

■ Depp, Johnny

Identification: American actor
Born: June 9, 1963; Owensboro, Kentucky

Johnny Depp's versatility, good looks, and charisma are often credited for his rise to superstardom; he is also revered for his ability to infuse characters with his own idiosyncratic humor and imagination.

Having found much success during the previous decade in *Edward Scissorhands* (1990) and other movies, Johnny Depp continued to prove his versatility in the 2000s. In 2001, he appeared as the 1970s cocaine kingpin, George Jung, in *Blow*, and Frederick Abberline, the opium-addicted investigator of Jack the Ripper, in *From Hell.* However, it was his role as Captain Jack Sparrow in the blockbuster film *Pirates of the Caribbean: The Curse of the Black Pearl* (2003), which made him well known to audiences worldwide. Basing his character's persona in part on the Rolling Stone's guitarist Keith Richards, Depp's original humor and dark allure won him his first Academy Award nomination. The movie won the People's Choice award for Favorite Motion Picture and grossed over $640 million globally. The sequel, *Pirates of the Caribbean: Dead Man's Chest* (2006), became the second-highest grossing film of the decade, generating over $1 billion. Depp, who had already been honored in 2001 as one of *People Magazine*'s "50 Most Beautiful People," was voted the magazine's "Sexiest Man Alive" in 2003.

Depp's success with the *Pirates of the Caribbean* audience led to highly acclaimed leading roles in other children's films, including *Finding Neverland* (2004), *Charlie and the Chocolate Factory* (2005), and *Alice in Wonderland* (2010). His singing role as the London barber in *Sweeney Todd: The Demon Barber of Fleet Street* (2007) was popular among adult audiences, and

Johnny Depp. (©iStockphoto.com/Frazer Harrison)

earned him a Golden Globe Award for best actor and his second Oscar nomination.

To round out the decade, Depp also narrated the documentary *Gonzo: The Life and Work of Dr. Hunter S. Thompson* (2008), and filled Heath Ledger's role in *The Imaginarium of Doctor Parnassus* (2009) after Ledger's death. In addition to his work as an actor, Depp has also worked as a film producer and screenwriter.

Impact

Depp has established himself as a Hollywood icon, achieving both critical and commercial success as an actor. He has starred in a wide variety of films, and become a favored collaborated or acclaimed director Tim Burton. In 2012, he appeared in a film adaptation of the television series *21 Jump Street*. The television series, which aired between 1987 and 1991, helped launch Depp's career as an actor.

Further Reading

Goodall, Nigel. *The Secret World of Johnny Depp.* London: Blake, 2011. Print.

Pomerance, Murray. *Johnny Depp Starts Here.* New Brunswick: Rutgers UP, 2005. Print.

Smith, Patti. "The Crowded Mind of Johnny Depp. *Vanity Fair* February 2011:48. Print.

Sally Driscoll

■ Desperate Housewives

Identification: Prime-time soap opera about several women who reside on the fictional suburban street Wisteria Lane
Creator: Marc Cherry (b. 1962)
Date: October 3, 2004–May 13, 2012

Desperate Housewives premiered on the ABC television network in 2004. With an average of twenty-three million viewers in its first year, the show became one of the biggest hits of the 2004–5 television season. The show later won several major awards, including the Golden Globe for best comedy in 2005 and 2006.

An hour-long television show mixing comedy, drama, and mystery, *Desperate Housewives* begins with the unexpected suicide of Mary Alice Young (played by Brenda Strong), a wife and mother who lived on Wisteria Lane. Many of the show's major characters are introduced to the audience at her funeral, including divorcée Susan Mayer (Teri Hatcher), homemaker Bree Van de Kamp (Marcia Cross), executive turned stay-at-home mom Lynette Scavo (Felicity Huffman), and former model Gabrielle Solis (Eva Longoria). Mary Alice watches over her friends and neighbors from beyond the grave, serving as the show's narrator as the characters cope in the wake of her death and eventually discover the reason for her suicide. She continues to narrate the drama in the subsequent seasons, helping to reveal the secrets that the housewives desperately try to keep from their friends, neighbors, and families.

Desperate Housewives was created by television writer Marc Cherry, who had previously created the comedy series *The 5 Mrs. Buchanans.* Cherry has explained in interviews that he developed the idea for the series after talking with his mother about how lonely she felt while she was raising three children.

Inspired by his mother's experiences, Cherry decided to write a soap opera that focused on women in the suburban United States. Several networks passed on the pilot; however, ABC decided to produce the show, airing the first episode in late 2004.

Impact

Although its ratings dropped to an average of about twelve million viewers by 2009, *Desperate Housewives* remained one of the top twenty programs on television throughout the decade, and it continued to receive nominations for Emmy Awards, Golden Globes, and Screen Actors Guild Awards. The show helped revitalize interest in prime-time soap operas and also served as the inspiration for the Bravo reality series *The Real Housewives of Orange County*, which premiered in 2006 and in turn inspired several spin-offs set in various locations throughout the United States.

Further Reading

McCabe, Janet, and Kim Akass, eds. *Reading* Desperate Housewives: *Beyond the White Picket Fence*. London: Tauris, 2006. Print.

Weinman, Jaime. "How Will We Remember *Desperate Housewives*?" *Maclean's*. Rogers Communications, 5 Aug. 2011. Web. 6 Aug. 2012.

Wilson, Leah, ed. *Welcome to Wisteria Lane: On America's Favorite Desperate Housewives*. Dallas: BenBella, 2006. Print.

Rebecca Sparling

■ Díaz, Junot

Identification: Dominican American author
Born: December 31, 1968; Santo Domingo, Dominican Republic

Díaz is a Pulitzer Prize–winning author whose works have appeared in a number of US publications, including the New Yorker. *He also serves as the fiction editor at the* Boston Review *and is a creative writing professor at the Massachusetts Institute of Technology (MIT).*

A native of the Dominican Republic, Junot Díaz achieved early success with *Drown* (1996), a collection of short stories. He received the 2002 PEN/Malamud Award for excellence in short story writing and the 2003 US-Japan Creative Artist

Junot Díaz. (Courtesy WBUR)

Fellowship from the National Endowment for the Arts. He took nearly a decade to complete his critically acclaimed debut novel, *The Brief Wondrous Life of Oscar Wao* (2007); Díaz repeatedly started and stopped work on this novel. For *Oscar Wao*, he received a number of awards, including the National Book Critics Circle Award, the John Sargent Sr. First Novel Prize, and the 2008 Pulitzer Prize for Fiction. Díaz also contributed to the screenplay of the 2002 film *Washington Heights*. Díaz's second collection of short stories, *This Is How You Lose Her*, was released in September 2012.

Díaz's experiences as an immigrant to the United States guide his work. Both *Drown* and *Oscar Wao* describe the difficulties of immigrants navigating their new worlds, and Díaz uses a blend of different genres, languages, and character perspectives to underscore this theme. In *Oscar Wao*, Díaz draws parallels between science fiction—including time travel and genetic manipulation—and the political history of the Dominican Republic to illustrate the trials of life in the Caribbean.

The shadow of former Dominican dictator Rafael Trujillo permeated Díaz's childhood—his father had been a military policeman—and influences his fiction as well. Díaz describes *Oscar Wao* as an examination of rape culture, beginning with the European colonization of the Caribbean and extending to modern dictators.

Impact

Díaz's work is known for its exploration of race and gender. He cites Toni Morrison and Octavia Butler as important influences, and he has drawn attention and interest to their earlier works while expanding on some of their themes. Díaz's work is important for examining the historical and intergenerational legacy of oppression and marginalization, and for chronicling the modern immigrant experience in the United States.

Further Reading

Dandicat, Edwidge. "Junot Díaz." *Bombsite.* BOMB Magazine, 2007. Web. 10 July 2012.

Jaggi, Maya. "Junot Diaz: A Truly All-American Writer." *Independent.* Independent.co.uk, 29 Feb. 2008. Web. 10 July 2012.

Moya, Paula M. L. "The Search for Decolonial Love, Part I." *Boston Review.* Boston Review, 26 June 2012. Web. 10 July 2012.

—. "The Search for Decolonial Love, Part II." *Boston Review.* Boston Review, 27 June 2012. Web. 10 July 2012.

Josephine Campbell

■ DiCaprio, Leonardo

Identification: American actor and environmentalist
Born: November 11, 1974; Los Angeles, California

DiCaprio earned critical acclaim for his role in 1993 film What's Eating Gilbert Grape, but earned prominence as an actor playing romantic leads, first in Romeo + Juliet (1996) and then in Titanic (1997). One of the most successful and best-known actors of his generation, DiCaprio is also an avid environmentalist.

After starring in director James Cameron's blockbuster film *Titanic* (1997), Leonardo DiCaprio became one of the most sought after actors in Hollywood. In 2002, he worked with director Martin

Leonardo DiCaprio. (©iStockphoto.com/Franco Origlia)

Scorsese for the first time in the film *Gangs of New York.* That same year, he starred in *Catch Me if You Can,* for which he was nominated for a Golden Globe. In 2004, DiCaprio and Scorsese worked together for a second time when DiCaprio accepted the role of eccentric billionaire Howard Hughes in *The Aviator,* which depicted the recluse's early, troubled days. DiCaprio was nominated for an Academy Award for his role as Hughes. He also won a Golden Globe for the role. Scorsese awarded DiCaprio a lifetime achievement award at the 2005 Santa Barbara International Film Festival.

DiCaprio and Scorsese worked together for a third time in *The Departed* (2006). The film was named best picture at the 79th Academy Awards. DiCaprio was nominated for a Golden Globe and a British Academy of Film and Television Arts (BAFTA) award for his work in the film. DiCaprio also received numerous award nominations in 2006 for his work in the politically charged thriller *Blood Diamond.* In 2008, DiCaprio and his *Titanic* costar Kate Winslet appeared in *Revolutionary Road,* a drama about a married couple in the 1950s.

In addition to his accomplishments as an actor, DiCaprio is a vocal supporter of various environmental causes. In 1998, he and his family started the Leonardo DiCaprio Foundation, which works toward securing a future for the earth and its inhabitants. DiCaprio also serves on the boards of the Natural Resources Defense Council (NRDC) and Global Green, USA. In 2000, he hosted an Earth Day celebration and interviewed President Bill Clinton about global warming. In 2007, DiCaprio wrote and narrated a documentary film entitled *The 11th Hour.* The film discusses global warming, and includes interviews with experts Stephen Hawking, David Orr, and former Soviet Union leader Mikhail Gorbachev. In 2010, he starred in the film *Inception.* DiCaprio played former FBI director J. Edgar Hoover in the 2011 biopic *J. Edgar.*

Impact

DiCaprio has leveraged his celebrity to try and increase awareness about environmental issues. He remains one of the most popular and successful actors in the entertainment industry.

Further Reading

Furgang, Kathy. *Leonardo DiCaprio: Environmental Champion.* New York: Rosen, 2008. Print.
"Leonardo DiCaprio Biography." *People.* Time Inc., 2012. Web. 13 July 2012.
Wight, Douglas. *Leonardo DiCaprio: The Biography.* London: Blake, 2012. Print.

Gina Kuchta

■ Digital reading

Definition: The practice of reading content such as books and magazines on electronic reading devices (e-readers)

Digital reading increased in popularity during the 2000s as e-readers grew lighter and more streamlined as well as more affordable. The development of online electronic book (e-book) retailers as well as standardized file formats for e-books further contributed to the increasing viability of digital reading.

In the early 2000s, the widespread adoption of digital reading was hindered by the fact that many e-readers were large and expensive and had little storage capacity. For example, the Rocket eBook weighed twenty-two ounces and held only ten books but cost five hundred dollars at launch. As public interest in digital reading increased, a number of companies began to create more lightweight devices with greater storage capacity and improved screens. These devices included the Sony Reader, released in 2006, and the Amazon Kindle, released in 2007, both of which featured E Ink displays designed to mimic the look of printed text on paper. The Kindle's advantage lay in Amazon's established e-commerce system and user base, which quickly adapted to purchasing and reading e-books. The bookstore chain Barnes & Noble released its own e-reader, the Nook, in 2009. The Nook ran the Android operating system and featured dual E Ink and color LCD displays. The device enjoyed a similar advantage to the Kindle in that it was based on an existing content infrastructure.

As new e-readers were introduced, the issue of file format presented a challenge to readers of digital content. E-books in certain proprietary formats could only be read on specific devices, and such devices were often incompatible with books in other formats. The Mobipocket format (later purchased by Amazon) and Sony's BroadBand eBook competed with various open formats (standardized as electronic publication, or EPUB, in 2007) and the widespread but proprietary Adobe Portable Document Format (PDF). The Palm Media eReader format (PDB) was supported on a number of devices, including the Nook, while the proprietary AZW format was compatible only with Amazon's Kindle. By 2009, EPUB seemed to be the leading standard, challenged primarily by Amazon's proprietary format. Many devices also supported PDF, but the format was seen as limited because it did not reformat text to fit on different screens.

As the leading e-reader manufacturers continued to compete, many consumers—particularly outside of North America—bypassed the need for e-readers altogether, preferring instead to read on mobile phones. The adoption of digital reading in the United States was particularly influenced by the introduction of the iPhone in 2007. Several popular reading apps emerged for the device, including eReader and Stanza.

Impact

Changes in technology, the publishing industry, and consumer behavior during the 2000s set the stage for an unprecedented level of digital reading, introducing the channel to the mainstream of media consumption and accelerating the shift from print to electronic media in the United States. The release of the iPad in 2010, as well as the introduction of similar touch-screen tablet devices, further bolstered digital reading in the early part of the next decade.

Further Reading

Gomez, Jeff. *Print Is Dead: Books in Our Digital Age.* New York: Macmillan, 2009. Print.

Kasdorf, William. *The Columbia Guide to Digital Publishing.* New York: Columbia UP, 2003. Print.

Kerry Skemp, MA

■ *District of Columbia v. Heller*

The Case: US Supreme Court ruling upholding the Second Amendment right of individuals to possess firearms in their homes in the District of Columbia

Date: Decided on June 26, 2008

A suit filed against the District of Columbia in 2003, challenging the meaning of the Second Amendment in relation to an individual's right to bear arms, eventually made its way to the US Supreme Court. In District of Columbia v. Heller, *the Supreme Court ruled that the District of Columbia's gun ordinances were unconstitutional.*

In 2003, six residents of Washington, DC, including federal security officer Dick Anthony Heller, challenged the District of Columbia's gun laws, which were enacted in 1976. The ordinances banned the registration of handguns, required licenses for all other firearms, and required that guns be kept "unloaded and disassembled, or bound by a trigger lock." The lawsuit stated that these laws violated the US Constitution's Second Amendment, which allows citizens to possess handguns in their homes for self-defense.

The US District Court for the District of Columbia dismissed the case—then known as *Parker v. District of Columbia*—on the grounds that the Second Amendment only applied to organized armed forces, such as the National Guard, and not to individuals. The court also dismissed all the plaintiffs from the suit except Heller because the laws were never enforced against the others. (Heller had been denied a handgun permit.) Heller appealed to the US Court of Appeals for the District of Columbia Circuit. The appeals court was faced with deciding whether the Second Amendment specifically applied to groups, such as a militia, or to individuals. On March 9, 2007, the court ruled that the Second Amendment protected an individual's right to bear firearms and reversed the prior decision. The appeals court also decided that the District of Columbia's laws were unconstitutional because they did not allow the use of handguns for self-defense in the home. The District appealed this decision to the US Supreme Court. On June 26, 2008, the Supreme Court upheld the decision of the appeals court, ruling the District of Columbia's gun laws unconstitutional.

Impact

District of Columbia v. Heller marked the first time since *United States v. Miller* (1939) that the Second Amendment was challenged in a US Supreme Court case. The Supreme Court's decision to uphold the ruling of the US Court of Appeals for the DC Circuit protected an individual's Second Amendment right to bear arms. The ruling also invalidated the District of Columbia's gun-ban laws from 1976, which the courts said violated the Second Amendment.

Further Reading

Chemerinsky, Erwin, et al. *After Heller: The New American Debate about Guns.* Washington: Cato Institute, 2008. Print.

Duggan, Paul. "Lawyer Who Wiped Out D.C. Ban Says It's About Liberties, Not Guns." *Washington Post.* Washington Post, 18 Mar. 2007. Web. 15 Aug. 2012.

Duke Law. "District of Columbia v. Heller." *Duke Law.* Duke University, n.d. Web. 9 Aug. 2012.

Legal Information Institute. "District of Columbia v. Heller (07-290)." *Legal Information Institute.* Cornell University Law School, n.d. Web. 10 Aug. 2012.

Angela Harmon

■ DIY culture

Definition: Acronym for "do it yourself," indicating a tendency toward self-sufficiency

Initially used in the 1950s to describe home renovation projects undertaken by nonprofessionals, the term "do it

yourself" has come to include music, arts and crafts, and publishing. Particularly in the 2000s, DIY products has become an increasingly popular alternative to homogenous, foreign-made, and mass-produced goods, and DIY culture represents a reaction against the surrounding culture of consumerism and corporatism.

With its roots in self-sufficiency, DIY culture encourages individuals to create, rather than to purchase, items needed in their lives. The trend in the 1950s for home improvement gave rise to the popularity of stores such as IKEA, which sell furniture in pieces to be assembled at home. Also interested in the self-made, punk bands carried DIY culture into the 1970s as a way to retain creative and managerial control of their music. Rather than rely on a record label, punk bands often preferred to self-produce records, create homemade merchandise, and self-publish zines. The zines of the 1970s became the how-to manuals popularized in the 2000s, such as the Complete Idiot's Guide and For Dummies series, which teach average Americans the basics of carpentry, computer languages, and many other skills.

While cultural interest in DIY built over the decades, the 2000s witnessed this casual interest becoming a movement. The DIY movement represents a reaction against mainstream culture. In response to globalization, it encourages people to shop locally. In response to corporate businesses, it supports independent shops. Concerns about environmental pollution have prompted crafters to refurbish used or unwanted items that would have otherwise been discarded. DIY culture counters consumerism with creativity and technology with the handmade. Ironically, it was the rise of technology and the expansion of the Internet that allowed the DIY movement to flourish as widely as it did.

The Internet allowed the DIY movement to expand to the wider marketplace. Not only did it provide a marketplace for goods, it also fostered the sharing of ideas. Throughout the 2000s, websites such as Craftster (2000) and Pinterest (2009) allowed users to browse DIY items and share them with others, while sites such as Etsy (2005) and Ravelry (2007) provided a forum for creators to sell their wares and to network with each other.

The Bike Dump offers reconditioned bikes, repairs, parts, advice, and "One Less Car" bumper stickers. (Courtesy Peter Blanchard)

Impact

With its emphasis on cost saving, DIY culture has grown in popularity in the late 2000s, following the economic downturn of 2008. Popularized by television shows like TLC's *Project Runway* and those on the DIY Network, DIY projects air throughout American homes. As the economic recession set in, a growing distrust of large corporations resonated with Americans and inspired many to create their own futures, with DIY projects becoming a means toward entrepreneurship.

While DIY culture in the 2000s catered to home improvers, gardeners, language learners, wedding planners, and crafters, rising education costs are promoting a new subset of DIY: students. As classrooms become digitized, the possibility of DIY higher education will likely become an increasingly popular alternative to traditional colleges and universities in the coming decade.

Further Reading

Kamenetz, Anya. *DIY U: Edupunks, Edupreneurs, and the Coming Transformation of Higher Education.* White River Junction: Chelsea Green, 2010. Print.

Levine, Faythe, and Cortney Heimerl. *Handmade Nation: The Rise of DIY, Art, Craft, and Design.* New York: Princeton Architectural, 2008. Print.

Lucia Pizzo

■ Domestic and offshore oil drilling

Definition: Oil extraction by drilling that occurs on land within the continental US, including Alaska, or offshore in the oceans or gulfs off the coast of the US

Although oil extraction peaked in the US in 1970, drilling for oil still takes place both within the continental US and offshore in the oceans and gulf that surround the country. In the 2000s, oil prices increased dramatically and some feared that oil had reached peak production rates worldwide. This oil crisis provoked significant changes to drilling during the decade, whereby new technologies opened up previous trapped oil reserves, and the ban on certain offshore drilling was lifted. As the US is the leading consumer of oil in the world, new ways to both conserve and produce oil gained prominence.

For most of the first decade of the 2000s, the US policy towards oil drilling under President George W. Bush, a former oil executive, focused on opening up protected domestic areas to drilling and finding concession from foreign oil importers. Any other types of energy policy, such as measures to reduce fuel consumption, the advocacy and advancement of renewable energy and policies to reduce climate change were rejected in favor of more drilling. This changed towards the end of the decade after the oil price shock of 2007–8. Under President Barack Obama's administration, there were more efforts aimed at fuel efficiency and other energy conservation techniques, along with ways to promote alternative and renewable energy sources.

New Domestic Reserves—Hydraulic Fracturing and Shale Oil

By the middle of the decade, new technologies were emerging in oil and gas extraction that opened up new areas of the continental United States to drilling ventures. The Bakken formation is found under Montana, North Dakota, and parts of southern Canada, and is part of the Williston Basin. Although it has been known since the 1950s to be home to a considerable reservoir of shale oil, it is difficult to extract, however. The technology oil extractors use to release it is known as hydraulic fracturing, or "fracking," and involves either drilling vertically and/or horizontally and injecting a high pressure liquid known as drilling

mud into the well to crack the rock formations to release the oil or gas. Although not new, this technology had been improved so that it became economical to use it. By 2008, extraction efforts were increasing in the Bakken, and a drilling mini-boom was well on its way. The oil reserves in the Bakken are estimated to be somewhere between 200 and 300 billion barrels; in 2006, proven oil reserves in all of the United States were said to be only 21 billion barrels. By 2009, Colorado and the West were also seeing an oil boom, with 33,000 new wells approved from 2001 to 2008. There are additional shale oil reserves all over the country that the oil industry is reevaluating given higher oil prices and improved extraction processes.

Another new potential reserve of oil is based in the United States' Arctic National Wildlife Refuge. The refuge is comprised of more than 19 million acres on the northern coast of Alaska on the Beaufort Sea, part of the Arctic Ocean. In 1998, the US Geological Survey estimated that between 5.7 billion and 16 billion barrels of oil might be technically recoverable from a subsection of the ANWR. Throughout most of the 2000s, Congress went back and forth on the issue of opening up the refuge to drilling. Republicans were in favor of drilling in the refuge, while Democrats repeatedly blocked their efforts in Congress over concerns about the impact drilling could have on the area's wildlife and fragile ecosystem. Alaskans themselves were largely in favor of drilling in the refuge, as each Alaska resident receives an annual dividend check from a permanent fund financed by oil lease revenues.

"Drill, Baby Drill"—Domestic and Offshore drilling

After the oil price shock that occurred in July 2008 when oil prices rose sharply to a high of $145 per barrel, concerns about national energy independence and security began to be voiced by many Americans. One of the potential types of drilling that could lead to increased energy independence was offshore drilling, which takes place off the coast of the continental United States in oceans or in the Gulf of Mexico. As gasoline prices hit record highs of over $4.00 in the summer of 2008, President George W. Bush lifted a 1990 ban on offshore drilling brought in by his father, President George H. W. Bush. Congress allowed its annual ban on portions of offshore drilling to expire in September 2008.

Offshore drilling is multijurisdictional, with state governments controlling drilling from the coast to about 3.3 miles out to sea (ten miles in Texas and Florida's Gulf coast). The federal government then controls the region out to about 230 miles (known as the Outer Continental Shelf or OCS), when it becomes international waters. Offshore reserves of technically recoverable oil (not proven) have been estimated to be ninety-three billion barrels, with fifty-nine billion barrels offshore of the lower forty-eight states.

The Republicans began to include increased domestic and offshore drilling as a policy plank. "Drill, baby, drill!" became a campaign slogan during the 2008 presidential election. Although popularized by Republican vice-presidential candidate and Alaska governor Sarah Palin, the slogan originated with Maryland's lieutenant governor Michael Steele.

Even if the ban on offshore drilling remains lifted, which is by no means a certainty, it takes many years before an offshore oil operation can receive the proper government permits and licenses and can then be built. Offshore oil located in deep water is also difficult, and dangerous, to extract. Given these restrictions, as well as significant environmental concerns, it is unlikely that offshore drilling will solve US oil supply problems in the short-term.

Environmental Concerns

Oil drilling carries with it certain environmental risks that have been popularized in the 2000s, especially regarding the issue of climate change. There are many who say that oil drilling and refining are helping to cause climate change. There are also significant concerns about the potential polluting activities of oil drilling, especially as it relates to water. Fracking in particular has caused environmental concerns, including some who say that there is increased seismic activity in areas where the extraction process occurs. Some research supports this theory, but as the technology is still quite new, more research is needed before results are confirmed. Although some suspect that chemicals used in the fracking process are toxic, the mix of chemicals used does not need to be reported. Furthermore, because fracking occurs far below the water table, the process has been exempted from the Safe Water Act.

Offshore drilling too has had environmental issues, especially when it comes to oil spills. Oil spills can be harmful to fish, and seafood, as well as birds, mammals, and plant life. It can also contaminate beaches and other coastal areas. In 2005, an estimated 595 oil spills occurred in the Gulf of Mexico and along the Gulf coast. These spills released releasing more than nine million barrels of oil, making it one of the worse environmental disasters in the United States at the time.

Impact

North Dakota, Montana, and other areas where domestic oil drilling has increased have enjoyed an economic boom that has led to increased employment opportunities as well as higher tax revenues. At the same time, citizen groups made up of concerned landowners and others were established to advocate against fracking because of environmental concerns, especially the contamination of the water table and food supplies. There is an emerging concern that fracking could contaminate underwater aquifers, and therefore the drinking water supply for many Americans. The BP oil spill in the Gulf of Mexico in the spring of 2010 all but silenced the Republicans' rallying cry of "drill, baby, drill!" Americans are still in the process of finding a balance between drilling previously untapped resources and addressing the environmental impact in affected areas.

With oil prices hovering around $80 per barrel at the end of 2009, the US policy of relying on significant amounts of imported foreign oil became costlier for the United States. It also constituted a security threat, as some exporting countries, such as Iran, Iraq, and Venezuela, were not always in a positive relationship with the United States. Advocates of domestic drilling argued that it could provide a short-term solution to the America's energy security problem. By the end of the decade, Americans were actively trying to reduce oil consumption by driving smaller, more fuel-efficient cars. Additionally, because increased drilling alone cannot solve the energy independence issue, the Obama administration began advocating for more affordable alternative and renewable sources of energy to be developed as well.

Further Reading

Cappiello, Dina. "Spills from Hurricanes Stain Coast." *Houston Chronicle.* Hurst Communications, Nov. 13, 2005. Web. 9 Dec. 2012. Discussion of the environmental damage caused by Hurricanes Katrina and Rita across four southern states in 2005.

Houseknecht, Dave, Brenda Pierce, and Alex Demas. "USGS Oil and Gas Resource Estimates Updated for the National Petroleum Reserve in Alaska (NPRA)." *USGS.* USGS, 26 Oct. 2010. Web. 9 Dec. 2010. Most recent findings from the US Geological Survey on undiscovered oil reserves in Alaska, finding that previous reports vastly overestimated the reserve, and that most of it was recoverable gas, not oil.

LeFever, Julie, and Lynn Helms, Lynn. "Bakken Formation Reserve Estimates." North Dakota Department of Mineral Resources, Bismarck, ND, 2010. PDF file. 9 Dec. 2012. A government report from North Dakota that refutes earlier estimates of reserves in the Bakken and puts forward new increased estimates.

Legesse, David. "Shale Oil Boom Takes Hold on the Plains." *National Geographic.* National Geographic Society, 28 September 2011. Web. 10 Dec. 2012. A good, basic description of the shale oil boom in the United States, especially in the Colorado area.

Mills, Robin M. *The Myth of the Oil Crisis: Overcoming the Challenges of Depletion, Geopolitics, and Global Warming.* Westport: Praeger, 2008. Print. This book, written by an oil industry insider, counters the theory of peak oil by stating that oil reserves are growing and have not peaked.

Moscou, Jim. "A Toxic Spew?" *Newsweek.* Newsweek/ Daily Beast Co., 19 Aug. 2008. Web. 9 Dec. 2012. An article that sets out the some of the environmental issues with fracking.

US Energy Information Administration. "Impacts of Increased Access to Oil and Natural Gas Resources in the Lower 48 Federal Outer Continental Shelf." *US Energy Information Administration.* US Dept. of Energy, 2009. Web. 9 Dec. 2012. Federal government report discussing the reserves in the OCS and the repercussions for developing these undersea oil fields.

Lee Tunstall, PhD

■ Dot.com bubble

Definition: A boom in the stock value of Internet-based companies during the late 1990s and early 2000s

Internet-based companies reached their peak stock market value in the early 2000s. In what has been dubbed the dot-com bubble, the stock prices of Internet companies soared during this time as investors forecasted the vast potential of the World Wide Web. They were encouraged by the confidence many placed in the flourishing Internet industry. As a result of such confidence, many were careless with their analyses and ignored the usual assessments involved in stock market investing. When many of the dot-com companies failed to thrive, investors lost millions of dollars.

Investors placed their confidence in the booming dot-com business during the late 1990s. Spurred by low interest rates and rising stock prices, investors provided a glut of venture capital to countless Internet companies. Companies used the capital to fund massive public awareness campaigns, and many paid millions of dollars for advertisements during Super Bowl XXXIV in January of 2000. The money was also spent on lavish corporate offices and to pay bonuses to employees. This uncontrolled spending would quickly bring the companies to ruin. Many investors failed to consider a company's potential to make a profit and solely relied on the high value of stock prices.

After several years of fast-rising stock prices, web-based companies foundered. On March 10, 2000, the NASDAQ Composite index topped 5,000. The Federal Reserve's increase in interest rates spurred the eventual deflation of the dot-com bubble. Within three months, stock prices were on the downturn. During this period, the market value of Internet companies fell by 50 percent. These companies were spending their venture capital faster than expected. One European venture, Boo.com, spent more than $188 million developing a global online megamall. Unable to recover its expenditures, Boo.com was liquidated. Such companies were dependent on the interests of the stock market, which failed to keep up. As these companies began to run out of funds, stock prices continued to plummet. Many venture capitalists panicked and sold their stakes before the businesses had time to recover. Such actions worried other investors and contributed to further losses.

Early 2000s Recession

By 2001, stock prices had fallen so low that many companies were filing for bankruptcy. Stock market favorites like Pets.com, eToys, and Priceline had seen their stock prices drop more than 99 percent. Some entrepreneurs profited before the burst, however, by selling their companies for massive profits. Most companies were not so fortunate. Celebrated start-ups like Webvan.com accumulated hundreds of

Pets.com Announces Withdrawal from Internet

On November 7, 2000, Internet pet supply store Pets.com announced to its shareholders that it was closing down. The company explained that it was ceasing operations because it was losing money and had failed to find a purchaser or financial backer. Its losses amounted to $147 million. The closedown would be gradual, the company said, but 255 of its 350 employees would be laid off immediately. Pets.com announced it would sell the majority of its assets, including its inventory, web site address, and its Sock Puppet brand. This dog puppet mascot had become nationally known during the previous summer. Pets.com sold the puppet to toy stores nationwide and featured it in television commercials. The closure marked a disappointing end for a company that initially looked destined for success and received significant investment from large Internet retailer Amazon.com.

Though there were several reasons for the failure of Pets.com, it became one of the more noteworthy flops, if not the most recognizable due to the company's high-profile marketing and the widespread decline in the fortunes of Internet companies that began in 1999.

millions of dollars in initial public offerings. Webvan.com was at one time worth $1.2 billion. Despite intense promotion—including branding on the seat cup holders at the San Francisco Giants' ballpark—the company was never able to attract enough customers to match its expenses and shut down in July of 2001.

The dot-com bubble burst also contributed to a recession early in the decade. From 2000 to 2002, the market value of NASDAQ companies lost more than $5 trillion in paper wealth. The terrorist attacks of September 11, 2001, helped contribute to the ever-falling stock prices. The crash lasted more than three years.

A New Dot-com Bubble?

The NASDAQ eventually made a slight recovery and by 2006 had rebounded to $3.6 trillion. Venture

capitalists became much more cautious as well. During the first quarter of 2006, investments totaled one fifth of the amount invested in the first quarter of the 2000 bubble.

Dot-coms saw an upsurge in stock prices in 2009. Companies such as Netflix and Amazon saw their market value climb to an all-time high in late 2009. Even companies such as Priceline began to recover, with stock prices increasing 140 percent and selling for nearly $180, a significant increase from the 2000 low of $6 per share. Even though many considered the possibility of another dot-com bubble, most experts agreed that the surge in stock prices was significantly different from the increases seen in the early 2000s. That these companies also survived the steep economic downturn of the late 2000s also helped to increase investors' confidence.

Impact

Despite the many drawbacks and losses seen in the aftermath of the dot-com bubble, many positive developments emerged as a result of the excessive investments made by venture capitalists. Companies such as Google and Amazon would not have succeeded without the capital they received during this bubble period. The event produced some of the most beneficial technology the world had seen and the Internet became the most predominant resource for connecting people and products around the world.

Further Reading

"The Dot-Com Bubble Bursts." *New York Times.* New York Times Co, 24 Dec. 2000. Web. 21 Dec. 2012. An overview of the events leading up to the dot-com bubble burst.

Gaither, Chris, and Dawn C. Chmielewski. "Fears of Dot-Com Crash, Version 2.0." *Los Angeles Times.* Los Angeles Times, 16 July 2006. Web. 21 Dec. 2012. Weighs the possibilities of a second dot-com crash as investors banked on Internet companies.

German, Kent. "Top 10 Dot-com Flops." *CNET.* CBS Interactive, n.d. Web. 21 Dec. 2012. A list of the top dot-com busts of 2000 and 2001.

La Monica, Paul R. "Internet Bubble 2.0? Not So Fast." *CNN Money.* Cable News Network, 26 Oct. 2009. Web. 21 Dec. 2012. Argues that another surge in stock prices differs significantly from the bubble.

Langdana, Farrokh. "Federal Reserve Policy from the Dot-com Bubble to the 'Subprime Mess': A Story of Two Ups and Two Downs." *Rutgers Business Law Journal* 6.1(2009): 56–65. PDF. Rutgers University. Web. 21 Dec. 2012. Examines how Federal Reserve policymakers reacted to America's economic needs before and after the burst of the dot-com bubble.

Willoughby, Jack. "Up in Smoke." *Leonard N. Stern School of Business.* New York University Stern, n.d. Web. 21 Dec. 2012. Willoughby responds to his earlier article predicting how Internet companies would drain their venture capital before turning a profit.

Cait Caffrey

Protesters gather at Paseo de los Héroes in Tijuana, calling for an end to Mexico's bloody drug war. (Courtesy of Fronteras Desk)

■ Drug war in Mexico

Definition: Violence between rival drug cartels and the Mexican military beginning in 2006

The 2006 election of Mexican President Felipe Calderón marked an end to the Mexican government's long passivity in its decades-long struggle with the illegal drug trade and the armed cartels that have profited from its existence. Calderón's offensive stance would give rise to reoccurring clashes between the government and the cartels and mass killings between rival cartel factions that would plague the country throughout the 2000s.

Calderón Election and Operation Michoacán

Felipe Calderón was elected president of Mexico by a small margin over rival Andrés Manuel López Obrador in September of 2006, at a time when drug-related violence in Mexico was occurring at staggering rates. Over two thousand people were killed that year as a result of cartel-related violence, nearly double the homicide rate of 2001.

The fashion in which drug-related murders were being executed had also taken a significantly violent turn, with beheadings, execution-style killings, and discoveries of mass graves becoming the norm. Desecration of bodies was beginning to be widely utilized by cartels as a means of intimidation to rival gangs, police and military forces, and the general public. Police and journalists who attempted to thwart or shed light on the violent clashes between cartels were also increasingly targeted.

The Mexican state of Michoacán, coincidentally the home state of newly elected President Calderón, had experienced the brunt of the violence, with over a quarter of Mexico's drug-related homicides taking place there in 2006. Much of Michoacán's Pacific coast had become a key staging area for large amounts of cocaine and heroin intended for sale in the United States.

On December 12, 2006, just eleven days after his inauguration to the Mexican presidency, Calderón deployed four thousand troops to Michoacán to arrest known drug dealers, conduct raids of drug transport facilities, and establish security checkpoints on major highways. Operation Michoacán resulted in dozens of arrests and the seizure of weapons, communications equipment, and the destruction of thousands of acres of illegal marijuana and opium fields.

The scale of Calderón's operation and defiant use of Mexican military force was the boldest attempt ever made by the Mexican federal government to crackdown on the drug cartels, which had operated with relative impunity for decades. Unlike drug enforcement operations conducted by previous administrations, Calderón insisted that one of the major goals of his presidency would be not simply to disrupt or minimize drug trafficking in Mexico, but to fully and permanently dismantle each cartel. By the end of his first year in office, over 45,000 Mexican troops had been deployed in the government's war with the cartels.

Mexico's Cartel Network

Between six and eight major drug cartels have been in competition for territory, production zones, smuggling routes, and political sway in Mexico since the 1950s. The cartels have deep geographic, cultural, and familial ties, and they have fostered strong alliances and fierce rivalries across the country.

By 2006, the nation's most powerful cartel was Los Zetas, an organization that operated primarily across the country's eastern gulf coast. The cartel was founded by deserted Mexican military commandos, and throughout the 2000s was widely considered to be the most technologically advanced and violent drug-related organization in the world. Northwestern Mexico has historically been controlled by the Sinaloa cartel, while the country's southwestern region has been dominated by the Michoacán-based Knights Templar cartel.

Throughout the decade, Mexican drug cartels operated with an efficiency and technological capability that rivaled, if not surpassed, many of the nation's legitimate business enterprises. Cartels constructed elaborate recruiting campaigns targeted at members of police forces and Mexican armed services, promising higher pay and swifter opportunities for promotion, protection, and power. Evidence also revealed that many of Mexico's cartels held quarterly business meetings, kept complex ledgers on financial proceedings, and took council-like voting sessions on key assassination attempts or violent offensives. The ferocity of their violence and disregard for civilian casualties led many experts to dub the organizations "narco-terrorists."

Analyses of Mexico's cartel system by Mexican government bodies, international drug prevention organizations, and independent journalists throughout the 2000s shed light on the intricately complex system of management and logistics that

kept these organizations in power. Throughout the 2000s, Mexican drug cartels began to take on the characteristics of large-scale private militias backed by savvy international corporations.

Role and Impact of the United States

Widespread consumption of illegal drugs in the United States remained the number one source of income for Mexican drug cartels throughout the 2000s. While Mexico is not the sole producer of illegal drugs sold for consumption in the United States, a large majority of contraband produced outside the United States, including those from a variety South American countries and from nations as far away as Afghanistan, made their way to American cities throughout the decade through the US-Mexican border on cartel-controlled smuggling routes.

With an American populace consumed by new fears of terrorism in the wake of the September 11, 2001, terrorist attacks, a sputtering economy, and high unemployment, the drug war in Mexico—despite the ferocity of its violence and swiftly escalating death toll—was not necessarily a hot-button issue in American politics during the 2000s, particularly outside of border states. Politicians in American states sharing a border with Mexico, however, were vocal in their concern, particularly in the latter part of the decade, when violence began to spill over from Mexico into border towns in the United States.

In October of 2007, President George W. Bush announced a $1.6 billion dollar aid package to Mexico to assist in the effort to combat the cartels. Dubbed the Mérida Initiative, the package, comprised of planes, helicopters, weaponry, surveillance equipment, and computer software, received widespread support from both Democrats and Republicans in Congress.

American support to Mexico would not come without controversy. In the late 2000s, a plan by US officials to secretly coordinate arms purchases with Mexican cartels as a means to trace the arms back to high-level cartel officials—called gunwalking—was uncovered. The mismanaged initiative, known as Operation Fast and Furious, caused considerable embarrassment to US security officials, particularly when it was discovered that weapons involved in the scheme had led to the deaths of numerous Mexican police officials as well as a US Border Patrol agent in 2010.

Strategies at Decade's End

In 2008, Mexico's National Defense Department unveiled an outlined an agenda to create divisions in the cartels' organizational hierarchies through the provocation of internal confrontations, in hopes of promoting their self-destruction from within.

Mexican diplomatic tactics were largely seen as half of the solution by decade's end. In addition to the United States being the largest market for Mexican drug cartels, Mexico's status as the United States' second largest trading partner and as its fourth largest oil supplier—as well as increasing impacts to US national security—led many policymakers to consider the Mexican drug war a two-state problem.

A wide variety of US legislation had a direct impact on the Mexican drug war throughout the 2000s, notably the country's lax requirements regarding the sale and purchase of automatic weapons, which Mexican analysts attribute with helping to arm the cartels. While American politicians continued to attempt to reach consensus on the issue of illegal immigration from Mexico, the cartels began to make their presence known in this contentious arena as well, often bribing officials with promises of sending them to the United States and by utilizing illegal immigrants as a means to transport drugs into the United States.

Plans have also called for a national-level replacement for the numerous local police and government officials who have long since surrendered to cartel influence. With the cartels expanding their criminal operations into human trafficking, extortion, and money laundering by the end of the 2000s, the effectiveness of continued arrests and direct engagement of the cartels began to be questioned.

Impact

The illegal drug trade has remained problematic throughout the world for decades. However, few nations were impacted by the corruption, violence, and fear inherent in the drug war during the 2000s more than Mexico. Since its inception, the Mexican drug war has remained the central issue in Mexican culture and politics and an ominous blot on its international reputation.

The rampant corruption surrounding local levels of Mexican government was so inerasable that by decades end, many Mexican political analysts and international crime prevention scholars wondered if it was a system that could ever be fully cleansed. A 2008 report by the US Justice Department indicated the presence of Mexican drug cartels in over two hundred US cities, leading many analysts to wonder if the increased domestic threat might set the groundwork for increased US involvement in years ahead.

Further Reading

Farrell, Courtney. *The Mexican Drug War*. North Mankato: ABDO, 2012. E-book. Web. 8 Oct. 2012. A detailed examination of the drug war in Mexico, including US involvement. Covers the history behind the drug war up through future impacts on society.

Frantz, Ashley. "The Mexico Drug War: Bodies for Billions." *CNN World*. Cable News Network, 20 Jan. 2012. Web. 8 Oct. 2012. Discusses the violence of drug cartels and the deaths that have occurred as a result.

Llana, Sara Miller. "With Calderón in, a New War on Mexico's Mighty Drug Cartels." *Christian Science Monitor*. Christian Science Monitor, 22 Jan. 2007. Web. 8 Oct. 2012. Details Felipe Calderón's crackdown on drug trafficking and his work toward rooting out police and government corruption.

McKinley Jr, James C. "US Is Arms Bazaar for Mexican Cartels." *New York Times*. New York Times Co., 25 Feb. 2009. Web. 8 Oct. 2012. Focuses on the sale of American guns to Mexican drug cartels.

Potter, Mark. "Mexico's 'War Next Door' Linked Directly to United States." *NBCNews.com*, NBCNews.com, 13 Dec. 2010. Web. 8 Oct. 2012. A discussion of Mexican drug traffickers who have crossed the border into the United States, and the impact of these traffickers.

John Pritchard

E

■ Early 2000s recession

The Event: Economic recession in the United States that ended the era of unprecedented expansion that began in the early 1990s
Date: March to November 2001

The United States suffered an economic recession lasting from March 2001 to November 2001. The downturn—during which the gross domestic product declined 0.3 percent and unemployment rose to 6.3 percent—has been attributed to several events, including the bursting of the dot-com bubble in 2000, the terrorist attacks of September 11, 2001, and a series of accounting scandals that came to light in the early part of the decade.

Ideally, a recession occurs when gross domestic product (GDP) growth is negative for two or more consecutive quarters (a quarter lasts approximately three months). Recessions are regular events in an economic cycle that also includes expansion, boom, and contraction, though some are worse than others for a number of reasons. The nonpartisan National Bureau of Economic Research (NBER) declares a recession or, more accurately, confirms when one is occurring.

According to the NBER, the United States experienced an unprecedented economic expansion from March 1991 to March 2001. The latter date marks the beginning of the early 2000s recession, which lasted for eight months at the beginning of President George W. Bush's first term. The NBER measures monthly rather than quarterly data, in conflict with the "real" definition of a recession, which stipulates negative GDP growth for two or more quarters. This is important to note because there was some controversy about which president (the outgoing Democrat Bill Clinton or the incoming Republican Bush) should take the blame for the recession. Many Republicans referred to the early 2000s recession as the "Clinton Recession." This argument was fueled by a 2004 report by the Council of Economic Advisors

(CEA), which stated that the recession began several months before the March 2001 date originally reported by the NBER, and, thus, at the end of President Clinton's second term. The blame game continued for some years, though even if the recession did begin under President Bush's watch, it would be inaccurate to say that he caused it with his policies because he had only been in office for two months when it started. The larger issue was that the CEA, a government agency, usurped the authority of the nonprofit, nonpartisan NBER, to whom other administrations had deferred historically. The CEA's report proved to be beneficial to President Bush, who, by this time, was running for reelection.

Michael Feldstein, president of the NBER, expounded on how he determined the start date of the early 2000s recession (and the end of expansion) in an article for the *Boston Globe* written a month after the recession's low point on December 4, 2001. (To clarify, the end of the recession was not determined by the NBER until 2003.) Feldstein noted that the rise and fall of production, sales, employment, and income usually happens in a parallel fashion, and that the end of the economic expansion in 2001 would have been easy to pinpoint if this had been the case (which it had not). According to Feldstein, industrial production peaked in September 2000 around the same time as sales in manufacturing and retail. The NBER based the start date of the recession on employment, which peaked during the first quarter of 2001, in March. Feldstein notes that the GDP did not turn down until the third quarter of 2001.

Contributing Factors

While several of the major events to which the recession is attributed—the collapse of the dot-com bubble, the September 11 terrorist attacks, and the accounting scandals at Enron and WorldCom—could not have been predicted, economists had been anticipating an economic downturn during the boom of the 1990s, which boasted both low inflation and low unemployment. One contributing factor to the recession seemed almost counterintuitive. Deflation, or a steady drop in consumer prices, brought on by a government surplus coming out of the Clinton years was associated with slow economic growth. Recession.org attributes this point to the economist John Maynard Keynes, the father of Keynesian economics. Keynes suggested that deflation brought on by a budget surplus begets slow growth because the government is "hoarding" a large amount of money. (The same reasoning applies when consumers, during a recession, save more than they spend.) Ben Bernanke, the chairman of the Federal Reserve during the Obama administration, addressed the National Economics Club in November 2002 on the dangers of deflation, a cause, he argued, that contributed to Japan's economic slump in the 1990s. Deflation also brings down consumer demand; if prices fall at a steady rate, consumers will put off making purchases as they wait for even lower prices, which slows both growth and, during a recession, recovery.

Another factor in the recession was the hysteria surrounding Y2K, or the Year 2000. Culturally, there was much ado about the new millennium, but in the business world, companies were seriously worried that their technologies might not be able to weather what many believed would be a widespread Y2K bug. The problem, they postulated, was that older computers would break down when the date changed from 99 to 00 because the computers, many believed, would miscalculate the date as the year 1900, possibly placing a century's worth of data at risk. (In truth, no one really knew what would happen or how much information would be lost in the event of a crash.) To prepare for this purely hypothetical, and in the end nonexistent, threat, companies and consumers rushed to replace their old technologies. Of course, after the uneventful date passed, the cash flow that had flooded the technology sector in 1998 and 1999 dried up. Most companies were already "up to speed," so there was little demand for new technology products.

The Y2K scare was tied to a large catalyst for the early 2000s recession: an overvaluation of stock in tech and Internet companies. As more money was spent on new computers and computer software, stock prices for tech companies rose and investors scrambled to get in on the action. Thus, the dot-com bubble was born. People invested in companies that were not turning a profit, and brokers who should

have known better were encouraging them to cash in on what was increasingly becoming a gold rush. Warren Buffett, the chairman and CEO of Berkshire Hathaway, who many consider to be among the most successful investors in history, predicted the outcome of the tech boom but was widely ridiculed for his stance. Supporters of the boom argued that the (ultimately faulty) business models of the new tech companies were indicative of a "new economy." According to a 2001 article (titled "Warren Buffett: 'I Told You So'") from the *BBC News*, Buffett thought that many investors harbored unrealistic expectations for the future success of the tech market based on the enormous amount of money many made during the late 1990s.

Despite the warning signs, the tech bubble effectively burst on March 10, 2000, when the NASDAQ hit an all-time high of 5,048.62 points (the intraday trading number is slightly higher) more than double its value from the year before. After that day, the market began a downhill slide and many new tech companies closed for good.

With the tech industry still in decline throughout 2001, the terrorist attacks on September 11 dealt a startling short-term blow to the economy. In the immediate aftermath of the tragedy, according to a 2002 congressional report titled "The Economic Effects of 9/11: A Retrospective Assessment," it was widely believed that the attacks pushed the already weak economy into a recession, but the report argues that this is not the case. However, the Dow Jones Industrial Average suffered its largest one-day point loss (685 points, or 7.1 percent) when it reopened on Monday, September 17. (This loss was surpassed on September 29, 2008, heralding the second recession of the decade, when the Dow Jones suffered a loss of 778 points, or 7 percent.) Damages from the attack to the financial district in New York City also contributed to a detrimental effect on the economy.

In October 2001, news broke that the Enron Corporation, an American energy company, had been lying about its massive profits. One of the largest and most politically influential companies in the United States, Enron declared bankruptcy in the wake of its multilayered scandal. Similar accounting scandals followed in 2002: Telecommunications giant WorldCom submitted what was then the largest bankruptcy filing in US history; Tyco International's executives were accused of stealing $150 million from the securities company; and Global

Crossing, a telecommunication and computer networking company with questionable bookkeeping practices, collapsed early in the year. The unprecedented scandals made investors more cautious, even suspicious, and they withdrew from the stock market in droves. According to George A. Akerlof and Robert J. Shiller, authors of the book *Animal Spirits: How Human Psychology Drives the Economy, and Why It Matters for Global Capitalism* (2009), many found faith in the housing markets where they need not trust accountants.

Impact

In 2003, the NBER's Business Cycle Dating Committee released a report stating that the economy reached its trough in November 2001. In economic terms, a trough marks the end of a decline in growth, though the committee said that economic conditions in 2002 and 2003 remained unfavorable. Many people refer to the early 2000s recession as the "2001 recession," but describing it as the "2001–2003 recession" would be more accurate because of its long-lasting effects on unemployment. For example, the unemployment rate peaked at 6 percent in 2003. According to the Economic Policy Institute (EPI), the 2001 recession was followed by extended job loss which increased rates of long-term unemployment. The EPI's brief, "The Rising Stakes of Job Loss" (2005), compared the 1990 recession and the early 2000s recession. The brief determined that following all other post-World War II recessions, it took the economy an average of twenty-one months to recover the jobs lost in the downturn. In the 1990 recession, it took the economy thirty-one months to "reclaim peak employment" levels, and in the 2001 recession, it took forty-six months.

The data points to a historically weak recovery, though the recession itself was relatively mild. In fact, it was surprising just how mild it ultimately was given the incredible length of the expansion that preceded it. However, in the wake of the recession, the term *jobless recovery*—coined during the 1990 recession—applied, and it gave rise to concerns that recovery from the two consecutive recessions was indicative of a larger trend. Indeed, a similar picture emerged after the 2008 recession.

In hindsight, many Americans believed that President Bush's tax cuts of 2001, 2002, and 2003 helped stimulate the economy out of the recession because they preceded the recovery. According to the Tax Policy Center, this is not the case. The center attributes the economic turnaround to several factors. By October 2001, the Federal Reserve had cut interest rates to a forty-year low. The rates caused a number of homeowner's to refinance their mortgages, and paying a lower monthly rate on their home, consumers were able to spend more on other goods. Government spending also increased as the United States began its military campaign in Iraq and, after the tech industry bottomed out following the collapse of the dot-com bubble, investors returned to tech companies in 2003.

Further Reading

Akerlof, George A., and Robert J. Shiller. *Animal Spirits: How Human Psychology Drives the Economy and Why It Matters for Global Capitalism.* Princeton: Princeton UP, 2009. Print. Argues that economists often overlook human emotion and behavior in their calculations.

Feldstein, Martin, and Kathleen Feldstein. "From Recession to Recovery." *Boston Globe.* New York Times Co., 4 Dec. 2001. Web. 27 Nov. 2012. Explains the factors that contributed to the NBER's decision to label the 2001 economic downturn a recession. Discusses the possible duration of the recession.

Lowenstein, Roger. *Origins of the Crash: The Great Bubble and Its Undoing.* New York: Penguin, 2004. Print. Traces the events leading up to the stock market crash of the early 2000s to the 1970s.

Martel, Jennifer L., and David S. Langdon. "The Job Market in 2000: Slowing Down as the Year Ended." *Monthly Labor Review* Feb. 2001: 3–30. Print. Compiled by the Bureau of Labor Statistics. Report looks at the slowing of the economic expansion that lasted from 1990 to the end of 2000.

Molly Hagan

■ eBay

Definition: Online auction site

The auction website eBay increased in popularity throughout the 2000s, becoming one of the most influential online retail venues among American consumers. The company's expansion into international markets and introduction of new retail ventures further cemented its status as one of the world's most popular websites by the end of the decade.

Created by computer programmer Pierre Omidyar and businessman Jeffrey Skoll and originally known as AuctionWeb, the online auction house eBay launched on September 3, 1995. During the 2000s, the company developed into a multibillion-dollar international business and expanded into a number of new markets. The company launched one of its most successful new ventures, eBay Motors, in April of 2000, allowing users to buy and sell used cars in the online marketplace. Despite warnings from critics who argued that selling used cars online was too ambitious, eBay Motors sold two million vehicles by 2006 and became the most visited site of its kind with over twelve million visitors per day, surpassing its main competitor, Yahoo! Autos.

In 2002, eBay purchased PayPal, an electronic payment service, for $1.5 billion. In the years following the acquisition, PayPal became a preferred method of online payment and was adopted by a number of other major online retailers, including Blue Nile, Dell, and Yahoo!'s shopping sites. In 2007, PayPal handled almost $50 billion in payments, a one-year growth of more than 30 percent, reflecting the increasing use of electronic payment services. In June of that year, eBay partnered with GE Money, the financial services unit of General Electric, to launch an eBay MasterCard rewards credit card.

Although eBay remained the dominant online auction site in the United States throughout the 2000s, the company nevertheless faced a number of challenges during the decade. Changes to eBay's fee structure and feedback system made in 2008 caused user dissatisfaction, negative press, and boycotts. In March of 2008, chief executive officer Meg Whitman resigned from her position, although she remained on the board of directors, and was replaced by John Donahoe. In October of that year, the company announced that it was laying off a 10 percent reduction of its global workforce and acquiring several online businesses. The economic downturn of the late 2000s and the resulting decrease in consumer spending further challenged eBay during the period.

Impact
The founding and evolution of eBay not only changed the recreational life of Americans, allowing hobbyists, collectors, and bargain hunters to buy and sell a variety of goods online, but also redefined the online business model. Although the economic climate of the late 2000s challenged eBay, the auction site remained one of the most successful Internet companies into the next decade, attracting millions of users.

Further Reading
Gilbert, Sara. *The Story of eBay*. Mankato: Creative, 2012. Print.
White, Michele. *Buy It Now: Lessons from eBay*. Durham: Duke UP, 2012. Print.

Linda M. Kelley

■ E-books

Definition: Book-length works in electronic, or digital, format that are read on e-readers, smartphones, tablets, and desktop computers

In the early 2000s, e-books became popular among consumers with the arrival of digital devices that could display text on small screens. E-books of popular titles were first offered to public library patrons, and print books became searchable on the web through Amazon.com and Google. Enhanced e-book reading began with the arrival of e-ink and e-readers. E-books have transformed the publishing industry, the retail market, and the reading experience.

E-books (electronic books), which are book-length works in digital format, are read on smartphones, tablet and desktop computers, and on dedicated e-readers, which are portable electronic devices for reading digital books and other digital texts. Some e-books are first published as printed books; other e-books are first produced in digital format. More and more e-books are being produced as e-books only. All of these factors have changed how books are published, sold, and read.

Brief History
In the 1960s, computer scientists developed what were called hypertext editing and file retrieval systems, which involved document hyperlinking and graphics. These systems are considered by many to be the first e-books. In 1971, Michael S. Hart founded Project Gutenberg, the first digital library. Hart wanted to make literary works in the public domain (books without copyright restrictions) freely available through electronic means. Project Gutenberg remained one of the most popular websites for free e-books during the 2000s.

In 1992, Sony marketed a book reader that was available on computer discs. Book Stacks Unlimited, an online bookstore, was also created in 1992. Other online databases began to offer users thousands of free e-books and other digital texts.

In the mid-1990s, small publishers began to use the web as a marketing tool by making books available on the Internet. Libraries in the United States began offering specialized, technical e-books in 1998, but these e-books could not yet be downloaded by library patrons.

Widespread and incompatible e-reader formats were developed in the 1990s, but some consensus was reached in 1999 with the Open eBook (OEB) format, which was replaced by the electronic publication (EPUB) format in the mid-2000s. Several other e-book formats began to be used during the 2000s as well, including Kindle, Mobipocket, PDF, plain text, and HTML.

The 2000s

In July 2000, Stephen King became the first bestselling author to publish an online-only work, the novella *Riding the Bullet*. Authors have since followed King's precedent-setting decision, publishing their own fiction and nonfiction works as e-books and spearheading what was then a nascent self-publishing industry.

The year 2001 saw the beginning of what became the largest e-book, Wikipedia, a web-based encyclopedia of millions of articles in dozens of languages. Wikipedia inspired a strong connection between e-books, digitization, and digital publishing, as well as the desire to build a universal digital library. This universal library grew during the decade, involving Google Books, Project Gutenberg, the Internet Archive, the Digital Public Library of America, and others.

The year 2003 is considered a turning point in the history of e-books, which at this time were read primarily using Adobe Acrobat Reader (in a form best known as PDF, or portable document format). Adobe's reader was especially easy for the consumer to download, and it was free. As early as 2001, Adobe had partnered with Amazon to sell two thousand in-copyright books in digital format. In late 2003, Adobe opened an online bookstore.

Also in 2003, public and school libraries began to offer popular works in the e-book format, expanding availability from specialized books for select professions to popular novels for all patrons. With e-books, library holdings began to rise exponentially. The use of e-books by library patrons rose steadily since 2003, although many people remained unaware of their existence.

Cellphones, smartphones, and personal digital assistants (PDAs) of 2003 could display text, opening the door to widespread e-book consumption. The first use of e-ink technology in 2004 made small-text display far more readable, leading to the development of the popular e-readers of Sony, Amazon (Kindle), and Barnes and Noble (Nook). The most popular readers of the 2000s included Kindle, Kobo, Nook, and Sony Reader, as well as text viewers for iPhone, iPod Touch, Android, BlackBerry, and Palm OS.

In October 2003, Amazon launched its "Search Inside the Book" feature. One year later, Google announced a collaboration with major publishers to share book excerpts online. Google then began a digitization (book scanning) project in collaboration with major libraries in late 2004, called the Google Print Library Project. Later named Google Books, the project was halted by Google in late 2005 in response to being sued for violation of copyright. The case was settled in November 2009, but it has remained controversial, especially among writers and publishers, who believe Google retains too much control over copyrighted material.

In 2007, Amazon launched its first generation Kindle, an e-reader that could also download e-books and other digital media through a wireless network. E-books were first sold through Apple's iPhone in 2008, and Barnes and Noble announced its Nook e-reader in 2009.

Publishing and Consumerism

Amazon dominated the sale of e-books during the decade, even offering its own publishing service, CreateSpace, to persons who decide not to have their works published through traditional means. The advent of e-books has allowed anyone with a computer to become a published author; indeed, it became possible for anyone to become a publisher. E-books thus spurred a new type of publishing industry. However, while this industry has led to success for a number of self-published authors, it has also allowed for potentially poorly written books—as self-published authors lack traditional editors—and many small, web-based publishers, some better, and more legitimate, than others.

The ease with which e-books can be produced has had both positive and negative effects. E-books had at first negatively affected the publishing industry. Large traditional book publishers were slow to catch on to the emergence of e-books in the early to mid-2000s, allowing online retailers such as Amazon and Barnes and Noble to capture the attention of consumers eager for new products and new experiences. Small Internet publishers also began to flourish. Although the traditional print publishing industry took longer to begin producing books in digital format, the practice grew rapidly during the decade. E-books became new, exciting products because of their portability, ease of availability, and inexpensiveness. They take up very little space—except on one's digital device or in the cloud—and can be printed on demand, if so desired.

Although many e-books are self-published without being edited or proofread, often leaving typographical and factual errors intact, they remain popular. Many e-books can be purchased for 99 cents, and still others can be purchased for well below the typical hardcover cost of $25. Along with the popularity of online retailers and with mega-bookstores, e-books had an early role in the closing of many independent bookstores, which could not match the prices, variety, and availability of e-books.

Impact

When Amazon first sold its Kindle in 2007, the company offered more than ninety thousand e-books in its Kindle store. More than one hundred of these e-books were on the New York Times Best Sellers list. By 2010, global e-book sales by all retailers reached nearly $1 billion, and Amazon reported that, for the first time, its e-book sales outnumbered its sales of physical books. By 2009, Wikipedia comprised more than three million articles. These numbers represented a new era in publishing, marketing, and reading.

E-books, although popular with consumers, retailers, and the new breed of publishers, present technological concerns involving issues of digital preservation, future compatibility, digital rights, transferability and copying, and alterability. Furthermore, e-books on Kindle and Apple's iTunes,

for example, are cloud based, meaning they are not located on the consumer's digital device; instead the seller maintains the product on its own computer servers. In effect, Amazon, Apple, and other e-book retailers redefined what it means to own a book.

Publishers can alter their e-books at will, meaning they can be easily changed. This leads to multiple versions of the same work. Some have argued, however, that alterability is good for publishing and for consumers, as e-books can be updated or revised when necessary, making the reading experience better for the consumer.

E-books have even inspired online manifestos for the rights of e-book buyers and users. One manifesto calls for the right to "a proper cover," "a Table of Contents," and "proofreading," elements that are mainstays of traditionally printed books.

Further Reading

Brophy, Peter. *The Library in the 21st Century: New Services for the Information Age.* London: Lib. Assoc. Pub., 2001. Print. Considers the changing role of libraries in the twenty-first century in light of increasing use of electronic resources and digital technology.

Hayles, N. Katherine. *Electronic Literature: New Horizons for the Literary.* Notre Dame: U of Notre Dame P, 2008. Print. The first systematic survey of the field of electronic literature. Includes CD-ROM, *The Electronic Literature Collection*, Vol. 1, ed. by Hayles, Nick Montfort, Scott Rettberg, and Stephanie Strickland.

Kelly, Kevin. "Scan This Book!" *New York Times.* New York Times Co., 14 May 2006. Web. 10 Aug. 2012. A comprehensive article examining e-books in the context of the development of what has been called a universal digital library, an ideal encouraging the digitization of all human knowledge.

Lombreglia, Ralph. "Exit Gutenberg?" *The Atlantic.* The Atlantic Monthly Group, 16 Nov. 2000. Web. 10 Aug. 2012. An early look at the significance of e-books and digital publishing.

McGuire, Hugh, and Brian O'Leary, eds. *Book: A Futurist's Manifesto—A Collection of Essays from the Bleeding Edge of Publishing.* Sebastopol, CA: O'Reilly Media, 2012. Web. 10 Aug. 2012. Argues that e-books are now integral to and inseparable from publishing.

Desiree Dreeuws, MA

■ E-commerce

Definition: The buying and selling of products or services by businesses and individuals over electronic systems, like the Internet, using desktop computers, laptops, smartphones, and other devices

Electronic commerce (e-commerce) grew rapidly in the late 1990s, but the dot-com bust in the early 2000s saw a dramatic contraction for most of these companies. Those that survived the crash modified their business plans, placing a greater emphasis on generating revenue, and by decade's end, they had regained their former prominence. In addition, new types of companies and methods of access were created during the 2000s.

E-commerce has its beginnings with electronic data interchange (EDI) in the 1960s. In 1980, Michael Aldrich developed a text display device called the Teleputer, which supported the first online shopping, a concept he had invented the previous year through the modification of a television set. After the development of the Internet in the 1990s, a small number of companies—including online retailer Amazon.com, auction website eBay, and search engine Google—opened up for business on the web. However, most sales still took place in stores, by mail, or over the phone. The major question early e-businesses needed to answer—an important one for e-businesses in the 2000s as well—was how to generate revenue. For businesses that had a large web presence, like retailer Sears, the e-business's revenue was part of the entire company's revenue. For businesses that existed primarily on the web, three revenue models developed. Companies like Amazon.com made most of their money from sales, companies like eBay made most of their money charging for a service, and companies like Google made most of their money from advertising. An important secondary source of income for most e-businesses was from selling information about its users.

E-businesses, as with all businesses, are largely defined by a set of business processes. These include marketing, sales, promotion, purchasing, logistics, and an electronic payment system. In the 2000s, most e-commerce was web-based, meaning that these businesses did not have physical stores—also called brick-and-mortar businesses—where customers could shop in person. For Internet businesses, website promotion is an important activity. Websites promote themselves by using a combination of mass media techniques; thoughtful website design, such as the addition of free features to attract customers to the site; and search engine positioning, including the use of meaningful key words in the site's code. Many e-business sales processes are defined by a supply chain. A typical supply chain includes several phases: acquisition of the product, promotion of the website, fulfillment of the order, customer delivery, and customer support. Optimizing the supply chain was an important way of increasing profitability for many e-businesses in the 2000s.

Toward the end of the 2000s, a revolution in technology changed the nature of e-commerce. First, Facebook and other social media websites began to be used in e-commerce. A business could use social media to advertise itself and keep customers engaged by providing updates about the business and its products, by running contests, and by announcing other promotional activities. Second, the popularization of the smartphone and the tablet computer at the end of the decade would enable customers to access an e-business from more than just a personal computer with an Internet connection.

Catalog Stores and Online Sales

The development of the international telephone system led to a number of companies moving part or all of their selling to a catalog phone-order system, rather than just using a catalog mail-order system. With the development of the World Wide Web in the 1990s, some of these companies and a number of new ones moved some or all of their sales activity online. The modern credit card was introduced in 1946, improved to include fairly secure purchases in the 1990s, and standardized to a secure payment card industry (PCI) system in 2004. With this infrastructure in place, Internet commerce became common in the 2000s. After Facebook became available to anyone over thirteen in 2006, online sales companies increasingly made use of a Facebook presence to attract customers to their main web stores; some would later support sales directly on Facebook as well. Facebook also introduced Marketplace in 2007, a free classified advertising platform.

No other company is more identified with online sales than Amazon. Founded by Jeff Bezos in 1995 as an online bookstore, it later expanded to sell other products, advertizing itself as the world's largest mass marketer. Amazon offers more products and enjoys larger sales volume than any other online retailer. The company also manufactures and sells the Kindle e-reader, first released in 2007. As with other e-readers, a customer can purchase books directly from the Kindle device, rather than via a desktop or laptop computer. One of the unique features of Amazon is the support it provides to others who want to set up a web-based business under the Amazon umbrella. This support includes website design assistance, a packaged checkout system, and an easy-to-use fulfillment system.

Dell, eBay, and L.L. Bean are typical examples of online retailers. eBay, founded in 1995, is best known for its online auction as a way of supporting customer-to-customer (C2C) sales, although it also became a multinational company involved in both online and traditional sales of a wide range of products. In addition, eBay has acquired, or purchased a major interest in, a number of businesses, including the online payment system PayPal (1995), 25 percent of classified ad service Craigslist (2004), international Internet phone service Skype (2005), and online ticket trader StubHub (2007). Dell, founded in 1984 by Michael Dell as a personal computer vendor, during the 2000s became an international seller of computers, computer support services, and other electronic devices, both in stores and online. Among the company's successful acquisitions are Alienware (2006), which gave the company gaming sales expertise, and Perot Systems (2009), which added considerable mainframe support expertise. L.L. Bean is a privately owned mail-order, online, and brick-and-mortar sales company. Founded in 1912 in Maine as a catalog store specializing in outdoor products, the company expanded in the 2000s to sell a wide range of products, many of them on the web. L.L. Bean's expansion as a multichannel sales company proved successful during the decade.

Service-Oriented E-commerce

By the 2000s, businesses had moved much of their infrastructure to the web, including EDI, as business-to-business (B2B) e-commerce. The multinational corporation General Electric accomplishes many of its transactions over the web as B2B e-commerce, including collecting and analyzing bids for many of its supplies. B2B transactions can reduce business overhead. For example, the Federal Reserve provides support, including information, to small banks automatically with several custom B2B applications.

Business-to-consumer (B2C) e-commerce can also reduce the cost of providing information to customers for companies like eHarmony, where customers automatically enter their data, search the site for information about other people, and initiate a contact. Wikipedia, founded in 2001 by Jimmy Wales and Larry Sanger, is probably the most famous B2C e-business that provides information to its customers as a service.

In addition to providing information as a service, many e-businesses provide other services to their customers. During the 2000s, MSN, Yahoo, AOL, and Google provided free e-mail, as well as many other services including search engines, free applications, and web storage. Craigslist, founded by Craig Newmark in 1995 as a limited set of services, became a leading online classified advertisement site in the 2000s, with sections devoted to jobs, housing, personals, and résumés, among other things. Another example of an e-business providing a service is Skype, a proprietary voice over Internet Protocol (VoIP) phone service, founded in Europe in 2003. Skype allows users to communicate by voice, video, and instant messaging across the world. A third example is GSI Commerce, whose service is support for building an e-business. Founded in 1995 and sold to eBay in 2011, it specializes in developing and running websites for physical stores.

While many other types of e-businesses provide a service over the Internet, financial service companies are typical of most of these. Online banking is provided by companies such as ING Direct, while Morgan Stanley and virtually all other brokerage firms let their customers view all of their accounts online; some even support online trading. Insurance of all types are advertised online, but state regulations often encourage an agent to draw up a physical policy, which includes a written contract with multiple disclosures.

A final example of e-businesses that provide a service is the use of e-commerce by issue-oriented organizations, political action groups, and politicians. Issue-oriented organizations and political action groups are organized around a cause and often use a website to disseminate information and collect donations. Virtually all politicians use a website and e-mail to inform their constituents of their views, provide them with services, and seek donations. As social media and mobile Internet access became commonplace in the late 2000s, all of these groups began to use Web 2.0 tools to improve their communications with constituents. In addition to the traditional use of the web, these groups use Facebook to organize supporters, video-sharing site YouTube to personalize appeals of their messages, and microblogging site Twitter to create a feeling of community, thereby dramatically changing the way they interact with their constituents.

Impact

At the beginning of the 2000s, e-businesses were primarily catalog stores and informational websites that were used by computer gurus. Access was almost exclusively on desktops and occasionally on a laptop.

After the dot-com bust of 2000, these businesses modified their business practices, becoming easier to access, and by the end of the 2000s, they were being used by non-experts as well as gurus. Many new types of e-businesses were successfully introduced in the 2000s. One of these, social media—including Twitter and Facebook—also became used to advertise and promote traditional e-businesses.

As the 2000s came to a close, many e-businesses were transitioning into multichannel businesses: ones with a storefront, a website, and a Facebook business page. The flexibility to expand sales across multiple platforms was the new business norm by the end of the decade. The popularization of smartphones, tablets, and cloud-computing technology at the very end of decade led to the expectation of being able to access information instantly and from anywhere. To accommodate this desire, many e-businesses that achieved success during the 2000s began developing a mobile presence for their customers. Location-directed smartphone applications (apps) would quickly gain in popularity. E-businesses would also make the sale of their goods and services easily accessible via tablets such as the iPad (introduced in 2010).

Further Reading

Kerpen, Dave. *Likeable Social Media: How to Delight Your Customers, Create an Irresistible Brand, and Be Generally Amazing on Facebook (& Other Social Networks).* New York: McGraw-Hill, 2011. Print. Describes how to use social media successfully to boost the popularity of one's e-business.

Lewis, Robin, and Michael Dart. *The New Rules of Retail: Competing in the World's Toughest Marketplace.* New York: Macmillan, 2010. Print. An in-depth discussion of the transformation of the retail industry, due to new technologies, globalization, and a changing marketplace. Provides examples of industry successes and failures. Focuses particularly on what will help new businesses succeed.

Pope, Clark, and Khushpreet Kaur. "Is It Human or Computer? Defending E-Commerce with Captchas." *IT Professional* 7.2 (2005): 43–49. Print. Discusses the security side of e-commerce for the business owner. Specifically covers how captchas can help businesses distinguish computer spammers and bots from actual human customers.

Rodrigues, Rodrigo, and Peter Druschel. "Peer-to-Peer Systems." *Communications of the ACM* 53.10 (2010): 72–82. Print. Discusses peer-to peer-systems, including file sharing, data storage, and scientific computing systems.

Schneider, Gary P. *Electronic Commerce.* 10th ed. Boston: Course Technology, 2013. Print. Covers the dynamics of the entire e-commerce field. Stresses how e-commerce is constantly evolving and discusses the latest business strategies and technologies.

George Whitson, PhD

◾ Economic Growth and Tax Relief Reconciliation Act of 2001

The Law: Federal law providing a range of temporary tax breaks to the American people
Date: June 7, 2001
Also known as: EGTRRA, Bush tax cuts

On June 7, 2001, President George W. Bush signed the Economic Growth and Tax Relief Reconciliation Act of 2001 into law. The federal government had been running record budget surpluses in the late 1990s. Many in the US government felt that these surpluses resulted from excessive taxation, and they wanted a vehicle to provide compensatory tax breaks to the American population.

In the final years of Bill Clinton's presidency, the US federal budget ran major surpluses, the first since 1969. The surpluses were due to several factors. These were years of robust economic growth, so corporations and individuals were paying more in taxes due to higher earnings. This combined with the effects of the Omnibus Reconciliation Act of 1993, which modestly increased corporate taxes and income tax, particularly for wealthier citizens.

The Clinton-era surpluses were contested in the 2000 presidential election. Democratic candidate Al Gore sought to use the surpluses to protect the Social Security system, which faced long-term shortfalls. Republican candidate George W. Bush argued that the surpluses resulted from excessive taxation. He wanted to give the money back to the people who had apparently paid too much in taxes.

Once elected, Bush made this form of tax relief a priority. Along with most Republicans, he sought to focus the tax cuts on the wealthier Americans impacted by the Clinton-era tax increases. However, Democratic politicians pressured Republicans to include tax breaks for other income levels.

The resulting legislation contained many changes. It created a 10 percent rate to replace the 15 percent rate and provided that the difference in tax liability for 2000 be refunded by check to taxpayers in 2001. It gradually lowered the 28 to 36 percent brackets by three percentage points and the highest tax bracket from 39.6 to 35 percent.

Among other things, the bill increased tax credits for dependent care, children, employer-provided child care, and adoption. It increased deductions for certain educational expenses and retirement contributions. It also increased the standard deduction for joint returns, eliminating the so-called marriage penalty. Further, it increased exemptions from estate and gift taxes. Importantly, the legislation included a sunset provision stipulating that the changes to tax law would cease on January 1, 2011.

Impact

The Economic Growth and Tax Relief Reconciliation Act of 2001 became law during a time of strong economic growth, but it is estimated to have cost the government approximately $1.4 trillion during the recession that began in 2008. This was a factor in creating record federal deficits. Nonetheless, its expiration has proven highly controversial, and President Barack Obama renewed the Bush tax cuts for two years in 2010.

Further Reading

Bancroft Library. "2001 Economic Growth and Tax Relief Reconciliation Act." *Slaying the Dragon of Debt.* University of California, Berkeley, 7 Mar. 2011. Web. 14 Dec. 2012.

Manz, William H. *Legislative History of the Economic Growth and Tax Relief Reconciliation Act of 2001.* Buffalo: Hein, 2002. Print.

"Summary of Provisions Contained in the Conference Agreement for H.R. 1836, The Economic Growth and Reconciliation Act of 2001." *Joint Committee on Taxation.* United States Government, 26 May 2001. Web. 14 Dec. 2012.

Adam J. Berger, PhD

■ Education in Canada

Definition: The administration and delivery of a specified curriculum within the system of schools throughout Canada

The education system in Canada functions to produce young adults prepared to undertake their roles as citizens in the broader context of Canadian society. The 2000s saw a significant increase in the demand for secondary-language immersion programs, particularly in Ontario, Newfoundland and Labrador, and British Columbia. Despite an overall decrease in student enrollment over the decade, funding for public education held relatively steady, resulting in a significant increase in per-pupil spending. At the end of the decade, Canada was named the most-educated country in the world.

The basic level of education delivered by school systems in Canada is federally mandated and is a guaranteed right in the Constitution Act. Canada's education system has accordingly seen few changes in its essential structure. The responsibility for delivering public education in Canada is accorded to the governments of the provinces and territories. Within each province and territory, a provincial Ministry of Education funds the operation of public schools within their individual jurisdiction, typically through a number of local area school boards. While the Constitution Act guarantees the right to education under the auspices of the Catholic faith as well as nondenominational public schools, the Province of Ontario remains the only province in Canada to publicly fund both Catholic and nondenominational school systems. This caused considerable controversy in the early 2000s when the United Nations Human Rights Committee claimed that Ontario's policy of publicly funding Catholic schools, but not other religious schools, was discriminatory. In 2007, the Public

Education Fairness Network was formed to pressure the Ontario government to fund all religious schools that meet provincial curriculum standards. Despite several legal challenges to publicly funded Catholic schools throughout the decade, Ontario has upheld the funding of Catholic schools as constitutional.

Canada, being officially a bilingual English- and French-speaking nation, has a number of publicly funded French-language school systems that operate in various regions of the country. In addition, the demand for secondary-language immersion programs in public schools increased significantly throughout the decade. Between 2000 and 2009, the number of Canadian students enrolled in a secondary-language program increased by 14 percent. New Brunswick is the only province that experienced a decrease in the number of students enrolled in such language programs during the 2000s.

Although the basic curriculum is consistent, there are regional differences in the overall curriculum reflective of the nature and society of the various regions. All school systems, whether publicly or privately funded, are required to deliver at minimum the standard curriculum designated by their respective Ministry of Education. Successful completion of a secondary school education is the minimum education standard throughout Canada, although the realities of the modern labor market increasingly demand postsecondary education and many professions require the successful completion of a university-level degree. As of 2011, approximately 50 percent of the Canadian population had attained some level of postsecondary education.

The administration of colleges, universities, and other postsecondary facilities in Canada is typically governed by a separate government ministry, such as Ontario's Ministry of Training, Colleges and Universities. These ministries oversee the funding and operation of academic institutions and trades training within their respective provinces. They also serve as the regulatory agency for those various institutions.

The Teaching Profession

Elementary and secondary school teachers in Canada are required to hold a minimum qualification of a bachelor's of education degree from an accredited teachers college, with more advanced positions such as principal requiring a master's of education degree or other specialist qualification. Admission into an accredited teachers college pro-

gram normally requires completion of a university undergraduate degree as a prerequisite. Graduates with the bachelor's of education degree can then apply for employment with the various education administrations that exist within the provinces. A Board of Education, or the equivalent body, consists of a number of elected members and is responsible for administering the staffing and operation of schools, and teachers enter into a labor and management relationship with the Board under which they are employed. Each province accordingly has a number of teachers unions, federations, and associations that represent their corresponding constituent members.

The number of full-time educations, including teachers, administrators, and other support staff members, increased by 7 percent from 2000 to 2009, with the largest increases occurring in Saskatchewan and Nunavut. In addition, the student-educator ratio decreased in all provinces over the course of the decade, with an average of approximately sixteen students per educator across the country.

Costs of Education

Public education through the completion of a secondary school diploma is provided freely to Canadians who meet age and residency requirements. The costs of delivering the public education system in Canada are recovered through taxation at both the federal and provincial levels. Provincial tax revenues are used directly in the funding of education, while a portion of federal tax revenues is allotted to the various provinces as "transfer payments", part of which is designated for the support of education.

There are approximately 15,500 publicly funded schools across Canada, the actual number changing continually as old and underutilized schools are eliminated and new schools are built. Of these, fully two-thirds (about 10,100) are elementary schools and some 3,400 are secondary schools. The remaining 2,000 schools are mixed elementary and secondary schools. In addition to these there are numerous private and faith-based schools that do not receive public funding.

Throughout the decade, increasing costs of education drove provincial governments to seek means of reducing costs. Methods included school zone amalgamations and individual school closures, elimination of high-cost capital equipment where appropriate (such as removal of certain playground equipment that incurred high liability and maintenance costs), and renegotiation of teaching and non-teaching staff contracts. In Ontario, a notable experiment was carried out with the construction of twinned public and Catholic secondary schools that share technical areas, which would have otherwise been duplicated at considerable cost had the two schools been constructed as entirely separate entities. Thus at the beginning of the decade, for the 2002–2003 school year a combined total of C$72.3 billion was spent on public and private education, with C$42.7 billion going toward elementary and secondary education, C$24.4 billion for college and university education, and C$5.2 billion for trade and vocational education. Public expenditures represent 82.3 percent of the total spent for the 2002–3 school year. By mid-decade, for the 2005–6 school year, the total public expenditure on education increased to C$75.7 billion, while public expenditures on elementary and secondary education dropped to C$40.4 billion. Public expenditures for special retraining and language training were boosted to C$4.6 billion, and increased to C$30.6 billion for postsecondary education. A significant portion of the increases was due to the implementation of programs designed to help the unemployed and underemployed in Canada to obtain training that would enable them to reenter or improve their position in the national labor force. While public expenditures on education remained relatively steady throughout the decade, the number of school-aged children enrolled in publicly funded schools decreased by 5 percent between 2000 and 2009, largely due to demographic changes in the size of the school-aged population. This contributed to a significant increase in per-pupil spending over the decade.

Despite this overall increase in spending per pupil, significant disparities in funding existed in Canada and a number of school districts struggled with the issues of overcrowding and underfunding. Cost-cutting measures implemented through the decade by various provincial agencies were the cause of considerable operational difficulties in several school systems across Canada. The principal complaint throughout the decade, particularly in Ontario (the most heavily populated province in Canada), was the growing discrepancies between the money provided by provincial governments for school operation according to their set funding formula and the actual costs of school operation. The funding formula used by government provided a fixed amount of funding per "pupil place" based on the number of pupils a

school was built to accommodate, whereas many schools were overpopulated.

Impact

Canada's education systems are fundamental to the development of future adult citizens who will comprise the Canadian labor force and fulfill roles in all sectors of Canadian society. As Canada plays an increasing role in world leadership, it is essential that the education system provide the best and most forward-looking education possible. According to a report released by the Organization for Economic Cooperation and Development in 2011, Canada is the most-educated developed country in the world, with more than 50 percent of the population attaining postsecondary education. The realities of modern economies demand an ever higher level of basic education, however, and it has been increasingly argued that the level of education provided freely should be extended through the undergraduate university degree or its equivalent. Education costs represent the second largest expenditure by provincial governments, next to health care, and there is little inclination to increase that expenditure at the expense of other programs. Education therefore continued to be a target for cost reductions throughout the decade, at the same time that means of making education more effective were sought.

Further Reading:

Bayefsky, Anne F., and Arieh Waldman. *State Support for Religious Education: Canada versus the United Nations.* Leiden: Nijhoff, 2007. Print. This book discusses the controversial topic of public funding in Canada for religious education, which the United Nations views as discriminatory.

Bowlby, J. Brenda, Catherine Peters, and Martha Mackinnon. *An Educator's Guide to Special Education Law.* Aurora: Aurora Professional, 2001. Print. This book provides a detailed explanation of the requirements of special education throughout Canada, in accord with provincial and federal human rights legislation.

Council of Ministers of Education, Canada (CMEC). "Education in Canada: An Overview." *Council of Ministers of Education, Canada.* CMEC, n.d. Web. 11 Nov. 2012. This website provides a concise summation of the overall state of education in Canada, with links to many other education-related resources.

Levin, Benjamin Ruvin. *Governing Education.* Toronto: U of Toronto P, 2005. Print. This book provides a unique combination of informed analysis and detailed accounts of events by participants involved in the governance of education in Canada.

McMullen, Kathryn, and Riley Brockington. "Public School Indicators for Canada, the Provinces and Territories, 2000/2001 to 2008/2009." *Statistics Canada.* Statistics Canada, 24 June 2011. Web. 18 Nov. 2012. This report summarizes major trends in education in Canada from the 2000 through 2009, including demographic and curriculum changes.

Richard M. Renneboog MSc

◼ Education in the United States

Definition: The academic and social context of American schools and the state and federal policies and events that affected the curriculum, funding, safety, and general efficacy of schools during the 2000s

The face of education in the United States changed drastically in the 2000s through the implementation of new federal policies, increases in spending, and increased violence and bullying in schools. Although education systems are generally run by states, education is a nationwide issue affecting every citizen as well as the direction of political campaigns and federal legislation.

Basic education, in both the public and private school systems, in the United States is broken into thirteen grades, or years, beginning with kindergarten and followed by the first through twelfth grades. Generally, elementary school consists of kindergarten through sixth grade; middle school, or junior high school, is grades seven and eight, although in some areas and districts, junior high school includes sixth grade or ninth grade. Finally, high school, or senior high school, is the four final years of basic education, grades nine through twelve. While this is the traditional model for schooling in the United States, some students attend alternative programs, such as charter schools, or are homeschooled by parents or tutors. While the curriculum may vary to some degree, by the end of the twelfth grade, students are expected to have a general foundation of knowledge across many subjects. Then, after the

completion of required classes, a high school diploma or a general education degree (GED), is awarded to students—although not all students reach this level, as attending school is only required by law until a person's sixteenth birthday. If students choose to continue with their education after obtaining their diploma or GED, they may apply to attend a community college, a four-year university, or a trade school. These options vary from person to person and depend on their skill sets and own personal goals and ambitions.

Major Educational Reforms

Most changes and decisions concerning education and public schools are made at the state level and are voted upon by the local population as propositions every few years. A few changes have been put into effect at the federal level, however, marking nationwide changes to schools and the education system. One of the most well-known changes was the No Child Left Behind Act created in 2001 by President George W. Bush, in concert with Congress, and passed in 2002. No Child Left Behind was a new and enlarged installment of a 1994 federal mandate entitled Elementary and Secondary Education Act, taking on many more topics and a breadth of control that had not been seen in federal education legislation before. Essentially, this education reform created mandated school testing for every student in every school in order to determine proficiency in reading, mathematics, and science, which would be assessed through standardized testing. Progress and "proficiency" is determined across all grades and sociocultural markers, and if a school is found to have failed in any category then it is officially deemed in need of improvement.

Almost immediately after No Child Left Behind was initiated, it met with strong opposition. Most of the opposition stemmed from the requirement that schools had to progress sufficiently each year, toward the ultimate goals of literacy and proficiency in mathematics and science for all students by 2014, and that schools would be sanctioned if they did not meet their annual progress goals. While several education organizations—such as the Business Coalition for Excellence in Education and the American Federation of Teachers, which both worked with Congress and the president to create and to pass the legislation—agreed with this policy, many other groups concerned with education did not approve. Requiring

George W. Bush signs the "No Child Left Behind" Act into law. (Tim Sloan/AFP Photo/Getty Images)

annual tests would cost a significant amount of money for the states and the school districts, but the act did not provide money to cover these costs, which angered school administrators and local legislatures. Debate continued into the next decade about the legality and practicality of some of the provisions of the law, but many of the provisions continued to be implemented unchallenged because they were viewed as extensions of previous federal education reform.

After enacting No Child Left Behind, President Bush and Congress passed several more education reforms, namely those that dealt with ensuring proper education for individuals with special needs, although some work was also done to improve education research. During his second term in office, President Bush spent more time working to make American students competitive internationally in academics, especially in science and technology. According to the National Center for Education Statistics, a test was given to many students in twenty-nine countries in 2003, 2006, and 2009 to analyze the level of students' reading abilities. While this test specifically focused on reading and reading comprehension, its results indicated that only 9 percent of

American students in 2003 scored a 625 or higher (the top level) compared to 16 percent of students in New Zealand and 11 percent in Sweden. The National Center for Education Statistics reported that US students had shown no change in proficiency, even with the education reforms, while several other countries had either improved or declined. By the end of Bush's presidency in 2008, whether or not No Child Left Behind had actually increased proficiency in any area of study was subject to debate.

When President Barack Obama took office in 2009, emphasis on education policy took a backseat to policy aimed at combating nationwide economic instability; however, the American Recovery and Reinvestment Act included funds for education in order to aid in state and local budget issues. This solution was short-term, however, as it was scheduled to end in 2011.

Funding for Schools

In conjunction with federal and state policies, funding for education has been a focus of many elections, both local and national. Whether the issue was appropriations for primary schools or grants available to college students in place of loans, spending drastically increased during the 2000s. This increase was mainly controlled by the Department of Education, but the total amount of money available was $29.4 billion in 2000. This amount increased nearly $11 billion by the next year and topped out for the decade at $58.4 billion in 2006. However, in 2009, the short-term funding provided by the American Recover and Reinvestment Act elevated the Department of Education budget to $155.4 billion. In 2010, the education budget was reduced to $64.1 billion.

Funding for colleges was part of the budget, but alternative funding options existed for college and university students, including scholarships and tuition remission. Individual states sometimes also offer grants for students who attend college in their home state; an example of such funding in the Cal Grant in California. Federal loans, such as the Stafford and Perkins loans, offer better interest rates and a more flexible repayment schedule than private bank loans, although that is another route to take in order to finance an education.

Violence in Schools

Following the Columbine High School massacre in 1999, school violence, and the media coverage of it,

increased, making it a topic closely aligned with education policy in the United States. While the Columbine massacre was not the first instance of student violence, it was the largest and most public. It also set a precedent that was replicated through the 2000s. Between 2000 and 2009, more than one hundred school-related shootings occurred. There was no clear upward or downward trend in violence, although school shootings became more common in the 2000s than in previous decades. The website Schoolsecurity.org details deaths in and around schools by school year. There were thirty-one deaths in 2000–1, seventeen in 2001–2, sixteen in 2002–3, forty-nine in 2003–4, thirty-nine in 2004–5, twenty-seven in 2005–6, thirty-two in 2006–7, sixteen in 2007–8, and thirteen in 2008–9. School violence seemingly increased in the decade's middle years and fell off again in the latter part of the decade. Even though statistics do not seem to show a significant decrease in school violence, awareness of the problem was amplified throughout the decade and continued into the next.

Impact

In the 2000s, education was taken out of the hands of the states, to some degree, in an attempt by the federal government to regulate standards for all students. With the enactment of No Child Left Behind, as well as a moderate amount of increased money for schools, scholastic proficiency should have increased across all sections of society, but growth was not seen in standardized-testing results. While some students benefited from the program, the top and bottom percentages of students seemed unable to take advantage of the program in meaningful ways. This fact may have been partly the result of the increase in economic hardship for families in the late 2000s (especially for immigrant families and those with special-needs children). It seems, however, that improvements in education in the United States were hindered by increased violence in schools and insufficient budgets. Education reform is an issue that will continue to be addressed, possibly by local government and school districts or through federal law, in order to attain the high levels of literacy and analytical knowledge that was the goal of previous education reforms.

Further Reading

Federal Education Budget Project. "Education in the Federal Budget." *Federal Education Budget Project.*

New America Foundation, 22 Mar. 2012. Web. 2 Nov. 2012. Provides concise analysis of education budget with data provided by governmental sources.

Hopkins, Katy. "Four Overlooked Ways to Pay for College." *U.S. News and World Report.* U.S. News & World Report LP, 7 July 2011. Web. 7 November 2012. Reports on traditional and less-known options on how to pay for college.

Manna, Paul. "Management, Control, and the Challenge of Leaving No Child Behind." Department of Government at College of William and Mary. PDF file. 4 Nov. 2012. Discusses the management and approach to the study of government policy implementation.

McGuinn, Patrick. "The National Schoolmarm: No Child Left Behind and the New Educational Federalism." *Publius* 35 (2005): 41–68. Print. Discusses the role of the federal government and the No Child Left Behind Act in the US system of education.

National School Safety and Security Services. "School Deaths and School Shootings: 2005–2006." *School Security.* National School Safety and Security Services, 1996–2007. Web. 4 Nov. 2012. Provides a breakdown of deaths per year resulting from school-related violence.

Anna Accettola

John Edwards. (Courtesy Joey Gannon)

■ Edwards, John

Identification: American politician and US presidential candidate in 2004 and 2008
Born: June 10, 1953; Seneca, South Carolina

First elected to represent North Carolina in the US Senate in November 1998, Democrat John Edwards has worked on a wide range of legislation dealing with education, prescription drugs, corporate governance, and campaign finance reform. In 2003, Edwards announced his candidacy for the Democratic presidential nomination, but instead became the running mate for Massachusetts Senator John Kerry.

Although always interested in the possibility of a political career, it wasn't until 1998 that successful attorney John Edwards made the decision to run for public office. He surprised the political establishment by winning the race for the North Carolina US Senate seat on his first attempt, taking office in 1999.

Environmental issues were high on Senator Edwards's agenda. In his home state, he proposed regular testing to ensure compliance with antipollution laws, along with stronger penalties for noncompliance. Senators Edwards cosponsored an amendment to the 2003 Energy Bill to block the Bush administration from weakening existing clean air laws. He was outspoken about Environmental Protection Agency (EPA) efforts to eliminate pollution controls on energy-producing plants.

Edwards was instrumental in crafting the No Child Left Behind educational initiative in 2001. He also worked on other education legislation, including measures to pay for the first year of college for all American students, grant financial incentives to prospective teachers, and increase pay for all educators.

Following the September 2001 terrorist attacks against the United States, Edwards asked that tax cuts be delayed in order to fund increased security, believing that the money could be better spent collecting information and uncovering terrorist plans in order to safeguard the nation.

Edwards chose not to run for the Senate again in 2004. Instead, on September 15, 2003, he announced his candidacy for the presidency of the United States. He lost in the primaries to Senator John Kerry of Massachusetts. Soon after, Kerry invited Edwards to be his running mate, and the decision was announced to the nation on July 6, 2004. The candidates lost the November election to President George W. Bush and Vice President Dick Cheney.

On December 28, 2006, Edwards declared his candidacy in the 2008 presidential election. Shortly after, in March, he announced that his wife Elizabeth had been diagnosed with a recurrence of bone cancer. Doctors stated the new metastasis was treatable, but not curable. After much deliberation, Edwards and his wife chose to continue with his 2008 presidential campaign. The couple's decision set off a nationwide debate related to the working life of those diagnosed with cancer. Throughout the debate, Elizabeth Edwards continued to affirm her belief that her sickness should not deter her husband's candidacy and that she should not allow herself or her husband to be defeated by the disease. Some critics raised questions about whether or not Edwards, if elected, would able to remain focused on the duties of the presidency given his wife's illness. Elizabeth Edwards succumbed to cancer in 2010.

Edwards finished second in the 2008 Democratic Party caucus in Iowa, earning nearly 30 percent of the vote. In the 2008 New Hampshire primary, Edwards finished third, earning 17 percent of the overall vote. Edwards finished a very distant third in the Nevada caucus, surprising many analysts. He earned less than 3 percent of the vote while Hillary Clinton and Barack Obama each earned over 45 percent.

Edwards earned over 14 percent of the vote in the Florida primary—finishing third again behind Barack Obama and Hillary Clinton. On January 30, 2008, Edwards officially ended his candidacy. He later announced his support for Barack Obama.

On August 8, 2008, Edwards confirmed long running rumors that he engaged in an extramarital affair with a former campaign staff member, videographer Rielle Hunter. It was later confirmed that the couple had a child together.

Impact

Edwards's political career was in its infancy at the dawn of the 2000s. By 2010, he had run for president twice, campaigned as the vice presidential nominee for the Democratic Party once, and, as a senator, took part in crafting some of the most important legislation of the decade. However, his legacy will likely be defined by the scandal that rocked the final years of his career. Edwards faced charges of violating campaign-funding laws relating to an alleged cover-up of his affair; he was found not guilty on one count, and

the remaining charges were dropped following mistrial in May 2012.

Further Reading

Duffy, Michael. "John Edwards: The Natural." *Time.* Time Inc., 19 July 2004. Web. 29 Oct. 2012.

Leahy, Michael. "For John Edwards, isolation is a symbol of his downfall." *Washington Post.* Washington Post, 11 Apr. 2012. Web. 29 Oct. 2012.

Severson, Kim and John Schwartz. "Edwards Acquitted on One Count; Mistrial on 5 Others." *New York Times* 1 Jun. 2012: A1. Print.

Terri McFadden

■ Eggers, Dave

Identification: American author, publisher, editor, educator, and philanthropist
Born: March 12, 1970; Boston, Massachusetts

A major force in contemporary American literature, Dave Eggers is an award-winning author and an advocate for human rights and education. He has been referred to by critics as the "voice of Generation X."

Dave Eggers had already achieved some success as founder of the publishing house McSweeney's and its associated literary journal when his fictionalized memoir, A Heartbreaking Work of Staggering Genius (2000), became a *New York Times's* best seller and a Pulitzer Prize nominee. The book details Eggers' challenges with raising his younger brother "Toph" after their parents died of cancer when Eggers was a senior in college. The book's experimental style thrust Eggers into the limelight as "the voice of Generation X."

Eggers used the proceeds from *A Heartbreaking Work* to further develop the McSweeney's brand, which is known in particular for publishing contemporary novels and works of humor. He also cofounded the Voice of Witness series, dedicated to nonfiction on human rights issues, such as *Surviving Justice: America's Wrongfully Convicted and Exonerated* (2005).

Eggers also founded the 826 Valencia writing center for underprivileged children and teenagers in San Francisco. The organization was later renamed 826 National after an enthusiastic cadre of teachers, students, and authors opened centers in

Dave Eggers. (Courtesy David Shankbone)

additional cities. A volunteer himself, Eggers's passion for encouraging reading led to the first edition of *The Best American Nonrequired Reading* (2002), which became a successful annual anthology.

After publishing *What Is the What* (2006), a National Book Critics Circle Award finalist about Sudanese refugee Valentino Achak Deng, Eggers cofounded a Sudanese educational organization in Deng's name. His 2009 novel *Zeitoun*, about an Arab American's experiences during Hurricane Katrina in New Orleans, won the American Book Award. The book also led to the founding of the Zeitoun Foundation, which worked to assist rebuilding efforts in the city in the years following the storm. Eggers's affinity for combining literary pursuits with philanthropic projects earned him a place the *Utne Reader's* 2008 list of "Fifty Visionaries Who Are Changing Your World."

During the 2000s, Eggers also edited several short story collections, and cowrote the film adaptation of Maurice Sendak's childrens' book *Where the Wild Things Are* (2009). He also collaborated with his wife, Vendela Vida, on the screenplay of *Away We Go* (2009).

Impact

Eggers' innovative and self-referential writing style has inspired a generation of writers. His promotion of other contemporary authors represents a unique investment in American literature. By redirecting the profits from award-winning books into nonprofit organizations, he has demonstrated unusual selflessness, compassion, and generosity. His founding of 826 National has targeted some of America's least advantaged children and teenagers by providing tutoring and support for their creative endeavors. The organization has published anthologies written by students, and has inspired other established authors to become involved with their efforts. *The Best American Nonrequired Reading* series promotes reading as a satisfying leisure time activity to adolescents throughout the country. Eggers published *A Hologram for the King* in 2012.

Further Reading

Cooke, Rachel. "From *Staggering Genius* to America's Conscience." *Observer.* Guardian News and Media, 6 Mar. 2010. Web. 27 Aug. 2012.

Hamilton, Caroline D. *One Man Zeitgeist: Dave Eggers, Publishing and Publicity.* London: Continuum International, 2010. Print.

Sally Driscoll

■ *Ehime Maru* and USS *Greeneville* collision

The Event: Marine accident involving a US Navy submarine that killed nine people
Date: February 9, 2001
Place: Off the coast of Oahu, Hawaii

The USS Greeneville, *a nuclear submarine operated by the US Navy, was conducting a rapid surfacing drill when it struck the* Ehime Maru, *a Japanese fishing vessel. The submarine split the smaller ship's hull, killing nine people. The accident caused international outrage and strained relations between the United States and Japan.*

On February 9, 2001, the USS *Greeneville* was positioned off the coast of Oahu, Hawaii. The submarine was carrying sixteen civilian visitors from Pearl Harbor that day. The commanding officer of the *Greeneville*, Scott Waddle, reportedly felt pressured to get the guests back to shore on time and rushed through mandatory safety procedures while conducting a high-speed surfacing drill for the visitors.

When the submarine surfaced, it struck the under-side of the *Ehime Maru*. The fishing vessel was transporting fifteen students and instructors from a high school in Uwajima, Japan, as well as twenty crew members. The *Ehime Maru* sank within five minutes of the collision. The US Coast Guard was dispatched to the scene, and rescuers saved twenty-six people. In the end, nine people were missing and presumed dead, including four high school students.

Following the incident, the US Navy launched a public investigation, and Waddle was relieved of his command of the USS *Greeneville*. A report issued by the National Transportation Safety Board found that the accident was the result of inadequate communication among senior officers prior to the commanding officer's decision to perform the surfacing drill. In addition, the report indicated that crew members had not adequately managed the civilian visitors, who were a distraction.

Waddle was eventually found guilty of dereliction of duty and negligent hazarding of a vessel. Still, he was honorably discharged and allowed to retire with his full rank and pension intact. Five other members of the *Greeneville* and several shore-based officers were also reprimanded.

Impact

In an effort to repair relations with Japan, the US Navy launched a $60 million operation to recover the victims' remains. After 425 dives, Navy divers recovered all but one of the bodies. The Navy eventually agreed to a settlement of $16.5 million with the victims' families and the survivors of the crash. In addition, a memorial was set up in Honolulu, Hawaii, to honor the victims. The Navy also started giving case studies of the incident to commanding and executive officers in the hopes of preventing similar accidents in the future.

Further Reading

Gordon, Mike. "*Ehime Maru*: A Year Later." *Honolulu Advertiser*. Honolulu Advertiser, 8 Feb. 2002. Web. 7 Aug. 2012.

Japan Times Online. "*Ehime Maru* Victims Honored." *Japan Times Online*. Japan Times Ltd., 11 Feb. 2011. Web. 7 Aug. 2012.

National Transportation Safety Board. "Collision between the US Navy Submarine USS *Greeneville* and Japanese Motor Vessel *Ehime Maru* near Oahu, Hawaii February 9, 2001." *National Transportation Safety Board*. National Transportation Safety Board, 29 Sept. 2005. Web. 7 Aug. 2012.

Rebecca Sparling

■ Elections in Canada

Definition: The selection of members of government bodies through the process of casting ballots

In Canada, elected representatives make up the body of parliamentary governments on the federal, provincial and municipal levels. The duty of parliamentary representatives is to determine official policies and to devise, discuss, and enact legislation that becomes law, thus determining the direction of Canadian society.

Representatives in Canadian government bodies are elected to serve through elections held independently on the federal, provincial, and municipal levels. Federally, during most of the 2000s, the area of Canada was subdivided into 308 electoral districts, or ridings. The same electoral method is used in both provincial and municipal elections, with the corresponding area being subdivided into a number of specific ridings. Several different candidates may stand for election in any particular riding, representing as many different political parties in federal and provincial elections, while municipal elections are nominally nonpartisan. All elections in Canada use a "first past the post" method, in which the candidate who has garnered the largest number of votes cast in his or her riding is deemed to have won that election, even if that number is not a majority.

The Canadian Electoral System

The Canadian federal government, which is located in Ottawa, the capital of Canada, consists of the House of Commons, whose members are elected by general vote, and an appointed Senate. The party that wins the most seats in the House of Commons leads the country, and the leader of that party generally becomes the prime minister. Each member in the House of Commons must have been deemed the victor in an election held in his or her particular riding. Provincial governments are elected in the same manner, but there are no corresponding provincial senates. Each provincial parliament is located in the capital city of the province or territory. At the municipal level, representatives are elected to be members of city and municipal councils or trustees of local boards of education, where such exist. Elected members may hold a seat in only one level of government at any one time.

At the beginning of the 2000s, the number of federal ridings, also known as constituencies, numbered 301. Each riding corresponds to one seat to be held by an elected representative in the House of Commons. Increasing population numbers and the changing distribution of population over time necessitate both the addition of seats and the reordering of the electoral districts to achieve representation by population. This process occurs after each ten-year census. In 2002, following the dissolution of the Parliament then in session, the number of ridings was increased to 308; a similar adjustment process took place in 2012. When electoral districts are defined, the commission charged with the task ensures that each has a generally equivalent population, with some exceptions for extraordinary circumstances of geographic area and sparse population.

Party Politics in Canada

Canada has several different political parties, each of which may field a candidate in any electoral district. The principal parties in federal and provincial elections are the Conservative, Liberal, and New Democratic Parties. Nominally equivalent parties function at the provincial level, though there are differences in political platform between the federal parties and their provincial counterparts. Two additional parties represent the interests of Quebec alone: the federal Bloc Québécois and the provincial Parti Québécois. In addition, there are several minor parties recognized by Elections Canada. To achieve standing as an official party in Parliament, a candidate party must win a minimum of four seats in any particular general election.

When an elected member vacates his or her seat during an election term, at any level of government, a by-election must be held in that particular electoral district to determine a new representative. The results of a by-election may change the balance of power within the elected government body, especially if it affects the number of seats held in such a way that a minority government (in which the ruling party holds the most seats but not a majority of seats) becomes a majority government, or vice versa.

Federal Political Landscape

At the federal level of politics, Canada began the decade governed by Prime Minister Jean Chrétien, leader of the Liberal Party. In 2000, the Liberals were reelected to a third majority government under Chrétien. Paul Martin replaced Chrétien as leader of the Liberal Party in 2003; in the federal general election the following year, the Liberal Party was reelected again, but with a minority of seats.

The Conservative Party, led by Stephen Harper, came to power in 2006, though it, too, failed to win a majority. As a minority government, the Harper Conservatives faced a number of threats. In 2008, following the reelection of the Conservatives as a minority government, the Liberal Party, now led by Stéphane Dion, structured a deal with the New Democratic Party and the Bloc Québécois to form a coalition government that would displace the Conservatives. In response, Prime Minister Harper sought the prorogation, or adjournment, of Parliament until January 26, 2009. After the prorogation was granted by the governor general—who serves as the representative of the Canadian monarch, also the monarch of the United Kingdom, in this case Elizabeth II—Dion resigned as Liberal leader and was replaced by Michael Ignatieff. Under Ignatieff, the Liberals agreed to support the Conservative budget, thereby signaling the end of the coalition. Led by Harper, the Conservatives remained in power as a minority government through the end of the decade.

Provincial Political Landscape

Provincial politics proved to be more dynamic through the 2000s, as the new territory of Nunavut entered its first decade following its official separation from the Northwest Territories in 1999 and the other provinces and territories responded to the dynamics of economic change. In Ontario in 2003, the Liberal Party, led by Dalton McGuinty, handily displaced the previous Progressive Conservative government, which had begun to lose support in 2000 and fell even more out of favor when leader Mike Harris resigned in 2002, to be replaced by Ernie Eves. In Alberta, longtime Progressive Conservative premier Ralph Klein retired from politics in 2006, while the Alberta oil sands project—the mining of crude oil from massive reserves in northeastern Alberta—ushered in a boom period that continued throughout the decade. The movement of people to Alberta from other parts of Canada, and from Ontario in particular, combined with the preexisting political effects in the latter to see Ontario become a "have-not" province—that is, one that receives equalization payments from the federal government to make up for a lack of tax revenue. In 2009, Ontario received an equalization payment for the first time ever, a marked change from its longtime position as the driving force of the Canadian economy.

In Quebec, separatist sentiments decreased through the decade to the point that federalist politics again became a major political force. In the 2008 federal election, a New Democratic MP was elected in Quebec for the first time, presaging a major upset in 2011, when the New Democratic Party would pick up an unprecedented fifty-nine seats, largely at the expense of the traditionally dominant Bloc Québécois.

Impact

The effects of the policies and laws enacted by the government of Canada throughout the 2000s, along with the dynamics of party politics, will extend well into the future for Canada. The Harper Conservative government set several precedents that were not entirely popular in Canadian politics, proroguing Parliament on two separate occasions and involving Canada in what many came to regard as a scandal in the F-35 Joint Strike Fighter program. Many of the provinces were also affected by unpopular and heavy-handed decisions by elected government representatives, particularly Ontario and Quebec, where massive debt and corruption were later revealed. Jurisdictional squabbles between provincial and federal governments served to disrupt the long-term stability of Canadian politics, while the realities of global economics exerted many different influences on the direction of the nation.

Further Reading

Elections Canada Online. Elections Canada, n.d. Web. 19 Dec. 2012. Maintains an archived record of election results, electoral districts, representatives, and information relevant to elections in Canada.

Gidengil, Elisabeth, Neil Nevitte, André Blais, Joanna Everitt, and Patrick Fournier. *Dominance and Decline: Making Sense of Recent Canadian Elections.*

Toronto: U of Toronto P, 2012. Print. Provides comprehensive and comparative accounts of Canadian elections from 2000 through 2008.

Milner, Henry. *Steps toward Making Every Vote Count: Electoral System Reform in Canada and Its Provinces.* Peterborough: Broadview, 2004. Print. Presents analyses by qualified observers regarding the growing movement for electoral reform in Canada.

Redistribution Federal Electoral Districts. Elections Canada, n.d. Web. 19 Dec. 2012. Provides a complete history of the redistribution of electoral districts in Canada and a full description of the redistribution process.

Tindal, C. Richard. *A Citizen's Guide to Government.* 3rd ed. Toronto: McGraw, 2005. Print. Provides a thorough, concise description of the Canadian political system, including the details of the electoral process.

Richard M. Renneboog, MSc

■ Elections in the United States, 2000

Definition: Presidential, congressional, and gubernatorial elections held November 7, 2000

The year 2000 saw the election of Republican George W. Bush after a prolonged recount and unprecedented Supreme Court decision decided the race between Bush and Democrat Al Gore thirty-six days after Election Day. In the US Senate, the Democrats enjoyed a majority until the inauguration of President Bush, when Vice President Dick Cheney broke the existing 50–50 tie. In the House of Representatives, the Republicans retained their majority.

In November of 2000, President Bill Clinton, first elected in 1992, was finishing his second and last term. Clinton's administration had fared well—by the time he left office the government boasted a budget surplus—but his legacy, particularly by the end of his presidency, was marred by an extramarital affair with White House intern Monica Lewinsky that resulted in his impeachment. Clinton's record as well as his character flaws played a significant role in the 2000 election as Democrats, particularly Vice President Al Gore, sought to distance themselves from the president. Gore was named the Democratic Party's presidential nominee following the withdrawal of his sole rival, New Jersey senator Bill Bradley, from the race.

Presidential Campaign

The Republican Party nominated George W. Bush, governor of Texas and son of former president George H. W. Bush (1989–93). In winning his party's nomination, Bush defeated former undersecretary of education Gary Bauer; businessman Steve Forbes; Utah senator Orrin Hatch; and former diplomat Alan Keyes, among others, though it was widely recognized that Arizona senator John McCain was Bush's strongest competitor leading up to the nomination. After the primaries, Bush selected veteran politico Dick Cheney, who had served as secretary of defense under the first President Bush, as his running mate. Gore strategically chose Connecticut senator Joe Lieberman, who became the first Jewish candidate to be part of a major-party presidential ticket. Lieberman was also one of the first Democrats to chastise President Clinton publically for his indiscretions.

Third-party candidates in the 2000 presidential race included Ralph Nader for the Green Party, Pat Buchanan for the Reform Party, and Harry Browne for the Libertarian Party. Among them, the left-leaning Nader, a longtime consumer activist, arose as the most viable candidate, though he was barred from the national debates. Nader's support of issues such as national healthcare, a livable wage, and environmental protection resonated with voters, so much so that nearing the election, the Gore campaign began to use the slogan "A Vote for Nader is a Vote for Bush," alluding to a potential spoiler effect. In the general election, he and his running mate, American Indian activist Winona LaDuke, garnered 96,837 votes, or 1.6 percent of the vote, in the contentious state of Florida. Nader earned more votes than Bush's margin of victory over Gore in New Hampshire as well. For years after the election, including during the 2004 presidential election, in which he also ran, many Democrats blamed him for siphoning off votes from Gore and ultimately contributing to Bush's victory.

The race between Gore and Bush was tight going into the last months of the campaign. Early on, Bush placed an emphasis on education, which was enticing to Democrats and independent voters. He pushed equally hard for two conservative goals, tax cuts and the partial privatization of Social Security, despite Democratic opposition. But overall, Bush made aggressive efforts to reach out to voters outside his base with his "compassionate conservative" rhetoric. Bush also did not fail to position himself in opposition to Clinton. He charmed voters with his easygoing persona, and as an evangelical Christian, he carried 68 percent of the white evangelical vote in the general election.

Against the affable Bush, Gore was seen as pedantic and wooden. His persona was especially problematic during the three debates, in which his eye-rolling and audible sighing became the focus of his performance. Whether he had won the debates with his arguments did not matter to many voters; he had lost in appeal. Additionally, Gore's antitobacco stance hurt him among Southern voters. Still, a number of groups rallied around Gore, sinking millions of dollars into ads and voter turnout initiatives, among them the environmentalist group the Sierra Club and the NAACP National Voter Fund. In the end, Gore failed to establish a clear persona or extricate himself from Clinton's shadow, though his popularity among African Americans, among whom he garnered 90 percent of the vote, and other groups kept the race close throughout the election.

Election Night, the Florida Recount, and *Bush v. Gore*

The 2000 presidential election was one of the most eventful in United States history, and news organizations hurried to report every new development. At about 7:50 p.m. on November 7, major television news channels such as CNN, NBC, and CBS, as well as the Associated Press, projected Gore as the winner of Florida, ten minutes before polls closed in the state's western panhandle, which falls in a different time zone. The news organizations retracted the call at about 9:54 p.m. At approximately 2:17 a.m. on November 8, the major networks projected Bush as the winner of the state of Florida and the election. Gore called Bush to concede the election, but CNN reported at 3:40 a.m. that Gore had called again to retract his concession. About twenty minutes later, both projections—Florida and the election for Bush—were retracted.

Much of the information that led the networks to make their calls was sourced from the Voter News Service (VNS), a polling organization collectively owned by the major news networks that relied heavily on exit polls, which tended to be unreliable.

Presidential Election Results

Presidential Candidate	Vice Presidential Candidate	Political Party	Popular Vote		Electoral Vote	
George W. Bush	Richard Cheney	Republican	50,460,110	47.87%	271	50.4%
Albert Gore Jr.	Joseph Lieberman	Democratic	51,003,926	48.38%	266	49.4%
Ralph Nader	Winona LaDuke	Green	2,883,105	2.73%	0	0.0%
Patrick Buchanan	Ezola Foster	Reform	449,225	0.43%	0	0.0%
Harry Browne	Art Olivier	Libertarian	384,516	0.36%	0	0.0%
Other			236,593	0.22%	0	0.0%

Source: Dave Leip's Atlas of U.S. Presidential Elections.

The misreporting as well as the closeness of the race contributed to the perception among some Americans that Gore was a "sore loser" for retracting his concession. Others believed that the early Gore call in Florida discouraged potential Republican voters in the state.

Confusion reigned for more than a month after Election Day. Votes were too close to call on election night in Wisconsin, Iowa, and New Mexico, but public attention remained on Florida, where discrepancies in the state's ballots abounded. In Palm Beach County, it appeared that an unusually large vote for third-party candidate Buchanan was the result of a confusing "butterfly ballot," a two-page ballot that was difficult for many voters to interpret. Chads, the bits of paper punched out of punch card ballots, were examined and deemed to be "dimpled," "pregnant," or "hanging"—that is, improperly or incompletely punched out—as poll workers tried to sort through remaining ballots elsewhere.

The closeness of the race automatically triggered a recount by Florida law. As limited recounting began, Bush held a tenuous lead numbered in hundreds of votes, out of nearly six million votes cast. On November 12, lawyers from the Bush campaign began a lawsuit to end the recount. Several federal judges turned the case down and allowed recounts to continue, but on November 24, the US Supreme Court agreed to hear Bush's appeal. On November 26, Florida secretary of state Katherine Harris, a cochair of Bush's Florida campaign, certified Florida's vote for Bush, though the recount had not

been completed. Gore's lawyers contested the result the next day, triggering a court battle over the manually recounted votes that Harris did not include in her recount. Although Bush began preparations for his administration in late November, the legal maneuvering continued until December 12, when the Supreme Court ruled to end the recount in the historic Bush v. Gore. The per curium decision (literally meaning "by the court"; the justices did not delineate any single majority author) was based on the equal protection clause of the Fourteenth Amendment. Gore conceded the election the following day.

Ultimately, Gore received 266 electoral votes; twenty states as well as Washington, DC; and 48.38 percent of the popular vote with 50,999,897 votes. Bush received 271 electoral votes; thirty states; and 47.87 percent of the popular vote with 50,456,002 votes. (There are 538 votes in the Electoral College; one elector abstained from casting a vote.) This outcome, in which a candidate won the popular vote but lost the electoral vote, had last occurred in the presidential election of 1888, when Benjamin Harrison defeated incumbent Grover Cleveland.

Congressional and Gubernatorial Elections

In the US Senate, the 2000 elections resulted in a 50–50 split between Democrats and Republicans. When such a split occurs, the vice president's party claims the majority. Upon Bush's inauguration, Vice President Cheney gave the Republican Party the advantage. However, Republican senator Jim

Jeffords of Vermont became an independent and began caucusing with the Democrats in mid-2001, thus changing the balance in favor of the Democratic Party.

There were several notable Senate races. In Missouri, Governor Mel Carnahan, a Democratic senatorial candidate, died in a plane crash while campaigning in October. With his name still on the ballot, Carnahan posthumously won the election against Republican John Ashcroft, who would later serve as attorney general in the Bush administration. Carnahan's widow, Jean Carnahan, served in her husband's stead until 2002, when she narrowly lost the seat in a special election. In New York, Hillary Clinton became the first sitting First Lady to run for (and win) public office, defeating Republican senator Rick Lazio in a contentious and expensive race.

In the House of Representatives, Republicans retained their majority, though they lost several seats to Democrats. Eleven states held gubernatorial elections, but West Virginia became the only state to change parties in the governor's house when Bob Wise, a Democrat, defeated incumbent governor Cecil H. Underwood, a Republican.

Impact

The 2000 elections changed the way news organizations reported on election results and sparked a larger debate about the Electoral College, particularly among Democrats, who argued that Gore won the popular vote and thus should have won the election. The election also had an impact on the voting process. In 2002, Congress passed the Help America Vote Act (HAVA), which required states to offer up-to-date voting equipment, voter registration databases, provisional voting, and complaint procedures. In addition, the Supreme Court's ruling in Bush v. Gore established a cultural precedent in terms of how elections are decided and prompted a dramatic increase in the number of lawsuits brought over election issues.

Further Reading

Allen, Neal and Brian J. Brox. "The Roots of Third Party Voting: The 2000 Nader Campaign in Historical Perspective." *Party Politics* 11.5 (2005): 623–37. Print. Discusses Nader's 2000 campaign in relation to the campaigns of other third party candidates throughout history and concludes that voters who cast ballots for Nader likely would have voted for another third party candidate or not voted at all, contrary to the arguments of some Democrats.

Dershowitz, Alan M. *Supreme Injustice: How the High Court Hijacked Election 2000.* New York: Oxford UP, 2001. Print. Argues against the Supreme Court's decision in Bush v. Gore and discusses the events that led up to it.

Konner, Joan, James Risser, and Ben Wattenberg. "Television's Performance on Election Night 2000: A Report for CNN." *CNN.* Cable News Network, 29 Jan. 2001. Web. 29 Nov. 2012. Analyzes the various failings of the television news organizations in their election night coverage.

Posner, Richard A. *Breaking the Deadlock: The 2000 Election, the Constitution, and the Courts.* Princeton: Princeton UP, 2001. Print. Provides a defense of the Supreme Court's decision in Bush v. Gore from the perspective of a US Court of Appeals judge and law professor.

Rakove, Jack N. *The Unfinished Election of 2000: Leading Scholars Examine America's Strangest Election.* New York: Basic, 2001. Print. Compiles essays from scholars dissecting the numerous peculiarities of the 2000 election.

Toobin, Jeffrey. *Too Close to Call: The Thirty-Six Day Battle to Decide the 2000 Election.* New York: Random, 2001. Print. Chronicles the unprecedented recount and court case that decided the 2000 election.

Molly Hagan

■ Elections in the United States, 2004

Definition: Presidential, congressional, and gubernatorial elections held November 2, 2004

In 2004, Americans reelected Republican president George W. Bush. Much like the presidential election that preceded it, though without the prolonged recount and court battle, the 2004 election came down to the electoral votes of a single state. The Republican Party also picked up seats in the Senate and in the House of Representatives.

The 2004 election was largely a referendum on the policies of President George W. Bush throughout his eventful first term. Less than a year into his presidency, the United States was attacked by terrorists

Democratic presidential nominee Senator John Kerry (right) with vice-presidential nominee Senator John Edwards at the Democratic National Convention, Boston, July 29, 2004. (AP Photo/Steven Senne)

affiliated with the international network al-Qaeda on September 11, 2001. The United States invaded Afghanistan in 2002 and in March of the following year invaded Iraq, alleging that Iraqi president Saddam Hussein was harboring weapons of mass destruction, although no such weapons were ever found. The wars continued through 2004 and proved to have a significant influence on that year's elections.

Presidential Campaign

While Bush, as the incumbent, received the Republican nomination with little opposition, a number of politicians emerged as contenders in the Democratic primary election. Vermont governor Howard Dean emerged as the early front-runner for the nomination, winning support for his opposition to the war in Iraq. Dean was one of the first candidates to run a successful fundraising campaign on the Internet. However, Dean's popularity waned, in large part because of media portrayals of him as angry and prone to gaffes. By March, Massachusetts senator John Kerry was the only candidate left standing in a field that once included Dean, General Wesley Clark,

Missouri representative Dick Gephardt, Ohio representative Dennis Kucinich, Connecticut senator and former vice presidential candidate Joe Lieberman, and Reverend Al Sharpton. After the collapse of Dean's campaign, Kerry's most fierce competitor was North Carolina senator John Edwards, who withdrew from the race after Super Tuesday. In July, Kerry announced that he had chosen Edwards, a moderate, young southerner, as his running mate. At the Democratic National Convention later that month, Illinois senate candidate and future president Barack Obama gave the keynote address that changed the course of his political career.

Foreign policy was the dominant issue of the campaign, along with the newly declared War on Terror. During his first term, Bush was criticized for his aggressive unilateral policies. Though several countries backed the United States–led invasion of Iraq—most notably Great Britain and Australia—many others were largely opposed to the action. The photographs of tortured prisoners at the Abu Ghraib prison in Iraq that emerged in early 2004 also had a devastating effect on foreign perceptions of the United States. The fact that much of the election revolved around these events and discussions of foreign policy is unsurprising in its context but historically unusual. In 2003, a Gallup poll reported that terrorism and the economy topped the list of extremely important issues to Americans in the upcoming election, with more Republicans citing terrorism and more Democrats citing the economy.

Kerry, a veteran politician, called for more caution in the Middle East and advocated repairing damaged relationships with US allies. The then-junior senator had voted to go to war in Iraq in 2002, though when he announced his campaign for president, he said that he had done so simply to threaten the use of force. He stuck by the vote based on the evidence that was presented to him at the time—namely, the information that suggested that Iraq had weapons of mass destruction. Still, in 2003, Kerry voted against providing $87 billion in funding for the wars in Iraq and Afghanistan. Kerry tried to explain that he did not want to fund the wars on borrowed money and had voted for a defeated measure that would scale

Presidential Election Results

Presidential Candidate	Vice Presidential Candidate	Political Party	Popular Vote		Electoral Vote	
George W. Bush	Richard Cheney	Republican	62,040,610	50.73%	286	53.2%
John Kerry	John Edwards	Democratic	59,028,439	48.27%	251	46.7%
Ralph Nader	Peter Camejo	Independent	463,655	0.38%	0	0.0%
Michael Badnarik	Richard Campagna	Libertarian	397,265	0.32%	0	0.0%
Other			363,579	0.30%	0	0.0%

Source: Dave Leip's Atlas of U.S. Presidential Elections.

back the Bush tax cuts to fund the wars. Nevertheless, the voting issue and others led opponents to describe Kerry as a "flip-flopper" who wavered on the issues. In addition, Kerry's speaking style was considered by some to be stiff or wooden, and his modifiers and complex explanations were seen as less assured than Bush's grand proclamations.

Kerry's military service became the focus of a massive smear campaign funded by a group called Swift Boat Veterans for Truth. As a young man, Kerry volunteered to serve in the Vietnam War, where he spent some time commanding a swift boat; he earned a bronze star, a silver star, and three Purple Hearts for his service. When he returned to civilian life he became an antiwar activist and testified before the Senate Committee on Foreign Relations about war crimes committed by US soldiers. During the 2004 election, members of Swift Boat Veterans for Truth led attacks on Kerry's military record, claiming that Kerry had lied about the actions that earned him his medals. Further investigations yielded little evidence to support their claims, and a number of prominent veterans, including Republican senator John McCain as well as Kerry's crewmates, defended the candidate. In the years after the 2004 presidential election, the term *swiftboating* came to be used to describe a particularly vicious political smear campaign.

Groups that were independent of either campaign yet clearly endorsed or denigrated one of the candidates played an unprecedented role in the election. According to the Federal Election Commission (FEC), independent groups spent more than $400 million in the lead-up to the 2004 election. Many were classified as tax-exempt organizations and were thus allowed to collect unlimited contributions. Such organizations were not subject to FEC spending regulations, but they were prohibited from advocating for or against a particular candidate. In 2006, the FEC fined several organizations, including Swift Boat Veterans for Truth and the liberal organization MoveOn.org, for violating this rule.

Exit Polling and Election Night

As the official results came in on election night, it became clear that leaked reports during the day, particularly the raw results from exit polls around the country, had favored Kerry by an erroneous margin. According to a report published in the *Washington Post*, the national exit poll showed Kerry with a lead of 51 percent to Bush's 48 percent on election night before the votes were counted. The official election result showed that Bush received 286 electoral votes and 50.7 percent of the popular vote with 62,040,610 votes, while Kerry received 251 electoral votes and 48.3 percent of the popular vote with 59,028,444 votes.

Although less dramatic than the previous presidential election, the 2004 election was likewise decided by the electoral votes of one state. In 2004, that state was Ohio, and much as in Florida in 2000, the voting and vote-counting processes in Ohio came under national scrutiny. Ambiguous legislation, varying standards, long lines, and faulty voting machines were just a few of the problems reported across the state, which Bush won by two percentage points. Despite the arguments of some Kerry supporters, however, most experts agreed that the Ohio result was not a case of widespread partisan disenfranchisement, though they argued that a number of policies disproportionately affected poor voters and that partisan leaders were given too much power in decisions concerning the electoral process.

Congressional and Gubernatorial Elections
Republicans made gains in both the Senate and the House in 2004. Before the election, Republicans had a slim majority in the Senate with fifty-one seats. They gained four more seats in the election, further solidifying their majority. Notable senatorial campaigns included the Illinois race, in which Democrat Barack Obama defeated Republican Alan Keyes. In the House, Republicans ended election night with 232 seats, up from 229 seats before the election. Democrats, however, won six of the eleven governor's races. Additionally, initiatives to ban same-sex marriage passed in eleven states.

Impact
The election was a resounding victory for Republicans and for President Bush, who viewed his victory as an indication that he had earned political capital throughout his campaign. News organizations once again reevaluated the way they reported on elections, most notably becoming much more cautious about reporting exit polls. Polling organizations similarly evaluated their approach to handling exit polls, seeking to prevent leaks of data to the media. The 2004 election also laid the groundwork for the ubiquity of the Internet, which would become a key factor in the next presidential election, in political campaigns.

Further Reading
Ceasar, James Wilbur, and Andrew E. Busch. *Red Over Blue: The 2004 Elections and American Politics.* Lanham: Rowman, 2005. Print. Analyzes the outcomes of the 2004 presidential, congressional, and gubernatorial elections and discusses their effects.

Cohen, Roger; Sanger, David E., and Steven R. Weisman. "The Bush Record: Challenging Rest of the World with a New Order." *New York Times.* New York Times, 12 Oct. 2004. Web. 3 Dec. 2012. Provides an in-depth look at the foreign policies of the Bush administration during the president's first term.

Denton, Robert E, ed. *The 2004 Presidential Campaign: A Communication Perspective.* Lanham: Rowman, 2005. Print. Collects a number of essays on issues pertaining to the 2004 presidential election and campaign, focusing in particular on rhetorical strategies, advertising, and other forms of political communication.

Liptak, Adam. "Voting Problems in Ohio Set Off Alarm." *New York Times.* New York Times, 7 Nov. 2004. Web. 5 Dec. 2012. Features interviews with officials and scholars regarding the voting problems in Ohio during the election.

Morin, Richard, and Claudia Deane. "Report Acknowledges Inaccuracies in 2004 Exit Polls." *Washington Post.* Washington Post, 20 Jan. 2005. Web. 4 Dec. 2012. Reports on the official analysis of number discrepancies in exit polls during the 2004 election.

Williams, Andrew Paul, and John C. Tedesco, eds. *The Internet Election: Perspectives on the Web in Campaign 2004.* Lanham: Rowman, 2006. Print. Collects a variety of essays discussing the role of the Internet in the 2004 election, focusing in particular on campaigning and promotion.

Woodward, Bob. *Plan of Attack: The Definitive Account of the Decision to Invade Iraq.* New York: Simon, 2004. Print. Reports on the events leading up to the Iraq War, which became a key area of contention among candidates during the 2004 elections.

Molly Hagan

◼ Elections in the United States, 2008

Definition: Presidential, congressional, and gubernatorial elections held November 4, 2008

In 2008, Democrat Barack Obama defeated Republican John McCain to become the first African American president of the United States. Democrats solidified their majority in the House of Representatives and attained a substantial majority in the Senate.

As President George W. Bush's second term in office approached its end, candidates from both major political parties struggled with the legacy of his administration. Military action in Afghanistan and Iraq, begun during Bush's first term, continued into the 2008 election season, and the recession that had begun in late 2007 brought economic issues to the

Presidential candidate Barack Obama; his wife, Michelle; and his children Sasha (left center) and Malia (right center) greet the audience at the Democratic National Convention, Denver, Colorado, August 28, 2008. (Library of Congress/ LC-DIG-highsm-03848/Photograph by Carol M. Highsmith)

forefront. Democratic politicians largely distanced themselves from Bush and his policies, while Republicans were at times split on whether to stand by the sitting president. The issues of foreign policy and the economy, as well as many Americans' desire for a significant change in leadership, proved crucial to both the presidential election of 2008 as well as the congressional and gubernatorial elections of that year.

Presidential Campaign

Due to the "front-loading" of the primary calendar, candidates began campaigning around Thanksgiving 2007. For the Democrats, the Iowa Caucus, held on January 3, was a major blow to New York senator Hillary Clinton, who had been the presumptive nominee through the end of 2007. Clinton came in third in the race, with North Carolina senator John Edwards, who had been Senator John Kerry's running mate in the previous presidential election, taking second place. Illinois freshman senator Barack Obama defeated both Clinton and Edwards by a large margin. As the Democratic primary progressed, Clinton and Obama emerged as fierce competitors for the nomination. Despite the enormous pressure put on Clinton to withdraw from the race, she did not concede until June 7, several days after Obama officially clinched the nomination on June 3. After garnering the nomination, Obama selected Senator Joe Biden, who had also run in the primaries and

was known for his foreign policy expertise, as his running mate.

Among Republicans, the field included longtime Arizona senator and across-the-aisle favorite John McCain, former New York City mayor Rudy Giuliani, former Arkansas governor Mike Huckabee, and former Massachusetts governor Mitt Romney, among others. In another surprise finish—Giuliani had been the early favorite—Huckabee won Iowa in January. McCain, the eventual nominee, made a comeback in the polls after winning New Hampshire later that month. He won enough delegates to assure his nomination after winning the primaries in Ohio, Rhode Island, Texas, and Vermont on March 4.

McCain, who had also been a contender in the 2000 primary, seemed a solid choice among Republicans. A veteran of the Vietnam War who had spent several years in captivity, McCain boasted years of experience in the Senate and was widely respected and seen as an honorable politician by members of both parties. Though he was never mistaken for a Democrat, during his long tenure in the Senate McCain made an effort to reach across the aisle on issues ranging from campaign finance reform to global warming. However, the political climate of the 2008 election was not amenable to moderation, and McCain often seemed at war with his familiar persona and the new ultraconservative rhetoric. Seeking to rally the party, McCain hired staffers who had worked on the same Bush campaign that had smeared him in 2000 while calling himself a party "maverick," and his campaign exploited wedge issues such as gun control and abortion. McCain solidified his new brand of conservatism when he chose the little-known Alaska governor Sarah Palin as his running mate. The first woman to run on a national Republican ticket, Palin had a folksy manner of speaking that appealed to the party's base in ways that McCain did not, and she garnered a large fan base. Her lack of experience was apparent, however, and many of her statements to the press were detrimental to the McCain campaign's credibility among voters.

The Internet and the Financial Crisis

Although the McCain campaign used the Internet to connect with voters and express its messages, the

Presidential Election Results

Presidential Candidate	Vice Presidential Candidate	Political Party	Popular Vote		Electoral Vote	
Barack H. Obama	Joseph R. Biden, Jr.	Democratic	69,499,428	52.87%	365	67.8%
John S. McCain, III	Sarah H. Palin	Republican	59,950,323	45.60%	173	32.2%
Ralph Nader	Matt Gonzalez	Independent	739,278	0.56%	0	0.0%
Bob Barr	Wayne Allyn Root	Libertarian	523,433	0.40%	0	0.0%
Other			750,660	0.57%	0	0.0%

Source: Dave Leip's Atlas of U.S. Presidential Elections

Obama campaign was far more adept at harnessing that forum to win votes. Former Vermont governor Howard Dean, who ran in the 2004 Democratic primary, had been the first major candidate to raise money by asking supporters for small donations via the Internet. The Obama campaign improved upon this strategy and used it to great effect. Obama and his team were able to utilize forums such as YouTube for free advertising, and social media websites such as Facebook brought Obama closer to young voters, a vast majority of whom threw their support behind him. Signaling a growing trend, the Pew Research Center reported that more people had gone online to get political and campaign news as of June 2008 than during the entire 2004 election.

Despite Obama's popularity, the race was still considered fairly close until September, when the financial crisis took both candidates—and the electorate—by surprise. Although politicians, and the public to an extent, had been aware of the ongoing economic downturn, the collapse of the investment bank Lehman Brothers, one of the largest in the country, in September of 2008 triggered a financial meltdown that became the focus of significant public and media attention. At the end of the month, McCain announced that he was suspending his campaign and returning to Washington to focus on the crisis, while the Obama campaign took a more measured approach.

Unlike in the two presidential elections prior, voting on election day 2008 was a relatively smooth process throughout the United States. Voter turnout was the highest it had been since 1968. Official election results reported that Obama received 365 electoral votes and 53 percent of the popular vote with 69,498,516 votes, while McCain received 173 electoral votes and 46 percent of the popular vote with 59,948,323 votes. Obama ultimately bested George W. Bush's 2004 record, receiving the highest number of votes in history.

Congressional and Gubernatorial Elections

Democrats made significant gains in the House of Representatives, increasing the party's majority by twenty-one seats. The Democratic Party achieved a near supermajority in the Senate, holding a total of fifty-seven seats to the Republican Party's forty-one; the additional two seats were held by independent senators who caucused with the Democrats. In one particularly contested Senate race, Democrat Al Franken defeated incumbent Minnesota senator Norm Coleman by a fraction of a percent following a mandatory recount. While most states holding gubernatorial elections either reelected the incumbent or elected a governor belonging to the same party as the previous one, the governorship of Missouri switched parties following the retirement of Republican governor Matt Blunt and the election of Democrat Jay Nixon.

Impact

The 2008 elections had a significant effect on the ways in which political candidates mobilized and connected with their supporters. Obama's use of the Internet, as well as his efforts to reach younger voters, allowed him to develop a strong base of supporters that would enable him to succeed in his bid for re-election in 2012.

Further Reading

Cain Miller, Claire. "How Obama's Internet Campaign Changed Politics." *New York Times.* New York Times, 7 Nov. 2008. Web. 10 Dec. 2012. Discusses the ways in which the Obama campaign's use of the Internet changed the way political campaigns are handled.

Grann, David. "The Fall: John McCain's Choices." *New Yorker.* New Yorker, 17 Nov. 2008. Web. 10 Dec. 2012. Explores the reasons for McCain's defeat in the 2008 election, focusing in particular on his turn toward right-wing rhetoric.

Heilemann, John, and Mark Halperin. *Game Change: Obama and the Clintons, McCain and Pain, and the Race of a Lifetime.* New York: HarperCollins, 2010. Print. Provides an up-close look at the 2008 election based on hundreds of interviews conducted in 2008 and 2009.

Magleby, David B., and Anthony Corrado, eds. *Financing the 2008 Election: Assessing Reform.* Washington: Brookings Inst., 2011. Print. Compiles essays focusing on the issue of campaign finance in the 2008 election, in particular discussing campaign finance reform.

McKinney, Mitchell S., and Mary C. Banwart, eds. *Communication in the 2008 US Election: Digital Natives Elect a President.* New York: Lang, 2011. Print. Collects essays discussing digital communication strategies, including fundraising and advertising initiatives, during the 2008 election.

Prah, Pamela M. "Will States Fix the 2012 Primary Process?" *Stateline.* Pew Center on the States, 6 May 2008. Web. 10 Dec. 2012. Discusses the effect of the front-loading of the primaries.

Rainie, Lee and Aaron Smith. "The Internet and the 2008 Election." *Pew Internet.* Pew Research Center, 15 Jun. 2008. Web. 9 Dec. 2012. Reports on record Internet usage by candidates even before the general election was underway.

Molly Hagan

■ Elections in the United States, midterm

Definition: Congressional elections that took place in 2002 and 2006

While some congressional elections take place at the same time as a presidential election, others take place two years into a president's term. These latter elections are known as midterm elections. Such elections often serve as important gauges of the popularity of the sitting president and at times result in major shifts in congressional majorities.

The United States' election system is designed to prevent the nation from being faced with a completely new Congress and president every few years. The members of the House of Representatives are elected every two years, the president every four, and senators every six. For the same reason, senators do not seek reelection en masse; instead, only one-third of Senate seats open every two years. Because of the staggered Senate election schedule and the two-year House term, every president may face a significant change in the makeup of Congress halfway through his or her four-year term. The results of these midterm elections are typically thought to reflect the electorate's approval or disapproval of the president's performance and agenda during the first two years of his or her term.

2002 Midterm Elections

When Texas governor George W. Bush narrowly won the presidency in 2000, he faced a divided Congress, with the House under Republican control but the Senate in Democratic hands. However, the terrorist attacks of September 11, 2001, unified Congress behind Bush as he sought to destroy the global terrorist network al-Qaeda and worked to revitalize the nation's economy during a recession. By the summer before the 2002 midterm election, Bush was riding a wave of popularity, bolstered by support for his proposal to create the landmark Department of Homeland Security. In a national poll taken shortly before the elections, Bush enjoyed a public approval rating of 63 percent, the second-highest approval rating held by a US president since the end of World War II. Even major financial scandals such as the 2001 collapse of the energy company Enron, which had ties to the administration, did not significantly affect Bush's popularity immediately after the September 11 attacks.

Compared to congressional elections held in presidential election years, midterm elections are typically characterized by low voter turnout, particularly among independent voters. In light of this fact, the 2002 midterm elections resulted in a landslide victory for Republican representatives and senators who had aligned themselves with Bush. Republican voters came out in record numbers, as did independents who approved of Bush's actions during the post-September 11 crisis, while Democrats failed to muster strong support from their base. The president led his party to majorities in both the House and the Senate, the first time a first-term president had done so since 1934.

2006 Midterm Elections

Soon after the 2002 midterm elections, President Bush was given support by the international community to target the regime of Iraqi president Saddam Hussein, whom many intelligence experts believed was developing weapons of mass destruction. Although Americans were not as unified behind Bush's pursuit of military action in Iraq as they were for his pursuit of al-Qaeda in Afghanistan in 2001, voters stood with the incumbent president during his 2004 reelection campaign.

By the 2006 midterm elections, however, many voters had come to disagree with Bush's policies. The toppling of Hussein's regime was quick, as promised, but US military action in Iraq continued. Meanwhile, a series of high-profile scandals, including the discovery that the intelligence on Hussein's weapons program had been false, dramatically undercut Bush's public image. Congress, which had been under Republican control since 2002, also lost favor among many voters.

Across the country, Republicans sought to distance themselves from Bush, but their attempts to do so largely fell short, as Democratic candidates, bolstered by heavy infusions of campaign contributions, hammered home to voters their opponents' connections to the Republican Party and, by extension, to Bush. The Democratic Party took control of the House of Representatives during this election, while Democratic gains in the Senate resulted in a 49–49 tie that was broken by the presence of two independent senators who aligned themselves with the Democratic caucus.

Impact

The midterm elections of the 2000s demonstrated the significance of midterm congressional elections for a sitting president. The 2002 elections showed strong voter support for President Bush, who was able to assemble a Republican Congress in his first term. Meanwhile, the 2006 midterm elections demonstrated the dramatic fall from grace Bush experienced during his second term, as Congress returned to Democratic hands largely because of the unpopularity of the sitting president.

Further Reading

Fineman, Howard, et al. "How Bush Did It." *Newsweek* 18 Nov. 2002: 44. Print. Discusses the wave of popularity that bolstered President Bush during the 2002 midterm election and how he was able to use it to further his agenda.

Jacobson, Gary C. *A Divider, Not a Uniter: George W. Bush and the American People.* London: Longman, 2007. Print. Describes the political partisanship and shift in public opinion that characterized the 2006 midterm elections.

—. "Terror, Terrain, and Turnout: Explaining the 2002 Midterm Elections." *Political Science Quarterly* 118.1 (2003): 1–22. Print. Discusses the political landscape that helped define the landmark 2002 midterm elections.

"Putting His Presidency Together Again." *Economist* 9 Nov. 2006: 29–32. Print. Reviews the issues that contributed to President Bush's unpopularity and the subsequent congressional changes that occurred during the 2006 midterm elections.

Tumulty, Karen, and Mike Allen. "Republicans on the Run". *Time.* Time, 26 Mar. 2006. Web. 4 Dec. 2012. Discusses the preparations made by both Democratic and Republican candidates in the months leading up to the 2006 midterm elections.

Michael P. Auerbach, MA

■ Electronic health records

Definition: A technologic collection that encompasses all aspects of a person's health and medical care

Electronic health records (EHRs) are storage databases of individual health information that can be typed, scanned, or voiced into a template or free form content-management system. At their most basic, EHRs contain medical history, laboratory test orders and results, prescription history, physician visit notes, and insurance information.

Although considered interchangeable with electronic medical records in some discussions, electronic health records (EHRs) actually imply a larger portfolio and benefit to patients and providers. Unlike an individual office's medical records on paper

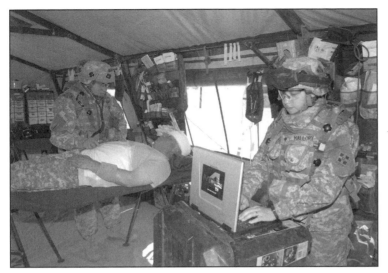

A medical unit use the Medical Communications for Combat Casualty Care (MC4) system to document patient care. (U.S. Army Photo)

or in a computer system, EHRs are distinguished as shareable, patient-owned content, with an ultimate goal of collecting and providing medical information on one patient to any provider, anywhere. EHRs are considered the biggest medical-records change of the 2000s, with the potential for even greater reliance on electronic data management into the twenty-first century.

Putting Paperless Records into Practice

Building upon paper-to-electronic transitions of individual, closed-loop medical records found in private physicians' offices and hospitals, EHRs have been embraced in part for their potential to interconnect different providers in an effort to improve patient care. In theory, EHRs are collections of medical data from office electronic medical records that follow patients across care; evidence-based care implementation and avoidance of duplicate care, particularly laboratory or prescription ordering, are two potential benefits. EHRs have the potential to save money for providers, patients, and businesses alike, and increasing the availability of compatible networking systems will likely further that effort.

By the end of the 2000s, EHRs were being used by around 44 percent of office-based physicians in their practices, up from 17.3 percent in 2002, according to the Centers for Disease Control and Prevention (CDC). Physicians in large health-maintenance organizations or health centers adopted EHRs more often than physicians in single or small-group practices. Practitioners older than fifty years of age were generally less likely to implement electronic record keeping, in part because of the steep learning curve, time, and costs required to implement a new electronic operating system. Even by 2009, 78 percent of office-based physicians and 91 percent of hospitals equipped for EHRs were not fully utilizing their capabilities. In fact, 59 percent of physicians polled by the CDC who reported using electronic record keeping actually used them as stand-alone, self-contained records, not as electronic documents for sharing data among caregivers.

EHRs were developed to increase the availability of shared medical information for improved patient care. They first emerged in medical groups like the Medical Center Hospital of Vermont and the Mayo Clinic in Rochester, Minnesota, in the 1960s, and their possibilities grew in the 1990s as electronic records were shared more broadly within provider networks. Compared with office-based business software that saves medical records in a closed loop, EHRs have the potential to become an open but secure network of patient health data. Barriers to development of these EHR systems include start-up financial and time considerations, consistency and interchangeability of systems used by different providers, security of personal information, and uniform quality and accessibility.

Government Regulatory Incentives

As early as 1991, the Institute of Medicine set a goal of switching entirely to EHRs, with no reliance on paper records, by 2001. The move from paper to electronic format has been slower than planned, but efforts were continually promoted during the 2000s. In his 2004 State of the Union address, President George W. Bush officially established the widespread adoption of EHRs as a primary public health goal, saying the move would reduce medical costs, prevent errors, and increase efficiency of care. In 2004, the Office of the National Coordinator for Health Information Technology (ONC) was founded to supervise efforts toward moving patient data management into an electronic era. The Centers for Medicare and Medicaid Services (CMS), which oversees multiple financial and regulatory aspects of state and national health care, gave support to EHR development soon after. By 2009, as part of the ONC effort, the Nationwide Health Information Network was being developed and tested to explore and manage the secure transfer of health care–related data over the Internet.

Only by the end of the decade did government efforts begin to impact EHR practices. The American Recovery and Reinvestment Act of 2009 was a broad economic stimulator that included the Health Information Technology for Economic and Clinical Health (HITECH) Act, which established a financial commitment to and timeline for implementation of EHRs. HITECH remedied the slow acceptance and inconsistency of EHRs by mandating EHR use by providers and hospitals by 2015 and defining appropriate methods of using electronic record keeping to share data and improve care. The CMS provided the industry highly detailed descriptions of meaningful use of EHRs, and the ONC became responsible for explaining health information technology—and EHRs specifically—to the public as well as evaluating the impact and efficacy of EHRs in use.

With guidelines and incentives from HITECH and other government resources, a new goal of total EHR use by 2014 has been put in place. Though only 16 percent of hospitals in 2009 reported having adopted an EHR system, the incentives and penalties set forth in the HITECH Act indicate that the majority of hospitals will institute paperless systems in the decade to come. Hospitals and large provider groups will most likely be the first to adapt to HITECH and CMS requirements because their greater resources likely include existing electronic systems that can be adapted to meaningful-use standards with relative ease.

Impact

EHRs used in the 2000s differed significantly from those introduced in the 1990s, largely because of the improved technological support of the twenty-first century. Although personal EHRs have the potential to improve health-care administration and many in the field consider them the foundation of good twenty-first-century health care, their true benefits will emerge slowly in the decades ahead. In practice, by the end of the 2000s, use of EHRs remained closed within each provider group; as government and private-business stakeholders develop

and implement smoother, more patient-friendly health information technology programs, ubiquitous electronic systems will develop. Lower costs and improved interchangeability will further efforts to achieve the seamless sharing of patient health data among all care providers, thus enabling optimal, efficient care.

Further Reading

Davis, Cynthia, and Marcy Stoots. *A Guide to EHR Adoption: Implementation through Organizational Transformation.* Chicago: HIMSS, 2012. Print. Industry textbook for provider groups and businesses that explains the advantages of electronic record keeping and advises professionals on transition methods that are beneficial for providers and patients.

Jones, Spencer S., et al. "Electronic Health Record Adoption and Quality Improvement in US Hospitals." *American Journal of Managed Care* 16.12 (2010): SP64–71. Print. Report on the potential patient-care benefits of implementing electronic record keeping.

Liang, Louise L., ed. *Connected for Health: Using Electronic Health Records to Transform Care Delivery.* San Francisco: Wiley, 2010. Print. A Kaiser Foundation publication for members and general patients that describes how and why providers are switching to electronic record keeping systems. Also addresses safety and privacy considerations.

Skipper, Jamie. *Individuals' Access to Their Own Health Information.* Washington: US Office of the Natl. Coordinator for Health Information Technology, 2012. PDF file. A consumer-oriented guide to maximizing electronic health records, both for sharing with providers and for compiling a personal best picture of health and care.

United States. Govt. Accountability Office. *Electronic Health Records: Number and Characteristics of Providers Awarded Medicare Incentive Payments for 2011.* Washington: GAO, 2012. PDF file. Description of government-collected data about the growing use of EHRs in response to incentive and regulation programs implemented in the 2000s, introduced with a review of EHR basics.

Vaiana, Mary E. "Will Adoption of Electronic Health Records Improve Quality in US Hospitals?" Santa Monica: RAND, 2011. PDF file. Fact sheet summarizing the findings of Jones et al.

Nicole Van Hoey, PharmD

■ Emanuel, Rahm

Identification: American politician
Born: November 29, 1959; Chicago, Illinois

Emanuel's no-nonsense political approach has earned him the nickname of "Rahmbo" among his colleagues. With a diverse background that includes both ballet and investment banking, Emanuel does not fit the typical mold of a political powerhouse. In addition to serving as Mayor of Chicago, he has served under two US presidents and as a member of the US House of Representatives.

By the beginning of the millennium, Rahm Emanuel was well known in Washington, DC. After working as a senior advisor to President Bill Clinton for two terms, Emanuel returned to his hometown of Chicago and pursued a career in investment banking. President Clinton appointed him to the board of the Federal Home Loan Mortgage Corporation (Freddie Mac) in 2000. That same year, he returned to politics, mounting a successful campaign for a seat in the House of Representatives as the representative from the Fifth District of Illinois.

During his tenure in the House, Emanuel was appointed to the Financial Services Committee, which provided oversight to such institutions as Freddie Mac. During the US mortgage crisis that began to escalate in 2003, the committee launched an investigation against Freddie Mac. Emanuel did not attend the hearings, however, due to his past employment at the organization.

Emanuel was selected chairman of the Democratic Congressional Campaign Committee in 2005. His brash and sometimes acerbic personality resulted in occasional conflicts with caused clashes with colleagues. Emanuel helped orchestrate the Democratic takeover of the House in 2006, winning the approval of many of his peers.

During the 2008 Democratic presidential primary, Emanuel faced a conflict of loyalties. He had established a personal and professional relationship with both front-runners, Senator Hillary Clinton and Senator Barack Obama. He did not publicly endorse a candidate until after the 2008 primaries, when he announced his support of the primary winner, Obama. Eventually, Emanuel joined Obama's election team. President Obama selected Emanuel as his chief of staff in late 2008.

Rahm Emanuel. (Courtesy Viewminder)

Impact

While serving as President Obama's chief of staff, he helped the president shape the health care legislation that eventually led to landmark health insurance reform. He also helped coordinate important economic and foreign policy. In February 2011, Emanuel ran successfully for the office of mayor of Chicago. As mayor, Emanuel has pledged to work on decreasing violence in the city. He remains one of the most influential politicians in the Democratic Party and in American politics.

Further Reading

Baker, Peter, and Jeffrey Zeleny. "Emanuel Wields Power Freely, and Faces the Risks." *New York Times.* New York Times Co., 15 Aug. 2009. Web. 10 July 2012.

On The Issues. "Rahm Emanuel Issues Positions." *On The Issues.* OnTheIssues.org., 1999–2011. Web. 10 July 2012.

Stephey, M. J., and Kate Pickert. "Rahm Emanuel." *Time,* 6 Nov. 2008. Web. 10 July 2012.

Cait Caffrey

■ Emergency Economic Stabilization Act of 2008

The Law: A bill that allowed the secretary of the US Department of the Treasury to purchase and insure troubled financial assets to provide stability and help prevent further disruption in the economy through incentives
Date: October 3, 2008
Also known as: Troubled Assets Relief Program

The US financial crisis of 2007–08 resulted in the near collapses of large financial institutions, such as banks and the housing market. The crisis also led to a decline in consumer spending and downturns in stock markets around the globe. In response to this crisis, the US government passed the Emergency Economic Stabilization Act on October 3, 2008. The goal of the bill was to prevent large financial institutions from collapsing and to provide economic relief to consumers and taxpayers.

From 2007 to 2008, the United States experienced its worst financial crisis since the Great Depression of the 1930s. Beginning in 2006, the value of securities within the real estate market were on the decline, and by 2008, evictions and foreclosures had sharply increased. Financial experts have stated that the crisis was caused by several factors, including the failure of credit-ratings agencies to forecast the risk of mortgage-related finances and interest-rate spreads. The financial crisis led to a large increase in unemployment, a drop in consumer spending, and the near collapse of large financial institutions.

The US federal government enacted several emergency and short-term responses to the crisis. One of these was the Emergency Economic Stabilization Act of 2008. The plan was proposed by Secretary of the Treasury Henry Paulson and was backed by President George W. Bush. Under the proposal, the federal government would purchase $700 billion of financial assets such as mortgage-backed securities and use $250 billion to begin the Troubled Asset Relief Program (TARP), which is the program used to purchase and insure troubled assets. The Department of the Treasury was allowed to modify home loans and to let tenants stay in rental properties despite risk of foreclosure. The act also restricted some executive compensations such as bonuses based on company earnings. Anything spent by the treasury secretary under the act required judicial and congressional review.

The act was met with protests across the United States, the largest of which was in New York City, where more than one thousand people protested around the New York Stock Exchange. Citizens who opposed the act argued that their tax dollars should not be used to bailout banks and people with the wealthiest positions. The act also met opposition from several politicians. Two of the major criticisms among politicians were that the act was too costly and that it did not provide relief to the middle class. Illinois senator Barack Obama, who was elected US president the following month, supported the bailout.

Impact

The Emergency Economic Stabilization Act had mixed results. Many US banks such as Bank of America and Citigroup used the bailout to pay down their debts, purchase other businesses, or invest in other ways to further the banks and their executives, rather than increase loans to stimulate the economy. At the end of the 2009 fiscal year, the US annual budget deficit had surpassed $1 trillion. A report by a congressional oversight panel on January 9, 2009, found that there was no evidence that TARP had been used to prevent further foreclosures.

Further Reading

Herszenhorn, David M. "Bailout Plan Wins Approval; Democrats Vow Tighter Rules." *New York Times.* New York Times Co., 3 Oct. 2008. Web. 28 Oct. 2012.
McIntire, Mike. "Bailout Is a No-Strings Windfall to Bankers, if Not Borrowers." *New York Times.* New York Times Co., 17 Jan. 2009. Web. 28 Oct. 2012.
Patrick G. Cooper

■ Eminem

Identification: American rap artist, record producer, and actor
Born: October 17 1972; Kansas City, Missouri

One of the first white musicians to become a best-selling rapper, Eminem's music career has been marked by success as well as notoriety. In the mid-2000s, he put his career on hold to deal with personal struggles including alcohol and drug abuse before making a comeback toward the end of the decade.

In May 2000, Eminem released his second album, *The Marshall Mathers LP*. The record was an instant success, becoming one of the fastest-selling rap albums of all time. *Marshall Mathers* features several hit songs, including "The Real Slim Shady," "Stan," and "The Way I Am." The album garnered Eminem the 2001 Grammy Award for Best Rap Album, his second win in the category. The success, however, did not come without controversy. Many songs from the album featured profane, violent lyrics and homophobic themes, sparking outrage and protests. Industry analysts speculated that Eminem's performance with openly gay artist Elton John at the 2001 Grammy Awards was an attempt to change his anti-gay image.

Despite experiencing tremendous success as a recording artist and performer in the early 2000s, Eminem struggled in his personal life. He divorced his wife, Kim Scott Mathers, in 2001. That same year, he received probation for an assault incident. He used issues from his personal life as creative inspiration. His next album, *The Eminem Show* (2002), proved immensely popular among fans and critics, and earned him another Grammy.

In 2002, Eminem turned to acting, starring as a white rapper in the semi-autobiographical film *8 Mile*. Eminem earned an Academy Award in 2003 for the song "Lose Yourself," a track from the movie's soundtrack. In 2004, he released his fourth album, *Encore*. Like his previous works, this album stirred controversy. However, it was also surrounded by rumors that Eminem was preparing to retire from music. The release of a greatest hits album, *Curtain Call: The Hits* (2005), further stoked retirement rumors.

The tumult in Eminem's personal life caused him to take a hiatus from music. In 2005, he sought treatment for prescription drug dependency. The following year, he remarried his ex-wife—only to divorce again a few months later. Eminem again turned to alcohol and drugs. After an almost-fatal overdose in December 2007, he again sought treatment. Two years later, he returned to recording music , and released the albums *Relapse* (May 2009) and *Relapse 2* (August 2009).

Impact

Eminem was one of the first Caucasian rappers to succeed in a predominantly African American musical genre, winning acclaim from critics and artists of varied ethnic backgrounds. Although his lyrics have often been offensive and his personal life chaotic, he has developed a loyal fan base and earned numerous awards.

Since his comeback in 2009, Eminem has continued his work as a best-selling rapper and influential record producer. In addition to his *Relapse* albums, both of which went platinum, he has collaborated with rapper Royce 5'9" on *Hell: The Sequel* (2011) and is at work on a solo album.

Further Reading

Eminem and Sacha Jenkins. *The Way I Am*. New York: Dutton, 2008. Print.

"Rolling Stone Artists: Eminem." *Rolling Stone*. Rolling Stone, 2012. Web. 6 July 2012.

Angela Harmon

■ Employment in Canada

Definition: The percentage of Canadians gainfully employed throughout the nation, subject to seasonal and regional variations

The economy of Canada is driven by the efforts of individuals working for pay in many different economic sectors. Within each sector and area of employment there is also differentiation between production and administration activities.

Throughout the 2000s, the economy of Canada remained relatively stable in comparison with that of other nations, most notably the United States. Business between these two nations amounts to about 1.5 billion dollars per day, most of it in the form of raw materials, agricultural products, intermediate goods, and finished goods. Correspondingly, overall employment rates in Canada throughout the decade also remained relatively consistent. Within the overall rate, however, some notable trends are observed as individual sectors adjusted to changes in market demand. In manufacturing, production employment in Canada decreased by 4.1 percent per year over the decade, and administrative employment in the same sector increased by 0.7 percent per year.

Job Stability

One indicator used by Statistics Canada to monitor employment in Canada is job stability, defined as the likelihood that an employee will maintain the same job for a four-year period. In 2008, this probability was pegged at 56 percent overall, indicating that 56 percent of employees had the same job in 2008 that they had in 2004. In the manufacturing sector, however, this probability had fallen to just 48 percent, the lowest since 1992. As a result of the economic slowdown that occurred in 2008, layoffs in manufacturing and other sectors increased significantly. This trend is seen as the primary reason for the decrease in employment in manufacturing and other sectors during that time. Coupled to this are significantly longer periods of unemployment for workers who had been laid off, a factor that tends to compound unemployment-rate figures by extending the period over which reduced employment levels are recorded. Accordingly, following the injection of "stimulus spending" into the Canadian economy, employment increased by 1 percent in 2010, instead of decreasing. The principal factor driving the decrease in manufacturing employment, particularly through the period of 2004 through 2008, was the loss of factory jobs in the automotive industry in Ontario and in textile and clothing mills in Quebec. Model changeovers and weak sales in the automobile industry, as well as plant shutdowns and relocations by American parent companies, combined to impact manufacturing employment negatively in the latter half of the decade, as manufacturing employment fell from 15 percent of total employment in 2002 to just 12 percent in 2007, recovering slowly from that level at the end of the decade. At the same time, however, overall earnings across all sectors increased, mainly as the result of large increases in high-paying jobs in the management, finance, government, education, and applied-science sectors.

Employment in Other Sectors of the Economy

Through the first half of the decade, the downward trend in employment that had marked the 1990s underwent a significant reversal. The main driver of this change was the development of the Alberta oil sands project; the price of imported oil rose to the point that crude extraction made the oil sands a competitive source. As the decade progressed, better means of extracting crude oil were developed, making the oil sands an even more attractive and competitive source of petroleum for the North American market. Throughout the 2000s, Canada supplied some 87 percent of the natural gas imported by the United States, along with some 2.4 million barrels of crude oil per day. According to Canadian government figures, approximately one thousand companies of all sizes and from almost every state and sector of the US economy directly supply goods and services to the oil-production industry in Canada. Employment in the oil and gas industry and other sectors, particularly in western Canada, shifted dramatically to full-time employment beginning in 2003, with part-time employment dropping off outright as more people were able to obtain full-time employment. The double-digit growth of the oil and gas industry continued throughout the decade and into the next.

Other Canadian mining industries also experienced increased growth in the latter half of the decade, as metal prices began a continual climb to record high levels driven by the need for specialty metals in electronic devices and the demand for construction metals such as iron and aluminum in other parts of the world. In 2005 alone, employment in other mining industries increased by no less than 16 percent overall. Mineral mining, particularly the Saskatchewan potash industry, experienced similar growth fueled by demand for the products in agricultural and other applications.

Impact

Employment in Canada is the foundation of the Canadian economy, and it enables the various social programs that are provided by Canadian federal and provincial governments. Canada's universal health care system is the primary beneficiary of funds generated through taxation from employment, administered by each province in conjunction with funds transferred from the federal government. Other social "safety net" programs are dependent upon high employment for their viability, including the Employment Insurance, Canada Pension Plan, and Old Age Security programs. Additionally, the growth in Canada's economic power, directly related to employment levels in the nation, has enabled Canada to become a significant economic player on a global scale as trade relationships are developed with other nations outside of North America.

Further Reading

Canada. Statistics Canada. *The Daily*. Statistics Canada, 18 Oct. 2012. Web. 4 Dec. 2012. Provides analyses of Canadian employment statistics, with breakdowns by sector and region. Issues are archived for research and historical purposes.

Krahn, Harvey J., Graham S. Lowe, and Karen D. Hughes. *Work, Industry, and Canadian Society*. 6th ed. Toronto: Cengage, 2011. Print. Examines Canadian employment patterns and trends and several other aspects of employment in Canada, drawing heavily on Statistics Canada for numerical data.

Jackson, Andrew. *Work and Labour in Canada: Critical Issues*. 2nd ed. Toronto: Canadian Scholars, 2009. Print. Examines many aspects affecting employment in Canada, both cause and effect, providing a valuable introduction to the sociology of work.

Tsounta, Evridiki. "Why Are Women Working So Much More in Canada? An International Perspective." International Monetary Fund, Apr. 2006. PDF file. Examines the role of the tax and benefit system in Canada and suggests that similar policies elsewhere would have similar benefits in other countries.

Richard M. Renneboog

■ Employment in the United States

Definition: Employment rates in the United States experienced a number of significant fluctuations during the 2000s

Employment figures are critical to gleaning an understanding of the state of the US economy. During the 2000s, a number of fluctuations occurred in US employment figures. These trends were reflective of a short recession at the start of the decade, a period of recovery during the mid-2000s, and a major recession in the decade's latter years.

Employment rates (including wages and hours) provide a gauge of the state of the economy. During the 2000s, the US economy experienced a number of fluctuations. The changes in the US employment profile could be framed in three distinct periods: a slight increase in the unemployment rate beginning

Employment in Major Sectors of the U.S Economy, 2000-2010

Sector	Number Employed (Millions)		% Change
	2000	2010	
Agriculture	2.4	2.1	–1.1
Mining	.5	.66	2.3
Construction	6.8	5.5	–2.0
Manufacturing	17.3	11.5	–4.0
Services, total	107.9	112.7	0.4
Trade, transport, utilities	26.2	24.6	–2.8
Information	3.6	2.7	–2.9
Finance	7.7	7.6	–0.1
Professional and business services	16.7	16.7	0.0
Educational services	2.4	3.1	2.8
Health care and social assistance	12.7	16.4	2.6
Leisure and hospitality	11.9	13.0	0.9
Other services	5.9	6.9	0.2
Government	20.8	22.5	1.3
Federal	2.9	3.0	0.4
State and local	17.9	19.5	0.9

Source: United States Department of Labor Bureau of Labor Statistics

in 2001, a modest recovery between 2003 and 2007, and then a major spike in unemployment rates beginning in 2008.

The Recession of 2001

The recession of 2001 was relatively modest, at least in comparison to other major economic downturns that have occurred in the United States since the Great Depression. It was a vexing recession—economists were not even sure when the downturn began until several years later. Typically, employment rates are seen as a major indicator of a recession—unemployment rates rise within a few months of a recession's start. However, unemployment rates during the 2001 recession rose less rapidly and severely, in many respects matching the rate of growth in the country's gross domestic product (GDP).

To be sure, the recession of 2001 was still significant—employment rates fell during this eight-month economic and fiscal slump. In fact, employment rates were sluggish to recover, even as the economy emerged from recession. Although the economy as measured by GDP started to slowly recover, employment struggled to grow along with it, leading many economists to deem the upturn following the 2001 recession a "jobless recovery." Many people who lost their jobs at the start of the recession remained unemployed for longer-than-expected periods. This trend affected state economies throughout the country. State governments, which are responsible for paying unemployment insurance for their respective unemployed workers, paid considerably more than usual each budget year on unemployment insurance, adding to budget shortfalls that persisted for several years after the recession came to a close.

The Post-September 11 Recovery

In the years that followed the recession of 2001, unemployment rates were slow to decline. It took eighteen months for employment rates to show improvement even though the recession itself lasted less than half that time. It took twenty-two months (from the start of the recession in March 2001 through September 2003) for job growth to return to a sustainable rate again. Since the Great Depression, the only comparable lag in job growth during a recession was in 1991, when it took a year for employment figures to improve to sustainable rates.

The post-recession recovery may have seen employment rates improve, but the recovery was uneven. Wages were not on the rise when weighed against inflation. Additionally, many industries had different rates of recovery as well. Manufacturing jobs were still difficult to find in 2003, for example, while the transportation industry (severely affected by the terrorist attacks of September 11, 2001) did not see job growth until later in the decade. One of the sectors seeing the most significant improvement by 2003 was construction and real estate, which were bolstered by a strengthening housing market.

The Late 2000s Recession

The post-2001 recession recovery did not last beyond 2007. The collapse of the housing bubble, coupled with the financial crisis of 2008, contributed to the deepest recession in the United States since the Great Depression. Virtually every industry sector was affected severely during this period, which became known as the Great Recession. Employment shrank slowly during the recession's earliest stages, held afloat in part by the economy's continued growth and the recession's limited industry impacts. However, when the financial crisis took hold in 2008, employment rates quickly plummeted across the economy.

Construction and manufacturing were among the first industries to see job losses, a typical trend during a recession. Thereafter, the real estate and financial sectors, as well as the professional and business services, transportation, and even government sectors all saw dramatic layoffs during this recession. Only critical-service sectors, such as health care and education, added jobs but this growth was slowed significantly in comparison to previous years.

The recession did not just cause job losses (approximately 8.8 million jobs from 2008 through 2010); in many cases, it changed the nature of the jobs that remained as well. Work hours, for example, decreased as employers attempted to rein in costs. By the end of the decade, employee hours had not yet returned to the levels at which they rested during the pre-recession years. Wages and benefits were also affected by the economic climate, with many employees making concessions in order to avoid widespread layoffs. Furthermore, this recession was considerably longer than previous recessions, making job recovery a process that would continue well into the next decade.

Impact

The US economy relies on the strength of its employee base. It is for this reason that, when analyzing the economic recessions, analysts look to job losses and gains as key indicators of the conditions that exist in the economy. The 2001 recession was modest, but had a significant impact on jobs for several years after the recession began. There was a modest period of recovery following that recession, but it was quickly undone by the much deeper and broad-reaching Great Recession of the late 2000s. In addition to the jobs themselves, employment figures during the 2000s included wages, benefits, and hours worked, all of which were significantly affected by the fluctuations that marked that decade.

Further Reading

Goodman, Christopher J., and Steven M. Mance. "Employment Loss and the 2007–2009 Recession: An Overview." *Monthly Labor Review*. 134.4 (2011): 3–12. Print. Outlines the breadth of effects the 2007–9 recession had on US employment.

Maxfield, Julie Hatch. "Jobs in 2005: How Do They Compare With Their March 2001 Counterparts?" *Monthly Labor Review* 129.7 (2006): 15–26. Print. Provides an extensive, sector-by-sector review of employment conditions in the years following the 2001 recession.

Vroman, Wayne. "The Recession of 2001 and Unemployment Insurance Financing." *Federal Reserve Bank of New York Economic Policy Review* 11.1 (2005): 61–79. Print. Describes employment trends during the 2001 recession.

Michael P. Auerbach

■ Energy drinks

Definition: Beverages concocted to increase energy, usually through caffeine

Although energy drinks have been in circulation in the United States since the mid-1900s, not until the early 2000s did the drinks enjoy widespread consumption. Their integration into American culture has caused an industry boom as well as attracted greater concern regarding the drinks' potential health risks.

Typically reliant on caffeine to boost stamina, energy drinks in the United States primarily target younger Americans. The drinks are most widely used by teenagers and those under thirty-five and appeal to a largely male consumer base. Like coffee and tea—which are not considered "energy drinks" since their caffeine is naturally occurring—energy drinks are marketed to students in order to provide extra energy to study or to complete homework and athletes hoping to enhance athletic and mental acuity.

Following early attempts at energy drink production, Red Bull, an Austrian drink, was introduced in the United States in 1997. It was joined by other popular energy drinks such as Monster, Rockstar, Hype,

and Full Throttle. Massive industry growth in the early 2000s surpassed all previous decades, growing from $8 million in sales in 2001 to $5.4 billion in 2007. The decade also witnessed new trends in packaging. While energy drink containers grew larger, providing multiple servings per can to accommodate caffeine restrictions, energy "shots" were condensed into smaller, more concentrated cans. In 2007, the industry also began to produce energy drink powder and tablets to be mixed with water.

As the drinks grew in popularity, critics began to assess their negative effects on health. Pharmacists and hospitals had initially hailed the drinks as a beneficial supplement to boost patients' energy levels. In the 2000s, however, medical professionals began to view the drinks as potentially harmful.

Excessive energy drink consumption has been reported to cause death, seizures, dehydration, deterioration of tooth enamel, and is known to interfere with heart and brain function. When the industry marketed a line of drinks with added alcohol, these effects were compounded. Furthermore, energy drinks can mask the effect of alcohol, leading a consumer to believe he or she is sober when in actually that is not the case. After a popular brand, Four Loko, was banned in several states, the product was reintroduced in 2010 without the caffeine and was no longer marketed as an energy drink.

Impact

In response to the potential dangers of energy drink consumption, many countries, including France, Norway, and the Philippines, have banned them. While the drinks are still readily available in the United States, critics have called for greater regulation through the Food and Drug Administration. Further regulation and research have been particularly needed, as the long-term effects of massive consumption of energy drinks are unknown.

Further Reading

Brody, Jane E. "Scientists See Dangers in Energy Drinks." *New York Times*. New York Times Company, 31 Jan. 2011. Web. 12 Oct. 2012.

Seifert, Sara M., et al. "Health Effects of Energy Drinks on Children, Adolescents, and Young Adults." *Pediatrics* 127.3 (14 Feb. 2011): 511–528. Web. 12 Oct. 2012.

Storey, Maureen. "American Beverage Association Statement on Pediatrics Article on Energy Drinks."

American Beverage Association. American Beverage Association, 14 Feb. 2011. Web. 12 Oct. 2012.

Lucia Pizzo

■ Energy Policy Act of 2005

The Law: Federal law that made sweeping changes in almost every sector of the energy industry
Date: Signed August 8, 2005

The US Energy Policy Act of 2005 authorized government subsidies, loan guarantees, and tax breaks for producers of both conventional and alternative energy as well as a variety of conservation measures. The act made significant changes to US energy policy and raised numerous issues regarding the future of renewable and nonrenewable energy in the United States.

Introduced as the debate over future US energy policy was escalating, the Energy Policy Act of 2005 was intended to address concerns about the scarcity of energy resources by encouraging increased production of both conventional and unconventional sources of energy. The bill was introduced in the House of Representatives on April 18, 2005, and passed three days later, while the Senate passed a version of the bill in June. Both houses of Congress approved a modified version of the bill in late July, and President George W. Bush signed it into law on August 8, 2005.

The act authorized loan guarantees for energy production methods that minimize or avoid creation of greenhouse gases, including nuclear energy, so-called "clean coal" technology, and renewable energy sources such as wind, solar, geothermal, and hydroelectric power. The act also increased the amount of ethanol required in gasoline sold in the United States, provided tax breaks for property owners installing energy-efficient features in homes and commercial buildings, offered tax incentives to purchasers of hybrid automobiles, and extended the duration of daylight saving time. Provisions calling for the revision of auto emissions standards and permitting drilling for oil in the Arctic National Wildlife Refuge were stricken from the bill prior to passage.

Some provisions of the Energy Act of 2005 sparked controversy and prompted accusations that the act favored fossil-fuel producers and failed to provide sufficient environmental protections. The act controversially included tax breaks for producers of fossil fuels and incentives for oil companies drilling in the Gulf of Mexico, called for research into the potential effects of shale oil extraction on public lands, and made gas and oil companies exempt from portions of the Safe Drinking Water Act.

Impact

Despite the broad scope of the Energy Policy Act of 2005, many of its provisions had not yet been implemented by the end of the 2000s, largely because of a lack of funds. Other provisions were rapidly implemented but produced mixed results. The mandated increase in the ethanol content of gasoline, for example, created short-term disruptions in gasoline supplies as refineries struggled to accommodate the changes. Provisions such as incentives for purchases of hybrid automobiles experienced modest short-term success as purchases of these automobiles increased and escalating competition among automobile manufacturers resulted in a wider variety of hybrid automobiles entering the marketplace.

Further Reading

Daynes, Byron, W., and Glen Sussman. *White House Politics and the Environment: Franklin D. Roosevelt to George W. Bush.* College Station: Texas A&M UP, 2010. Print
United States Congress Senate Committee on Energy and Natural Resources. *Energy Policy Act of 2005.* Washington: BiblioGov, 2010. Print.

Michael H. Burchett

■ Energy Policy of the United States

Definition: Debate over exploring sources of domestic oil and investing in alternative energy resources

The rising cost of oil was a major contributor to the economic issues that surfaced during the 2000s. Instability in the Middle East, coupled with the devastation of Hurricane Katrina and increasing demand for oil, sent crude prices skyward during the decade. This situation spurred heated debates in the United States about both utilizing domestic oil sources and investing in alternative energy sources.

In the early 2000s, members of the Organization of the Petroleum Exporting Countries (OPEC) decided to raise prices on crude oil. This decision was the starting point for a consistent and dramatic increase in the price of oil during that decade. Among the factors that maintained this trend were the continued instability of the Middle East, Hurricane Katrina (which disrupted the offshore drilling platforms in the Gulf of Mexico) and other weather events, and the demands of the industrialized world. The near-crisis situation fostered a renewed debate in the US government about the nation's energy policy, as leaders argued for the implementation of a new policy that reduced the country's dependence on foreign oil and invested in stable (and environmentally friendly) fuel sources.

Exploring Domestic Sources
The decision by OPEC to raise the per-barrel price of oil was criticized by many observers, who considered the move little more than a demonstration of the organization's power. However, most of the world's leading consumers of oil (including the United States) were not among the leading producers of this invaluable resource, and they, therefore, relied heavily on imported oil. Thus, the United States and other foreign-dependent oil consumers were helpless in the face of both OPEC's decision and general instability in the Middle East. In fact, although the main motivations for the US-led invasion of Iraq—toppling Saddam Hussein's dangerous regime and combating terrorism—were subject to debate, a stable Iraq (which is among the world's leaders in oil production) had tremendous implications for the price of crude oil.

The instability of the Middle East and other major oil-producing regions led many US political leaders to call for the pursuit of domestic energy sources. This idea sparked a major debate in Washington, DC, as environmentalists squared off against advocates for domestic oil exploration. Environmentalists argued that the two main areas given focus for exploratory drilling and oil extraction—the Arctic National Wildlife Refuge in northern Alaska and along the Atlantic coastline—presented risks to local wildlife, water supplies, and their ecosystems. On the other hand, advocates argued that such concerns were groundless, as modern exploratory drilling and extraction technologies have minimized the environmental impact of oil production. Furthermore, these advocates stated,

the risks were outweighed by the potential to reduce American dependence on foreign oil.

Investing in Alternative Fuel Sources
Another important part of the US energy policy debate during the 2000s was the topic of alternative energy sources. This notion was based on the idea that oil and coal (the two biggest sources of energy in the United States) may have become too expensive and environmentally damaging, and that the United States would benefit from investing in other sources of energy. Even tapping into US-based oil wells in Alaska and the Atlantic coastline, some argued, would not reduce the cost of oil, as the technologies needed to locate, extract, and transport these reserves would be far more expensive than simply importing barrels from the Middle East.

Meanwhile, a growing number of alternative and renewable energy sources entered the energy policy debate. For example, ethanol, a chemical produced from corn, was given increased attention as both a cost-effective and environmentally friendly alternative to oil. Other sources of energy, such as wind and solar power, became part of the debate as well. These alternative resources gave rise to an entire "green energy" industry that became increasingly relevant in the energy policy debate. Although expensive and controversial, even nuclear power was considered worthy of inclusion in the discussion as the country debated a new direction in its energy policy.

Impact
The cost of energy has long been a critical factor in the US economy. During the 2000s, as the cost of oil rose far above reasonable levels, it became clear to American politicians that a major change in energy policy was necessary. Many proposals, including exploring domestic sources and investing in alternative sources of energy, were debated throughout the decade. By the end of the 2000s, although the issue remained important, a new American energy policy was still in the developmental stage.

Further Reading
Geri, Laurance, and David E. McNabb. *Energy Policy in the US: Politics, Challenges, and Prospects for Change.* London: Taylor, 2011. Print. Provides an overview of the energy policy debate, including a review of the many different proposals raised during the 2000s.

Johnston, John Bennett, Jr. "All of the Above: New Directions in Energy Policy." *Juniata Voices* 9 (2009): 27–29. Print. Argues in favor of drilling in northern Alaska and along the eastern US seaboard as part of a new energy policy.

Lovins, Amory B., and L. Hunter Lovins. "Fool's Gold in Alaska." *Foreign Affairs* 80.4 (2001): 72–85. Print. Argues against increased domestic oil exploration as part of the new energy policy, stating that imported oil is less expensive than domestically produced oils.

Michael P. Auerbach

■ Enron collapse

Definition: A scandal that caused the bankruptcy of Houston-based Enron Corporation, a leading energy company

A publicly traded natural gas and commodities company, Enron grew swiftly through diversification and innovation. Its stock rose dramatically. However, the company was riddled with fraud. In 2001, stock values plunged, and Enron was forced to file bankruptcy. Thousands of Enron employees lost jobs and pensions, investors were bilked for billions, and several company executives were imprisoned.

Enron began honestly in 1985 as an energy supplier via a network of North American natural gas pipelines. The company added capabilities by building or acquiring electric power plants around the globe and expanded into such enterprises as petrochemicals, plastics, pulp and paper, broadband, and water. The company lobbied successfully for natural gas trade deregulation, and it made enormous profits by supplying electricity at inflated prices. Throughout the 1990s, the value of Enron stock soared, topping more than $90 per share in August of 2000.

How the Downfall Began

Not all Enron efforts were profitable. Many ventures—such as the massive Dabhol power project in India—were disastrous failures. However, to present the false impression the company was booming and to keep investments pouring in, Enron engaged in dubious, unethical, or downright fraudulent business practices.

The company built a complicated web of special purpose offshore shell companies to boost apparent income and asset value and to disguise significant losses. Arthur Andersen, a large and respected Chicago-based accounting firm, assisted Enron for years in altering their bookkeeping in exchange for multimillion-dollar auditing and consultation fees. Executives at Andersen were also found to have shredded documents to conceal the company's involvement in Enron's scheme. As a result of these deceptive accounting practices, investments rolled in, and top Enron officers collected enormous salaries and bonuses based on expected performances that never materialized.

A significant part of Enron's plan involved the willing and active participation of important political figures. Enron was a major contributor to the campaigns of US president George W. Bush and US senator Phil Gramm, who streamlined legislation benefiting the company. Senator Gramm was husband of Wendy Gramm, chair of the Commodity Futures Trading Commission (CFTC), who in the early 1990s changed rules governing energy futures trading to Enron's advantage. She later accepted a seat on Enron's board of directors and served on its Audit Committee, both highly paid positions within the company. President Bush, the Gramms, Vice President Dick Cheney, Treasury Secretary Paul O'Neill and other influential individuals were instrumental in spearheading, at Enron's urging, federal deregulation of energy markets in late 2000.

Policies that eliminated oversight allowed Enron to shift its emphasis to power brokerage and to freely manipulate the energy supply in major markets. In California, for example, the company engineered more than thirty-five rolling blackouts that interrupted or withheld power in the state. Hundreds of thousands of business and private customers were subsequently forced to pay inflated prices for electricity. Before tougher energy regulations were instituted in mid-2001, Enron gouged billions of dollars from customers and contributed to a national energy crisis. Once regulations were instituted, a massive revenue stream dried up, and Enron's shaky financial situation was exposed.

The Crash and the Aftereffects

Enron came under scrutiny in early 2001 after a series of articles in respected financial publications raised questions about the company's suspicious income, profits, and debt accounting practices.

The Enron complex in Houston, Texas. (Courtesy eflon)

Enron's empire was ready to collapse. In August of that year, Chief Executive Officer (CEO) Jeffrey Skilling resigned—after selling his shares of company stock for more than $30 million. Other top executives similarly divested themselves of their holdings for enormous sums of money as the company crumbled.

Enron received a brief reprieve on September 11, 2001, when terrorist attacks on the World Trade Center moved the spotlight away from the company's practices. In the interim, the company sold some assets and issued "corrected" accounting reports for previous years of operation in a desperate attempt to support its financial profile and maintain investor confidence. The ploy did not work, and by late October 2001, the price of Enron stock had plunged to $20 per share. The company's credit rating was downgraded, which further reduced investments. In November, the Securities and Exchange Commission (SEC), the federal stock market regulatory agency, announced it would begin a formal investigation of Enron.

After a proposed buyout fell through, further lowered credit ratings, and a flurry of negative media reports were printed, the end came quickly for Enron. With its stock worth just pennies per share, the company filed for bankruptcy on November 30, 2001, and applied for Chapter 11 protection two days later. Four thousand Enron employees immediately lost their jobs. Most of 15,000 other employees—whose pensions were based on the value of now-worthless Enron stock—lost everything they had saved.

Top Enron executives were subsequently tried for fraud, money laundering, conspiracy, and other crimes. More than a dozen received prison terms. Arthur Andersen lost its Certified Public Accountant (CPA) license, costing its 85,000 employees their jobs. Enron founder Kenneth Lay, facing a long confinement for his role in the scandal, died in 2006 before being sentenced.

Impact

Enron's bankruptcy, the largest in US history at the time, was soon surpassed when WorldCom folded in 2002 and was further dwarfed by the bankruptcies of Lehman Brothers and Washington Mutual Bank in 2008.

In a class action lawsuit, former Enron employees each received about $3,000 in compensation for lost pensions. Shareholders similarly recovered a fraction of nearly $75 billion they lost. In the wake of the scandal, new legislation—especially the Sarbanes-Oxley Act of 2002—was instituted to strengthen corporate accounting standards and practices.

Further Reading

Brody, Keith, and Sancha Dunstan. *The Great Telecoms Swindle: How the Collapse of WorldCom Finally Exposed the Technology Myth.* Mankato: Capstone, 2003. Print. An exploration of a corporate downfall that surpassed the Enron's in size and scope.

Eichenwald, Kurt. *Conspiracy of Fools: A True Story.* New York: Broadway, 2005. Print. A detailed account of the collapse of Enron.

Gray, Kenneth R., Larry A. Frieder, and George W. Clark, Jr. *Corporate Scandals: The Many Faces of Greed.* St. Paul: Paragon, 2005. Print. Discussion and analysis of corporate malfeasance affecting American economy.

Henn, Stephen K. *Business Ethics: A Case Study Approach.* Hoboken: Wiley, 2009. Print. Examines the business practices behind various corporate scandals.

McLean, Bethany, and Peter Elkind. *The Smartest Guys in the Room: The Amazing Rise and Scandalous Fall of Enron.* London: Portfolio Trade, 2004. Print. Focuses on the personalities of individuals involved in the Enron scandal.

Jack Ewing

■ Extraordinary rendition

Definition: The abduction and transport of persons to foreign jurisdictions that allow torture, which is illegal under American statutes and a violation of international law; by contrast, "rendition" is the legal, constitutional transfer of a person between jurisdictions

In an effort to protect the nation following the September 11, 2001, terrorist attacks, the United State government expanded a secret program of extraordinary rendition instituted in the 1990s. Central Intelligence Agency (CIA) operatives apprehended suspected terrorists in domestic or overseas locations and then flew them to countries where torture was allowed, in order to extract information by any means about past or future terrorist acts.

One of the least publicized, least understood aspects of US foreign policy is the government's involvement in secret activities. From the beginning of its history—acting on the principle that desperate times demand desperate measures—the United States has undertaken numerous surreptitious operations in national interest. Most such practices are clandestine because the object of the action is to remain undetected. Since the beginning of the Cold War, however, an increasing number of US secret operations have been covert: planned and executed in a manner primarily intended to hide the identity of entities behind the activity. The National Security Act of 1947 legally empowered the CIA, upon presidential approval, to enact covert operations for political and military objectives; other agencies such as the Federal Bureau of Investigation (FBI) or the Diplomatic Security Service (DSS) may be called upon for assistance. Such covert activities, which the US government could plausibly deny, may include sabotage, assassinations, or support for the subversion or overthrow of foreign governments. Some operations are only revealed long after they have been enacted, via media disclosure or Freedom of Information Act (FOIA) requests; other covert operations, protected under the blanket of "national security," may never be known.

An Antiterrorism Measure

Early publicized instances of extraordinary rendition carried out with US government approval occurred following the initial terrorist attack on New York City's World Trade Center. In February 1993, a truck bomb exploded in the subterranean parking garage under the North Tower, killing six people and wounding hundreds. Extraordinary rendition, with President Bill Clinton's approval, was subsequently used to apprehend a number of the perpetrators on foreign soil and transport them to the United States, where they stood trial, were convicted, and were imprisoned for their crimes.

The administration of President George W. Bush reinstated and stepped up the technique of extraordinary rendition after the attacks of September 11, 2001. Between 2001 and 2004, when the media became aware of the program, dozens of terrorist suspects were kidnapped and detained—the full number of individuals apprehended and detained may never be known, but more than 1,200 CIA flights have been documented. During that time, several major changes in policy were instituted. Abductions were often carried out without the knowledge, cooperation, or approval of foreign countries where suspects were found. More significantly, prisoners were not returned to the United States for questioning, thus their treatment was not closely monitored. Instead, blindfolded, shackled, and sedated suspects were transported to prisons in different locations—Egypt, Syria, Jordan, Morocco, Pakistan, Afghanistan, Uzbekistan, Poland, and Romania were popular—or to secret US government–run "black sites" in foreign countries. Prisoners were often subjected to harsh interrogation tactics: placed in stressful positions, sexually humiliated, or water-boarded.

In principle, American extraordinary renditions conducted in the twenty-first century served several useful purposes. They prevented suspects from participating in acts of terror. In some cases, they provided valuable information about planned acts of future terrorism.

The most successful renditions involved two operatives closely identified with al-Qaeda: Khalid Shaikh Mohammed, who planned the September 11 attacks, and Abu Zubaydah, who directed a terrorist training facility in Afghanistan. Each of the men was separately abducted and detained in Pakistan. Closely interrogated, both provided details about additional figures connected with terrorist groups, and both were coerced into revealing plans for future plots.

Other cases, however, were spectacular failures: through mistaken identity, innocent people were kidnapped and tortured. Khaled al-Masri, for example, a Lebanese-born citizen of Germany, was kidnapped in Macedonia. Though it soon became obvious that he was not the person the CIA thought he was, al-Masri was held and tortured for several months in Afghanistan, then transported to a remote location in Albania and released to make his way home on his own. An Egyptian-born resident of Italy, Hassan Mustafa Osama Nasr (also known as Abu Omar), was kidnapped in Milan—dozens of bystanders witnessed his abduction—and flown to Egypt for detention and interrogation. Such clumsy intelligence agency operations not only embarrassed the supposed professionals who carried out the captures, but also jeopardized American diplomatic relationships with friendly nations.

Reactions to Extraordinary Rendition
Once the media became aware of the American extraordinary rendition program, the policy and the CIA faced increasing public scrutiny and criticism. Between early 2005 and 2009, numerous reports appeared in domestic and foreign news outlets revealing further details of specific examples of the practice. Government investigations were conducted in many countries. These uncovered evidence that officials at various foreign airports—in France, Germany, Ireland, Portugal, Spain, Sweden, the United Kingdom, and elsewhere—had colluded or cooperated in illegal CIA-operated flights en route with kidnapped suspects to detention facilities. Various human rights groups, including Human Rights Watch, American Civil Liberties Union, and Amnesty International, soon became involved. Protests were lodged, not only for the ostensible condoning of torture, but also for placing American military personnel at potential risk of similar treatment in retaliation. The United States was publicly condemned for engaging in multiple violations of the European Convention on Human Rights and the United Nations Convention against Torture.

The Italian government went further, in the case of Abu Omar, who was detained and interrogated in Egypt for four years before being released and allowed to return home. Italian prosecutors collected a mountain of evidence left behind during a particularly sloppy rendition operation: forged identity cards, genuine American passports containing the actual names of the agents, and statements from witnesses who had observed the abduction. The Italian

courts issued arrest warrants (which were not honored, since the agency involved was locked into a policy of denial) and proceeded to trial. During the trial, the whole conspiracy was uncovered, revealing widespread collusion between American and Italian agents. In 2009, the Italian court convicted more than twenty CIA operatives and a US Air Force officer in absentia—the first agents ever to be publicly tried and found guilty for participating in the American extraordinary rendition program.

Impact
When properly planned and executed, extraordinary renditions have proven useful in the war on terror—a conflict in which the normal rules of engagement have been set aside. Such renditions provide the option of immediate detention in the face of imminent acts of terror that simply cannot wait for the legal process to take effect.

In the wake of public exposure and widespread condemnation, the American rendition policy was closely examined internally in order to make changes aimed at maintaining secrecy, preventing mistakes, and ensuring humane treatment of suspects within acceptable limitations. American-operated black sites were to be discontinued, future suspects would instead be transported to jurisdictions where they were wanted for crimes, and suspects would receive full legal protection during prosecution. Other recommendations adopted included adherence to stricter tactical and operational procedures, assignment of the most experienced agents in carrying out renditions, and closer scrutiny of intelligence gained—since in the process of interrogation, it was discovered that some prisoners will say anything to escape torture.

As the decade drew to a close, the rendition policy began to be more closely monitored by the US government. In 2009, President Barack Obama signed executive orders that retained the rendition policy while also promulgating stricter controls allowing the president to approve or disapprove individual cases. The order also increased the level of oversight regarding the humane treatment of individuals during apprehension, transportation, and detention.

Further Reading
Daugherty, William J. *Executive Secrets: Covert Action and the Presidency.* Lexington: UP of Kentucky,

2006. Print. Explores the relationship between American presidents and the intelligence community from an historical perspective.

Gough, Roger, Stuart McCracken, and Andrew Tyrie. *Account Rendered: Extraordinary Renditions and Britain's Role.* London: Biteback, 2011. Print. An exposé that reveals details of the United Kingdom's collusion in American extraordinary renditions.

Grey, Stephen. *Ghost Plane: The True Story of the CIA Rendition and Torture Program.* New York: St. Martin's, 2007. Print. A detailed, well-documented exploration of the American rendition program from 1997 onward.

Murray, Mark J. "Extraordinary Rendition and U.S. Counterterrorism Policy." *Journal of Strategic Security* 4.3 (2011): 15–28. Print. Defines terms, discusses controversies, and provides case histories of post–September 11 US extraordinary renditions.

Shulsky, Abram N., and Gary J. Schmitt. *Silent Warfare: Understanding the World of Intelligence.* Dulles: Potomac, 2002. Print. Argues for the necessity of intelligence agencies and describes the principles and procedures for gathering, analyzing, and managing information.

Zimmer, Brenden M., ed. *Extradition and Rendition: Background and Issues.* Hauppauge: Nova Science, 2011. Print. Examines the history, laws, and processes involved in the transportation of persons between jurisdictions.

Jack Ewing

F

■ Facebook

Definition: The world's largest online social-networking website where users can connect and share with friends

Reaching 350 million users around the world by the end of the 2000s, the social-networking site Facebook brought people together in unprecedented ways and provided innovative sharing and communication tools. Nevertheless, the site and its policies have also raised concerns about privacy and safety.

When Facebook was released in 2004, several predecessors and early competitors already existed. Friendster, a social network for finding people with similar interests (with the possible intention of dating), was founded in 2002 by Jonathan Abrams and Rob Pazornik. The year 2003 saw the launch of MySpace, a media-heavy site that let users customize their profile pages. LinkedIn, a social-networking site for business professionals, was also launched in 2003.

In addition to more general social-networking sites, campus-specific social networks were being founded at many colleges and universities in the early 2000s. The first was Club Nexus, launched at Stanford University in 2001, but Columbia University and several other schools also offered similar services, many of them created and managed by students. There were also several social networks aimed at college students in general, including the Daily Jolt and Collegester.com. Despite Facebook's late start compared to its competitors, the site ultimately gained the largest user base of all social-networking sites, becoming one of the highest-trafficked sites of the decade.

Facebook's Beginnings

Harvard University student Mark Zuckerberg developed two websites in 2003 that would set the stage for the service that became Facebook. Course-Match, which helped students determine their courses based on what others were taking, and Facemash, which allowed people to compare images of fellow students, were immediate hits and proved that college students were ready to take their socializing online.

Based on the popularity of these two sites and Zuckerberg's initial experiments with image-commenting capabilities, the first version of Facebook was launched on February 4, 2004, at TheFaceBook.com, allowing students to create profiles and connect with other students. Within a day of the launch, between twelve hundred and fifteen hundred people had signed up for the service.

Dispute over Origins

Substantial dispute surrounds the origin of the idea of Facebook. Many different individuals—primarily fellow Harvard students—have claimed various levels of involvement in developing the service. Zuckerberg's friends and collaborators Eduardo Saverin, Chris Hughes, and Dustin Moskovitz are widely credited with significant early involvement, although Saverin was eventually ousted in less-than-amicable circumstances.

Twin brothers Cameron and Tyler Winklevoss founded HarvardConnection (later renamed ConnectU), a campus social network, with Divya Narendra in December 2002. Mark Zuckerberg apparently agreed to work on HarvardConnection but did not complete the work and instead launched Facebook. The Winklevosses and Narendra sued Facebook in September 2004 for breach of contract, eventually reaching a settlement in February 2008.

Another Harvard student, Aaron Greenspan, developed a campus social network at Harvard called houseSYSTEM in 2003. Part of houseSYSTEM was called the Universal Face Book, and the service offered event calendars and photo albums. Greenspan has repeatedly alleged that Facebook was his idea and filed a petition to cancel the Facebook trademark, which was settled in 2009.

Growing beyond Harvard

After approximately one month of exclusive access for Harvard students, Facebook opened up to Stanford, Columbia, and Yale. By June, the site had extended access to users at forty different colleges and universities.

The early popularity of Facebook stemmed from a number of factors, including widespread Internet access, which was initially more readily available on college campuses than to the general population, and a focused target demographic of college students who constantly socialized, had many social connections, and were willing to share personal information online with others. Additionally, the site was frequently updated by its users, prompting nearly 60 percent of Facebook's users to visit the site daily and some 20 percent of users to visit the site more than five times a day.

Facebook grew quickly after its founding. Zuckerberg and cofounder Moskovitz moved to Silicon Valley and received their first funding—$500,000 from PayPal cofounder Peter Thiel—in June 2004. The site reached a million users by November 2004, narrowly missing a goal set by Thiel of 1.5 million users for the year. In Palo Alto, Zuckerberg connected with Sean Parker, the founder of the online music-sharing service Napster, who served as Facebook's president for a short but influential time.

Following the initial investment from Thiel, Facebook continued growing, attracting investment interest from venture capital companies. Zuckerberg turned down several acquisition offers, some from companies as large as Viacom, which wanted to combine the service with MTV.com. Interest in Facebook was sparked by its huge user base, rapid growth, high levels of repeat usage, and attractive demographic of users: young college students. Even the *Washington Post* displayed interest in investing in Facebook, but the venture capital firm Accel Partners outbid the news outlet by offering $12.7 million in funding in exchange for a 15 percent stake in the company. The investment would be crucial in acquiring the staff to develop the features and partnerships that would ultimately help Facebook become the dominant social network of the 2000s.

Basic Features

Facebook added many features throughout its evolution, but early core capabilities include the user profile, the wall, the status update, and notifications.

Facebook profiles include basic personal information, such as name, age, and gender; background information, such as hometown or schools attended; interests and hobbies; and other customizable information. Unlike many other social-networking sites, Facebook does not make it easy to find people through shared interests; the emphasis is on maintaining existing connections, not creating new ones. A user's wall is a profile section where other users can post greetings, links, or photos, while a status update is a message that a user can type into Facebook to be displayed to their friends on the site.

Facebook users typically receive notifications by email when other users write on their wall, "tag" (identify) them in photos, or send them messages. Notifications were key in building habitual Facebook use among members, prompting numerous site visits. In addition to more public communications such as wall posts, status updates, and comments, Facebook offers private communication options in messaging and chat.

Other ways to communicate on Facebook include groups and events. Users can create groups for general communication around a particular topic or cause, or schedule events ranging from birthday parties to protests. The vast range of Facebook events and groups shows the flexibility and power of the platform, which has often been used for purposes of political organization and activism.

Evolution of Key Features

By October 2005, Facebook had reached five million users—a large number that nevertheless paled in comparison to MySpace's twenty-four million users at the time. But in late 2005, Facebook unveiled a feature that may have been critical for the site to eventually surpass MySpace: the ability to upload and tag photos. Users could approve tagged photos or "untag" themselves from photos. Photos in which a user was tagged were linked to that user's profile. The tagging feature was the first of its kind and was key in attracting new users and getting existing users more involved with the site.

Another crucial feature was the news feed, which listed friends' latest activities (such as status updates, profile changes, or new photo uploads) and was introduced in September 2006. The news feed provided a central place for users to view all of their friends' Facebook activity. Many users reacted strongly against the feature for providing too much visibility into their online activities, but much of the backlash died down when Facebook introduced more ways for users to control which activities would be shared. Truly revolutionary in concept, the news feed transformed Facebook from being a place to view individual pictures or specific profile pages to being the go-to place for all updates from online friends.

Also in September 2006, Facebook opened up the service to all people over the age of thirteen with a valid email address. After open registration was enabled, the number of new Facebook accounts created each day nearly doubled, reflecting widespread interest.

Facebook Platform and Facebook Connect
By May 2007, 1 percent of all Internet time was spent on Facebook. In the same month, Facebook launched the Facebook Platform at its first annual f8 Developers Conference. The platform enabled software developers to create applications that integrated with the service, such as social games that could be played within Facebook. This accelerated the company's rise as users began to use more and more applications ("apps") that prompted them to log in to Facebook multiple times a day. By November 2007, more than 8,000 applications had been developed on the platform, a number that would rise to 33,000 by July 2008.

The success of the platform showed that Facebook's primary value proposition was not its features, but the connections between its users. The platform also offers a social graph, which features the connections between users and their shared interests. By offering up access to the social graph to other developers, Facebook was not risking its own success, but rather ensuring it, by selling its social data to other companies. After releasing the platform, Facebook no longer had to develop every type of functionality for the site, but rather could serve as the platform for excellent applications developed by others.

In late 2008, Facebook released Facebook Connect, a secure single sign-on system that allowed people to access any website using their Facebook login. This was not only convenient, but also enabled the social graph to tracking users' activity on other websites.

Advertising, Business Model, and Corporate Culture
By the fall of 2007, Facebook had fifty million users. Microsoft invested $240 million in the company as part of an advertising deal, taking a 1.6 percent stake

in Facebook. As the company continued to grow, Facebook hired former Google executive Sheryl Sandberg in 2008 to serve as chief operating officer. The company was first cash flow positive in 2009, due mostly to advertising.

Facebook represented a revolution in advertising because it provided not only a platform to broadcast advertising messages, but it also generated data to inform the successful targeting of those messages. For example, Facebook made it possible to target an advertisement about a running shoe sale in San Francisco only to users who live in the area and have indicated interest in running. This type of targeting was unprecedented and prompted significant experimentation by advertisers, but many Facebook users have expressed discomfort with the degree to which the information they share on the service can be used to target advertisements to them.

Despite its huge user base and advertising profits, Facebook is known for a casual work culture, with many young employees who dress in jeans and T-shirts. Zuckerberg in particular is known for often wearing a hooded sweatshirt and sandals. The Facebook offices are decorated with graffiti, including the company motto Move Fast and Break Things, which fosters a "hacker" culture of experimentation.

Privacy, Criticism, and Blocking
In addition to providing user data for advertisement targeting, Facebook has been widely criticized for perceived privacy infringements. Although users are typically able to limit the content they post to be visible only to friends on the site, these settings often default to sharing information publicly. This not only aggravates some users, but has also allegedly resulted in situations as serious as people losing their jobs due to content posted on Facebook.

In December 2009, Facebook changed all profiles to be public—meaning visible to anyone, even non-users and non-friends—by default, requiring users to change settings to keep their information private. Because many users preferred to keep their information visible to friends only, the switch angered many users and caused some to stop using the service. Several organizations joined a US Federal Trade Commission (FTC) complaint against Facebook for its lack of privacy protections.

Facebook's ability to open up connections between people who have fallen out of touch and to facilitate communication between such parties has been blamed for many divorces. Staying logged in to Facebook has also led to spouses discovering unwanted information, including private messages between users. A December 2009 study found that 20 to 33 percent of all divorce filings in the United Kingdom cited Facebook as a reason for the separation, reflecting a potential downside of widespread sharing.

Facebook has been blocked in many countries, including China and Iran in 2009, due to concerns about its role as a tool for political activism in opposition to parties in power.

Impact

By creating the largest social network in the world, Facebook revolutionized online communications, human connections, activism, and advertising. The site has helped people maintain connections with others in unprecedented ways and has even been used to mobilize grassroots political efforts. As the social network evolves, it will undoubtedly have new applications (and implications) for corporations, advertisers, law enforcement, and individuals.

Further Reading

Hill, Kashmir. "Facebook's Mark Zuckerberg: 'We've Made a Bunch of Mistakes.'" *Forbes*. Forbes.com, 29 Nov. 2011. Web. 9 Oct. 2012. Includes a list of the privacy-related problems uncovered by the FTC investigation of Facebook.

Kirkpatrick, David. *The Facebook Effect: The Inside Story of the Company That Is Connecting the World*. New York: Simon, 2010. Print. A comprehensive, extensively researched overview of Facebook's evolution, from Harvard onward.

Lacey, Sara. *Once You're Lucky, Twice You're Good: The Rebirth of Silicon Valley and the Rise of Web 2.0*. New York: Gotham, 2008. Print. Portrays Facebook as part of the Web 2.0 revolution in Silicon Valley. Also includes descriptions of other companies involved in the transition.

Mezrich, Ben. *The Accidental Billionaires: The Founding of Facebook: A Tale of Sex, Money, Genius and Betrayal*. New York: Anchor, 2010. Print. Focuses on unraveling the controversies around Facebook's origins.

Miller, Daniel. *Tales from Facebook*. Malden: Polity, 2011. Print. Examines the impact of Facebook on friendship, marriage, isolation and communication, business, and religious institutions in sociological and anthropological terms.

Kerry Skemp, MA

■ Fads

Definition: Popular trends in fashion, technology, business, and social activity

The 2000s saw the introduction of a number of popular fads into American society. Some of these fads gave way to long-term developments, while others fell victim to the economic downturn late in the decade or the changing tastes of consumers.

Between 2000 and 2009, the United States saw a wide range of fads, activities and products that were extremely popular but often for only a short period of time. Such fads existed within all aspects of society and included fashion trends and popular business practices. Some fads involved the use of new technologies to retain information and share it with others.

Real Estate

During the early 2000s, the US government attempted to encourage more citizens to purchase their own homes, an activity that would spur economic growth. Deregulation of housing lenders made it possible for more people, even those with limited incomes and poor credit, to purchase real estate with the aid of loans. The popularity of home ownership gave rise to the practice of "house flipping," in which investors would purchase a home, make some improvements to it, and quickly resell it for a profit.

House flipping was extremely popular, especially during the mid-2000s, when housing prices were at a high. It also boosted the economy, as it helped supply a great deal of business for the real estate and construction industries. Reality television programs such as *Flip This House*, *Flip That House*, and *Flipping Out* further served to popularize the practice. However, after the housing bubble collapsed late in the decade, due in large part to the decade's lending and borrowing practices, it became far more difficult for house flippers to continue to make money.

Fashion

A number of major fads characterized 2000s fashion. When the shoemaker UGG introduced a highly recognizable sheepskin boot to US consumers, film and television stars and other celebrities soon took to wearing them, leading to a boom in sales. While UGG

Matching Crocs for girls. (Courtesy of Peter Dutton)

boots had been on the market since the 1970s, they became widely popular by the mid-2000s. Meanwhile, another shoe reached its popularity apex in 2007. Crocs presented consumers with a porous rubber sandal that covered the foot but could be worn in the water or on wet surfaces. Sales skyrocketed by the summer of 2007 but soon plummeted, and in the years following, the shoe saw considerably less popularity.

One of the most widespread fads during the 2000s was the wristband. Worn to show support for a number of different charities, wristbands became enormously popular both as signs of social and political consciousness and as fashion statements. Cyclist Lance Armstrong's yellow rubber "Livestrong" bracelets, for example, raised funds for cancer research and education. Similar bracelets were introduced to support HIV/AIDS research and other causes. Eventually, many of these bracelets disappeared from the marketplace as people began to question whether the money raised by the sale of these popular accessories was actually going to the intended recipients. Still, Livestrong bracelets remained popular by the end of the 2000s.

Technology
Some of the fads of the 2000s led to long-lasting innovations. For example, personal digital assistants (PDAs), which had been on the market since the 1990s, saw increased popularity during the 2000s as their capabilities increased. While standalone PDAs fell out of favor, PDAs and cellular phones effectively merged to form smartphones, phones that featured web capabilities as well as cameras, video software, and global positioning systems.

Meanwhile, some new websites captured the public's favor, though their popularity tended to wane as new sites were introduced. In 2003, people gained the ability to share their thoughts as well as photos and preferred web links with their friends via a site called MySpace. A year after MySpace arrived on the web, college student Mark Zuckerberg and his colleagues introduced Facebook, which soon replaced MySpace as the dominant social networking site. Increased interest in social networking, a trend that outlasted the fads for individual websites, also led to the creation of the professional networking–oriented LinkedIn and the microblogging site Twitter. These sites continued to grow in popularity by the end of the decade.

Impact
Some of the fads of the 2000s, such as house flipping, decreased in popularity with the collapse of the housing bubble and the overall downturn of the US economy late in the decade. Others, such as Crocs, fell out of favor as the tastes and needs of the American consumer changed. Still others, such as social networking websites, had a profound impact on American culture and played a significant role in the evolution and use of technology that would continue into the next decade.

Further Reading
Berger, Arthur Asa. *Ads, Fads, and Consumer Culture: Advertising's Impact on American Character and Society.* Lanham: Rowman, 2011. Print. Discusses fads and the advertising and marketing strategies that created them during the 2000s.

Best, Joel. *Flavor of the Month: Why Smart People Fall for Fads.* Berkeley: U of California P, 2006. Print. Explains the social and cultural reasons why fads in businesses and other institutions take off.

Hallett, Vicky, and Marc Silver. "Strike Up the Wristband." *US News and World Report* 54.2543 (2004): 11. Print. Describes the different types of wristbands available during the 2000s and their connections to charitable organizations.

Smith, Martin J., and Patrick J. Kiger. *Poplorica: A Popular History of the Fads, Mavericks, Inventions, and Lore that Shaped Modern America.* New York: Harper, 2005. Print. Explores the history of fads in the United States, providing context for the new fads of the 2000s.

Villani, Rick. *FLIP: How to Find, Fix, and Sell Houses for Profit.* New York: McGraw, 2006. Print. Describes the fad of house flipping and the potential for earning large sums of money through the practice.

Michael P. Auerbach

■ *Fahrenheit 9/11*

Identification: Award-winning documentary critical of US President George W. Bush that faults his administration for misleading the public over the Iraq War
Director: Michael Moore
Date: Released June 24, 2004

Michael Moore's unabashed critique of President George W. Bush was released during the 2004 presidential election year, when opinions about the validity of the Iraq War and the president's leadership ability were significantly polarized. With its provocative news footage, creative assemblage, and investigative reporting tinged with humor, Fahrenheit 9/11 was praised by those on the left of the political spectrum, but deemed unpatriotic propaganda by those on the right.

For the title of *Fahrenheit 9/11*, Michael Moore drew upon Ray Bradbury's *Fahrenheit 451*, the classic literary work about censorship and the suppression of knowledge. Instead of "451," the temperature at which paper combusts, Moore uses "9/11", a reference to the terrorist attacks of September 11, 2001. The film begins with the contested election of George W. Bush in 2000. It then examines his past military record, business career, and relationship with the bin Laden family and other Saudis. The film portrays Bush as a dishonest, incompetent, and conflicted president. Without subtlety, *Fahrenheit 9/11* alleges that Bush's stated reason for going to war in Iraq—to disarm the country of weapons of mass destruction—was a smokescreen for a more personal motive. The film includes footage of President Bush reading to elementary school students, and being interrupted by a staff member who informs him of the terrorist attacks on New York and Washington, DC.

A production of Moore's Dog Eat Dog Films, *Fahrenheit 9/11* was supposed to be released by Disney's Miramax, until Disney backed out of the agreement. The film was then distributed by Fellowship Adventure Group, the company established specifically for

Producer Harvey Weinstein (second from left) and director Michael Moore (center from right) at the premiere of Fahrenheit 9/11. *(©iStockphoto.com/Pascal Le Segretain)*

Fahrenheit 9/11 by the owners of Miramax, Harvey and Bob Weinstein, along with Lions Gate Entertainment and IFC Films. Following its release, *Fahrenheit 9/11* won twenty-six awards and twelve nominations worldwide, including Favorite Motion Picture from the People's Choice Awards and the Palme d'Or, the highest honor at the Cannes Film Festival. The film became the highest-grossing documentary ever.

Impact

Regarded by many as the most thought-provoking and polarizing film of the year, if not the decade, *Fahrenheit 9/11* generated a national discussion over the Bush administration's reasoning behind the Iraq War, the validity of the USA PATRIOT Act, and the role of documentary films in politics. Many critics thought Moore was simply preaching to his previously well-established liberal audience, and that the film did little to change attitudes among centrist and conservative thinkers. President Bush was reelected in November 2004. Nonetheless, the film introduced the documentary genre as a tool of political communication for both major political parties in the United States.

Further Reading

Ebert, Roger. "Fahrenheit 9/11." *RogerEbert.com.* RogerEbert.com, 24 June 2004. Web. 29 Aug. 2012.
Scott, Bowles. *"Fahrenheit 9/11* Torches Box Office Records." *USA Today* 27 June 2004. Print.
Vesely, Milan. *"Fahrenheit 9/11." Middle East* 348 (Aug.–Sep. 2004): 18–19. Print.

Sally Driscoll

■ Fairey, Shepard

Identification: American artist
Born: February 15, 1970; Charleston, South Carolina

Shepard Fairey gained international recognition for his design of a poster of Barack Obama seen frequently during the 2008 US presidential campaign. Known to some as a street artist, and to others as a commercial graphic designer, his work sparked a national debate on the use of others' work in both commercial and artistic efforts.

At the start of the 2000s, street artist and graphic designer Shepard Fairey was working at BLK/MRKT, the design firm that he had cofounded in San Diego in the late 1990s. While at the firm, Fairey participated in guerilla marketing for companies such as Pepsi and Netscape. Fairey left BLK/MRKT to move to Los Angeles, where he and his wife Amanda started their own design firm, Studio Number One, in 2003.

During the mid-2000s, Fairey's work appeared in one-man shows and other exhibits in the United States and Europe. His work is part of the permanent collections of museums including the National Portrait Gallery in Washington, DC and the Victoria and Albert Museum in London, and the Museum of Contemporary Art in San Diego.

In early 2008, when California was anticipating the 2008 Super Tuesday presidential primary, Fairey and Yosi Sergant, a publicist, decided to create a poster to get out the Obama vote in California. Fairey and Sergant had spoken of the possibility of the campaign in 2007, but Fairey was reluctant to

Shepard Fairey. (Courtesy Adam Engelhart)

divert attention from Obama, or to jeopardize Obama's credibility because of his own past. He knew that his past arrests for street art might have been a problem for the campaign. After consulting with campaign organizers, the two went ahead and created a poster—it took Fairey about a day to create the poster and another to print out 700 copies. He sold 350 and gave away the remaining 350. The sale of the poster paid for a second printing of 4,000 which were handed out at rallies and events. The initial run of 700 posters read "Progress," but feedback from the campaign prompted Fairey to change the text to "Hope."

Fairey's portrait of Obama became part of the collection at the National Portrait Gallery shortly before Obama's inauguration. The image was chosen as the cover for national publications, including *Time* magazine's 2008 Person of the Year issue and *Esquire* (Feb. 2009). *Rolling Stone* commissioned a different portrait of Obama from Fairey for its August 2009 issue.

In February 2009, Fairey was on his way to the Institute of Contemporary Art, Boston, for the opening of his solo exhibition, "Supply and Demand" when he was arrested on outstanding warrants for illegally tagging property from his early street art campaign, "Obey," featuring an image of Andre the Giant. As part of his July 2009 plea bargain, Fairey pleaded guilty to three counts of vandalism and paid a two thousand dollar fine, banned himself from Suffolk County, Massachusetts, for two years, and issued an apology for posting his art without property owners' permission.

Fairey's move into mainstream corporate work has prompted some to question whether or not he has lost his edge as a street artist, while others point to his 2009 arrest as evidence that he has kept his edge. Still others have questioned the artistic value of work that is borrowed and adapted, as much of Fairey's work is. The Obama poster itself is an artistic adaption of a photo shot by Mannie Garcia while freelancing for the Associated Press. He has admittedly borrowed from Soviet and Chinese propaganda posters, art nouveau works, and the work of others, but claims that the work becomes original when it is "recontextualized."

Impact

Fairey, a self-described popular artist, gained national recognition after a poster he designed of then Senator Barack Obama helped get out the vote for the presidential candidate. Demand for the poster rose quickly, and Fairey's art met with a mixed critical response. Fairey openly acknowledges that he adopts images and graphics from other sources, often without giving credit to the original artist or creator. This practice sparked a national debate on fair use and artistic credibility and has opened Fairey up to lawsuits.

Further Reading

Arnon, Ben. "How the Obama "Hope" Poster Reached a Tipping Point and Became a Cultural Phenomenon: An Interview With the Artist Shepard Fairey." *Huffington Post.* HuffingtonPost.com, 13 Oct. 2008. Web. 22 June 2012.

Johnson, Ken. "Can a Rebel Stay a Rebel Without the Claws?" *New York Times.* New York Times Co., 17 Mar. 2009. Web. 22 June 2012.

O'Donoghue, Liam. "Interview: Shepard Fairey." *Mother Jones.* Mother Jones, Mar./Apr. 2008. Web. 22 June 2012.

Ann Cameron

◼ Faith-based organizations

Definition: A charitable organization affiliated with a religious group

The separation of church and state became a renewed source of debate after President George W. Bush expanded government funding to religious charitable organizations, or faith-based organizations (FBOs), in 2001.

Politically, the popularity of the term "faith-based" began with the Republican Party in the 1990s—most notably by Texas governor George W. Bush, who in a speech in 1996, said, "Government should welcome the help of faith-based institutions." The earliest known use of the term occurred in 1981, when Clarence Martin, a lobbyist for the Association for the Advancement of Psychology, used the phrase "faith-based values" to deride pervasive religious views in society, such as creationism. Linguistically, William Safire pointed out in a June 27, 1999, *New York Times* article that the term "faith-based organization" is largely political. As Reverend Bill Callahan of the Quixote Center in Maryland told Safire, "The language of faith-based signals to people our motivation while separating us from the institutions."

Office of Faith-Based and Community Initiatives

Following his inauguration in 2001, President Bush issued his first executive order to create the Office of Faith-Based and Community Initiatives (OFBCI) in the White House. A subsequent executive order stipulated that a number of government departments, including Justice, Education, and Labor, also establish a Center for Faith-Based and Community Initiatives. The third and most controversial executive order, in 2002, made it easier for religious organizations to receive money by allowing them to circumvent antidiscrimination laws.

The orders were a vast expansion of several laws that President Bill Clinton had signed in the late 1990s as a provision to welfare reform, collectively known as Charitable Choice, which said that religiously affiliated social organizations should not be excluded from competition for government funds, as the White House website explained, "simply because they are religious." The stipulation was the fruit of a political compromise between the president and Republican senator John Ashcroft. Previously, groups like Catholic Charities and Jewish Family Services could not compete with secular organizations for government funds unless they created a separate 501(c)(3) nonprofit and did not attempt to convert aid recipients or discriminate in their hiring practices. After Charitable Choice, these requisites were largely removed, though the Clinton administration interpreted the law more strictly than its successor, refusing money to organizations that could not or would not separate religious practices from their secular organizations.

When he created the OFBCI, Bush, himself an evangelical born-again Christian, was working from policies he had enacted as the governor of Texas, which were under the auspices of the Welfare Reform Act of 1996. Originally, President Bush's plan called for eight billion dollars in federal grants and vouchers for religious nonprofits that provided social services such as job training, food, and after-school programs. "The premise of the president's initiative," the *New York Times* wrote in a July 8, 2001, editorial, "is that some social services can reach some people more effectively if religious practice is a part of the service."

For religious groups who supported the plan, it was a triumph over discrimination; a wrong—that enormously beneficial programs had been systematically denied government funds because of the separation of church and state—had been righted. Some religious critics, however, argued that government money might distort the mission of the recipient organizations.

Others—secular and religious people alike—worried that the initiative set a troubling precedent in providing refuge for organizations with discriminatory hiring practices. The legislation, a part of the Charities, Aid, Recovery, and Empowerment (CARE) Act of 2002, stipulated that federal funds were to be used for secular purposes. However, the Texas Freedom Network, a Texas watchdog agency, pointed out that even though the same stipulation existed in the legislation Bush had instated in Texas, government and worship funds had inevitably intermingled. Furthermore, the *New York Times* wrote, the language of the legislation suggested that organizations could voluntarily proselytize to aid recipients, as long as that recipient had an alternative and secular organization available to them; this was known as the "opt out" provision. But it would be difficult for those in a substance abuse program or a juvenile delinquency program, for example, to claim that right.

In 2007, in *Hein v. Freedom from Religion Foundation*, a case involving the OFBCI and a group of atheists and agnostics, the US Supreme Court ruled that taxpayers could not challenge executive expenditures. The 5–4 decision reversed a 2006 ruling by the US Seventh Circuit Court of Appeals.

Impact
Faith-based initiatives and the OFBCI were viewed as a signature of the Bush administration, and many people expected that the election of President Barack Obama would be the end of them. However, President Obama, who made it clear during his 2008 campaign that he supported the program, kept the office and its policies in place, though he renamed it the Office of Faith-Based and Neighborhood Partnerships. In 2010, Obama signed an executive order to strengthen "the legal footing" of the government's relationship with faith-based organizations and encourage transparency.

Religious groups and others were divided on the success of the program under Bush. David Kuo, a former Bush aide and deputy director of the OFBCI, alleged that the office fell short of Bush's promises and ultimately became more about politics than good works. Kuo, an evangelical and contributing editor to the website Beliefnet, wrote about his time with the OFBCI in his book *Tempting Faith: An Inside Story of Political Seduction* (2006).

Further Reading
"Frontline: The Jesus Factor." *PBS*. WGBH Educational Foundation, 29 Apr. 2004. Web. 14 Dec. 2012. Interviews and transcripts from PBS's *Frontline* special on President George W. Bush's faith and its impact on his political career. Also discusses American evangelicals.

Kuo, David. *Tempting Faith: An Inside Story of Political Seduction.* New York: Free, 2006. Print. Written by a former Bush aid and director of the OFBCI who came away disillusioned with the administration and its faith-based mission.

"Mr. Bush's 'Faith Based' Agenda." *New York Times*. New York Times, 8 July 2001. Web. 14 Dec. 2012. An editorial that explores the intent of President Bush's faith-based initiatives.

Safire, William. "The Way We Live Now: 6-27-99: On Language; Faith-based." *New York Times*. New York Times, 27 June 1999. Web. 14 Dec. 2012. Discusses the rise of the term "faith-based" in 1999, two years before President Bush pushed his faith-based initiatives.

"The Texas Faith-Based Initiative at Five Years: Warning Signs as President Bush Expands Texas-Style Program at National Level." *Texas Freedom Network*. Texas Freedom Network, n.d. Web. 14 Dec. 2012. A Texas religious freedom and civil rights watchdog group reports on the successes and failures of Bush's faith-based programs in Texas between 1996 and 2001.

Molly Hagan

■ *Family Guy*

Identification: An animated sitcom about the Griffins, a family of quirky individuals living in the fictional town of Quahog, Rhode Island
Creator: Seth MacFarlane (b. 1973)
Date: Premiered on January 31, 1999

The success of Seth MacFarlane's Family Guy *can be attributed to its brainy wit and devoted fan base. MacFarlane's unforgiving humor and biting commentary on pop culture has led to the show receiving frequent praise as well as criticism.*

Family Guy tells the story of the outlandish Griffin family. MacFarlane voices the main character and family patriarch, Peter, an incompetent and bigoted man who gets involved in nonsensical situations. Peter's wife, the even-minded Lois, struggles to keep her family under control. Their children, Chris and Meg, are intensified versions of American misfit teenagers. Chris is overweight and dimwitted, much like his father. Meg fares no better as an awkward loner, desperate to fit in. The Griffins also have an infant son, Stewie, who relentlessly plots world domination. Stewie is only able to communicate with the family's talking dog, Brian, who stands upright and drinks martinis. Each episode parodies an aspect of contemporary American life, and the show is well known for its cutaway shots ridiculing popular culture.

Family Guy was nearly cancelled after only two seasons because of its low ratings. The show's network, FOX, decided to give it another chance, granting a third season. The show was placed in a time slot that competed with some popular shows, however, and the competition overwhelmed the animated series. *Family Guy* was officially cancelled in 2002.

The first three seasons of the show were released on DVD in 2003. Within a month, more than four hundred thousand DVDs had been sold. This caught the attention of network executives, and FOX renewed the show in 2004. The following year, *Family Guy* returned to FOX's regular lineup.

Impact

Family Guy has won many awards, including five Emmys and two Annie Awards. The show's treatment of controversial issues has generated criticism, however. The series is consistently admonished by the Parents Television Council (PTC), and many complaints against it have been filed with the Federal Communications Commission (FCC). The show was also involved in three separate copyright infringement lawsuits, though the cases were either dismissed or settled. Despite these reproaches, *Family Guy*'s popularity continued to grow during the decade.

Further Reading

Callaghan, Steve. *Family Guy: Stewie's Guide to World Domination.* New York: Harper, 2005. Print.
Corea, Andy I. "Copyright Lessons from *Family Guy*

Add Insult to Injury to Support Your Fair-Use Defense." *Tennessee Bar Association Intellectual Property Section* 2.1 (11 Dec. 2009): 3–4. *St. Onge Steward Jonston & Reens* (*SJSR*). Web. 4 Sept. 2012.
Flint, Joe. "Is 'Family Guy' Creator Seth MacFarlane Taunting the FCC?" *Los Angeles Times.* Tribune Interactive, 4 May 2010. Web. 4 Sept. 2012.

Cait Caffrey

■ *Fast Food Nation*

Identification: Bestselling exposé of the fast-food industry and its powerful influence on society
Author: Eric Schlosser (1959–)

Date: 2001 (book), 2006 (film) When the obesity rate among Americans had reached an epidemic proportion, E. coli was threatening the safety of the nation's beef supply, and illegal immigration had become a perplexing national issue, Eric Schlosser went behind the scenes of the fast-food industry to link these and other social problems with the "all-American meal." Written from a liberal perspective, Fast Food Nation *became one of the most polarizing, yet provocative books of the decade.*

Fast Food Nation begins with a history of the fast-food industry from the first McDonald Brothers Burger Bar Drive-In in the late 1930s to the globalization of McDonald's, Taco Bell, Subway, and other fast-food chains during the late twentieth century. Eric Schlosser details the government policies and business practices that have been responsible for the growth of the industry, and he goes behind the scenes to trace the policies and ethics related to the preparation and consumption of hamburgers and French fries, or what the industry calls "commodities."

Schlosser profiles animal cruelty at factory farms and the inhumane treatment of workers at slaughterhouses, where low pay and hazardous working conditions among a largely immigrant population have created ghettos overrun with crime and health problems. While *E. coli* was threatening the safety of the nation's beef supply, Schlosser faults the US government for its ineffective, bureaucratic safety system that failed to mandate recalls of tainted meat or to provide the resources necessary for adequate inspections of meatpacking plants.

Schlosser examines the lobbying conducted by the National Restaurant Association to fight against the raising of the minimum wage in an era in which its "real" value had decreased drastically, and he links the Republican refusal to raise the wage to the demise of the middle class. He investigates both the social implications of an exploited teenage workforce and the marketing campaigns aimed at children. Last but not least, the book links the obesity epidemic to the ubiquitous consumption of fast food.

Fast Food Nation evolved from articles first published in *Rolling Stone* in 1998 and became such a success globally that it was translated into more than twenty languages. A comedic-dramatic film based on the book was released in 2006 to additional acclaim.

Impact

Fast Food Nation raised the level of awareness that cheap food comes at the price of social welfare and health. Because the book was published during the George W. Bush presidential administration and a Republican-held Congress, it did not have an immediate legislative impact, although, in 2007, the new Democratic-majority Congress raised the minimum wage. However, the fast-food industry did respond to the bad publicity. Factory farms reduced the use of antibiotics and began to treat animals less cruelly. Fast-food restaurants added more salads and fruit to their menus, switched to healthier oils for cooking french fries, and began to post nutritional information, while support for farmers' markets, community supported agriculture groups, and natural, organic food stores soared.

Further Reading

Jones, Kristin M. "*Fast Food Nation.*" *Film Comment* 42.6 (2006): 73–4.

Slivka, Andrey. "You Want Fries with That?" Rev. of *Fast Food Nation*, by Eric Schlosser. *American Scholar* 70.2 (2001): 152–54.

Sally Driscoll

■ Federer, Roger

Identification: Professional tennis player
Born: August 8, 1981; Basel, Switzerland

Roger Federer is one of the top-ranked professional tennis players in the world. Some tennis observers believe that Federer, who is known for his court strategy, is the greatest player in history. Federer broke tennis player Pete Sampras's record of fourteen Grand Slam titles in 2009. This achievement makes him the unofficial greatest men's tennis player of all time.

On the heels of his wins at the Wimbledon Junior Championships, seventeen-year-old Roger Federer, the top ranked junior player in the world, began playing on the men's professional tour in 1998. By the end of 1999, Federer was the youngest player listed among the top 100 of the Association of Tennis Professionals (ATP) Tour.

During the 2000 season, Federer reached the finals of an ATP twice, first in Marseille and again at Basel. During that same year, Federer also represented his country at the Sydney Olympic Games. Though he did not take home a medal, it was there that he met tennis player Miroslava Vavrinec, who was on the Swiss women's team. They married in April 2009.

The year 2001 was a successful one for Federer. At nineteen years old, he earned the first victory of his professional career when he won the ATP singles title in Milan. He subsequently led Switzerland's Davis Cup squad to a victory over the United States in the tournament's opening round. Federer's performance

Roger Federer. (Courtesy Gaëtan Ferey)

led journalists to give him the nickname "Federer Express," which has stayed with him throughout his career.

Federer went on to beat 2001 Wimbledon favorite Pete Sampras before suffering a surprising loss in the next round to underdog Tim Henman. Henman beat Federer a second time later that year in the finals of an indoor tournament held in Federer's hometown of Basel. Nonetheless, by the end of 2001, Federer was the thirteenth best singles tennis player in the world.

Federer continued to climb steadily upward in international men's tennis rankings, although he failed to crack the top ten. It seemed like each time Federer pulled off an upset, he followed up the victory with a loss to a lesser opponent. In 2002, for example, Federer won his first Masters series event with a pair of crushing wins; a week later, he was eliminated in the first round of the French Open by a virtual unknown.

Then, in the summer of 2002, around the time of his twenty-first birthday, Federer experienced a tragic loss that helped change his attitude and, ultimately, his game. Federer's old coach and mentor, Peter Carter, had been killed in a car accident in South Africa. Carter had traveled there on safari, at Federer's urging, to celebrate the news that Carter's wife, following a yearlong battle with cancer, was free of the disease.

His former coach's death forced Federer to reevaluate his approach to life and to tennis. In 2003, Federer won six tournaments, including his first Grand Slam event. The brilliance of his game had finally conquered his erratic tendencies.

In 2004 Federer, who won that year's Wimbledon, US Open, and Australian Open championships, became the number one tennis player in the world. He would retain this status uninterruptedly for the next four and a half years. He went on to win several more Grand Slam titles, giving him a total of thirteen such wins as of late 2008.

In 2008, a twenty-seven-year-old Federer saw his five-year winning streak at Wimbledon broken by tennis player Rafael Nadal. Nadal also took over the world's number one ranking, displacing Federer from the top spot he had owned for 237 straight weeks.

Federer stated that his number one priority in the 2009 season would be to reclaim the status of Wimbledon champion. He achieved this goal, winning at Wimbledon and earning his fifteenth Grand Slam title—an all-time record. With his Wimbledon victory, coupled with his prior win at the 2009 French Open, Federer regained his number one world ranking. He headed into the US Open in September as the favorite and defending champion. When he advanced beyond the semifinals of that tournament, he cemented an unprecedented streak of having reached at least the semifinals or better in twenty-two consecutive Grand Slam tournaments, dating back to 2005. Federer, however, was bested in the finals of the US Open by Argentinean Juan Martín del Potro, who stunned the Swiss superstar in five sets.

Impact

Federer is one of the greatest athletes to ever play the game of tennis. His consistently superior performance and dynamic personal story made him one of the most popular professional athletes of his time. He became the highest earning tennis player of all time in 2008, holding almost $45 million in career earnings. Federer has appeared in the finals of every Grand Slam tournament since Wimbledon 2005, save one—the 2008 Australian Open.

Further Reading

Clarey, Christopher. "Federer at Flushing Meadows: Flickering or Flaming Out?" *New York Times* 7 Sep. 2012: B10. Print.

Foster Wallace, David. "Federer As Religious Experience." *New York Times PLAY*. New York Times Co., 20 Aug. 2006. Web. 29 Oct. 2012.

Price, S.L. "Is He The Greatest of All Time?" *Sports Illustrated*. Time Inc., 15 Jun. 2009. Web. 29 Oct. 2012.

Beverly Ballaro

■ Fey, Tina

Identification: American actor and screenwriter
Born: May 18, 1970; Upper Darby Township, Pennsylvania

Tina Fey's work as a writer, producer, and actor has helped drive the success of two award-winning comedies, the late-night variety show Saturday Night Live *and the sitcom* 30 Rock. *She has also written screenplays and acted in several films.*

In 1999, Tina Fey made history when she became the first female head writer for *Saturday Night Live*.

The 2000s in America

FIFA World Cup ■ 219

Tina Fey. (©iStockphoto.com/Dimitrios Kambouris)

In the 2000s, Fey also appeared on the show's main stage, becoming a coanchor of the show's comedy news segment "Weekend Update." In 2001, she won a Writer's Guild of America Award for her work on the "SNL Twenty fifth Anniversary Special." The following year, Fey was awarded an Emmy Award for Outstanding Writing for a Variety, Music, or Comedy program. In 2004, she was joined by Amy Poehler on "Weekend Update." The pair was the first female duo in the *SNL*'s history to star in the segment.

In 2002, Fey started to develop a sitcom about a head writer on a comedy show that loosely paralleled her own experiences at *SNL*. In 2006, she left her position as head writer for *SNL* to produce and star in the show, *30 Rock*. Her work as the show's executive producer and head writer has earned her three Emmy Awards for Outstanding Comedy Series, a Golden Globe for Outstanding Comedy Series and several other awards. For her role as the show's star, Liz Lemon, Fey won Emmy Awards for Outstanding Lead Actress in a Comedy Series in 2007 and 2008, a Golden Globe, and a Screen Actors Guild award.

Fey returned to SNL in 2008 to appear in a recurring role as Republican Party vice presidential candidate Sarah Palin. Critics and audiences alike praised Fey's comedic portrayal of Palin. Fey won an Emmy for Outstanding Guest Actress in a Comedy Series in 2009 for her performance.

Fey wrote and starred in the critically acclaimed 2004 film *Mean Girls*, which was based in part on Rosalind Wiseman's 2002 book *Queen Bees and Wannabees*. She also appears in the films *Baby Mama* (2008), *The Invention of Lying* (2009), and *Date Night* (2010). In 2011, she published a memoir entitled *Bossypants*.

Impact

In 2008, Fey was awarded the prestigious Mark Twain Prize for American Humor in 2008. Some have speculated that her success paved the way for other female comedy writers, such as Kristen Wiig and Annie Mumolo, creators of the 2011 film *Bridesmaids*. Fey remains one of the most popular actors and writers in entertainment.

Further Reading

Fey, Tina. *Bossypants*. New York: Little, 2011. Print.
Flowers, Arhlene A., Cory L. Young. "Parodying Palin: How Tina Fey's Visual and Verbal Impersonations Revived a Comedy Show and Impacted the 2008 Election." *Journal of Visual Literacy* 29.1 (2010): 47–67. Print.
Whalley, Jim. Saturday *Night Live, Hollywood Comedy, and American Culture: From Chevy Chase to Tina Fey*. New York: Palgrave, 2010. Print.

Leland Spencer

■ FIFA World Cup

Definition: Quadrennial men's and women's soccer tournaments held in rotating locations throughout the world by the International Federation of Association Football (Fédération Internationale de Football Association, or FIFA).

The increasing popularity of soccer as a spectator and recreational sport in North America in the 2000s resulted in expanded interest in the FIFA World Cup. Television coverage of the tournaments, coupled with strong showings by the Canadian and American women's teams, as well as the American men's team, further attracted North American audiences.

Canada takes on the United States at the 2003 Women's World Cup. (Courtesy Curt Gibbs)

The 2002 FIFA World Cup was hosted jointly by South Korea and Japan in May and June of that year, becoming the first World Cup to be held in two countries. The United States' upset victories over Portugal and Mexico earned the team a spot in the quarterfinals, where it was defeated by Germany, the eventual runner-up to Brazil. Due largely to the time difference between North America and the host countries, the matches broadcast in the United States received relatively low ratings for major sporting events.

In the fall of 2003, the United States hosted its second consecutive FIFA Women's World Cup. China was initially set to host the tournament, but an outbreak of the SARS virus in that country resulted in a last-minute change of venue. The heavily favored American team finished the tournament in third place, after runner-up Sweden and champion Germany. Canada's fourth place showing was the all-time highest finish for the team.

The far less dramatic time difference between the United States and host nation Germany resulted in record television ratings for the 2006 World Cup. North American viewership increased despite a poor showing by the US men's team, which scored just two goals and failed to record a win in group play. Nearly 16.9 million American viewers watched Italy defeat France in the final match, a 152 percent increase over the 2002 final.

The United States and Canada both qualified for the 2007 Women's World Cup in China. While Canada was eliminated in group play, the US team went on to its second consecutive third-place finish. Brazil was the runner-up, while the German women's team again took home the trophy.

Impact

By the end of the 2000s, the sport of soccer had experienced unprecedented growth in North America, in large part because of public interest in the FIFA World Cup. This resulted not only in increased youth participation in the sport but also in rising spectator interest in the North American professional league, Major League Soccer (MLS). The construction of new, soccer-specific venues in several major US cities and the expansion of MLS to include teams from the Canadian cities of Toronto, Montreal, and Vancouver further emphasized the growing popularity of the sport.

Further Reading

Lisi, Clemente. *A History of the World Cup: 1930–2010.* Lanham: Scarecrow, 2011. Print.

Longman, Jeré. "US Expects Soccer's Rise if It Hosts Cup in 2022." *New York Times.* New York Times, 27 Nov. 2010. Web. 21 Aug. 2012.

Williams, Jean. *A Beautiful Game: International Perspectives on Women's Football.* New York: Berg, 2007. Print.

John Pritchard

■ Film in the United States

Definition: Industry that creates motion pictures in the United States for distribution in cinemas both domestically and internationally

During the 2000s, the US film industry relied on technological advances to produce films with computer-generated special effects capable of depicting realistic settings, people, and places. At a time when digital technology allowed for quality film viewing on home entertainment systems, the industry also became more heavily invested in franchise films, with multiple sequels and 3-D effects, in order to keep attracting large audiences to cinemas.

The film industry in the United States is the largest in the world and includes both small, independent productions and multimillion-dollar blockbusters that are shown in movie theaters

Biggest Box-Office Draws of the Decade

1	*Avatar*	2009
2	*The Dark Knight*	2008
3	*Shrek 2*	2004
4	*Pirates of the Caribbean: Dead Man's Chest*	2006
5	*Spider-Man*	2002
6	*Transformers: Revenge of the Fallen*	2009
7	*Star Wars: Episode III—Revenge of the Sith*	2005
8	*The Lord of the Rings: The Return of the King*	2003
9	*Spider-Man 2*	2004
10	*The Passion of the Christ*	2004

Source: Box Office Mojo.

worldwide. Approximately five thousand full-length feature films were made in the United States between 2000 and 2009. From big-budget adaptations of comic books and novels to documentary films and dramas, the decade saw a considerable diversity of themes, styles, and genres. The assorted films of the 2000s are also notable for the revolutionary way in which they were recorded, produced, and distributed. Digital technology, in which computers are used to add or to create special effects or remove unwanted images in a movie, first came into widespread use in the 1990s; in the following decade, studios used this technology on an even greater scale to produce the kind of spectacle entertainment that typically has been best seen on a large screen in a movie theater. Additionally, studios lured moviegoers into theaters by offering blockbuster entertainment that utilized fully-realistic 3-D technology.

Digital Effects

The rise of special effects–laden movies harkens back to 1977, when *Star Wars*, written and directed by George Lucas, first impressed audiences with its stunning visuals and old-fashioned movie serial sensibilities. Yet as groundbreaking as the *Star Wars* trilogy was, it was made in an era when small models of space ships were used to create the illusion of giant battles in space and matte paintings gave actors stunning backdrops. In the 1980s, computer-generated imagery (CGI), which requires neither models

nor matte paintings, was first employed in a sampling of films and did not come into its own until the early 1990s. Pixar Studios released *Toy Story*, the first CGI feature-length animated film, in 1995.

The use of CGI became almost ubiquitous in the animated films of the 2000s. Pixar's feature-length animated films—including *Finding Nemo* (2003), *The Incredibles* (2004), *Cars* (2006), and *Up* (2009)—were so popular with children and adults that they nearly replaced traditional, hand-drawn animated movies. *Up*'s critical reception was so positive that it became only the second animated feature ever to be nominated for an Oscar for best picture.

CGI bolstered the box office success of many live-action films of the decade, including Ridley Scott's Roman epic *Gladiator* (2000), which also won the Academy Award for best picture; the popular *Harry Potter* films (2001–2011) adapted from J. K. Rowling's series of novels (1997–2007); and Peter Jackson's critically lauded three-film adaptation, from 2001 to 2003, of J. R. R. Tolkien's masterwork, *The Lord of the Rings* (1954–1955), the final installment of which, *The Return of the King*, won the Academy Award for best picture in 2003.

Perhaps the most significant example of the revolutionary shift toward digital filmmaking was in James Cameron's 3-D science fiction epic *Avatar* (2009), which exhibited the most cutting-edge technology to date. Filmed with 3-D cameras and using "motion capture" techniques in which live actors were recorded and their motions rendered onto computer-generated characters, the movie became the highest-grossing film of the decade, with worldwide box-office sales of more than $2.7 billion.

Digital technology also changed the way people watched films, from digital projection equipment in theaters to digital downloads of films onto home computers or handheld electronic devices. With these changes came the lifting of the physical confines of film reels, videotapes, and DVDs. Movies were now available to anyone, literally at any time.

Popular Adaptations

Hand-in-hand with the success of digital filmmaking was the increased popularity of film adaptation, which is the reworking of known story lines and

Science and engineering students at the Worcester Polytechnic Institute (WPI) in Worcester, MA, work on active motion capture for use in video game animations. (Photo by Melanie Stetson Freeman/ The Christian Science Monitor/Getty Images)

characters from written works to form the basis of a film. Of the top twenty highest-grossing movies of the decade, only one, *Finding Nemo*, was based on an original screenplay and story idea. All the others had been adapted from a separate, previously released source material. Among the most popular were adaptations of comic books. In 2000, Bryan Singer adapted the long-running *X-Men* comic (1963–) into a feature film that not only spawned three successful sequels during the decade (2003, 2006, 2009), but also fueled the growth of the superhero film genre.

The superhero films of the 2000s were more fully developed than their predecessors, aided by both digital special effects and directors and writers who had grown up with comics and appreciated their entertainment value. Among the most commercially successful and critically acclaimed adapted films of the decade were the three *Spider-Man* movies (2002, 2004, 2007) directed by Sam

Raimi and the two *Batman* films (2005, 2008) directed by Christopher Nolan. Other notable comic book movies were Zack

Synder's 2009 adaptation of *Watchmen* (1986–1987) by Alan Moore and Dave Gibbons; Sam Mendes's 2002 adaptation of *Road to Perdition* (1998) by Max Allan Collins and Richard Piers Rayner; and Terry Zwigoff's 2001 adaptation of *Ghost World* (1993–1997) by Daniel Clowes.

Movies based on popular novels were also largely successful throughout the decade, most notably the *Harry Potter* series and *The Lord of the Rings* trilogy. The *Shrek* animated series (2001, 2004, 2007), based on William Steig's 1990 fairytale picture book, and *The Chronicles of Narnia* (2005, 2008), the classic series of fantasy novels written by C. S. Lewis between 1949 and 1954, were also very successful.

Genres and Themes

Also distinguishing this decade in film were movie genres that had not been previously popular in American cinemas. During the 2000s, moviegoers flocked to theaters to watch documentaries such as *Fahrenheit 9/11* (2004), *Super Size Me* (2004), *March of the Penguins* (2005), and *An Inconvenient Truth* (2006). Film buffs also seemed more willing to watch movies recorded in a foreign language, including *Crouching Tiger, Hidden Dragon* (2000), a Chinese martial-arts saga; *The Passion of the Christ* (2004), an adaptation of the New Testament gospels filmed in Latin, reconstructed Aramaic, and Hebrew; and *Letters from Iwo Jima* (2006), a World War II drama recorded primarily in Japanese.

The decade also saw the reemergence of film genres that had long since been considered passé, most notably: the musical, with such hits as *Moulin Rouge!* (2001), *Chicago* (2002), *Dreamgirls* (2006), and *Mamma Mia!* (2008); and, the disaster movie, including *The Day After Tomorrow* (2004) and *2012* (2009).

Filmmakers also touched on the terrorist attacks of September 11, 2001, and its aftermath. The subject was approached directly in films such as *World Trade Center* (2006) and *Flight 93* (2006), and indirectly in movies such as *Syriana* (2005), *Jarhead* (2005), *Rendition* (2007), and *The Hurt Locker* (2008)—the latter of which won the 2010 Academy Award for best picture. Dramas like these, as well as documentaries about the day itself and the resulting global War on Terror, indicate that filmgoers were not solely seeking escapist entertainment throughout the decade.

Successful Directors

Many film critics and fans tend to define film eras based on the successes and failures of the directors who worked on them. One of the most celebrated directors and producers of the 2000s was Academy Award–winner Steven Spielberg, who experimented with various genres such as the science fiction films *A. I. Artificial Intelligence* (2001), *Minority Report* (2002), and *War of the Worlds* (2005); the comedies *Catch Me If You Can* (2002) and *The Terminal* (2004); and the historical drama *Munich* (2005). Although in his seventies, actor and director Clint Eastwood also produced a number of critically acclaimed films. His most notable films included the boxing movie *Million Dollar Baby*, which won the 2004 Oscar for best picture, as well as *Mystic River* (2003), *Letters from Iwo Jima* (2006), *Changeling* (2008), and *Gran Torino* (2008). Martin Scorsese, who has directed some of the most celebrated films of the last forty years—including *Taxi Driver* (1976), *Raging Bull* (1980), and *Goodfellas* (1990)—earned his first Academy Award for best director for the 2006 crime drama *The Departed*.

Younger directors also made their impact on the decade. Ethan and Joel Coen, who began their film careers in the 1990s, entered a prolific period in the 2000s with such notable films as *O Brother, Where Art Thou?* (2000) and *The Man Who Wasn't There* (2001). The Coen brothers earned their first Oscar in 2007 for *No Country for Old Men*, an adaptation of Cormac McCarthy's 2005 novel of the same name. Christopher Nolan directed some of the most critically-acclaimed and commercially-popular movies of the decade, beginning with the mystery/thriller *Memento* in 2000 and continuing with the crime drama *Insomnia* in 2002. These were followed by his successful revival of the Batman franchise in 2005 with *Batman Begins*. His films in the latter half of the decade include *The Prestige* (2006), a mystery/drama about a rivalry between two magicians, and *The Dark Knight* (2008), a sequel in the Batman series that has been ranked among the greatest superhero movies of all time.

Impact

Over the course of the last one hundred–plus years, the film medium has evolved from silent films to "talkies," from black and white to color, and from square screen to widescreen. The industry made another great leap in the 2000s when digital filmmaking freed filmmakers from the confines of sets and stages, allowing them to create worlds limited only by their imaginations. The infinite possibilities of digital filmmaking, however, has come with a price: the challenge studios have faced of keeping people going to theaters and paying for content when digital home-entertainment systems and direct downloads of film onto televisions, computers, and wireless devices makes theatergoing optional. Another challenge to the industry's bottom line in the digital age has been film piracy, a phenomenon that did not begin in the 2000s but accelerated during the decade due to the ease with which high-quality digital bootlegs of films can be procured.

Further Reading

Corrigan, Timothy, ed. *American Cinema of the 2000s: Themes and Variations*. New Brunswick: Rutgers UP, 2012. Print. A collection of essays that look at how filmmakers responded to real-life events of the decade, from the 9/11 terrorist attacks, to the devastation of New Orleans following Hurricane Katrina, to the election of Barack Obama in 2008.

Dixon, Wheeler W., and Gwendolyn Audrey Foster. *21st-Century Hollywood: Movies in the Era of Transformation*. New Brunswick: Rutgers UP, 2011. Print. Looks at the ways in which digital technology has transformed the manner in which films are made, viewed, discussed, and studied.

Hoberman, J. *Film After Film: Or, What Became of 21st-Century Cinema?* Brooklyn: Verso, 2012. Print. The author, a senior film critic at the *Village Voice* since 1988, looks at the impact of world events on American cinema in the last decade, as well as the ways in which digital filmmaking has all but replaced the traditional variety.

Loder, Kurt. *The Good, the Bad, and the Godawful: 21st-Century Movie Reviews*. New York: Thomas Dunne, 2011. Print. A collection of two hundred movie reviews by the former *The Week in Rock* host Kurt Loder, culled from the websites of MTV and *Reason* magazine.

Müller, Jürgen. *Movies of the 2000s*. Cologne, Germany: Taschen, 2011. Print. Part of Taschen's movies-by-decade series. Discusses the transformative ways American filmmaking has been changed because of digital technology and globalization.

Christopher Mari

■ Flash mobs

Definition: Utilizing the power of social media, flash mobs are groups of people who meet in a public space to perform a unique and oftentimes bizarre act for the purpose of entertainment

In a flash mob, participants converge at a predetermined place and time to perform a seemingly absurd act for a brief period. As fast as the people appeared, they disappear, oftentimes leaving bystanders confused and entertained. Marketing companies later mainstreamed the concept of a flash mob.

The concept of flash mobs evolved out of smart mobs, which are groups of people who converge in an area to make a political or commercial statement, a promotional practice first described by Howard Rheingold in his 2002 book *Smart Mobs: The Next Social Revolution*. The first flash-mob event occurred in June 2003 in Manhattan, New York, at a Macy's department store. Its creation is attributed to Bill Wasik, the senior editor of *Wired* magazine. Wasik arranged the flash mob by emailing approximately fifty people and telling them to gather at a shop in Manhattan. Wasik explained that he enjoys watching people come together suddenly, but he also created flash mobs as a comment on conformity in US society.

Flash mobs are commonly filmed and uploaded to the Internet. Many of them have garnered tens of millions of views. One of the most viewed flash-mob videos occurred in January 2008. More than two hundred flash-mob participants converged inside Grand Central Station in New York City and froze in place at the exact same moment. They held this for five minutes and then dispersed. This flash mob was organized by the comedic performance art group Improv Everywhere, which has organized several flash mobs throughout the United States.

Some of the largest flash mobs have included thousands of participants. The largest flash mob organized in the 2000s occurred on March 22, 2008. Thousands of people in cities around the globe participated in pillow fights all at the same moment. In New York City alone, more than five thousand people took part in this event, known as Worldwide Pillow Fight Day.

Flash mob supporting the Cluster Munition Coalition (CMC). (Courtesy ItCBL/Cluster Munition Coalition)

After they became popular, some companies began using flash mobs as a marketing tool. This became known as "flash-mob marketing." These events have been sponsored by a variety of companies, including T-Mobile and the Fox network. While flash mobs traditionally have an element of spontaneity, flash-mob marketing events are often heavily choreographed.

In July 2004, the term "flash mob" was added to the *Oxford English Dictionary*.

Impact

Many people involved in flash mobs argue that trying to attach any social or cultural significance to the phenomenon would be missing the point, but others see these events as a reflection of the power of modern communications technology. Those who participated in the Arab Spring, also known as the Arab Revolution, in 2010 used social media and flash-mob approaches to stage demonstrations and protests.

Further Reading

Athavaley, Anjali. "Students Unleash a Pillow Fight on Manhattan." *Wall Street Journal.* Dow Jones, 15 Apr. 2008. Web. 20 Oct. 2012.

Wasik, Bill. "My Crowd: Or, Phase 5—A Report from the Inventor of the Flash Mob." *Harper's* 312.1870 (2006): 55–66. Print.

Patrick G. Cooper

■ Food allergies

Definition: Serious immune responses during which mast cells react against proteins in foods and release immunoglobulin E or other antibodies, causing a range of symptoms from hives or wheezing to multiorgan, life-threatening anaphylactic shock

Allergic food reactions have been documented in varying forms for centuries; although allergy concerns focus most heavily on children, reactions can develop and occur in people of any age. Food allergy awareness is ubiquitous in the early twenty-first century because of increased prevalence and changes to public health efforts that affect every consumer, not just those with allergies.

In 2007, one in every twenty-six children in the United States experienced at least one food allergy reaction, according to the US Centers for Disease Control and Prevention. This population represents an 18percent increase from the 1997 rate of one in twenty-nine. Potential causes theorized by researchers include timing of introductory foods, hygiene, and genes, though no single factor stands out.

Complicating the increasing numbers of reactions is the sustained durations of allergies. Evidence-based research of the 1990s supported the widespread belief that food allergies in children were frequently outgrown as immune systems grew tolerant of allergens. The 2000s, however, saw fewer and later allergy resolutions than ever before. More children are maintaining dairy allergy, once outgrown as toddlers, into school years; peanut and shellfish are typically considered lifelong allergens.

In the United States, eight foods—including dairy, egg, peanut, and tree nuts—account for 90 percent of allergic reactions. Despite this consistency, treatment still relies on absolute avoidance. However, the Consortium of Food Allergy Research (CoFAR), founded by the National Institute of Allergy and Infectious Diseases, postulates that desensitization programs, successful with environmental allergens, might be effective for food allergies as well. Since its inception in 2005, CoFAR has developed oral immunotherapy studies to resolve egg and peanut allergies. A 2009–10 CoFAR study researched the possibility of a peanut vaccine.

Awareness of food allergy severity has led to important government protections for prevention as well. In 2004, the Food Allergen Labeling and Consumer Protection Act (FALCPA) mandated plain-language ingredient disclosure for the top eight US allergens in food products. Any packaged food sold in the United States is required to display these allergy triggers in a stand-out manner, such as using bold text or a separate statement about allergen content. However, labeling consistency remains poor, and enforcement sporadic. In addition, statements about cross-contamination or unusual allergies are only voluntary under FALCPA.

Impact
Food allergies became public health burden in the 2000s, especially in places where children congregate, such as day care centers and schools. As food allergies grow and remain a presence, considerations for product ingredients and labeling, immunotherapy, and food-timing recommendations will likely change.

Further Reading
National Institute of Allergy and Infectious Disease. *Guidelines for the Diagnosis and Management of Food Allergy in the United States: Summary for Patients, Families, and Caregivers.* Bethesda: US Dept. of Health and Human Services, 2011. PDF file.
Sicherer, Scott. *Understanding and Managing Your Child's Food Allergies.* Baltimore: Johns Hopkins UP, 2006. Print.
Wood, Robert. *Food Allergies for Dummies.* Indianapolis: Wiley, 2007. Print.

Nicole M. Van Hoey, PharmD

■ Food trends

Definition: Popular foods and food movements from 2000 to 2009

The 2000s saw an increased focus on food—where it came from, what was in it, and who was making it. Rising rates of diabetes and obesity in the United States and Canada boosted public interest in locally sourced, organic, and nutritious foods.

Students weigh greens harvested from the White House vegetable garden. (Official White House Photograph/Photograph by Samantha Appleton)

The release of Michael Pollan's book *The Omnivore's Dilemma: A Natural History of Four Meals* in 2006 marked a turning point in the way many Americans felt about industrial food production. In his iconic book, Pollan tracked four meals from source to table. The right book for the right time, it was ushered in by rising consumer interest in sustainability and the emergence of activist organizations devoted to addressing such issues as overfishing, genetically modified foods, and global warming. The term "locavore" to describe a person who eats locally sourced food became a part of the popular lexicon beginning in 2005. In 2009, First Lady Michelle Obama began cultivating a vegetable garden on the South Lawn of the White House, the first since Eleanor Roosevelt planted a victory garden on the White House grounds during World War II. The White House vegetable garden is used as a direct source of nutritious and hyper-local sustenance for the first family and guests of the White House, as well as a place to educate local schoolchildren about gardening and the benefits of fresh, locally grown foods.

Fast Food and Organic Food

The decade was one of contradictions in the fast-food industry. The push for more healthy options, which had been ongoing since the 1980s, intensified. The solution to meeting this growing demand appeared to be, more often than not, menu items that had the look and feel of nutritional fare but featured mostly the same caloric makeup as burgers and fries, such as salads that were loaded with nuts, cheese, or other fatty toppings. Other restaurants purposely moved in

the opposite direction, producing dishes that were almost satirical in their excess, such as Burger King's Enormous Omelet Sandwich and Quad Stacker.

Among the factors cited for contributing to the move toward healthier menu options were the rising rates of obesity and diabetes across the country. Many health advocates and lawyers took on fast-food companies using the techniques antismoking advocates had used to battle tobacco companies in the 1990s. The release of Morgan Spurlock's documentary film *Super Size Me* in 2004 led to increased awareness as well. For instance, soon after the release of the film, which was later nominated for an Academy Award, the McDonald's chain eliminated all of its "supersized" menu options.

Mid-decade, a low-carb craze took over the nation with the success of *The South Beach Diet: The Delicious, Doctor-Designed, Foolproof Plan for Fast and Healthy Weight Loss* by Arthur Agatston. A cardiologist by profession, Agatston was interested not in tightening readers' waistbands but in lowering their risk of heart attack and stroke. Recognizing the failure of the low-fat diet craze of the 1980s and 1990s, Agatston felt Americans were consuming far too many processed foods lacking in fiber, nutrients, and omega-3 fatty acids that promote heart health. The South Beach Diet begins with two weeks of a lean-protein diet that excludes alcohol, fruit, white rice, bread, pasta, and other foods. In the following weeks, small amounts of "forbidden" foods are reintroduced. A year after Agatston's book was published in 2003, it had gone back to print twenty-three times with more than 7.7 million copies in print.

A push among consumers moved organic products from the shelves of specialized or gourmet health-food stores into traditional supermarkets and grocery stores. The rapid expansion of Whole Foods Market grocery stores during the decade to cities across the country helped bring organic and fair-trade foods into the mainstream. Other grocery chains followed suit, including Wal-Mart. In 2005, Whole Foods became a Fortune 500 company. According to data from the Organic Trade Association, annual sales of organic food hit twenty-four billion dollars in 2009, representing a fivefold increase over the previous decade.

Celebrity Chefs

While celebrity chefs have existed in the past, the decade brought with it a new wave of interest in cooking as entertainment. Rachel Ray started the decade with a cooking show on the Food Network and ended it with a magazine, cookware line, and network daytime talk show. In the past, this kind of mass appeal would have been the exception; in the 2000s, it was the rule. Chefs such as Mario Batali, Bobby Flay, and Emeril Lagasse became household names. Both in and out of restaurants, chefs became brands. Some critics and food writers questioned the level of control these chefs could maintain over empires that sometimes stretched across the world and into merchandising areas not typically sought out by chefs of the past.

Impact

The popularity of the Food Network grew considerably in the late nineties, priming the pump for success in the 2000s. Television shows like the Food Network's *Iron Chef America* and Bravo's *Top Chef* turned chefs into contestants and cooking into competition. So while some popular shows like Ray's demonstrated cooking techniques, others elevated the process to something seemingly unattainable to the average viewer. Michael Pollen pointed out in the *New York Times Sunday Magazine* that the Food Network's target audience during these years shifted from viewers who loved to cook to viewers who loved to eat.

Meanwhile, the movement toward sustainable, local food led to a diversification of American eating habits. Many people ascribe to their food choices the way some might ascribe to a political belief. (Indeed, for many, the choice is political.) From local to vegan, eating is no longer simply a means of consumption; it is a personal statement about one's way of life.

Further Reading

Gogoi, Pallavi. "The Rise of the 'Locavore.'" *Bloomberg Businessweek*. Bloomberg, 20 May 2008. Web. 6 Dec. 2012. Discusses the rise of the local food movement.

Miller, Lisa. "Divided We Eat." *Newsweek*. Newsweek/Daily Beast Co., 22 Nov. 2010. Web. 6 Dec. 2012. An in-depth look at the relationship between food choices and socioeconomic class.

Parker-Pope, Tara. "Kid Goes into McDonald's and Orders . . . Yogurt?" *New York Times* 15 June 2009, New York ed.: D5. Print. Describes the changes in American eating habits in the 2000s and the changes made by fast-food restaurants in order to keep apace of the trend.

Pollan, Michael. *The Omnivore's Dilemma: A Natural History of Four Meals*. New York: Penguin, 2006. Print. Examines food fads and the future of American eating habits.

Shapiro, Ari. "Americans' Insatiable Hunger for Celebrity Chefs." *National Public Radio*. NPR, 5 Mar. 2005. Web. 14 Dec. 2012. Describes the increasing popularity and growing restaurant empires of celebrity chefs.

Molly Hagan

■ Foreign policy of the United States

Definition: The strategies the United States government employs to protect and promote its national interests and achieve its strategic goals in the world of international relations

For most of the first decade of the twenty-first century, the major thrust of US foreign policy was related to protecting the homeland against acts of aggression like the terrorist attacks of September 11, 2001. In response to these attacks, the United States fought two wars; advocated preemptive military action against nations that supported or harbored terrorists; and promoted the protection of human rights and the expansion of democracy and free trade.

US foreign policy in the first decade of this century was intrinsically linked to the terrorist attacks of September 11, 2001. On that day, nineteen men affiliated with the terrorist group known as al-Qaeda hijacked four commercial jet airliners, which crashed into the World Trade Center in New York City, the Pentagon outside Washington, DC, and a field in Shanksville, Pennsylvania. The attacks, which killed nearly 3,000 people, shifted the focus of US foreign policy from the promotion of free trade, human rights, and democratization, to the elimination of terrorist threats by way of intelligence analysis, covert military operations, and preemptive military force. This shift in American foreign policy alienated a number of longtime US allies, notably Germany and France. A number of foreign policy analysts considered it an adaptation of the type of proactive stance the US employed against Nazi

Working session at the U.S.-Islamic World Forum in Washington, DC. (Courtesy U.S.-Islamic Forum)

Germany during World War II (1939–45), and against the Soviet Union during the Cold War (1947–91).

US Foreign Policy Prior to September 11

On January 1, 2000, the United States was in the midst an extended period of relative peace. US foreign policy in previous decades had been framed by the Cold War—the sustained ideological battle between the America and its Communist rival, the Soviet Union. Although the Cold War did not involve direct military aggression between the United States and the Soviet Union, it manifested itself in numerous proxy wars worldwide. The two nations supplied their allies in these conflicts with arms and intelligence, in the effort to maintain support of their strategic vision on the world stage. The proxy conflicts included the Vietnam War (1957–75), the Bay of Pigs Invasion (1961), the Iran-Iraq War (1980–88), and the Arab-Israeli Conflict (1948–present).

The Cold War ended in 1991, following the collapse of the Soviet Union, and its loss of control over territories in Eastern Europe. The United States, now the world's sole superpower, began using its political and economic influence to promote free trade among nations and support the growth of democratic governments throughout the world, including Eastern Europe. During this same period, the United States was enjoying the longest sustained period of economic growth in its history. When Republican George W. Bush started his presidency in January 2001, his foreign policy team was focused on maintaining good economic and diplomatic relations with Russia and China. Additionally, the Bush administration wanted to secure a peace treaty between the Israelis and Palestinians, and build a missile defense shield that would protect the United States from nuclear attack.

The Global War on Terror

Few officials in the Bush administration considered terrorist activities, including those related to radical Islamic fundamentalists like the al-Qaeda terrorist network, to be a major concern for US foreign policy. This changed following the September 11 attacks, which destroyed the World Trade Center complex in New York City, and caused significant damage to the Pentagon, the headquarters of US Department of Defense. These terrorist attacks were the first act of aggression by a foreign enemy on US soil since the attack on the American naval base at Pearl Harbor in December 1941. In response to the attacks, which were considered an act of war, Bush launched the "global war on terror," targeting not only members of al-Qaeda, but also the governments of nations that harbored and supported terrorists, including the Islamic fundamentalist Taliban regime in Afghanistan.

In October 2001, a US-led military coalition (which included NATO member nations such as the United Kingdom, Germany, and France) began a campaign of air strikes against targets in Afghanistan. Although the airstrikes toppled the Taliban regime, some al-Qaeda forces, including bin Laden, retreated into the mountainous regions of Afghanistan, and organized a sustained guerrilla campaign against US-led forces. The hunt for bin Laden and other leaders of al-Qaeda and the Taliban would continue throughout the decade.

In announcing the global war on terror, the Bush administration reserved the right to act preemptively against threats to the US homeland. During a State of the Union address in January 2002, Bush described an "axis of evil," composed of three nations: Iraq, Iran, and North Korea. The Bush administration made clear its belief that each of these nations sought to harm US citizens and American interests worldwide. Although a US-led coalition of forces had successfully turned back Iraqi leader Saddam Hussein's invasion of Kuwait in 1991, several members of the Bush administration believed he was attempting to reconstitute his weapons of mass destruction (WMD) program—a violation of the ceasefire agreement Iraq had signed. Throughout 2002 and into early 2003, weapons inspectors from the United Nations sought to uncover Hussein's weapons program, but met with resistance from the Iraqi regime. In March 2003, the Bush administration and a coalition of allied forces, including the United Kingdom, decided to use military force to topple the Iraq government, believing Saddam Hussein to be too large a security threat to be left alone. The military invasion of Iraq did not have the same amount of international support as the military campaign against the Taliban in Afghanistan. Pointedly, the leaders of France

and Germany opted not to include their troops in the ranks of coalition forces, and were critical of the US action against Iraq. In addition, large demonstrations against the war effort occurred worldwide. Nonetheless, the United States conducted a massive air campaign, which was followed by a ground invasion. The Iraqi government was toppled, but no WMD were ever discovered inside Iraq. A Senate report released in July 2004 concluded that the United States had gone to war in Iraq on "flawed" intelligence and security data that had received wide circulation both domestically and internationally. Many critics alleged that the Bush administration had undertaken a military campaign against Iraq in order to secure US oil interests in the region.

At their outset, the wars in Afghanistan and Iraq were popular with the majority of American people, and the Bush administration was widely praised for its aggressive foreign policy in the wake of the September 11 attacks. Both wars, however, began to lose popularity as insurgent forces in both Afghanistan and Iraq began implementing covert guerilla attacks against coalition forces. Bush was reelected to a second term as president in November 2004, despite concerns among some voters about the flawed information that had led to the war in Iraq, the financial toll of both wars, and the causalities suffered by US forces. However, by November 2006, the wars had become a political liability for the Republican Party. Following the midterm elections, the Democratic Party regained control over both houses of Congress. That same month, Bush accepted the resignation of Defense Secretary Donald Rumsfeld, a key proponent and organizer of the administration's global war on terror. In January 2007, President Bush announced a new Iraq strategy, which brought thousands of additional troops (known informally as "the surge") to the Iraqi theater to provide security to a nation wracked with sectarian violence. The surge strategy helped to decrease violence in Iraq enough to help facilitate a withdrawal of American and coalition forces, which had been agreed to in December 2008 and was completed in December 2011.

Economic Concerns

In addition to conducting the global war on terror, the Bush administration sought to expand economic development in both industrialized and developing nations by liberalizing trade and fostering free markets. The Bush administration also substantially increased economic assistance to other nations during the decade, from approximately $13 billion at the start of the 2000s to an estimated $34 billion in 2008. While it failed to procure a peace agreement between the Israelis and Palestinians, the administration did strike a bilateral deal with Russia to decrease nuclear stockpiles left over from the Cold War. The Bush administration also worked with the international community to prevent nations like Libya and Iran from acquiring nuclear weapons. Finally, the United States strengthened its efforts against infectious diseases worldwide in the 2000s, becoming the single largest donor to the Global Fund to Fight AIDS, Tuberculosis and Malaria.

US foreign policy began to shift at the end of the Bush administration and at the start of the administration of President Barack Obama, as the wars in Iraq and Afghanistan began to wind down. The United States and the rest of the world began to focus on the growing global economic crisis. The crisis began in late 2007, but its full effects were not felt until September 2008, when numerous large banks teetered on the brink of collapse as billions of dollars in investments were lost on bad loans made during the recent housing boom in the United States and elsewhere. The resulting economic downturn—the first to hit the nation since the recession of the early 2000s—was the worst it had experienced since the Great Depression of the 1930s. The Great Recession, as it came to be known, was felt throughout the entire world economy, eliminating millions of jobs and wiping out billions of dollars in investments. From 2008 until well into the next decade, much of US foreign policy would focus on repairing the damage caused by the financial, crisis and looking for ways to prevent another one from occurring. In addition, the United States remains committed to ensuring political stability in Iraq and Afghanistan, providing both countries with military support and aid money.

Impact

The major change in US foreign policy following the September 11 terrorist attacks was a new focus on the threats of terrorist organizations like al-Qaeda. That shift in focus, however, came at a very great cost. In addition to trillions of American dollars spent on the war effort, over 6,700 US troops died in Iraq and Afghanistan. Hundreds of coalition forces, including troops from Great Britain, France, and Canada, also died in each theater. Tens of thousands of service members sustained injuries in each conflict, and the combined civilian death toll likely exceeds an estimated 150,000, with over 4.7 million Iraqis and 500,000 Afghanis displaced by war.

Unlike its past military adversaries, the United States faces an intangible enemy in the threat of global of terror. A single peace treaty, or a decisive victory on the battlefield, cannot permanently end terrorism, because it is not nation-state-based phenomenon, but a philosophy adhered to by a loose association of radical groups across the globe. The aggressive way in which the global war on terror was conducted in the 2000s magnified not only divisions between the United States and its allies over foreign policy, but highlighted the challenge posed to American military might when pitted against nontraditional terrorist militias in an urban setting.

America's inability to control violence in Iraq in the later 2000s, or secure the capture or killing of Osama bin Laden, stood in stark contrast to the country's massive political, military and economic power. US Navy SEALs killed bin Laden in Pakistan on May 2, 2011, but significant challenges related to Islamic fundamentalism and acts of terrorist violence remain. The amount of blood, treasure, and global political capitol expended by the United States during the war on terror of the 2000s led many foreign policy analysts to speculate that the country's position as a dominant world power was in decline.

When President Obama came to office in January 2009, he stressed the importance of America's military withdrawals from Iraq and Afghanistan, and sought to repair strained relations between the United States and its allies. Moreover, Obama sought to demonstrate to growing economic powers like India and China that the United States would work with them on issues related to security and trade, while serving as an advocate for human rights, representative democracy, and free-market economics. While is clear that America still has an important role to play on the world stage in light of the Arab Spring uprisings (2010–present), new sensitivities related to the financial stability of a globalized economy, and the ongoing threat of terrorist violence, it is unlikely to revisit the strategy of unilateral military action it deployed in the 2000s in the near future.

Further Reading

Ambrose, Stephen E., and Douglas G. Brinkley. *Rise to Globalism: American Foreign Policy Since 1938, Ninth Revised Edition*. New York: Penguin, 2010. Breaks down US foreign policy by presidential administrations from just prior to World War II through the post–September 11 world.

Herring, George C. *From Colony to Superpower: U.S. Foreign Relations Since 1776*. New York: Oxford University Press, 2011. Focuses on the evolution of American foreign policy from the inception of the republic to the early twenty-first century.

Kaufman, Joyce P. *A Concise History of U.S. Foreign Policy, Second Edition*. Lanham, Md.: Rowman & Littlefield, 2010. Overview of American foreign policy, including policy changes initiated in the aftermath of the September 11 terrorist attacks.

National Commission on Terrorist Attacks. *The 9/11 Commission Report: Final Report of the National Commission on Terrorist Attacks Upon the United States*. New York: W.W. Norton, 2004. Official government report written by the commission that investigated the causes of the September 11 terrorist attacks, and the immediate responses of the US government to the attacks.

Reeson, Greg C. *Stalemate: Why We Can't Win the War on Terror and What We Should Do Instead*. Lanham, Md.: Government Institutes, 2011. Presents a critical look at US foreign policy since September 11 and argues that many of the policies implemented in the Bush administration and carried on through the Obama administration will not lead to a US victory against radical Islamic fundamentalism.

Christopher Mari

■ Franks, Tommy

Identification: US Army officer
Born: June 17, 1945, Wynnewood, Oklahoma

As commander of the United States Central Command, General Tommy Franks led American and allied coalition forces in Operation Enduring Freedom against the Taliban forces in Afghanistan, and in Operation Iraqi Freedom.

Franks was born Tommy Ray Bentley in Wynnewood, Oklahoma, but was adopted at an early age by Ray and Lorene Franks. He spent his youth in

Tommy Franks. (U.S. Department of Defense/Photograph by Helene C. Stikkel)

several small towns in Oklahoma and in Midland, Texas. After two years at the University of Texas at Austin, Franks enlisted in the United States Army in 1965. After basic training, he was selected to attend the Army's Artillery and Missile Officer Candidate School at Fort Sill, Oklahoma. After graduating, he served a tour with artillery units in Vietnam. While in the Army, Franks later graduated from the University of Texas at Arlington, and received a master's degree in Public Administration from Shippensburg University. He has also graduated from the Army War College and the Armed Forces Staff College.

Franks served in a variety of positions as he rose through the ranks of the officer corps, including command posts in Germany and Korea. He also served for a time at the Pentagon as inspector general of the Investigations Division. In 1992, Franks was assigned to the Louisiana Maneuvers Task Force, an army think tank involved in planning the kind of military the United States would need in the post–Cold War world.

During the First Gulf War (1990–91), Franks, a brigadier general, served as assistant divisional commander of the First Calvary Division. In June 2000, Franks was promoted to the rank of four-star general and made commander in chief of the US Central Command, with responsibility for overseeing the American military in a large region from the horn of Africa to Pakistan in central Asia. After the terrorist attacks of September 11, 2001, Franks oversaw Operation Enduring Freedom, which toppled the Taliban government in Afghanistan. A key part of Franks's strategy in Afghanistan was joint efforts between civilian CIA operatives and Army Special Forces troops. In 2003, he commanded the invasion of Iraq (Operation Iraqi Freedom) which culminated in the overthrow of Saddam Hussein's regime. In Iraq, Franks stressed joint operations, with contributions from all the US service branches, as well as the forces of the cooperating foreign nations. His strategic goals were speed, flexibility, and the use of lethal firepower. However, some military and political analysts criticized Franks for failing to anticipate continuing attacks on US troops by informally organized insurgent militias that remained loyal to Hussein after the fall of the regime.

As the major offensive operations in Iraq wound down, Franks retired from the Army in July 2003, after thirty-eight years of service. Following his retirement, he founded the consulting firm Franks & Associates LLC.

Impact

Franks capped a distinguished career as an Army officer by serving in one of the most visible positions in the United States military, as commander of Central Command during the wars in Afghanistan and Iraq. Franks believed that the kind of joint-force effort he led in these conflicts was the embodiment of the type of military that the Louisiana Maneuvers Task Force had envisioned—a lean but lethal force that accomplished military objectives quickly and efficiently.

Further Reading

Bush, George W. *Decision Points*. New York: Crown, 2010. Print.

Franks, Tommy, and Malcolm McConnell. *American Soldier*. New York: Harper, 2004. Print.

Woodward, Bob. *Plan of Attack*. New York: Simon, 2004. Print.

Mark S. Joy

■ Franzen, Jonathan

Identification: American novelist and essayist
Born: August 17, 1959; Western Springs, Illinois

Dissatisfied with what he considered the degradation of the novel into mere entertainment, Jonathan Franzen sought to revitalize the form as a vehicle for social commentary and change.

Jonathan Franzen's determination to marry social critique and characters within the novel format stems from his 1996 essay "Perchance to Dream: In an Age of Images, a Reason to Write Novels." In the essay, Franzen relays his despair about the demise of the novel's power and commits himself to altering its course. Initially publishing *The Corrections* (2001) in response to his own critique, Franzen's subsequent works, including his memoir, continue to echo a consciousness that points both intensely inward and simultaneously speaks to larger cultural issues.

Franzen published *The Corrections* as a character-based social commentary. The novel speaks to cultural questions of drug use and whether it numbs life or makes it more bearable all by cementing the reader's investment in characters. By utilizing the trend among readers to seek entertainment in novels, "Franzen embeds [his thoughts about the world] in the lives of affecting human characters" (Eakin). He accepts the novel's approachability as a medium of entertainment while capitalizing on the attention of readers to relay his cultural critique. *The Corrections* received the 2001 National Book Award for Fiction and the James Tait Black Memorial Prize for Fiction in 2002.

In addition to *The Corrections*, Franzen's publications during the 2000s included the essay collection *How to Be Alone* (2002), his memoir *The Discomfort Zone* (2006), and a translation of Frank Wedekind's *Spring Awakening* (2007). Throughout the decade, Franzen continued to push the novel toward cultural relevance, turning to concern for the environment.

Jonathan Franzen. (Courtesy David Shankbone)

His interest in environmentalism was made acute by his fascination with birds. In his memoir, he relates his marital struggles—which ended in divorce—to displaced birds: "When two kestrels . . . began showing up on a chimney outside my kitchen window and bloodying their beaks on fresh-killed mice, their dislocation seemed to mirror my own" (Franzen 163). By visualizing himself and his life through these birds, Franzen formed the basis for his 2010 novel *Freedom*, in which humans and birds are continually displaced. The freedom to leave must contend with the inability to stay. In *Freedom*, as Franzen unveils the breakdown of relatable human relationships, he sets up a series of mirrors revealing the upheaval of humankind's relationship with the environment.

Impact

Franzen's work stands as proof that the novel as social commentary will endure. Rather than abandon the novel as a way to speak to social ills, he sought to make commentary about the larger world relevant. Instead of dismissing the novel as entertainment, he sought to use its power of captivation to direct a

reader's attention. Ultimately, by creating novels that speak to the intimate world of characters as individuals, Franzen found the means to speak to society as a whole.

Further Reading

Eakin, Emily. "Jonathan Franzen's Big Book." *New York Times*. New York Times Co., 2 Sep. 2001. Web. 13 Aug. 2012.

Franzen, Jonathan. *The Discomfort Zone*. New York: Picador, 2006. Print.

Lucia Pizzo

■ *Freakonomics*

Identification: A nonfiction book that uses economic theory to explain a number of social anomalies
Authors: Steven D. Levitt (b. 1967) and Stephen J. Dubner (b. 1963)
Date: Released on April 12, 2005

People do not generally make a connection between schoolteachers and sumo wrestlers, but writers Steven D. Levitt and Stephen J. Dubner make such an association acutely apparent in their book Freakonomics: A Rogue Economist Explores the Hidden Side of Everything. *The authors' text examines various social topics and makes some thought-provoking conclusions, such as how* Roe v. Wade *and violent crime are connected, or how a swimming pool is more dangerous than a gun.*

Steven D. Levitt, an economist known for his quirky approach to economics, met journalist Stephen J. Dubner in 2003 during an interview for the *New York Times Magazine*. Dubner was fascinated by Levitt's take on economics. The two bonded quickly, and Dubner's published article garnered Levitt much attention from *New York Times* readers. It also caught the attention of publishers who encouraged Levitt to write a book about his ideas. At first, Levitt was not interested; he had little confidence in his writing abilities and did not believe he had all of his theories worked out. After some deliberation, he decided to ask Dubner to help him write the book.

Levitt's goal was to challenge the conventional knowledge of his readers by using the language of economics to make sense of his ideas. A crucial idea Levitt and Dubner attempt to get across in *Freakonomics* is that economics can be understood as a study of incentives, the encouragement that drives individuals to make decisions. Expanding on this belief, the authors examine several topics in relation to economics, including drug gangs, real estate agents, campaign finance, and even the Ku Klux Klan. These examples help illustrate their atypical perspective in an area best characterized as "freakonomics," a term the two invented to summarize their theories. Levitt and Dubner assure their readers that all of life's obscurities can be resolved when approached from the right angle. The authors attempt to shift their audience's point of view so they may realize these possibilities.

Impact

Freakonomics was on the New York Times Best Sellers list for more than two years, selling more than four million copies worldwide. The book spawned its own blog on the *New York Times* website as well as a feature-length documentary and a radio show called *Freakonomics Radio*. In October of 2009, Levitt and Dubner published a second book, *SuperFreakonomics: Global Cooling, Patriotic Prostitutes, and Why Suicide Bombers Should Buy Life Insurance.*

Further Reading

Falvey, Meghan. "Weakonomics: Levitt Slinging Soft Old U-Chicago Stuff." *n+1*. n+1 Foundation, 25 June 2005. Web. 13 Aug. 2012.

Levitt, Steven D., and Stephen J. Dubner. *Freakonomics: A Rogue Economist Explores the Hidden Side of Everything.* New York: Harper, 2005. Print.

Schawbel, Dan. "Stephen Dubner on the *Freakonomics* Phenomenon." *Forbes.* Forbes.com, 30 Jan. 2012. Web. 13 Aug. 2012.

Cait Caffrey